English Ethnicity & Culture in North America

English Ethnicity &
Culture in North America

Edited by DAVID T. GLEESON

The University of South Carolina Press

Published by the University of South Carolina Press
Columbia, South Carolina 29208

www.sc.edu/uscpress

Manufactured in the United States of America

25 24 23 22 21 20 19 18 17
10 9 8 7 6 5 4 3 2 1

Library of Congress Cataloging-in-Publication Data
can be found at http://catalog.loc.gov/

ISBN 978-1-61117-786-2 (cloth)
ISBN 978-1-61117-787-9 (ebook)

CONTENTS

ACKNOWLEDGMENTS

First, thanks must go to my fellow collaborators Don MacRaild of Ulster University and Tanja Bueltmann of Northumbria University. They have been great colleagues and friends throughout our larger project, of which this collection is a part. The project is "Locating the Hidden Diaspora: The English in North America in Transatlantic Perspective, 1760–1950," funded by the Arts and Humanities Research Council (AHRC) of the United Kingdom (project grant AH/1001042/1), and it facilitated a lot of the research in this book. I am grateful to the AHRC for this support.

All of the authors included in this work have been a pleasure to work with, and I thank them for their promptness in responding to edits and deadlines. I am also grateful for the support of the staff members at USC Press who have guided this project to publication, especially Alex Moore, Lynne Parker, and Linda Fogle. Some elements of this book were presented in an exhibition to the public at the College of Charleston in the summer of 2013. Dean of Libraries John White and the archivist Anne Bennett were vital in putting that together. So too were my colleagues MacRaild and Bueltmann as well as Monika Smialkowska and Lesley Robinson from Northumbria University and Sally-Ann Huxtable from the National Museum of Scotland. Thanks also to Mary Battle of the Avery Research Center for her logistical support. While guiding this project I have also had lots of encouragement from my colleagues at Northumbria, especially Mike Cullinane, Brian Ward, and Sylvia Ellis.

My wife, Amy, and my daughter, Emma, are now used to me working at strange times on various research projects, and my son, Aidan, born in England, who came along appropriately enough during this one, is getting into the swing of my routines. As always, I thank them for their love, support, and patience.

Introduction

England in America

A s the purveyor of populist American politics, the candidate Andrew
Jackson of the newly formed "Democratic Party" had a biography written for his presidential run in 1828. The book told of his exploits on the
frontier, his fights against Indians, but also his hatred for the "English." He had
apparently first felt this abhorrence in the stories from his Irish-born mother. His
despising of England only increased after his violent confrontation with a British army officer during the American Revolution when the young Jackson had
refused to clean the officer's boots.[1] Later he rose to heroic stature for his defense
of the Mississippi River during the War of 1812 at the Battle of New Orleans when
he halted the assault of British forces. Indeed, according to one rival, it seemed
that his "killing 2,500 Englishmen at N[ew] Orleans" was his only "qualification" put forward for "the complicated duties of the Chief Magistracy" of the
United States.[2]

Of course Andrew Jackson's issues had been with Great Britain and the British government, and yet he and most Americans referred to their old enemy as
"England." This conflating of England with Britain was and is common in the
United States. The Britain against which the new United States defined itself was
the English version, not the Scottish, Welsh, or Irish ones. Jackson, for example,
did not consider his "Scots-Irish" parents as British even though this was their
and his, until 1783, legal status. The non-English could when they chose to, it
seems, define themselves as not British. This focus of hatred for England over
Britain seemed to permeate the American social classes. During the Civil War,
for example, the British consul in New York, a time of high tension between his
government and that of the United States, noted that in the city "it was safe to
describe oneself as Scots, Irish, or Welsh, but not British or English."[3]

Despite this long pedigree of Anglophobia among postcolonial Americans,
historians of ethnicity believe that the English, for social and cultural reasons, fit
easily into the United States. Indeed leading scholars of immigrants in America
have declared that in Americans' eyes, "the English had no ethnicity at all."[4] The
issue of Englishness was, on the face of it, even less present in British Canada.
Anglo-Canadians, many of them American Tories or their descendants, remained

loyal to king and country. But as Canada matured through the nineteenth century, to the point of becoming a dominion with some semblance of independence in 1867, the English and Englishness became more problematic. French Canadians in Quebec had rejected it, but even in Anglo-dominated Ontario, an increasing antagonism toward the English definition of "Britishness" grew. Canadians were still proud members of the British Empire, but they saw their western/frontier version of it as stronger than the more effete version back in the mother country. In Saskatchewan, for example, many British Canadians rejected "the hegemonic conflation of English with British."[5] The fact that a number of English arriving in Canada saw themselves as "Gentleman Emigrants" and the reality that many Canadians' British roots were Scottish or Irish only exacerbated differences, leading one immigrant to declare that "the Englishmen here [in Toronto] are much disliked."[6]

Admiration, however, for England and English culture remained. Indeed one literary scholar believed that in the United States it rose to the level of "Anglophilia." It was particularly strong in the burgeoning colleges of post–Civil War America. According to Henry Adams, Bostonians, for example, "always knelt in self-abasement before the majesty of English standards."[7] Shakespeare remained the paragon of literature for many North Americans, and the Magna Carta was the basis of American and Canadian liberty.[8] In addition economic connections were vital in taming U.S. Anglophobia. The United States needed loans from London to further its own growth and development. Leading businessmen and politicians sought to influence foreign policy in ways that emphasized understanding over prejudice and compromise over conflict.[9] This continued cultural appreciation and strong economic relationship had political consequences, including general American acceptance of the Canadian Confederation in 1867 and the Treaty of Washington in 1871, the latter settling disputes from the Civil War. This easing of tensions on the continent ushered in an era of better relations between Britain and the United States. There remained attempts to "to twist the lion's tail," especially in pursuit of Irish American voters, but respect for England and Britain remained and even extended to cooperation on mutually beneficial foreign policy issues. The diplomatic historian Bradford Perkins described a "Great Rapprochement" from 1895 to 1914 between "England" (Britain) and the United States that laid the foundation of what eventually became known as the "Special Relationship."[10]

Yet history rarely moves in straight lines. The course of Anglo-American diplomatic relations did not glide inexorably toward a special relationship, and neither were Anglo-American cultural connections accepted unequivocally as just new versions of England in North America. This collection explores some of these continued complicated links between England, its people, and its culture with North America in the nineteenth and twentieth centuries. In general these essays challenge the established view of the English as having no "ethnicity" and highlight the vibrancy of the English and their culture in North America.[11] This collection also challenges the prevailing notion of the English as "invisible im-migrants."[12] Recognizing the English as a distinct ethnic group, as are the Irish, Scots, and Germans, has implications for understanding American identity too, providing a clearer picture of how Americans often defined themselves in the context of Old World cultural traditions. Ultimately all of the work included here upsets the idea of a coherent, comfortable Anglo cultural mainstream and indi-cates the fluid and adaptable nature of what it meant and means to be English, American, and Canadian.

The English cultural roots of what became the United States and the Anglo-Canadian provinces provide fruitful research for understanding the "English-ness" of North America, but so too do the large numbers of English immigrants who moved to North America. According to the 1901 census, Canada had over 1.2 million residents of English origin. In what became the United States, the English were the largest immigrant group in the American colonies in the sev-enteenth century and later constituted 80 percent of the 2,760,360 people of specified national origins who left Britain for the United States between 1820 and 1910.[13] With over 2 million English migrants coming to America, some historians did notice their presence. Rowland Berthoff and William Van Vugt paid serious attention to English studies of British immigrants in the United States, especially to the English contributions to the industrial development of America.[14] Char-lotte Erickson dedicated a large portion of a monograph to the English. She, like Berthoff, did acknowledge the vital role of English immigrants in the industrial growth of the country, but she believed that their class identity was more impor-tant than their ethnic one. Thus she titled her work *Invisible Immigrants*, partly because many scholars had ignored them as a discrete group but also because they disappeared virtually seamlessly into the American mainstream.[15] Other works examined the role of the English in various outposts of the American Revolution, and they reported class and regional identity as the dominant forms of Englishness expressed.[16]

There were, however, those who expressed openly a sense of national Englishness in North America in the nineteenth and early twentieth centuries. Indeed the first record of an explicit society to express Englishness, as distinct from Britishness, appeared in colonial America with the founding of St. George's Society in Charles Town (now Charleston), South Carolina in 1733. Similar groups were founded in New York City and Philadelphia before the American Revolution. The revolution hindered the expansion of these English societies, but in the nineteenth century they spread quickly across the United States and into Canada. By the end of the 1800s the Royal Society of St. George had been founded to link North American English societies together and with England.

These groups were a strong symbol of English ethnicity similar to those of other immigrant societies in North America.[17]

In the first essay of this book, William E. Van Vugt highlights even further this ethnicity of the English in the United States. Through his study of the large letter database at the London School of Economics, originally compiled by Charlotte Erickson, he indicates clearly that the same push/pull factors of migration that affected other European migrants also affected the English. Although many had the advantages of language and work skills that other immigrants did not, the English also, for example, practiced the chain migration commonly seen in other American ethnic groups. The next two essays, one focused on the United States and the other on Canada, too show that the English in North America shared a common experience with other immigrants. Ethnic societies were key elements of support for immigrants both in social and economic terms. Erickson had dismissed the St. George's Societies as merely for elite English immigrants and isolated from the majority working-class community. In earlier work Donald M. MacRaild and Tanja Bueltmann challenged this view of St. George's Societies, but in their respective essays here, they both show that the public celebration of Englishness by the English transcended class boundaries.[18] MacRaild focuses on the Order of the Sons of St. George, which emerged in the late nineteenth century in the Middle Atlantic region. English workers set this group up explicitly to protect the interests of Protestant English workingmen. They did so because of the opposition they saw from another entrenched ethnic group among the American working classes, the Irish. They felt the ethnic pressure from Irish Americans and responded accordingly. Bueltmann examines the Sons of England, a group that represented working-class as well as bourgeois English immigrants in Canada. Her study of this group, which spread across the country, signifies that even in "British" Canada the English sought to distinguish themselves from others and used their ethnicity to further their own interests.

Kathryn Lamontagne looks at English ethnicity in the working-class culture of Fall River, Massachusetts, long recognized as a place of English settlement in the burgeoning industrial society of New England. Lamontagne's analysis of labor union activities highlights that English participation in them was driven as much by ethnic as class interests. Joseph Hardwick's essay assesses another element of English ethnic identity in North America: religion. Hardwick analyzes a continued strong English presence in the Episcopal Church after the American Revolution and reveals interethnic tensions and disputes over "American values" usually only associated with the Catholic Church in the United States.[19]

David Gleeson complicates further the idea that Englishness was easily assimilated into the United States. Focusing on one of the most culturally Anglophilic parts of the country, the South, during the tumultuous years around the formation of the southern Confederacy, he acknowledges that while many southern whites held the view that their region was in some ways an extension of "Old England," there was still substantial hostility to contemporary England and the English. Thus being part of the "Anglo-American" mainstream did not necessarily mean a warm welcome for England, the English, or English values. James McConnel's essay examines another, more physical example of Anglophilia in the United States: statues to English/British monarchs. A monument erected to an English king, for example Alfred the Great, was in some ways a symbol of increased transatlantic cooperation between the American and British governments, but ultimately these memorials were constructed to convey American and not English messages. They were not just mere acceptance of English values but instead were paeans to the greatness of the U.S. transformation of these principles into something purer and better than the originals.

The final three essays delve deeper into some specific examples of English culture in North America, specifically sport, folk traditions, and dance. Dean Allen analyzes that quintessential English game cricket and sees it as an important element in the maintenance of English culture in North America. Despite widespread Anglophobia on many parts of the continent, cricket remained popular and was surpassed only in the aftermath of the Civil War with the rise of baseball. English immigrants played a major role in this preservation of their culture across the Atlantic. Continuing on in chronological terms, Monika Smialkowska explains the increased interest in English folk customs through the historical "pageant" craze that gripped the United States in the late nineteenth and early twentieth centuries. This search for authenticity among Americans seemed merely to be aping a Victorian English craze to reenforce "Anglo-Saxon norms" among the "new" immigrants arriving by the millions from southern and eastern Europe. Smialkowska, however, finds this explanation too simplistic and posits that the movement was far more sophisticated culturally and politically than has been previously believed. Mike Sutton assesses the late twentieth-century revival of the English morris folk dancing tradition in the United States. The morris was initially resuscitated as part of the larger folk revival, but Sutton's firsthand anthropological study of contemporary morris "sides" shows that while giving a nod to English tradition, American dancers created something new and uniquely their own.

As Van Vugt's analysis of English immigrants in the United States is an appropriate place to begin this collection, so Sutton's essay is a fitting one to conclude it. Sutton confirms in many ways a belief shared by all of us involved in this project: that as with other ethnicities in North America, English culture did not disappear into a larger mainstream but instead was adapted, merged, and transformed into something hybrid. St. Patrick's Day, for example, began in North America as an exclusive ethnic festival for Irish immigrants, but it has been transformed into something that is as much, if not more, American as it is Irish. Preserved by ethnic associations for their future "hyphenated" genera-tions, this idea of a symbiotic assimilation of immigrant cultures in the U.S. and Canadian mainstreams is accepted by scholars.[20] We believe that this applies to English literature, pageantry, commemorations, cricket, and much more, and we hope that this initial foray will encourage others to pursue the numerous other sources of English ethnicity in the United States and Canada and how they were transformed on the western side of the Atlantic.

NOTES

1. Jon Meacham, *American Lion: Andrew Jackson in the White House* (New York: Random House, 2008), 11–12, 31–33, 37.

2. Henry Clay, quoted in David S. Heidler and Jeanne T. Heidler, *Henry Clay: The Essential American* (New York: Random House, 2010), 179.

3. Edward Archibald, quoted in Amanda Foreman, *A World on Fire: An Epic History of Two Nations Divided* (London: Allen Lane, 2010), 116.

4. Kathleen Neils Conzen, David A. Gerber, Ewa Morawska, George E. Pozzetta, and Rudolph J. Vecoli, "The Invention of Ethnicity: The View from the USA," *Journal of American Ethnic History* 12 (Fall, 1992): 3–41.

5. Marilyn Barber, "Nation-Building in Saskatchewan: Teachers from the British Isles in Saskatchewan Rural Schools in the 1920s," in *Canada and the British World: Culture, Migration and Identity,* ed. Phillip Buckner and R. Douglas Francis (Vancouver: University of British Columbia Press, 2006), 219.

6. Amy J. Lloyd, "'The Englishmen here are much disliked': Hostility towards English Immigrants in Early Twentieth-Century Toronto," in *Locating the English Diaspora, 1500–2010,* ed. Tanja Bueltmann, David T. Gleeson, and Donald M. MacRaild (Liverpool: Liverpool University Press, 2012), 135–49.

7. Eliza Tamarkin, *Anglophilia: Deference, Devotion, and Antebellum America* (Chicago: University of Chicago Press, 2008), 247–69, Adams quoted on 212.

8. Donald M. MacRaild, "The International Magna Charta Day Association," available at http://digitalcommunity.englishdiaspora.co.uk/?p=324, accessed October 1, 2014; Monika Smialkowska, "Conscripting Caliban: Shakespeare, America, and the Great War," *Shakespeare* 7 (2011): 192–207. See also Carolyn Harris, *Magna Charta and Its Gifts to Canada: Democracy, Law and Human Rights* (Toronto: Dundurn Books, 2015).

9. Jay Sexton, *Debtor Diplomacy: Finance and American Foreign Relations in the Civil War Era, 1837–1873* (New York: Oxford University Press, 2005).

10. Bradford Perkins, *The Great Rapprochement: England and the United States, 1895–1914* (New York: New Atheneum, 1968); Kathleen Burk, *Old World, New World: The Story of Britain and America* (London: Little, Brown, 2007), 299, 562.

11. For more information on the overall project, see www.englishdiaspora.co.uk, accessed October 15, 2014.

12. See note 15.

13. Series A-14, A125–103, Section A: Population and Migration, Statistics Canada, available at http://www.statcan.gc.ca/pub/11-516-x/sectiona/4147436-eng.htm#cont,

accessed October 1, 2014. In the United States the Scots accounted for 488,789 (17.7 percent) and the Welsh for 59,540 (2.2 percent). A further 793,801 did not specify origins. See 61st Congress, 3d Session, Doc. 756, *Reports of the Emigration Commissioners: Statistical Review of Immigration, 1820–1910,* vol. 3: *Distribution of Immigrants, 1850–1900* (Washington, D.C.: U.S. Government Printing Office, 1911), [William P. Dillingham], table 8, 13.

14. Rowland T. Berthoff, *British Immigrants in Industrial America, 1790–1950* (Cambridge, Mass.: Harvard University Press, 1953); William E. Van Vugt, *Britain to America: Mid-Nineteenth Century United States* (Urbana: University of Illinois Press, 1999); William E. Van Vugt, *British Buckeyes: The English, Scots and Welsh of Ohio, 1700–1900* (Kent, Ohio: Kent State University Press, 2006).

15. Charlotte Erickson, *Invisible Immigrants: The Adaptation of English and Scottish Immigrants in Nineteenth-Century America* (London: Weidenfeld and Nicolson, 1972). Erickson also completed an encyclopedia entry for the English in which she again downplayed the overt ethnicity of English immigrants, especially of those who were not in the working class. See "English," in *Harvard Encyclopaedia of American Ethnic Groups,* ed. Stephan Thernstrom, Ann Orlov, and Oscar Handlin (Cambridge, Mass.: Harvard University Press, 1980).

16. See, for example, Mary H. Blewett, *Constant Turmoil: The Politics of Industrial Life in Nineteenth-Century New England* (Amherst: University of Massachusetts Press, 2000); and Philip Scranton, *Proprietary Capitalism: The Textile Manufacture at Philadelphia, 1800–1885* (New York: Cambridge University Press, 1983).

17. Tanja Bueltmann and Donald M. MacRaild, "Globalizing St. George: English Associations in the Anglo-World to the 1930s," *Journal of Global History* 7 (March 2012): 79–105; Tanja Bueltmann, David T. Gleeson, and Donald M. MacRaild, "Invisible Diaspora? English Ethnicity in the United States before 1920," *Journal of American Ethnic History* 33 (Summer 2014): 5–30.

18. Erickson, "English"; Bueltmann and MacRaild, "Globalizing St. George."

19. Indeed the nineteenth-century Catholic Church in America has been referred to as an "Immigrant Church" often in conflict with native definitions of "freedom." See Jay P. Dolan, *The Immigrant Church: New York's Irish and German Catholics, 1815–1865* (repr., Notre Dame, Ind.: University of Notre Dame Press, 1992); John T. McGreevy, *Catholicism and American Freedom* (New York: W. W. Norton, 2003), 28–46.

20. Mike Cronin and Daryl Adair, *The Wearing of the Green: A History of St. Patrick's Day* (New York: Routledge, 2002). For the differing interpretations of assimilation that show it being a two-way rather than a one-way street, see Russell A. Kazal, "Revisiting Assimilation: The Rise, Fall, and Reappraisal of a Concept in American Ethnic History," *American Historical Review* 100 (April 1995): 437–71.

Relocating the English Diaspora in America

During the last decade or so of her career Professor Charlotte Erickson compiled an extensive database on 1674 English immigrants who settled in the United States of America between 1803 and 1916. Erickson was able to use only the data for Lancashire (177 cases) for her last book before her passing in 2009. This is an exploration of that database, what it tells us, and how it might be used for our continued quest to locate and understand the English diaspora in America. Erickson usually started with the U.S. county history biographies and then added data from passenger lists; marriage, birth, and death certificates; and parish registers as well as both British and American censuses for an unprecedented assembly of information on the migrants' origins, occupations, ages, religions, levels of education, prior moves within England, their parents' occupations and literacy levels, marriage details, their spouses' backgrounds, occupational changes in England and America, traveling companions, ports of departure and arrival, any family members they were joining, occupational and geographic changes in America, property values, and a wealth of other personal details from their biographies. This information allows us to track their social, occupational, and geographical changes in England and America, and to trace them from one identity to another.

Of course we cannot assume that such a sample faithfully represents all of the English immigrants of the nineteenth century, but it does provide revealing examples of these people, whose experiences and strategies may have been common, even typical. Furthermore the patterns that emerge—and the patterns that do not emerge—are useful clues for further research on the whole.[1] The database seems especially useful for investigating the relationship between industrialization and economic growth—the key changes of modernity—and migration from England to America.

ORIGINS

More than two-thirds of the 1,674 sample emigrants (1,149=69 percent) had their precise origins recorded. Those who left small villages were especially numerous in the 1840s and 1850s (60 percent of them left then), whereas those leaving towns and cities were more common in the 1860s and later. That is, as the English economy developed over the century, the people were leaving more urban areas—as expected. Their origins correlated strongly with their occupations. Those who left villages and village-dominated areas were more likely to be agrarians or craftsmen, in equal proportions. Villagers in industry, service, or the professions were comparatively rare. Those who left towns were less likely to ˙ be agrarians and more likely to work in crafts and, to a lesser extent, industry; virtually none of them were in commerce or the professions. All of this is to be expected and has been indicated in other studies. But when we look more closely at origins and occupations, the story gets more interesting.

OCCUPATIONS

A total of 1,288 of the migrants had their last occupations in England recorded. Their occupational profile follows in table 1.

TABLE 1. PROFILES FOR LAST KNOWN OCCUPATIONS
         IN ENGLAND (UNKNOWNS REMOVED)

  I. Agriculture
    261=20.3%
      54 farmers
      89 farm laborers
      78 farmers' sons
      40 misc.*
 II. Labor (presumed unskilled)
    115=8.9%
III. Service
    65=5%
IV. Preindustrial Crafts
    441=34.2%
      124 building
      128 mining
      58 food
      42 metal
      47 cloth
      23 wood
      19 misc.
  V. Industry
    205=16%
      92 textiles

(Table 1 continued)

        85 iron

        28 misc.

VI. Commerce and the Professions

    201=15.6%

        10 rail workers

        60 clerks

        69 commerce workers—dealers, brokers, agents, businessmen, etc.

        49 professionals—doctors, dentists, architects, clergymen, etc.

        3 gentlemen

        10 students

N=1,288 =100%

*Includes gardeners, cow keepers, farm bailiffs, shepherds, yeomen, etc.

SOURCE: Erickson Database, BLPES

AGRICULTURE

About 20 percent of the sample emigrants whose last occupations were recorded (261 of the 1,288) had left agriculture, broadly defined (see table 1). About the same percentage of the entire English labor force was in agriculture in 1851, so we do not see a disproportionate departure of agrarians. But of these emigrant agrarians, only one in five were clearly true farmers. The great majority were actually farmers' sons or farm laborers. Therefore the English agrarians were moving into American farming especially from the lower rungs of the agricultural ladder—farmers' sons and farm laborers, and so on. But all of these people had agrarian experience that they used to move to America to get their own land and acquire an independence and future that they probably could not have achieved in England.

About 9 percent of the sample migrants with known last English occupations were classified as unskilled laborers. Their biographies and other data show relative poverty and hard circumstances. Only about a quarter are known to have had education. It is also clear that many had at least some farm experience, though unskilled labor, sometimes factory labor, was their main occupation. Their agricultural backgrounds and aspirations explain why nearly half of them (52) entered some form of agriculture in their first American occupation. Of these, roughly half started in America as farm laborers; nearly as many started as farmers, though often as farm renters. Their success was modest in comparison with others', but nearly three-quarters ended up as farmers, most with their own farms. Few likely would have achieved this level of success had they stayed in England.[2]

A total of 808 migrants in the sample took up farming in America (see table 2). Of these, 605 had their last English occupations recorded, and an astonishing two-thirds (394=65 percent) left nonagrarian work in England to farm in America. Put another way, for every English emigrant in the sample who left agriculture (as their last occupation in England) for American farming, two had left nonagricultural work.[3] This is a huge proportion—perhaps exaggerated in the database. We can dig deeper into their history. The great majority of them apparently had not worked on farms before: only a little more than one in ten (13.5 percent) of these people had started out in English agriculture—usually farm labor or working for their farmer fathers—and then found nonagricultural work before leaving to farm in America.

TABLE 2. LAST ENGLISH OCCUPATIONS OF THOSE WHO WENT
INTO FARMING IN THE UNITED STATES

I. Agriculture
    215 (35%)*
        51 "Farmers"
        60 farmers' sons;
        75 farm labourers
        29 specialists/misc (mainly gardeners, shepherds, cow keepers, etc)

II. Labor
    83 (14%)*
        69 them "labourers" n.o.d. (not otherwise defined)
        14 specified (eg., lab factory, or lab mine
        Total cases with known last English occupation: 609
        N=808 (= 100%)
        *percentage of those with known last English occupation.

III. Service
    33 (6%)* various types

IV. Preindustrial Crafts
    152 (25%)*

V. Industry
    62 (10%)*

VI. Commerce and the Professions
    64 (11%)*
    Not known: 199

Total cases with known last English occupation: 605

N=808=100%

*Percentage of those with known last English occupations.

SOURCE: Erickson Database, BLPES

That the majority of those who ultimately farmed in America had left a nonagrarian occupation in England is significant. The most common last nonagrarian occupations were various preindustrial crafts, especially miners and building trades workers. These were mainly rural people who were connected with the agrarian economy and likely had some experience or connection with agriculture—one thinks of the lead miners who also did some farming in North Yorkshire, for example, but whose farm experience was not recorded. They were going to America mainly to fulfill their agrarian aspirations, and working in some form of skilled craft was an effective way to earn the capital necessary for passages, especially multiple family passages, and for getting established in farming.[4]

It appears that agriculture was the single most powerful draw for the sample migrants, as nearly half (808) ended as American farmers. The database offers a look at their employment history before emigration and reveals that only a handful (1%) of the emigrant farmers had started out in crafts or industry, became farmers in England, and then emigrated. Moving from crafts or industry to farming was harder to do in England than in America: of the 808 who became farmers in America, about a quarter (152=25%) had left crafts or industry in England. Others left English agriculture and did craft or industrial work in America only to take up farming there. An interesting example is a gardener named Francis Crowder. As a Mormon he emigrated from Buckinghamshire in 1873 with a group of other English emigrants to work in a smelter in Salt Lake City; but after that he moved to California to become a fruit grower, and he prospered so much that he became a "prominent capitalist" and opened his own bank.[5] The American environment and economy allowed many English immigrants to jump back and forth from crafts and industry to agriculture.[6] Their ability to make such repeated shifts indicates a flexibility and resourcefulness that enabled them to succeed in America.

GETTING STARTED IN AMERICA

The English who had no recorded prior agricultural experience before farming in America used a variety of strategies to move into farming. Most first worked in the American building trades, mining, or blacksmithing. Typical in the sample was a carpenter named Samuel Mayo, who left Suffolk for America in 1830 because, as he recalled, his wife induced him to emigrate. First he worked as a carpenter in New York, where his two children were born; then he moved to Cambridge in Lenawee County, Michigan, where he cleared heavily timbered land. By 1850 he had six children and real estate worth one thousand dollars, and by 1870 the value of his real estate had grown to sixty-eight hundred dollars plus a personal estate of nearly three thousand dollars.[7] Another case later in the century may seem far-fetched, but it is no more remarkable than many others. Frederic Clark, born in Sunderland (Durham) in 1874, was the son of George Clark, a marine engine builder and owner of George Clark Southwick Engine Works Ltd. His mother was the daughter of a Scots schoolmaster. Clark worked for two years in a law office in Sunderland and then for three years in another law office in London, and he was admitted to the bar in 1899. Between 1899 and 1901 Clark traveled around the world in an attempt to heal his weak lungs. After returning to England in 1901 to settle his father's estate and inheriting the business, he immigrated to California in 1902 at age twenty-eight to join friends who had become fruit growers there. After working with them he bought his own orchard and worked it with his brother. California seems to have offered the greatest occupational changes for Clark (among others), who though he was a wealthy and successful barrister, could pursue very different options in America.[8]

When immigrants from any nation came to farm in America, they most commonly started out as farm laborers. What seems to have set the English apart was their proclivity and ability to start out in some other occupation: surprisingly only 17 percent of the English who farmed in America started there as farm laborers.[9] More commonly they started in crafts, and in many cases we see the lines between agriculture and rural crafts blurred—in both England and America. Sometimes it is hard to define their occupations, especially when they switched to and from farm labor or combined farming with mining, blacksmithing, butchering, and/or carpentry. It was by crossing these blurred lines repeatedly that many made the most practical moves to farming in America.[10] Sometimes we get the sense that these people could do anything. George Stephenson was "reared to agricultural pursuits" in Lincolnshire but was a butcher by the time he immigrated to Ohio in 1851. There he worked at lumbering before becoming a foreman in a woolen factory only to return to butchering and then become a livestock dealer.[11] More either started out in some sort of craft or went directly into farming. If the immigrant agrarians had been desperately poor and unskilled, one would expect many more cases of people starting out at the bottom as farm laborers.

CRAFTS AND INDUSTRY TO AMERICAN AGRICULTURE

As noted, about a quarter of those who ended up farming in America had left crafts or industry in England. Rather few from crafts and industry chose to stay in that work in America—only 15 percent and 11 percent in crafts and industry, respectively. Most headed for farming or commerce and the professions, which is not surprising. Craftsmen and industrial workers usually had more to gain by switching to farming or commerce and the professions than by continuing with their old lines of work. Although crafts and industry could provide their own levels of independence and success, especially at the managerial level, more immigrants in the sample used crafts or industry in America as a stepping-stone to farming or commercial and professional work. English industrial workers were key players in the story of American immigration.[12]

A classic, mythical migration motif is that of people caught up in the industrial revolution finding redemption from industrial labor and urban squalor in farming their own land in America. Early writers simply assumed that the economic dislocations and technological displacement that accompanied industrialization pushed many of the victims to America. However, an opposite model suggests that those who benefited from Britain's growing industrial economy were more able to seize even greater benefits in America. Perhaps some combination of these two models was at play. After all, there was a wide variety of evolving industries, with many different, changing occupations, while swings in British and American economic growth also affected migration. The possibilities seem endless.

About 16 percent of the immigrants in the sample had left industrial work. About 10 percent ended up in American industry as their last occupation, although not all of these had left industrial work in England.[13] In fact, only about half of those who ended up in American industry had come directly from English industry, while about a fifth had come from a craft.[14] A few had actually left English farming and ended up in American industry, which shows the astonishing variety of options that were open to the English, more than any other immigrant group because of the advanced British economy. Relatively few industrial workers in the sample ended their days toiling in a factory: over a third became supervisors, owners, managers, and so on.[15] Industrial work was not often the long-term goal.

Among Britain's industrial workers, hand-loom weavers were often perceived as victims who suffered falling wages and diminishing control in the onslaught of the power-loom revolution. The database gives some support to this image but only in limited ways: there are only twenty-five weavers in the sample; seventeen of them emigrated before 1850. Once in America, nine began as weavers and a total of sixteen ended their careers in farming. But America was not necessarily an escape. Samuel Sutton stayed in textiles and thrived. He left Derbyshire in 1833 for Boston, Massachusetts, and was said to be a pioneer in the American hand-loom knitting industry. By 1860 he had nine thousand dollars in real estate and a personal estate valued at two thousand dollars.[16] Others, however, seem to have had little to show for their migration. In 1844 the forty-six-year-old Staffordshire silk weaver Charles Warmsley arrived in Grant County, Wisconsin, where his wife and children had settled two years earlier. His success story seems modest: the 1850 U.S. census enumerated him as a laborer living with his wife Sarah and four English-born children. In 1860 he was still a laborer with a mere $100 in real estate and a personal estate worth $250. One wonders if he had regrets about his move.[17]

Some stuck to weaving for a long time in America. John Barker was an overlooker of worsted mills in Leeds by age twenty-five and later in Bradford. In 1879, at age thirty-nine, he left with his wife and two children for Lawrence, Massachusetts, where he worked in a mill as a woolen weaver. He was enumerated there in 1880 as a section hand in a woolen mill, aged forty, with his English-born wife, Elizabeth, and three children, one of whom also worked in the mill. He was still there in 1900 and worked as a woolen weaver until 1909, when the family moved to Live Oak, California, for six years and then in 1915 to Pacific Grove, where he built a home. He was killed by an automobile in 1920.[18]

Two-thirds of the weavers eventually became farmers in America, and most seem to have had to overcome hardship first. They appear to have been some of the poorest migrants in the sample. The stocking weaver Samuel Reed left Leicestershire in 1826 and worked as a common laborer at a number of jobs, including on the Erie Canal, until he could take up unimproved land in Illinois, on which he struggled to survive living in a log shanty. Then he mined in California and returned to Illinois to become a street commissioner.[19] In 1842 James Hardy, a twenty-three-year-old weaver with some education, left Barnsley, South Yorkshire, with his servant wife, Sarah, and his parents; his father, Henry, was a yarn dealer. Eight years later he was living with and working for a New York–born farmer. By 1860 he was living in Wisconsin as a farmer in his own right with real estate worth three thousand dollars, as recorded in the census, along with Sarah and their seven children, who were all born in Wisconsin, as well as his aging parents. Twenty-nine-year-old John Williamson, a fancy goods weaver in 1851, left Bradford for America with his wife, also a weaver. They worked together for seven years, accumulated savings, and after working four years in New Hampshire moved to Fairfield, Iowa, and bought 50 acres of unbroken prairie land with their savings of $1,000. By 1870 they had $5,000 in real estate and a personal estate worth $1,750. By 1890 they owned 120 acres, and Williamson entered politics.[20]

COMMERCE AND PROFESSIONS IN AMERICA

Among all immigrant groups the English stand out for their high numbers in commerce and the professions, both before and after their migration. About 15 percent in the sample—201 of the 1,287 with identifiable last occupations in England—were in commerce or the professions. There is no doubt that on average these were an elite group: they had a higher rate and quality of education and training. Only a third—66—of them had no record of any education, and only a handful were self-educated, while many had attended selective boarding schools and academies. Others were classified as educated according to their marriage certificates and biographies. It appears that as time went on, greater proportions were members of this class: 27 percent for the last quarter of the century compared to 16 percent for the third quarter and 11 percent for the first half of the century.

Those in commerce and the professions, especially in the last quarter-century, included many with lofty occupations such as architects, doctors, various kinds of "dealers," businessmen, and lawyers, among others. Quite a few were clerks, but probably not the lowly types because it was widely known that America already had an oversupply of common clerks. In fact, some were government clerks and brokers—people who had means. For example, one person identified as a "clerk" was Norman Logan. He was born in Brixton to a father who was first a bank clerk and then a bank manager. Logan was educated at the Elizabethan School in Aldenham, Hertfordshire, and in 1881 he began a five-year position at a real estate firm in London. At age twenty-three, in 1887, he immigrated to California to take charge of his father's mining property, and then later that year he took charge of a mine in Placer County for a London syndicate. Two years after that he returned to England to launch a mine on the stock exchange, and he then returned to America to combine ranching, farming, and running businesses. Logan may have been exceptional, but other emigrant clerks of his time had impressive experience, some traveling the world and most finding enviable positions, often professional ones, in America.[21]

It is remarkable that about a quarter—23 percent—of the English in the sample from various backgrounds ended up in American commerce or the professions. The sources probably exaggerate this figure, but even half this number would be significant. It is doubtful that any other immigrant group came close to having so many entering this class. Two main explanations seem apparent. Because the British economy was the most advanced at the time, England had more people skilled and experienced in these areas and willing to relocate in order to maximize their opportunities. Additionally there had been a long Anglo-American relationship, with English merchants and professionals dominating American trade and the professions ever since the colonial period. The lack of language barriers and a residual cultural commonality opened more doors for the English. Of those who left commerce or the professions in England, nearly a third became American farmers—64 of the 201 with last occupations—and they were fairly evenly distributed over the century. However, about half of them remained in commerce and the professions, while quite a few others became supervisors in industry.

Among those in this group leaving for America in the last quarter of the century were three architects, all of whom eventually took advantage of the building boom in California. Burgess John Reeve had paid fifteen hundred dollars for his apprenticeship in London and practiced there for twenty-two years before heading to Kansas City in 1881 and then Los Angeles a year later to build business blocks.[22] Ernest Coxhead was similarly experienced and ended up as a church architect in Los Angeles. Charles Wardle Morton had studied in Paris and practiced as an architect in England before immigrating to New York in 1884 to open his own studio and then to Sacramento.[23]

In another case, Carrington Adrian Swete, whose father was a fellow at Worcester College, Oxford, went to sea as a boy and in 1894 settled in Bakersfield, California, only to leave three months later out of disappointment. Later that year he bought forty acres in Capay Valley to raise almonds and pears, but he found that life monotonous. In 1898 he went to gold mines in Cape Norne, Alaska, for eighteen months, and then he returned in 1899 to ranch with his brother, a machinist.[24] Swete's story is worth telling because that kind of restlessness and refusal to settle for something monotonous came up time and time again with professionals, miners, and people in other occupations—more so than signs of desperation or extreme hardship.

MOVEMENT IN ENGLAND BEFORE EMIGRATION

One tantalizing question for historians is the extent to which emigration was preceded by a move within England. Did prior moves and mobility encourage or facilitate immigration to America? Was migration within England a predictor of migration to America? Perhaps a move within England—to find work or to change an occupation—was a first step in a more drastic move overseas. The database gives some useful hints. We know that a quarter of the sample, 438, did not move prior to their immigration to America and that over a third of the total, 629 or 38 percent, did have a prior move, and we can investigate those prior moves. For the rest, a little more than a third, or 36 percent, there is no evidence either way, but surely many did. A reasonable estimate, then, is that around half of the immigrants had made a prior move, which is a large figure.

Most, 60 percent, of those whom we know had a prior move were under the age of thirty at the time of their migration to America. Those with a prior move were not necessarily inclined to change occupations: in fact most, 57 percent, did not change their occupations in England. About a quarter, or 28 percent, had changed their occupations as well as their locations in England. The rest, 13 percent, are uncertain. Looking at those who made a move in England prior to their move to America, we see no occupational group that showed a special inclination to do so.

COMPARING TYPES OF COUNTIES

England's great diversity complicates the study of its economic history. Erickson and others attempted to meet the challenge by dividing England's counties into four major types: low-wage agricultural; high-wage agricultural; low-wage industrial; and high-wage industrial. (Erickson, *Leaving England*, Table 3.11, pp. 119–21; Van Vugt, *British Buckeyes*, Tables 6–8, pp. 238–45.)[25]

Low-Wage v. High-Wage Agricultural Counties

The occupational profiles of the emigrants from high-wage and low-wage agricultural counties are quite similar.[26] In neither group do we see people changing from English agriculture to nonagricultural work before leaving England to farm in America. What does show in both is that people apparently without experience in crafts nevertheless started in America with crafts, often before switching to American farming. This underscores America's open labor market, especially in rural areas, where demands for rural crafts were high. One gets the sense that the English were highly adaptable, resourceful, and flexible; perhaps had connections or networks; and were using the most practical way to obtain their American land. This seems to have been particularly true of those leaving relatively high-wage counties, where there were higher wages for farm laborers and more prosperity for farmers.

There is no doubt that those leaving both high-wage and low-wage agricultural counties included some poor, even desperate people. For example, Charles Butcher's family had long worked as wool dealers and buyers but were virtually forced to emigrate from Devon in 1843 because of a "financial disaster," a common circumstance in the early 1840s textiles industry.[27] Those who left high-wage counties were not necessarily better off than those leaving the low-wage counties. For example, John Taylor lived in extreme poverty as a shepherd in Lincolnshire before he immigrated to Boston in 1853 to join a brother who had gone there six years earlier. Starting out as a railway laborer and then a gardener, he had a personal estate valued at a mere fifty dollars, according to the 1860 U.S. census.[28] William Bridge, a Methodist with no known education, was enumerated in Wittersham, Kent, in the 1851 census as a farm laborer age nineteen living in the house of his stepfather, who was also a farm laborer, and his mother, Sarah. His seventeen-year-old sister was a servant. Twenty-one-year-old Bridge arrived in Chicago in 1852 "a poor boy," and he worked as a farmhand for his brother George, who had preceded him. William saved enough to buy a team of horses and also worked in a woolen factory to buy his farm, and by 1883 he owned 176 improved acres.[29] In another example, William Jackson seemed desperate once he got to Syracuse, New York, from his native Leicester, and he worked at "anything he could find," including for a farmer for fifty cents a day.[30]

Some of these poor immigrants overcame their circumstances through repeated moves in America in their climb up the economic ladder. Thomas Hill was described as a poor man who in 1851 emigrated from Lincolnshire to Knox County, Illinois, where he worked on a farm and at a brickyard. Hill moved often, and after taking employment in various places he went to Peoria to work in a tavern for several years. He bought a farm near Princeville and then moved in 1860 to Manito, Mason County, where he rented a farm. He rented another farm in nearby Egypt and following that bought 80 acres in Tazewell County only to sell them six months later. Then he lived in Mason County for three years before buying 280 acres in Mahito. The 1870 census enumerated him there as a farmer age forty-four with his Illinois-born wife Nancy and seven children. Ten years later, in 1880, he was listed as a farmer age fifty-five with three sons, all farm laborers. He was still on the same farm in 1894.[31]

Robert Bell used classic understatement when he described his family as being in "limited circumstances." After his mother died in 1838, Bell herded sheep and saved money for eight years for his passage to America. Although he had lost his right hand in an accident, he went first to Dubuque, Iowa, where he was enumerated in 1850 as a farm laborer. In 1850 he left to work in a New Orleans hotel, and then in 1851 he began mining in California, where he managed to accumulate thirty-five hundred dollars by 1854. After returning to England to marry, he traveled to Wisconsin and bought land in Dodge County, where the 1860 census recorded him as a farmer age thirty-two with two thousand dollars in real estate and a personal estate valued at two hundred dollars, and living with his wife Jane, twenty-one, two children, his father, Joshua Bell, and a twelve-year-old English boy named John Darling, who was in school. Bell prospered: the 1870 census recorded him as a farmer with an impressive twelve thousand dollars in real estate and a two-thousand-dollar personal estate.[32]

The database offers glimpses of how creative and resourceful some of the poorer English were in acquiring their farms. William Cook described his father as poor and worked from a young age for the equivalent of $30 per year. After leaving West Ferry, Lincolnshire, in 1849 he chopped wood for $1.50 per day in Dodge County, Wisconsin. Then in 1854 he proceeded to Fillmore County, Minnesota, where he entered 80 acres of timbered land and made a prairie claim. After breaking 40 acres, he sold up around 1857 and went to Bloomfield, Iowa, where he bought 60 acres of wild land at $10 per acre. But he had to sell two horses just to make the down payment, and he borrowed money at 20 percent to buy oxen, paying off the interest by selling butter and eggs. His success was not as spectacular as Bell's: he was enumerated in Bloomfield in 1860 as a farmer with $1,600 in real estate and a personal estate of $400 living with his English-born wife Jane and three children. Ten years later he had $4,000 in real estate and a personal estate of $2,150. By 1886 he owned 160 acres.[33] An even more spectacular success was George Burkingshaw, who arrived in the United States in 1855 with "limited capital," which he invested in a small farm. Yet he was able to build a fine house and by 1879 had a "fortune" of $13,000 to $15,000.[34]

In recounting these personal stories we find much evidence of "chain migration," of family members joining others who had gone ahead and could make immigration affordable for their poor relatives and ease their transition. This was how Henry Parker, son of a Methodist preacher, did it. After working as a farmhand in Barrowley, Lincolnshire, and then at a foundry for six months, he joined his two brothers who were already in Iowa, arriving with another brother in 1870 with only 25 cents to his name. He started out working as a farmhand and then rented land for seven years. He moved to Silver Creek, Iowa, in 1880 and bought 160 acres. His father, George, joined them in 1883 to marry his brother's widow.

Low-Wage v. High-Wage Industrial

The rest of the English counties can be divided into low-wage and high-wage industrial ones.[35] About half of the emigrants leaving low-wage industrial counties hailed from Cornwall, which would be expected: Cornwall had the highest rate of emigration in the latter half of the century as its lead, copper, and tin mines approached exhaustion, while the upper Mississippi River Valley and upper Michigan opened their mines to exploitation. One observer in Cornwall remarked in 1881, "If you want to see our Cornish miners, you must go to Pennsylvania, to Lake Superior, to Nevada; you'll find very few of them in Cornwall."[36] Warwickshire's significant representation in America is more surprising perhaps. Of thirty-six immigrants from that county with known occupations only two had left agriculture—a farm laborer and a gardener—and fifteen had left crafts—mostly building trades workers and miners. Twelve were workers from a wide variety of industrial positions, and the rest were mainly professionals.[37]

As with the low- and high-wage agricultural counties, comparing the low- and high-industrial counties yields little of interest. The high- and low-wage industrial counties had much in common. There was little difference in emigrants' decades of departure: about half in both groups left in the 1840s or 1850s. In addition there was little occupational difference, although among the emigrants from high-wage industrial counties fewer had left agriculture, more had left crafts, and only slightly more had left industry or the professions. The main difference between emigrants from the low-wage counties and those from the high-wage industrial counties was their first American occupations: the low-wage emigrants were much more likely to start in crafts—46 percent versus 26 percent—while the high-wage emigrants were more likely to start out in industry or the professions. Perhaps this is a reflection of their average higher wages in England and their relative prosperity. In addition the high-wage industrial emigrants were less likely to enter American agriculture. More notable proportions of low-wage emigrants used crafts as a stepping-stone to American farming. Farm laborers sometimes started out in crafts in America, though more continued as farm laborers or even were farmers first.[38] In summary: there was little difference between emigrants from low- and high-wage agricultural counties and between those from low- and high-wage industrial counties. Maybe the American conditions were more significant.[39]

EDUCATION

The extent of the migrants' education is inherently interesting. Did those with education, who may have had more ambition and knowledge of America, tend to emigrate more than those without? The database contains some clues. Nearly half left no evidence either way: they may or may not have been educated. Of 915 with evidence in their records, fewer than 10 percent, or 87, appear to have been illiterate and uneducated, having signed their marriage certificates with marks rather than signatures, or their lack of education was noted in their biographies. Another 33, or 4 percent, were described as having "limited" or "meager" education; another 94, or 10 percent, were said to have "learned a trade." Adding those together, 214, or almost a quarter, seem to have had little or no education. An additional 135 were described as being apprenticed—often for a full seven years—or were "bound out" as apprentices, a situation that was often exploitative but usually brought useful skills. These people were probably literate, but if we are conservative and classify them as uneducated, that leaves an estimated 60 percent with formal education, and this does not count those who were probably literate but not formally educated. A surprising number had attended colleges and professional and private schools and academies. It is doubtful that any other immigrant groups had such a high rate. Predictably, the educated emigrants were overrepresented and clustered in the later years of the century, as education became more common and compulsory for youths in 1870. However, more than a quarter of the educated, or 28 percent, had left during the first half of the century.

When correlated with occupations, the education data are more informative. About 15 percent of those we know had formal education had left agriculture for their last English occupations.[40] A fifth, or 113, had been in commerce or the professions, and nearly all apparently were educated.[41] This is not surprising: one would expect that those in that elite class were more likely to have education. In America their education facilitated the immigrants' adjustment and rise to success in any field, including farming: fully a third—201, or 36 percent—with known formal education went directly into American farming. One gets the sense that the farmers had abilities as well as education that explain their success. There seems to be a correlation between education levels and shifting to American professions or farming.[42]

Among the individuals behind the data, for example, Henry William Wolseley's formal education was combined with wide travels and remarkable life experiences and elevated him in the social and professional hierarchy. He was the son of a Lancashire Anglican clergyman; was educated at St. Peter's College, York; and in 1863 went to sea on tea-carrying merchant ships for reasons of both health and adventure and became a ship's mate. He then immigrated to Chicago, studied law, and was admitted to the bar in 1874.[43] Another example is Charles Williamson, who came from a wealthy Bristol family and studied medicine in London and Paris. He was forced to work to continue his studies after his father lost the greater part of his fortune. After becoming a doctor he immigrated to Kansas in 1855, being attracted by the slavery issue, and as a physician at Mt. Pleasant he served antislavery forces during the territorial conflicts. During the Civil War he treated proslavery groups in order to gain information from Confederate forces.[44]

RELIGION

As with education, the database provides some useful information about the migrants' religions. It confirms the special prominence of nonconformists, or dissenters, and provides some clues for deeper research. About 60 percent of all the sample emigrants had known religious affiliations. Of these about a quarter were Methodists; an additional 2 percent were Primitive Methodists, a related denomination formed in 1811. Baptists numbered sixty-one—or 6 percent of those with a known religion—and nearly as many, fifty-seven, or 6 percent, were Mormons. The Methodists were largely rural and agricultural; about 40 percent were in crafts, and about a quarter were in agriculture.

Anglicans too formed about a quarter of those with known religion, but the strength of that affiliation is uncertain as the great majority claimed Anglicanism through "Anglican marriage" or "Anglican parents." Furthermore many of the Anglicans had left Cornwall, Lincolnshire, and the West Riding, where Anglicanism was not strong. So in fact the nonconformists, especially the Methodists, were overrepresented among the immigrants—a finding that has been made in other studies as well.

Until the late 1820s nonconformists and dissenters generally had a limited role in public life, often being discriminated against in officeholding, land tenure, and higher education. Because the 1830s were a time of immense social change, as urbanization and industrial growth brought a lot of hardship—perhaps the hand-loom weavers being the most notable—many turned to evangelicalism and joined churches that were less attached to the English establishment than Anglicans were. Dissenters and members of nonconformist churches seem to have been less attached to their country and could more easily consider expatriation, especially if they could join dissenters who had gone before them.

A look at the Methodists' origins supports the generally understood notion that nonconformity, especially Calvinism and Methodism, was most successful in more rural, austere, isolated places, especially mining districts, where Anglicanism did not run deep. That nonconformity helps explain the high rates of emigration there.[45] This includes Cornwall, Devonshire, the North Riding of Yorkshire, the West Riding, and Lincolnshire. Nonconformity apparently worked along with economic changes and information about American opportunities to encourage emigration.

Surprisingly only twelve clergymen—as their last English occupation—are included in the sample, and half of them were Mormon missionaries or preachers, compared with only a few Methodists. Furthermore only four remained as clergymen in their first American occupation; most of the rest went into farming or skilled work. One who did remain in the ministry was Robert Parrett, who trained for the Anglican clergy and had a benefice before emigrating in 1816. However, after a couple of years in New Jersey he moved to Posey County, Indiana, in 1819 to farm. Parrett converted to Methodism after the Wheeler brothers arrived from England to propagate Methodism, and he joined them as a circuit rider and preacher. In 1825 he settled in Evansville and organized its first Methodist church.[46]

Joseph Wheeler of the Wheeler brothers too is in the sample. He became a Methodist in his youth, was licensed to preach at age seventeen, and worked as a missionary in London before emigrating from England with his older brother, Rev. Richard Wheeler, to Vandenburgh County, Indiana, in 1818. The following year he went to Evansville intending to go to Albion, but he fell ill. He then became a circuit rider throughout the "Bluegrass" region and helped convert Parrett to Methodism. Together, based in Evansville, they rode the circuit and organized camp meetings. By 1834 Wheeler had settled in Mechanicsville, where he preached for thirty years.[47]

THE "BOOM" OF 1850–73

All of the variables looked at so far were of course dependent on the years of emigration, and I have started to explore this by comparing two conventional periods of English economic history: the so-called "mid-Victorian boom" of 1850–73 and the "Great Depression" of 1874–1900.[48]

Nearly half, 48 percent, of the emigrants in the database sample left during the so-called "mid-Victorian boom" of 1850–73. All but ten had a recorded last

American occupation, and they were not that different from the emigrants of the whole century. Like the whole sample, about 20 percent had left agriculture as their last occupation—the same proportion for agriculture for the whole male labor force in 1851. Also similar, only 16 percent of those in agriculture were clearly farmers, while just less than half, 40 percent, were farm laborers and a quarter, 28 percent, were farmers' sons—the remainder being shepherds, gardeners, and the like. From this we deduce that during the years of widespread agricultural prosperity successful, bona fide farmers were not leading the agrarian movement to America; rather it was those who found it hard to farm in England, especially if they wanted to own land, who were leaving. Quite a number of sons of well-to-do English farmers are in the sample, but few wealthy farmers themselves are represented.[49]

It was in many ways a golden age for agriculture, both in Britain and America, and the best time for people from all backgrounds—nonagricultural and agricultural alike—to become landowning farmers in America. Four in ten—325=41 percent—of the boom emigrants ended up in American agriculture, which is a higher percentage than for the migrants of the last quarter-century. About 40 percent of the "boom emigrants" who ended up in American agriculture had left English agriculture. About a quarter, 22 percent, left crafts, and 6 percent left some form of unskilled labor.[50] In comparison, of those who left during the first half of the century and who ended up in American agriculture only 31 percent had left agriculture as their last English occupation, and about the same percentage had left crafts. For both periods, remarkable numbers of people with or without known farming experience entered American agriculture.

As can be seen in the occupational history of those in crafts, in the third quarter of the century they comprised a third of the sample migrants, while they comprised 30 percent of the labor force in 1851 and 1881.[51] However, about a fifth of the sample craftsmen first worked as farm laborers, unskilled laborers, or industrial workers before turning to a craft in England and then leaving for America. Turning to a craft in England was a step up, and a step toward America.[52] Surprisingly, only a quarter—58 of the 225—of the craft workers who migrated to America during the boom years ended up in farming as their last occupation. About 40 percent remained in crafts, and about 1 in 5 ended up in commerce or the professions. Some turned to industrial work, usually as foremen, manufacturers, and so on. Altogether the data show a remarkable variety of options for people skilled in crafts and a significant persistence in that work in America.

DEPRESSION OF 1874

Some notable differences apply to the emigrants who left from 1874 to the 1890s, which were years of widespread depression in England. During the so-called

Great Depression of British Agriculture many people in English agriculture struggled to maintain profits in an age of free trade, global overproduction of grains, and cheap transport by steamships. Additionally both Britain and the United States experienced industrial depressions from 1873 to the 1880s. When we look at the "depression" emigrants' last English and first and last American occupations, some interesting patterns emerge (see tables 3–5).

TABLE 3. LAST ENGLISH OCCUPATIONS, 1874–1916

20 Agriculture=12%
6 Labor=4%
8 Service=5%
60 Preindustrial crafts (33 of these in mining)=36%
28 Industry=17%
44 Commerce and professions=26%
   32 Unknown
   N=198=100%

TABLE 4. FIRST KNOWN U.S. OCCUPATIONS, 1874–1916

37 Agriculture=20%
21 Labor=11% (mostly factory labor)
1 Service=0%
60 Preindustrial crafts (38 of these in mining)=32%
35 Industry=19%
33 Commerce and professions=18%
   N=187=100%

TABLE 5. LAST KNOWN U.S. OCCUPATIONS, 1874–1916

46 Agriculture=23%
5 Labour = 3%
5 Service=3%
47 Preindustrial crafts (23 of these miners)=24%
35 Industry=18%
59 Commerce and professions=30%
   N=197=101.1%

Only 12 percent left English agriculture, and most of these were farm laborers or farmers' sons. About a third were in crafts. Only 17 percent left behind English industry. For some, this was their first step, especially for craftsmen entering farming in America. We see that there was a shift to commercial and professional pursuits: nearly a third. This reflects the new modernizing American economy and declining opportunities in American farming but also the quality of the immigrants, especially their education and professional and commercial experience. Gradually more entered commerce and the professions, which one would expect as the immigrants achieved success and moved out of skilled labor or farming as they got older. The late-century immigrants who stayed in American industry were typically machinists building materials, manufacturers, mill and firm owners, engineers, superintendents, managers, and the like.[53]

THE WEST RIDING OF YORKSHIRE

The database can tell us about the emigrants' specific counties and regions. The West Riding of Yorkshire offers a good start. It was England's second most industrialized county after Lancashire, but the West Riding was more varied in terms of its industries and its adjustments to mechanization.[54] Additionally the West Riding contained large rural and agricultural areas where people often combined farming with weaving.

A total of 147 emigrants in the sample left the West Riding of Yorkshire. They had a broad range of occupations that reflected the extensive industrialization of the county. A third, 55, were industrial workers, about three-fourths of whom—39=72 percent—were connected with the textiles industries. The rest of the industrial emigrants were employed in the iron industry, all of them skilled, such as grinders, forge men, and machinists.[55] Thus those emigrating from the West Riding to America were quite varied but more industrial than those leaving other counties, with the exception of Lancashire.

TEXTILES TO AMERICAN AGRICULTURE

Half of the sample industrial emigrants from the West Riding entered American agriculture either immediately or after working for a while in America.[56] The transition from industry to American agriculture was especially prevalent among textiles workers: of the thirty-nine textiles workers in the sample only five went into textiles and stayed, while half, twenty, went into agriculture—most of them immediately and the rest after first working in textiles or some other work. The remainder went into a variety of occupations, especially mining or crafts. They seem to have been willing and able to endure great rigors to become American farmers. One typical example is Samuel Crawshaw, a thirty-nine-year-old clothier who immigrated to Philadelphia in 1828 and worked there for nineteen months, apparently to accumulate capital, and then bought uncleared land near Carbondale, Illinois, and began the backbreaking task of clearing a farm out of the virgin forest. Six years later he was still farming and served as a local preacher.[57]

Details of their American lives reveal certain strategies of how the textiles workers often went through phases to become successful farmers. Usually it meant working for farmers to acquire the knowledge necessary for American farming. Three textiles emigrants in the sample left Huddersfield, which was a major producer of woolens with a large population of weavers, many of whom were involved with the Luddite movement and other forms of resistance to the new machinery. There is no indication of any such distress or protest behind the sample emigrants' moves. Thomas Firth, who was born in nearby Lindley and married in 1819, was described as a "woolen manufacturer" and seems not to have been poor since he was able to emigrate with his children even during the depressed "hungry forties," in 1847—the year after his wife died. He went directly to New York City to work for a carpet manufacturing firm. In 1861 he left for Randolf County, Illinois, where he remarried and bought a farm, although three of his sons remained with the carpet firm, suggesting that the work there was good but that Firth was fulfilling a long-term goal of farming in America.[58]

If indeed roughly half of the emigrant textiles workers from West Yorkshire entered American farming, as the sample suggests, this high proportion can be explained by their complex backgrounds. Many textiles workers, especially weavers, had some experience with farming, perhaps had combined weaving with farming, and were going to America with some earnings to buy land. They were willing to work in textiles or other work first, but some went right into farming and even bought unimproved land, which required years of backbreaking work. The line between agriculture and industrial work was often blurred, which could actually assist these people's adjustments to change.

All but a few of the sample textiles workers who entered American agriculture did so in the 1840s and 1850s, the "golden age" of American farming when more and more good land was being made available and local markets could sustain family farms. They were settling in the American Midwest but also Pennsylvania and western New York. Some took up farming in Utah, reflecting the success of the Mormon mission in Yorkshire and Mormons' massive migration to that territory.[59]

TEXTILES TO TEXTILES

Roughly the same number of sample textiles immigrants remained in textiles as went into farming. Usually they and other industrial workers did the same line of work, but many rose to supervisory positions, sometimes soon after or upon their arrival. In fact, nineteen of the fifty-five industrial emigrants from the West Riding—more than a third—became superintendents, mill owners, managers, foremen, store owners, and the like. Most rose from humble origins such as that of weaver, but some had left Yorkshire with skills and experience that helped them rise in America.[60] Positions of authority could come easily to English immigrants, in part because of their reputation as leaders in textiles. The linen mill worker John Cuttle left Leeds in 1851 for Schenectady, New York, where he remarried—apparently his first wife having died since later he was recorded as living with his four English-born children. He rose quickly in his career. In 1852 he was in Fall River, where he was mill superintendent for the American Linen Company. Later he started a meat and grocery business and then became president of a publishing company.[61]

Four sample emigrants left from Honley, near Huddersfield. The most interesting case is that of Henry Marsden, who left at the height of the textiles depression in 1842 for Chicago to work as a woolen mill foreman. Living in Honley from 1832 to 1842, he was recorded as a clothier in 1833 and a weaver in 1836. He moved to Leeds and then Blackburn before immigrating to America. He described himself as a factory overseer immediately before his migration. In America his wife died after only two years, and he kept up his frequent moves, relocating at least three times. The 1860 American census recorded him as a farmer living with five children and having two thousand dollars in real estate and a personal estate valued at one thousand dollars. Marsden, like so many others, had a history of frequent changes in his place and occupation and an adaptability that suited him well in America.[62]

After the Civil War there were more cases of Yorkshire textiles immigrants rising to supervisory levels. William Taylor was a child of the Huddersfield mills, already working there by age nine. He and his wife were worsted weavers, and by 1874 he had become a partner in his worsted firm. He sold his share before emigrating at age thirty-two, in 1884, and so he must have had resources. After working for a short while in Ontario, he then became superintendent for mills in Rhode Island, Massachusetts, and Maine. He took time to tour the western states. The pattern of superintending mills in so many places suggests that perhaps he was being recruited, or at least was moving frequently to take better and better positions.[63]

CONCLUSION

In some ways the industrial emigrants from the West Riding reflected the larger population of English immigrants. Relatively few appear to have been moving to escape unemployment, technological displacement, or conflict with management, although some were moving out of poverty or needed employment. Desperation seems not to have caused many to emigrate; but America could still act as an escape route, even a safety valve, for those who did not relish a life stuck in factories. The significant shift from industry to American farming especially suggests something more positive. Farming one's own land during this time was an immensely powerful incentive, offering a fulfillment perhaps impossible to comprehend fully today. Landownership was a deeply held cultural ideal, especially for the English, for whom it had long been associated with voting rights and liberty. For many it was the best or only way not only to achieve a competency and independence but also to fulfill a moral, even spiritual quest. The English emigrants seem to have had long-term plans to take up farming in America and likely had been in contact with others who had gone before them. Probably the most notable fact and area for further research emanating from this preliminary study is the large movement into American farming of people who had little or no prior agricultural experience and how they succeeded.

At first it may seem improbable that people working in textiles or the iron and other industries so readily entered American agriculture. However, many of these people had originally left farming or farm labor to work in factories and had taken on industrial identities while maintaining aspirations to farm once the time was right. Some had combined weaving with farming and headed to America to fulfill their life ambitions. Yet many others seem to have had no prior experience with farming. For those in preindustrial crafts, the link with agriculture both in England and America was even greater.[64]

One widely shared characteristic among both agricultural and nonagricultural English emigrants was their continued mobility in America. Having made the move across the ocean, they seem to have been willing, even eager, to make more moves in the United States in order to fulfill their ambitions. One remarkable but not isolated case is that of Curtis P. Casson, a miller from Thorn who migrated to New Jersey in 1831 at age nineteen. Casson's skills at mill building took him many different places to live: he reported eleven moves in America. His and others' stories show a resourcefulness, perhaps even a restlessness, an ability to adjust, and a willingness and even eagerness to clear a farm.[65]

The industrial and preindustrial emigrants from the West Riding or any other part of England were apparently not content to be stuck in one place or job. Rather they seem to have been ambitious go-getters who wanted to make the most of their lives. As the data and sketches presented here indicate, these people made vital contributions to the American economy and society and were at the forefront of pushing the American frontier westward.

English immigrants achieved impressive upward social and economic mobility. Half ended up as farmers, almost all with their own farms, many of them large estates. The database perhaps exaggerates this feature, but probably not too seriously. For those from Lancashire, the West Riding, and most other places, American farming could indeed be an escape from industrial and urban life or from a rural life with limitations for the future. Probably no other immigrant group had such a high percentage that succeeded so spectacularly and remained so predominantly in American agriculture. All in all, this was a stunning group achievement for people aiming to own land and gain independence. This is one of the main stories behind the people in the sample. America could be a "safety valve" for rural artisans and industrial workers as well as unskilled laborers. They could not become farmers in England—especially not landowners—but they could in America. Any desperation seems to have been outweighed by higher aspirations and goals. In other words, they were motivated more by the American "pull" than by the English "push."

The project also underscores the complexity of the migrants. They are hard to pin down. They were more complex in their occupations and abilities than we originally thought. Even the database does not capture all of their changes, mutations, or skills. We should certainly not underestimate these people or their resolve. How do we comprehend fully people such as William Tonks, a blacksmith who left Staffordshire in 1856 and once in America walked across the Great Plains to get to Utah?[66] How do we understand others who endured incredible hardships in carving farms out of the American wilderness? America seems to have attracted a certain quality of English persons: those with ability and a fierce determination to succeed. For many that meant finding a way to get their land even if they had little or no farm experience. Like many other ethnic migrants in the country, they channeled all their efforts, resources, experiences—their very lives—to make it in America.

NOTES

1. Erickson did take great pains to achieve a sample that was as representative as possible by aiming for a proportionate number of cases for each county, as well as for years of high and low emigration, and covering the American counties that had both higher-than-average and lower-than-average populations of English as well as a balance between rural and urban places. The sample is likely biased toward the more successful immigrants and those who became farmers and members of the middle class, which we can take into consideration. In addition the American county histories are weighted toward the successful ones, or at last those immigrants who were eager to have their stories told in those histories. Also the southern states and most western states except California and Utah did not publish county histories. Therefore the American Midwest, the Atlantic states, New England, those counties hugging the Mississippi River, and California and Utah are the focus in the database, just as they were the focus of settlement for the vast majority of nineteenth-century English immigrants. See Charlotte Erickson Database, Archives and Special Collections, London School of Economics (hereafter referred to as LSE), London, England.

2. These English seem to have handled well the often Anglophobic attacks against "foreign ownership" in the American West. They may have known about the opportunities for purchasing land from the heavy involvement of British investors in the American West. For more, see Edward P. Crapol, *America for Americans: Economic Nationalism and Anglophobia in the Late Nineteenth Century* (Westport, Conn.:

Greenwood Press, 1973); Jay P. Sexton, *Debtor Diplomacy: Finance and Foreign Relations in the American Civil War Era* (New York: Oxford University Press, 2005), 249–51; James Belich, *Replenishing the Earth: The Settler Revolution and the Rise of the Anglo World, 1783–1939* (New York: Oxford University Press, 2009), 119.

3. Of these 394, 85 were laborers; 33 were servants; 152 were in crafts (i.e., 1 in 5—152 out of 808—of all whom farmed in America [total 808], left crafts in England); 62 were in industry (only 8 percent of the total 808); and 64 were in commerce or the professions. Of these 394, 46 were in agriculture before going into their nonagricultural work in England, before emigrating and doing American farming. There is no first occupation listed for 52 of them.

4. Of the forty-seven cases of those who did agricultural and then nonagricultural work in England before emigrating and farming permanently in America, a few characteristics emerge. Eighteen of them left farm labor for various forms of unskilled labor or worked for both farmers and nonfarmers; four were specifically factory laborers, in steel or engine works, or were road workers; six were in service; thirteen had entered crafts before their emigration, mainly building trades workers, miners, butchers, and others who traditionally lived near or on farms or could combine both; and only three were industrial workers, all of them in textiles from Stockton, Bradford, or Bolton, the heart of the industrial north. Iowa was over-represented as a destination, with twelve migrating there. Seventeen left England in the 1840s, fifteen in the 1850s, and six in the 1870s.

5. ID 983, LSE ("ID" refers to the person's identification number in the database). See also Charlotte Erickson, *Invisible Immigrants: The Adaptation of English and Scottish Immigrants in 19th-Century America* (London: Weidenfeld and Nicolson, 1972).

6. The database also shows that of 273 who had started in English agriculture, 69 of them then turned to nonagricultural work before leaving for America. Of these 69, 49 went into American agriculture.

7. ID 1595, LSE.

8. ID 1043, LSE.

9. Of the 808, 134—from a variety of last English occupations—started out as farm laborers in America. This is 16.6 percent of the 808.

10. Among many examples, see ID 77, 93, LSE. For blending carpentry and farming, see ID 937, LSE.

11. ID 446, LSE. For a similar case, see ID 569, 1034, LSE.

12. See, for example, Rowland Tappan Berthoff, *British Immigrants in Industrial America, 1790–1950* (Cambridge, Mass.: Harvard University Press, 1953).

13. Of the 178 English immigrants who went into American industry and stayed, the most common origin was the West Riding of Yorkshire, followed by Lancashire, and the most common occupation in England was in the iron industry, followed by textiles.

14. New York was the most common destination, followed by Massachusetts and Pennsylvania, which indicates that the industrial immigrants were staying where there were plentiful industrial jobs, while those entering agriculture headed for the Midwest and upper Mississippi River Valley. Fifteen went to Massachusetts, five to

New Jersey, twenty-eight to New York, and fourteen to Pennsylvania. Two of these went into agriculture first in America and then to the textiles work they had left in England.

15. Of the 205 industrial workers (last English occupation), 123 ended in America in industry or commerce and the professions, and of these 123, 51 clearly became owners, superintendents, partners, and so on.

16. ID 586, LSE.

17. ID 1275, LSE.

18. ID 1148, LSE.

19. ID 251, LSE. William Hill resorted to living in a stable while he sought land in Wisconsin after his emigration from Cheshire in 1842 (ID 1225, LSE).

20. ID 396, LSE.

21. ID 1094, LSE. Aldenham School in Hertfordshire is an English "public school."

22. ID 1099, LSE.

23. ID 1028, LSE.

24. ID 1115, LSE.

25. In this scheme the low-wage agricultural counties are Bedfordshire, Berkshire, Buckinghamshire, Cambridgeshire, Devon, Dorset, Hampshire, Herefordshire, Hertfordshire, Huntingdonshire, Norfolk, Northamptonshire, Oxford, Rutland, Shropshire, Somerset, Suffolk, Surrey, and Wiltshire. The high-wage agricultural counties are Cumberland, Kent, Lincolnshire, Sussex, and Westmorland.

26. In both groups of counties just under half (44–45 percent) of the emigrants started out in America in agriculture, about a fifth in crafts, and a tenth in commerce or the profession, respectively. For their final American occupations, again there were no significant differences: about two-thirds from both low- and high-wage agricultural counties ended up in American farming as their final occupation. The emigrants from low-wage agricultural counties were somewhat distinctive for leaving agricultural work in England, then starting out in crafts in America, and then finally returning to farming in America. The emigrants leaving high-wage agricultural counties were more clustered in the 1840s and especially the 1850s, whereas there were more low-wage agricultural emigrants in the 1830s and 1860s. The 1850s especially were common years for those leaving the high-wage counties—nearly half (45 percent), which may reflect the growing prosperity of the 1850s, even after the repeal of the Corn Laws opened up the British market to foreign grain. As for their occupations in America, the low- and high-wage agricultural emigrants were virtually identical. Nearly 40 percent of the emigrants who left the high-wage agricultural counties for America were in agriculture, as compared with 32.5 percent of those who left the low-wage agricultural counties. Of these agricultural emigrants, twelve were farmers, thirteen were farmers' sons, and thirty-four were farm laborers; there were also some described as gardeners and shepherds. As might have been predicted, the emigrants leaving the high-wage agricultural counties of England were mainly seeking a life of American farming: although 39 percent of them left agriculture in England, 44 percent were able to take up agriculture as their first occupation in America, while 65 percent ended up in agriculture as their last occupation.

27. ID 660, LSE. For a similar case, see that of William Hackett from Nottingham-shire in 1821, ID 751, LSE.

28. ID 456, LSE.

29. ID 61, LSE.

30. ID 67, LSE. Arthur Stubbs's father too emigrated "in desperate circumstances" from West Yorkshire, in 1851 (ID 285, LSE).

31. ID 154, LSE.

32. ID 440, LSE.

33. ID 441, LSE. In another case, Abraham Gould arrived from Kent with only 50 cents (ID 236, LSE). William Cousins too was poor (ID 444, LSE). In 1851 he arrived in America $100 in debt and settled in Eden (Low Moor) as a farmer. He was enumerated in Eden in 1860 as a farmer age forty-two with $870 in real estate and a $400 personal estate, a wife, three children, and a "domestic." Also registered in the household were an English-born adult male and three small children with two surnames who were born in Iowa. By 1879 he had 320 acres of farmland and two town plots valued at $30,000–$35,000. Cousins had retired by then.

34. ID 459, LSE.

35. The low-wage industrial counties are Cornwall, Gloucestershire, Leicestershire, Warwickshire, and Worcestershire. The high-wage industrial counties are Cheshire, Derbyshire, Durham, East Riding of Yorkshire, Lancashire, London/Middlesex, Northumberland, Nottinghamshire, West Riding of Yorkshire; see Charlotte Erickson, *Leaving England: Essays on British Emigration in the Nineteenth Century* (Ithaca, N.Y.: Cornell University Press, 1994), 120. I have included East Riding, Yorkshire, and West Riding, Yorkshire; it is not clear why Erickson omitted those. Also, I have not included North Riding for high-wage agriculture.

36. Quoted in Berthoff, *British Immigrants in Industrial America,* 59.

37. Only thirty-seven had known last occupations.

38. Of the one hundred farm laborers, thirty-nine also started out as farm labor-ers in America; twenty-five started out as farmers—either owners or renters; nine started in crafts; and the rest started in various forms of labor or are unknown.

39. Seventy-six of the low-wage industrial emigrants started out in crafts in America but then ended up in American agriculture. This is 32 percent of all the emigrants from these counties. Of these seventy-six, nine were blacksmiths, and all started out in America doing other work before moving to farming. All seventy-six became farm-ers of their own farms. Twenty were building trades workers, mostly carpenters; a few were cabinetmakers and bricklayers; thirty-three were miners; five were shoemakers; and four were stonemasons.

40. Seven percent (38) had left labor, 4 percent (20) service, 24 percent (133) crafts, and 14 percent (77) industry.

41. Information about their education is listed for 138 of those in commerce or the professions, and of these, 16 were apprenticed, 6 had "little" or "scant" education, and the rest were educated.

42. Thirty percent of those with known education ended up in commerce and the professions. A quarter of those known to be educated (132) went into American crafts.

43. ID 311, LSE.

44. ID 565, LSE. Williamson was a doctor in Mount Pleasant, Kansas until 1859, when he moved to St. Nicholas as surgeon to the Kansas militia during the Civil War. He moved in 1865 to Tecumseh and in 1867 made a homestead claim in Washington, where he was listed as a physician in 1870 with a personal estate of only one hundred dollars, a wife named Sarah, and six Kansas-born children. In 1873 he opened a drugstore in Washington. From 1871 to 1887 he was a U.S. pension surgeon but kept his drugstore.

45. David Hempton, *Methodism: Empire of the Spirit* (New Haven: Yale University Press, 2005), 93–94. Richard Carwardine, *Transatlantic Revivalism: Popular Evangelicalism in Britain and America, 1790–1865* (Westport, Conn., Greenwood Press, 1978), 10, 32–33, 10. A. D. Gilbert, *Religion and Society in Industrial England, 1740–1914: Church, Chapel and Social Change* (London: Longman, 1976). Hugh McLeod, *Religion and Society, 1850–1914* (Basingstoke, 1996).

46. ID 361, LSE.

47. ID 375, LSE.

48. The "boom" is of course problematic, even mythical. Historians such as R. A. Church have stressed that there is no true distinctive "historical unity" for these years, and yet with qualifications we can refer to a great "Victorian Boom" because prices and growth rose and living standards improved significantly. (Church: R. A. Church, *The Great Victorian Boom 1850–1873* [London: 1975]). "By 1851, the bulk of the population was, for the first time, sharing in the benefits of economic growth with a sustained rise in income per head"; see Colin Harvie and Martin Daunton, "Society and Economic Life" in Colin Matthew, ed., *Short Oxford History of the British Isles: The Nineteenth Century* (Oxford: Oxford University Press, 2000). Growth was most spectacular between 1853 and 1856, 1863 and 1865, and 1871 and 1873, although 1858 was a year of "profound depression." Generally, although the percentage of the labor force engaged in agriculture dropped from 22 percent in 1851 to 14 percent in 1871, it was a "golden age for British agriculture" with "'high farming' and high profits and with investment in new farm buildings, drainage, and herds of animals to fertilize the soil." (ibid., 53–54). But real wages rose significantly only from the mid-1860s on (ibid., 28, 74). Thus the third quarter of the century, which is widely viewed as a period of economic growth in England and America, was especially propitious for English farmers and farm laborers but also for those in rural crafts to pursue farming in America.

49. See cases ID 454 and 455, LSE; the latter's father farmed six hundred acres in Middlesex in 1849.

50. Some who were classified as common laborers at their time of emigration had first occupations as farmers. See William Robinson, who left Lincolnshire in 1844, ID 1267, LSE.

51. Erickson, *Leaving England,* table 3.6.

52. There was little difference between their first and last English occupations.

53. In 1890 more than 20 percent of the English and Welsh natives in the United States were farmers. The 1890 census also shows that adult male British immigrants were still more likely than other immigrants or native-born Americans to be working

in mining and various forms of manufacturing and much more likely to be engaged in textiles and iron and steel. Only 30 percent of the English immigrants of 1875–90 were classified as unskilled laborers—a percentage far lower than that for other immigrants of that time. See William E. Van Vugt, "British (English, Scottish, Scots Irish, Welsh) and British Americans, 1870–1940," in Immigrants in American History: Arrival, Adaptation, and Integration,4 vols., ed. Elliott R. Barkan (Santa Barbara, Calif.: ABC Clio, 2013), 2:235–44.

54. Both were dominated by textiles, but whereas Lancashire produced mainly cotton, the West Riding produced much woolen as well as cotton and was more involved with other industries that were undergoing change in the nineteenth century, especially steel and coal.

55. Only thirteen (under 10 percent) were from agriculture, mostly farmers or farmers' sons, but four specified as farm laborers. Only six were nonagricultural, presumably unskilled laborers, although one was specified as a railway laborer. These proportions were low for British emigration generally and reflect the higher proportions from the West Riding who were engaged in industry. A fifth were skilled craftsmen, mostly building trades workers, millers, tailors, and a few miners. Another twelve were clerks, bookkeepers, merchants, students, and the like.

56. Of the twenty West Riding industrial emigrants who entered American agriculture, fifteen were in textiles (six weavers, three clothiers) and the rest were classified as foreman, "woollen mill manufacturer," wool "worker," wool finisher, comber, or "fancy goods maker." The other five were in the iron industry, two of them blade grinders, one a smelter, one a pattern maker, and one a millwright.

57. ID 52, LSE. The 1850 census enumerated Crawshaw as a farmer in Jackson County with five hundred dollars in real estate; an English-born wife, Elizabeth, age fifty-nine; and one daughter, age sixteen, who was born in Illinois.

58. ID 323, LSE.

59. There were five Mormons in the West Riding sample, reflecting the Mormon mission there. Industrial areas undergoing significant changes that included technological displacement were ripe areas for Mormons. See ID 931, 935, 938, 964, 979, LSE.

60. See John Barker (ID 1148, LSE), who was a foreman, and Samuel Best (ID 588, LSE), a manager.

61. ID 641, LSE. Some immigrants rose even without experience in textiles: e.g., John Wilson, a Yorkshire bookkeeper, was given a job as an overlooker in an American carpet factory, for which he had no prior experience (Erickson, *Invisible Immigrants,* 249).

62. ID 1249, LSE.

63. ID 642, LSE. An early twentieth-century case was Samuel Best, who left in 1902. His father was working as a superintendent of a worsted mill in 1859 but an innkeeper in 1879. Best first went to Philadelphia to start a wool combing plant based on the English system. He became superintendent of the Hudson Worsted Company in 1909 and was still there apparently as late as 1927. Textiles workers were certainly not confined to either farming or their former lines of work; some turned to something completely different in America, often starting at the bottom and working to the top.

John Webster, a cloth dresser in a Leeds mill, emigrated alone in 1853 to pave the way for his family, who followed two years later. Webster migrated to Chicago and worked as a laborer for the Chicago Gas Light and Coke Company, but rather soon he became the assistant secretary of the company, and he died in 1866; see ID 452, LSE.

64. This was also Erickson's finding for those who left Lancashire; see her *Leaving England*, 231.

65. ID 1166, LSE.

66. ID 946, LSE. For similar cases, see ID 958, 952, LSE.

Ethnic Conflict and English Associational Culture in America

The Benevolent Order of the Society of St. George, 1870–1920

> I cannot feel that America is my country; I am made to feel a stranger here, and I am made to see that the English power, and the English influence and the English hate, and the English boycott against the Irish-Irishmen is [*sic*] to-day as active in America as it is in Ireland.

> Fenian and dynamite campaigner Jeremiah
> O'Donovan Rossa, *Rossa's Recollections, 1838–1898*

Between 1814 and 1860 some "three and a quarter millions of the natives of Great Britain and Ireland, 'a population for a kingdom,' have emigrated [*sic*] to this country," wrote Joseph C. G. Kennedy, superintendent of the U.S. census.[1] While the Irish dominated the latter part of this period, many English leavers added to America's already dominant Anglo-Protestant ethno-culture, thus strengthening the organic roots their forebears had first planted. Thus, while the emergence of the United States had been predicated upon violent rejection of British rule, there remained a primordial connection between motherland and new land through U.S. adherence to English socio-legal and constitutional traditions and via enormous British investment in American industry, transport, and commerce. This deeply entrenched Englishness stifled to the point of fury the zealous Fenian Jeremiah O'Donovan Rossa. Moreover the influence was practical and prosaic as well as cultural. English capitalists were widespread, with their investment crucial to early American industrialization. English workers attained better-paid skilled work far more regularly than their Irish counterparts did; indeed the ethnicity of O'Donovan Rossa's countrymen was synonymous with the lower end of the labor market.[2]

These factors were understandably anathemas to an exile such as O'Donovan Rossa. However, the historical and economic associations had a negative impact on English immigrants in some ways. For one thing, cultural hybridity or synonymy shaped how the English should be received in the United States and help explain why relatively so little has been written about English immigrants in the United States and why historians, assuming the veracity of these umbilical Anglo-American connections, have largely played down the ethnicity of the English.[3] Indeed some scholars have seen them as ethnically "invisible" because of their inherent similarity to their hosts.[4] Clearly there is much truth in notions of ease of transfer, for the English found much less that was alien to them than might have been true of the Ukrainian, the German, or even the Irish Catholic.

Yet ethnicity was a visible characteristic to many of the English. Like virtually every other immigrant group in the United States, they founded societies based on birth qualifications—exclusively for persons of English birth or descent and excluding all other nationalities, except sometimes the Welsh, who often were too few in number to found their own societies. These terms were applied to the various St. George's Societies set up from the early 1700s to disburse charity to the poorer and more unfortunate classes of their countrymen. The same also was true of the later Benevolent Order of the Sons of St. George (OSStG), a ritual-bound, initially clandestine, friendly society that emerged out of ethnic and class conflict on the Pennsylvania coalfields. Founded in 1870, the OSStG emerged amid the class struggle of workers and masters. Organized principally by the Miners Benevolent Association (MBA) and then by the Order of the Knights of Labor (KOL), the OSStG came to represent English and, to a lesser extent, Welsh workers' ethnic and class interests. In one sense these associations—whether charities or friendly societies—were set up simply to help their own communities. However, they also were laced with a degree of sectarian awareness. Some were exclusive to Protestants, in a sure-fire attempt to exclude Catholics, for which we may read "Irish"; others, such as the OSStG, were forged in the fires of English/Welsh/British-Irish conflict in industrial America. While the Irish initially lacked something in class and sectional power due to their socioeconomic status and workplace roles, they made up for some of this shortfall in their sheer numbers. In turn their numbers ensured that naturalization drives and political mobilization under the flag of the Democrats constituted a successful story that the English- or wider British-born—who were generally around one-third the number of the Irish-born—could not match. The balance of advantages and disadvantages made for a curious series of conflicts and fault lines, none of which have been adequately explored in a body of scholarship that downplays the very concept of a distinct English-born group. What unfolds here challenges this easy assumption.

This essay does not propose that the English were as universally ethnic as, for example, the Germans, whose array of societies and events covered seemingly all aspects of life.[5] What it does do is propose that not all English folks were universally comfortable or privileged in the new communities. While acknowledging the superior experiences of English people who were highly skilled workers, managers, and capitalists, it also suggests that many of their number were like many other immigrant groups in that they struggled against poverty and under-privilege to find a foothold in the new community. While ordinary English un-skilled agriculturalists, workers in pressed and dying handicrafts, political rebels, and lesser venture capitalists sought an idealized society in America, this type of utopianism was not a norm for average workers crossing the ocean. For them, a better life was realistically sought and negotiated in a world of difficulties and tribulations often little different from those at home, and sometimes far worse.

THE ETHNICIZATION OF THE ENGLISH IN AMERICA AND ITS CAUSES

Like their German, Scots, or Scandinavian counterparts, many expectant Eng-lish folks found U.S. capitalism no less severe than the system they had left behind. Among the skilled, there emerged a battle to protect the advantages in craft, workplace, pay, and conditions that they had migrated to expect. For the unskilled, or within the less technical forms of labor, workers could find them-selves strongly or wholly inadequately resourced for survival in the new country. At times St. George's Societies, which were planted in most major towns in the American Northeast and the Canadian Great Lakes region as well as in every major eastern port of entry, aided dozens of hard-up cases, collectively dispens-ing thousands of dollars annually. English workers also formed mutual self-help societies, such as the Order of the Sons of St. George, following the conventions of collectivism against hardship that they had known back home and which was central to community life in the United States. A significant minority of English emigrants, then, lived more normal and challenging immigrant lives than the ethnic history of the United States would ordinarily lead us to believe. Apart from those who fell on the charitable mercy of the social superiors, many thou-sands more contributed to rates of return emigration that were second only, in European terms, to those of the Italians.[6] Taken together, these variables suggest a far weaker and more varied relationship with the United States than integra-tionist models suggest.[7] This essay thus critically examines some of the issues around the perceived ease of English immigrants' transition into American life by exploring the sectarianism of English immigrant life and the continued place occupied by the Irish as mortal enemies of Britain.

The discussion here focuses on the OSStG. While conflict shaped the OSStG in the early years, the organization eventually flowered into a huge self-help as-sociation focusing on sociability and the public celebration of English roots. Un-like the St. George's Societies, the OSStG was not an ethnic charity. It was at first an example of working-class solidarity. It was born from sectarian fears and eco-nomic hardship and therefore took on an ethnic character, supporting English-men and Protestants but not Britons or Irishmen or Catholics. The OSStG shared at least its nationality qualification with the likes of the St. Patrick's Benevolent Association, which similarly combined collectivism and patriotism. In excluding Catholics, it was, however, more like Ulster's Orange Order. Taken together such organizations represented powerful forces of ethnocentric communalism and were not restricted to one or another national group. Most nationalities formed such groups, and the English were no exception.

The OSStG conformed to a powerful independent streak within English associational culture, aping the styles of craft, sectional, and ethnic fraternities they had known at home. Workingmen of substance joined together to protect themselves collectively against the vagaries of modern industrial life; they also joined because fraternity depicted them as improving, solid, and respectable. With mass emigration, "the idea of fraternity, and how to organize it, was one of nineteenth-century Europe's most visible exports to the New World."[8] One strategy was for friendly societies that gathered funds from members for the benefit of members to be transported overseas, as indeed many were.[9]

The European background to the OSStG was not its only explanation. America, as De Tocqueville observed, took the principle of "joining" to altogether new levels since enjoying the fruits of community required active participation in it.[10] In frontier communities fellowship was vital; among devout and Godly folk, confraternity had a dimension of religious fellowship. During the nineteenth century Americans could choose from an abundance of fraternities, societies, and clubs that united principles of charity, self-help, and civic consciousness, outstripping even the many possible associations available to Englishmen in the old country.

The OSStG was born out of a heightening ethnic consciousness. Indeed conflict between the English and the Irish, or between Protestants and Catholics, made accommodation with American capitalism still more difficult because it split the working class in ways that did not suit its wider interests. Such factors were far more noticeable in the United States than elsewhere. Britain had cheap Irish labor and landless rural migrants to break strikes and press down wages, but the United States had many more groups competing for survival, as well as slaves and former slaves, to weaken the prospects for worker solidarity. It was not that the binary division was purely on the lines of race and ethnicity, even if these cleavages were naturally most common. In the 1830s, for example, when Baltimore hat manufacturers sought to force down wages, they looked to "women and English and German immigrants, not freedmen or slaves."[11] America clearly offered infinitely greater opportunities to the poor Irish than their homeland did, but the same was not so clearly the case for English workers who made the same journey. Moreover, like the Irish and others, the English provided plenty of instances of poor workers desperate to secure work and pay with barely a thought to class-consciousness.

THE IRISH IMPETUS TO ENGLISH ETHNICITY

The desperate English cases filing before the stewards of the elite English charities, the St. George's Societies, in any of the major U.S. or Canadian cities further
undermined the imposition of a blanket narrative of English success. A further
factor playing against the ease-of-entry thesis was intense ethnic conflict between
the English and the Irish in industrial America. With Britons vastly outnumbered
by the Irish, these conflicts did not have the one-sided feel that might have been
noticed simultaneously in sectarian conflicts between Irish immigrants and British nativists in the cities of northern England or Scotland.[12] While some intra-
ethnic English-Irish cooperation might have been noticed in the Working Men's
Party in Philadelphia and New York in the late 1820s, this was not the common
narrative.[13] Indeed the Great Famine in Ireland (1845–50) greatly worsened
relations, as in these years the Irish suffered the most difficult transition into
American life. While the English workers trained in Britain's industries formed
the aristocracy of the American labor force and "received favoured treatment,"
the Irish were "left to fend for themselves."[14] Additionally the Irish faced intense
prejudice and often clashed with working-class Britons and Yankees.

Irish immigrants did not, however, stand still; in the fast-boiling cauldron
of 1860s American cities they pursued naturalization, citizenship, and attendant
voting rights with alacrity. Then, deploying their sheer weight of numbers effectively, the Irish exerted political power that the English and British failed
to match. From there the Irish were able to issue challenges to British rule in
Ireland: Fenianism, dynamite schools, financial support for all nationalist organizations, and the lobbying of American politicians all—each strategy enjoyed
impressive support from the increasingly organized and confident Irish in U.S.
cities.[15]

The pressures exerted by the Irish complicated the lives of the English and
sometimes brought them under severe duress. However, these factors did not
make the Englishman's lot in the United States worse than that of the average Irish immigrant: far from it. Even as late as the early twentieth century,
the Dillingham Commission reported the superior social status of the English,
for example, as foremen and works' managers.[16] Not even three generations of
postfamine settlement could put the Irish precisely on a par with the English.
Irish women married so much later than their British counterparts that it encouraged endogamous marriage among the Irish because potential partners of other
ethnicities were partnering much earlier.[17] Nevertheless poverty and lack of skill
were common within the English group. Challenges presented by Irish—and
often American—hostility to the British Empire created tensions for the English.
Such factors contributed to the formation, by English workingmen in the United

States, of ethnic associations that strongly resembled those of the Irish and Scots, thus suggesting at least a degree of group identification in response to external pressure.

The mass emigrations of the 1840s during the Irish Great Famine amplified all negative relations between the English and the Irish. In 1846 the *Liverpool Times* divided the Irish into "the emigrants of hope" who went to the United States or Canada and "the emigrants of despair" who languished in Britain.[18] In the industrial and commercial cities of Liverpool, Manchester, and Glasgow and in many dozens of smaller urban centers, Irish Catholics were met with hostility from English, Welsh, Scots, and Irish Protestants. Sectarian tensions marked communal life, stratified employment opportunities, and segmented community life along ethno-religious lines. Irish Catholics overwhelmingly were unskilled and occupied the least secure, most ill-paid work.[19] In the United States such hope as the *Liverpool Times* imagined was filtered through initial hardship but then was distilled into stronger and clearer opportunities for advancement than Britain offered. Additionally the sheer volume of emigrants in the generations before, during, and after the Great Famine cemented what was one of the largest European immigrant groups in the United States.

Not every aspect of life pointed to the easier task of English transition into American society. Conflict pressed upon the English as their numbers shrank relative to other, much faster-growing communities. The Irish Famine of the 1840s intensified differences and divisions between the Irish and the English, and the emerging schism would take on a new character in the United States as the hunger, want, and disease that ravaged Ireland sent forth huge numbers of Irish across the Atlantic to America. These were not just regular Irish emigrants: their numbers were vastly larger than before; their social circumstances were more pinched than any group leaving Ireland before or since; and they understandably came with smoldering political grievances. America was just the place to hone that sense of injustice into something less mute. By 1860 the Irish constituted more than half the foreign-born population in four of America's five largest cities: New York, Philadelphia, Brooklyn, and Boston. The number of English-born in these four cities combined was less than half the 203,740 Irish-born population in New York alone. The contrast was even more dramatic in New York, where the English-born numbered 27,082: one-seventh of the Irish community and only a little more than one-quarter of the 119,984 German-born in the city.[20]

Even in key states of English settlement, in 1860 the Irish-born outnumbered them 1.33 million to 0.35 million—a ratio of 3.5:1 in favor of the Irish.[21] In 1880, long after the Great Famine, New York's 198,595 Irish-born outnumbered the English-born in that city (29,664), Philadelphia (26,315), Brooklyn (20,324), Chicago (13,045), and Boston (8,998) by more than two to one.[22] As table 1 shows, in the principal cities containing English ethnic associations, the Irish outnumbered their British counterparts by between 2:1 and nearly 5:1. (See table 1.) This marked a substantial contrast to what the British were used to at home. Only London, Liverpool, Glasgow, and Manchester had Irish-born populations that could match those in the United States—except New York, which outstripped all of them—but of course even in the northwest of England, where in 1851 they constituted 8.6 percent of the population, the Irish-born were no more than a noticeable minority. In U.S. cities the British- , English- , and Scottish-born were immigrants too, and their respective communities were almost universally dwarfed by the Irish-born.

In fact the only communities where the number of British came close to that of the Irish counterparts were in the textile centers, such as Fall River, Massachusetts, and mining communities, such as Scranton, Pennsylvania, where British technical and labor know-how were fundamental to industrial takeoff and sustenance. Utica, New York, a textile town on the Erie Canal, attracted a diversity of Britons.[23] The Welshman William Davies, writing from there when it was a town of five hundred dwellings in 1821 and the canal was still two years from completion, anticipated the positive effects that would be enjoyed there when Lake Erie and the Hudson were connected.[24] Such developments clearly helped give the town a strong British character, with particularly the Welsh heavily represented in its population of eight thousand or so in the 1830s.[25] While New York State was an important part of the textile sector, New England was dominant in the American textile industry. By midcentury that region contained half of the largest mills and three-quarters of the country's spindles. Massachusetts, New Hampshire, and Rhode Island were major regional centers.[26]

Here the English, mostly from Lancashire, not only brought their technical skills but also established trades' unions, English societies, and churches and introduced culinary and cultural customs. The same was true of Yorkshire folk introduced to the worsted (woolen) industry to 1860s Lawrence, also in Massachusetts.[27] By the 1850s, however, both the Yankee and English mill girls were being threatened by waves of Irish immigrants, who rapidly came to dominate the New England textiles labor force.[28] Meanwhile in the postbellum United States, "practically the entire English silk industry was transferred by skilled British immigrants from Macclesfield and Coventry to Paterson, New Jersey."[29] Although unions were less strong in New Jersey than in Massachusetts, nevertheless in the late 1840s and early 1850s English mule spinners and native-born workers formed alliances that sought to embrace all workers in the face of severe employer hostility. The English characteristically also made donations to strikers in their native Lancashire in the mid-1850s.[30]

As the historian Mary Blewett has shown in her classic study of New England politics, among the immigrants were many who entered the country with a

TABLE 1. BRITISH-BORN AND IRISH-BORN IN THE MAJOR
U.S. CENTERS OF ENGLISH ASSOCIATION ACTIVITY
(OVERVIEW, 1860–1900)

	% Eng	% Brit	% Irish	British-born	English-born	Scots-born	Irish-born	Welsh-born	TOTAL	No of Cities
1860	12.3	15.5	69.1	137,622	109,711	27,911	615,564		890,808	25
1870	15.5	20.6	79.4	182,769	137,033	35,145	704,033	10,591	886,802	28
1880	18.2	23.8	76.2	222,165	169,967	40,671	711,443	11,527	933,608	26
1890	22.6	30.4	69.6	325,750	242,111	70,556	744,767	13,083	1,070,517	32
1900	24.6	32.9	77.1	352,410	264,192	71,270	719,704	16,948	1,072,114	34

SOURCES: Bureau of Census data, 1860–1900. The cities chosen (25–34 in number) qualify by having English associations and being big enough to warrant individual recording in each relevant census.

heightened sense of class-consciousness, including immigrant mill workers from Lancashire and Yorkshire equipped with deep traditions of trade unionism, sympathies for Chartism, and a determination to resist the excesses of capitalism.[31] They dreamed of being free of the shackles of a class-ridden society in England, but America presented many blocks to such aspirations. Moreover, as the nineteenth century ended and the twentieth began, English and Irish immigrants were grouped together by nativists, whose ire was directed not at Celtic paupers but at southern Europeans, Asians, and Hispanics.[32]

SECTARIAN ASSOCIATIONALISM

British labor historians have characterized the British and the Irish as workers divided by both class and ethnicity. The division is a superficial one that downplays or ignores the many Irishmen who played leading roles in British labor organizations; but it has the advantage of neatness since sectarian conflict so often outmatched all other associations when British—whether English, Welsh, or Scots—and Irish workers came together.[33] The same spark of conflict could also be seen in the United States; indeed this was acutely the case in the anthracite regions of Pennsylvania in the 1860s and 1870s, when a movement of violent, prototrade unionists, mostly Irishmen, imported some of the techniques and tactics of Donegal and Tipperary Ribbonism to industrial and communal relations in the new community. These were the Molly Maguires. As with the strategies adopted by later Fenian operatives, the Mollys used legitimate fronts to hide their activities. The core of activists was dedicated to vigorous, sometimes violent collectivism in which the mystique of the oath- and ritual-bound secret society was blurred with primitive trade unionism. In Pennsylvania specifically the Mollys were an Irish element of the miners' trade union, the Workers' Benevolent Association.

These men began to seek reprisals for discrimination and poor working conditions against Welsh and English foremen, policemen, and workers, whom they held responsible. What Kevin Kenny described as a more specific story of the emergence of a protean trade union movement others—both contemporaries and historians working prior to Kenny—viewed as an essentially Irish Catholic, pronationalist conspiracy of secrecy and violence.[34] While this analysis is correct, the ethnic aspects cannot be ignored, especially when viewing matters from the English or Welsh perspective. Indeed the most recent study of this episode of clandestine collectivism on the part of the Irish framed it within both ethnic and class forms of behavior.[35] The Mollys were not, however, some isolated sect. Indeed in English and Welsh eyes, matters were made worse by the wider community's apparent contempt shown for the rule of law. Irish men and women with no apparent connection to the Mollys apparently kept quiet about their identity, while "two of the known murderers and their families were quietly spirited away from the processes of the law."[36]

This Pennsylvania violence sounds an interesting note because of the balances of ethnicities on the coalfields at the time. In Scranton in 1870, when Molly Maguire violence was in full flow, the Irish only slightly outnumbered the British (see table 2). In 1880 they had stretched their slight superiority. By 1890 the roles had been reversed, a trend that continued in 1900. In none of these census years, however, was the balance strongly in favor of one group or the other. Only the English or Scots, if assessed alone, were weak minorities. However, the evidence suggested that they acted in concert against the Irish. Overall we can see in Scranton a much closer set of figures than in most other American settlements. Not only were Welsh mine workers proportionately more numerous than in virtually any other settlement in the United States, but they and the English also dominated the grades of managers, overseers, and foremen. As well as this, the Welsh were counted numerously among the police, magistrates, and other officeholders. Numbers are one thing, but attitudes are another. Not only did the British match the Irish in number, but they also used their control of the key levers of power within the mines and the community to victimize the Irish. Meanwhile the Irish struggled against the English, mostly Cornish, and especially Welsh power brokers in the mining districts.[37]

TABLE 2. BRITISH- AND IRISH-BORN POPULATIONS OF SCRANTON, PENNSYLVANIA, 1860–90

Born in	England	Wales	Scotland	Britain	Ireland	Irish—British Ratio
1870	1,445	4,177	366	5,988	6,491	1.08:1
1880	1,558	3,616	301	5,475	6,772	1.23:1
1890	3,065	4,890	575	8,530	8,340	0.97:1
1900	3,692	4,621	576	8,889	7,198	0.81:1

SOURCES: Bureau of Census, 1870: *Ninth Census*, vol. 1: *The Statistics of the Population of the United States* [. . .], "Nativities of the Population of Principal Cities," table 8—"Fifty Cities," 388–89; 1880: *Statistics of the Population of the United States at the Tenth Census*, table 16—"Foreign-born Population of Fifty Principal Cities," 540; 1890: *Report of the Population of the United States at the Eleventh Census*, table 34—"Foreign-born Population Distributed According to Country of Birth for Cities Having 20,000 Inhabitants or More," 670–71, 674–75; 1900: *Census Reports*, vol. 1, *Twelfth Census of the United States*, table 35—"Foreign-born Population Distributed According to Country of Birth for Cities Having 25,000 Inhabitants or More," 796–803.

A sense of injustice caused some Irish workers to respond with violent and murderous reprisals. What emerged in 1860s Scranton was a context for a more equal and protracted struggle than was the case when one community was hopelessly outnumbered by the other. The state of lawlessness was extreme, and murders were numerous. Police were drafted in from Philadelphia, for example in 1875 when a dozen arrived to protect workers of the Lee and Wilkesbarre Coal Company at Summit Hill, Ashton, Pennsylvania.[38] Yet the crimes went on. This was partly blamed on the inaction of the state authorities—something the press in Fort Wayne, Indiana, contrasted with the determined anti–Ku Klux Klan operations in the South.[39] The mainstream Catholic community stood against the Maguires. At his service on December 21, 1875, at the Catholic church in Mahoney Plain, Pennsylvania, the Reverend Daniel O'Connell "read a letter from the archbishop of Philadelphia, which was a formal excommunication of the society known as the Molly Maguires, otherwise the Ancient Order of Hibernians."[40]

Labor dimensions of Irish ethnicity represented dimensions of struggle in the old country. Indeed 1870s Scranton was the focal point for overlapping and connected traditions of labor organization. The town and its mining environs gained national notoriety for harboring a movement of violent, prototrade unionists, mostly Irishmen, who imported some of the techniques and tactics of Donegal and Tipperary Ribbonism—of which the original Molly Maguires were part—to industrial and communal relations in the new community. As with the strategies adopted by later Fenian operatives, the Mollys used legitimate fronts to hide their activities.[41] The core of activists proffered vigorous, sometimes violent collectivism in which the mystique of the oath- and ritual-bound secret society was blurred with primitive trade unionism.

Molly Maguire activity excited another element of interest. Some of these Pennsylvanian Irish workers were still British subjects and so drew the attentions of the British consul general. R. C. Clipperton noted the "the well-remembered 'Molly Maguires'" as "an organisation of assassins said to be a wing of the Ancient Order of Hibernians."[42] He noted that British and some American workers of English descent got together to form the Benevolent Order of the Sons of St. George as a counter to the Mollys after "three Englishmen were brutally murdered in the coal regions" of Pennsylvania.[43] Kenny in fact tabulated sixteen killings carried out between 1862 and 1875. All of the victims except two miners were authority figures: a policeman, a burgess, and a justice of the peace outside the pits; and a mine owner and numerous superintendents, foremen, and watchmen within the industry. The nationalities were split: four Americans, one Welsh American, three Welsh, two Cornish, one Scottish, one Irish, and four unknown.[44] The focus on American and British figures of authority excited considerable unease and undoubtedly enhanced ethnic attachments. The killings were partly fired by enduring sectarian violence between Irish and Welsh workers, Mollys on one side and "Modocs" on the other.[45] The Welsh and Irish were split by class, with the Welsh occupying higher occupational grades and most management positions; they also parted on politics, with the Welsh favoring the Republicans and the Irish being strong Democrats.[46]

Despite the obvious attraction of an ethnic explanation for the rise of the OSStG, there also is a different interpretation. In this alternative version of events the impetus for the organization was dated precisely to unfortunate events on the evening of June 4, 1870, when after a boozy pub crawl a Cornish man named Benjamin Jaco accidentally locked his roommate, Williams, out. Williams apparently swore to get even with Jaco, and some weeks later the two men argued in a pub "frequented by Englishmen," and Williams shot Jaco dead.[47] It was said that the English then gathered under the leadership of Thomas R. Lyddon to ensure that the dead man, who had no friends or family in the United States, was given a decent burial. Other sources credited Joseph Davenport and William Maylin with the society's foundation.[48] A civic history of Scranton noted the presence of these two men and another ten as the founders who received the first charter.[49] The sources also discussed the issue of justice. The same narrative claimed that Williams had many influential friends in Scranton who were likely to protect him.[50] Corruption certainly seems to have been a common beef on the coalfields in these times, with Welsh and English magistrates, cops, and managers roundly condemned. Certainly, regardless of origins, the Irish, Welsh, and English lined up in ethnic blocs, using whatever influence they had among officeholders or the general population to protect their interests at the expense of the others. Usually these expressions of collective self-interest fell along ethnic axes.

Clandestine Irish ethnic activism also blurred with more traditional class-based notions of worker resistance to capitalism. The Molly Maguires, for instance, were an offshoot of the Workers' Benevolent Association (WBA). While the Mollys engaged in clandestine violence against employers and authorities, arousing Welsh and English fear and enmity, the WBA sought to control labor supply, wage levels, and workers' conditions. The WBA collapsed under sectional and sectarian division and fierce resistance from employers and authorities, and it was replaced, from the late 1870s, by the Order of the Knights of Labor (KOL). Here we find perhaps the organization with the closest apparent structure to the OSStG. The KOL was at first a clandestine, ritual-bound, pseudo-Masonic-type organization.[51] It suffered the same weaknesses as the WBA, bearing some of the hallmarks of the Mollys but more of the OSStG, in being clandestine, ritual-bound, and seemingly sectarian. It also drew the admonishment of the clergy, whose denunciations kept a certain portion of Irish Catholics out of its orbit.[52] Crucially, it differed from the OSStG in being pronouncedly Irish and Catholic. The leader of the KOL in Scranton was Terence V. Powderly, a second-generation Irishman who was later a Clan na Gael and Land League activist. Working his way up the structures of the KOL, he was in 1878 elected mayor of Scranton on the Greenback-Labor card.[53] Powderly's KOL was growing in Scranton and on the wider coalfield at just the time when the OSStG, with its similar ritualized structure and apparatus, was consolidating around English Protestant miners' interests. Meanwhile, Powderly faced the charge from Allan Pinkerton, among others, that the Knights of Labor were simply a resurgence of the tyrannical Molly Maguires.[54] Given Powderly's heritage and roles, the charge was easily laid.[55] Certainly the initial base of support for the Knights of Labor in the mid-1870s came from Irish Catholics. Five years later Powderly was of the opinion that most members were Catholic.[56] Under such circumstances, accusations of association with the Mollys were both obvious and likely; moreover English workers were highly unlikely to have joined.

Ethnicity certainly was an impermeable barrier for the OSStG. From its inception in 1870, the organization, like Canada's Sons of England, excluded other Britons and the Irish: only Englishmen, their sons, and their grandsons were admitted. Even otherwise usually fellow-traveling Irish Protestants could not be admitted. Catholics were barred. Protestant values were repeatedly stressed. Moreover secret initiation rituals were maintained. In fact the OSStG looked rather like an Englishman's Orange Order, with its religious exclusivity, sashes, aprons, rituals, secrecy, and parades. Furthermore the anti-Irishness that led to the formation of the OSStG in the first place did not disappear. In the face of continued and heightened Irish nationalism, this dimension was retained and sometimes grew.

Whatever the precise trigger, the OSStG gained a reputation for vigilance against the Irish. Members announced themselves as an exclusively English, Protestant, and ritual-bound organization; in many ways they were the inverse of the Mollys but with the same focus on exclusivity and secrecy. While it is no surprise to find that the Irish fell back on a century-long tradition of clandestine resistance to the perceived exercise of arbitrary power, this was more of a novelty for the English. English class fault lines had resulted in sometimes highly organized, clandestine behavior among English trade unionists, radicals, and rural redressers; but organizing on ethnic lines was new. What the English, many of whom were Cornish, and their Welsh neighbors faced in these anthracite coalfields was an imported Irish tradition of clandestine resistance to authority.

THE OSSTG SPREADS

At first the OSStG was small and relatively regionally limited. It also was, like the KOL, constrained by its clandestine dimensions. In the early months of 1870 and 1871, it primarily spread within Pennsylvania, as Hazleton, Pittston, Carbondale, Mahonoy City, and other places planted lodges; in all of these places there was

English and Welsh conflict with the Irish. As early as January 1872 a regional Grand Lodge was organized on the coalfield, with a "full board of officers."[57] That same year a great change occurred when the organization spread to New York and New England. A decision was made in August 1872 to found a Supreme Lodge at Providence, Rhode Island.[58] Sources also point to developments much farther afield, with a flourishing culture in Utah, in Salt Lake City, Ogden, and elsewhere.[59] As with the KOL, the OSStG shifted emphasis and moved away from the closed ritual of the secret society. The OSStG and the KOL had from an early point emphasized benevolence and collective self-help, and this aspect was strengthened in the 1870s for the OSStG and in the early 1880s for the KOL. In the latter decade the church relaxed its proscription of trades' union membership by Catholics, a fact aided by the KOL's abandonment of secret rituals of entry and conduct.[60]

The OSStG of the later 1870s began to focus on cultural dimensions of ethnicity, specifying that "the families of the various lodges meet together socially on stated occasions, thereby keeping live the English love of the country and the festivities of her fête days."[61] In addition the social class of the OSStG was extended in the early 1880s. This was reflected, for example, in the decision by the New York St. George's Society to make an annual donation of $150 for a labor bureau—an act that showed the strong relations between these two different types of English organizations. The bureau was organized by the OSStG, which counted among its members "a great many employers of labour" who were behind the idea of harmonizing labor supply and demand.[62]

Early in the same decade, a great change occurred when the organization spread to New York and New England. In 1882 it was reckoned to have 7,000–8,000 members nationwide.[63] In August of the same year the decision to found a Supreme Lodge at Providence, Rhode Island, was made.[64] By the end of the century the OSStG had lodges and members from Montana and Utah to the Eastern Seaboard. During the early 1880s the order spread rapidly. In just nine months between August 1883 and June 1884, it had grown from 125 lodges to 159 and membership had increased from 11,643 to "about 17,000." One report claimed proudly that the OSStG "is swelling at the rate of 5,000 to 6,000 members yearly—a wonderful growth when the restricted field from which membership can be taken is considered."[65] That same year lodges had received $85,895 and had disbursed $28,730 "for sick and funeral benefits and donations." Nearly $20,000 was invested, mostly in U.S. government loans. Importantly, the OSStG by the mid-1880s was located in thirteen states. Pennsylvania (50), New York (20), and New Jersey (9) had the most lodges; the others were Massachusetts, New Hampshire, Connecticut, Ohio, Illinois, Iowa, Michigan, Wisconsin, Kentucky, and Virginia.[66]

Alongside these men there also emerged, in 1885, an Englishwomen's organization in Cleveland, Ohio.[67] By the 1890s women's lodges were engaged in joint St. George's Day services and celebrations with male societies in New York and other cities as well as organizing their own soirees, concerts, and fundraisers.[68] As the century drew to a close, local organizations could be large. In 1895 Chicago alone could muster over one thousand members gathered for the annual OSStG parade on a Sunday close to St. George's Day.[69] The following year terrible weather reduced the parade to six hundred members of twenty-four lodges.

Progress did not stop there. At the ninth convention, held in 1897 in Syracuse, journalists reported claims that the OSStG had 40,000 members. Englishness was still lauded, with each member wearing "elaborate badges of the order with the famous words: 'Honi Soit Qui Mal Y Pense,' the motto of the English order of the Garter."[70] In 1901 the order seems to have moved to triennial conventions of the Supreme Lodge. That year eleven states—Pennsylvania, New Jersey, Massachusetts, Rhode Island, Connecticut, New York, Ohio, Illinois, Michigan, Montana, and California—were represented at the Philadelphia convention.[71] Six years later Trenton, New Jersey, welcomed delegates from all over the country. Included in their business that year, 1907, was the intention to create a state funeral fund and a move to biennial conventions.[72] Boston hosted the convention of 1913, when a local man, William F. Barlow, was elected supreme president. Barlow, it was said, had worked hard to make "Massachusetts . . . the banner jurisdiction," which he seemed to have achieved. The article reported how membership there had climbed to 5,318, an increase of 273 in 1913, whereas in Pennsylvania, the normal lodestar of the OSStG, there had been a 126-member decline to 5,300. That said, both states were considered to be "in a very prosperous condition, both financially and numerically."[73]

English societies, like their Irish or German counterparts, launched newspapers. One such was the reactionary, anti-Catholic *Anglo-Saxon*, which in 1877 "was declared 'the official organ of [the] St George's union of North America'" and had strong associations with the OSStG's working-class equivalent in Canada, the Sons of England—an organization that is explored in Tanja Bueltmann's essay in this book.[74] The OSStG developed its own periodical, the *St. George's Journal*, which it published in Philadelphia between 1876 and 1891. The OSStG also launched the short-lived *English-American*, published in New York, which ran for just one year, 1884–85. During the 1890s the foundation of the Royal Society of St. George was accompanied by the launch of the *English Race*, a monthly periodical distributed to branches of the society and also to kindred groups that were unaffiliated. Among the latter was the St. George's Society of Toronto, which received copies and also requests for copies from other societies.[75]

After World War I there was a notable shift in the emphasis of the OSStG—a shift that can be discerned in the emergence of still another new periodical. In 1919 Ernest H. Bennett, of the OSStG's Anglo-Saxon lodge, edited a short-lived monthly called the *English-Speaking World,* which covered a dizzying array of Anglo-American organizations, initiatives, and activities, including news of the OSStG.[76] This journal pointed to a turn in the OSStG's mission from patriotic friendly society to a collection of politically Anglo-Saxonist agitators. After the war, then, the only real change was a now much more prominent fourth force. On top of the St. George's Societies, the OSStG, and the Sons of England, the Royal Society of St. George, which was founded in England in 1894, was now making its presence felt as a global force that wished to unify the various societies.[77]

By the 1920s the OSStG had long since thrown off its image as a secret society and had nearly doubled in size from that of the 1880s—although claims of sixty thousand to seventy thousand members seems 30 percent too high.[78] For many membership societies, the interwar period marked a high peak of activity. It was at this point that the OSStG had broadened its appeal still further to persons of a higher socioeconomic class. Now civic leaders and small and medium businessmen—and not just miners, textile hands, and other blue-collar men—were part of the scene. It is possible that this development was part of a bleeding of members from the St. George's Societies to the OSStG; certainly there was a feeling on the part of the much smaller, elite-focused St. George's Societies that they should "absorb the young" because "benevolence alone is not sufficient[;] benefits must also accrue."[79]

Other changes were discernible in this period, not least a further strengthening of a more comfortably off leadership class. Examining the major lights in the Upper Peninsula of Michigan at the time gives us an insight that may be used to generalize. Evidence shows a network of men there who were active in three or more societies, with certain key ones—the OSStG plus the Freemasons, the Elks, and the Knights of Pythias—recurring in most cases. James H. Dale, an English-born florist of Houghton, Michigan, was typical. A self-made man who worked his way up in the horticultural industry, he became owner of his own company. Dale was a classic nineteenth-century joiner: Masons, Elks, Knights of Pythias, the Society of American Florists, Sons of St. George, and others at times called on his exertions as a solid member. Dale had numerous aspects in common with his fellow Sons of St. George members. Frank Elsworth Keese, superintendent at the Oliver Iron Mining Company in Upper Michigan and the grandson of an Englishman, was in the Sons of St. George as well as a Freemason and a Knight of Pythias. This was true as well of William Trebilcock, son of a Cornishman, a stationary engine man, and later a greenhouse manufacturer. In addition to the Sons of St. George and the Knights of Pythias, Trebilcock joined the Oddfellows, the Macabees, and Modern Woodmen of America. William J. Billing, a motor sales company owner, was the son of a Cornish miner and joined the Sons of St. George. Judge John G. Stone of Houghton, Michigan, was in the Sons of St. George, the Freemasons, the Elks, and the Knights Templar. The case of James H. Thomas, who too was descended from English immigrants, is interesting: he was a funeral director in Calumet and a member of the OSStG and several other confraternities, while his wife joined the Rebekahs, the Eastern Star, and the Phythian Sisters and was active in charitable circles.[80] The men described were not politicians, mayors, ambassadors, or consuls but rather businessmen, traders, and sturdy, largely self-made men. They were the classic, successful, second-generation sons and daughters of immigrants. In the United States, former Cornish miners produced offspring who became funeral directors, wholesale florists, or medium-sized business owners and who, despite their new comfort and privilege, retained connection to the friendly societies and clubs that their fathers had founded and nurtured.

ANTI-IRISH DIMENSIONS OF ENGLISH ETHNICITY IN AMERICA

Anti-Irish and anti-Catholic prejudices united all British Protestants, English or not. Indeed with strong Calvinist and chapel traditions, Scots and Welsh were capable of even more fiercely anti-Catholic and anti-Irish rhetoric than their English counterparts were. This was observable in the sectarian tensions that occurred in Britain;[81] in addition it was a fundamental feature of the urban American fabric. The Welshman John H. Evans in a letter to John Richards, vicar of Llanowddin, Montgomeryshire, in 1842 wrote of both the good and bad things for immigrants about the state of New York. Among the good, he recalled, "I do not think that they punish thieves with death as often as they do in England." Among the bad, he reported in matter-of-fact tones that "it is generally said there is no great punishment for killing an Irishman."[82] Irish Protestants have tended to be overlooked in assessments of the creation of the type of anti-Catholic culture that affected Irish immigrants in Britain and the United States. In the 1880s, long after Evans's observation, it was said that Irish Protestants became exaggerated nativists in organizations such as the American Protective Association to distinguish themselves from their Irish Catholic countrymen. As a consequence, wrote an Irish Catholic editor, "Wherever there is a street-preaching riot, or an attack on Catholic Church or convent, be sure that certain faithful *Irish* Calvinists are foremost among the enlightened Protestants upon the ground."[83] Middle-class Englishmen were no less susceptible to anti-Irish tendencies than were their working-class fellow countrymen.

It is hardly a leap of faith to imagine that the Irish would have dreamed of revenge against Britons. A sense of anger and hostility resulting from Anglo-Irish relations and personal experiences of poverty and hunger affected ethnic relations in American cities, often to the detriment of the English. Whereas in Ireland or Britain such dreams might yield a sullen, festering, and fruitless ambition, the United States freed Irish immigrants to seek revenge that might actually be wrought. Moreover, American ethnic politics provided voice for such feelings. According to Robert Ernst, the list of undimmed grievances harbored by the Irish included "all things English, including the hapless English immigrant in America."[84] In 1874 during his address to the Baltimore St. George's Society, the treasurer railed against the mistreatment of out-of-work Englishmen by Irish policemen: "Few Englishmen would credit the oppression and tyranny which their countrymen have to undergo in this boasted land of freedom." He continued, "The boast 'Britons never shall be slaves' will be a mockery when any Fenian policeman or Magistrate can incarcerate an Englishman as a felon to 'feed fat his ancient grudge' imported from the Emerald Isle."[85]

When the Irish introduced Ribbon-Hibernian societies to the new communities of settlement, which they did in Britain as well as in the United States, they were, in their minds, natural resisters to the pressures of capitalists and bosses, who in America were surrogates for landlords in Ireland.[86] They had an absolutely clear sense in which the Irish were shaped by ethnic as well as class considerations. They did not simply graduate from ethnic-consciousness to class-consciousness, as would suit most Marxist interpretations. The historian David Emmons in his study of the Irish in Butte, Montana, expressed the belief that the Irish were so involved in feelings of nationalism and anti-Britishness that ethnicity often undermined their class concerns. For him, prejudices based on historic injustices at home explained Irish workers' ultimately limited interest in pan-ethnic class solidarities. Emmons stated persuasively, "There were enormous differences between the [mutualist] Sons of Italy, say, or the Sons of St George, and the [ethno-political] Clan na Gael, and the conclusion is inescapable that the history of American labor—as surely as that of the English—would have been different had the Anglophobic Irish not been so early and dominant a component of the working classes of both nations."[87] To Emmons, the Irish were caught in a suspicion-filled half-light, viewing no one—not the English, Germans, or others—as allies in matters of class. Consequently, "the Irish worker was an unlikely candidate for working-class radicalism."[88] That said, Emmons showed elsewhere that there also was a world of difference between the society ethos of the Catholic Ancient Order of Hibernians, which was friendly, and that of the Fenian Clan na Gael.[89]

It is also true that the English gave the Irish, in Britain and America, plenty of reasons to stick to their nationalist credentials and remain aloof from pan-ethnic affiliations. Casual anti-Irishness and derogatory assumptions were commonplace. At the usual St. George's Day dinner in 1883, the presence of guests from the Hibernian Society did not prevent the Baltimore St. George's Society from discussing Anglo-Irish political matters.[90] In particular they were interested in Phoenix Park, where on May 6, 1882—some eleven months previously—Lord Frederick Cavendish and his undersecretary, T. H. Burke, had been murdered.[91] President Spencer of the Baltimore St. George's Society made mention of the tragedy in a light-hearted way. During a toast to "Old England," and drawing up the Irish American bombing campaigns in Britain,[92] he commented, "Unfortunately John Bull had a crown in which there is an emerald, and he has just found out it contained dynamite [Laughter.] Irishmen are not alone responsible for this. There are influences at work that foster these fearful conspiracies in every country, and it behooves Americans to go hand in hand to suppress them."[93] On the same night in April 1883, as their countrymen in Baltimore made mention of the Phoenix Park murders, members of the New York's St. George's Society too listened to talk of dynamite. This time a clear attempt was made to soothe potential tensions, albeit in a different way. Their president, Mr. Hill, pointed out that the government of the city of New York dated to a charter of the late seventeenth century: "its author was an Irishman, pure and simple, and he made it before dynamite was invented." This was a worthy, reasoned, and sensible comment in such an Irish city, and one guaranteed not to embarrass Judge Jack Shea, of the Friendly Sons of St. Patrick, who was one of several responding to a toast to "Our Sister Societies." "There are occasions when silence is the safest eloquence," he said, "and this was one." Perhaps this too was a reference to the dynamite bombing campaigns. He could see no reason why his society should not celebrate St. George's Day and "remarked with pride of the great weight Ireland had in the formation and evangelization of the British nation."[94] Ancient history was the safest site for common ground.

Ethnic issues became less pressing after the collapse of the Molly Maguires in the mid-1870s. The political and laborforce tensions that had prompted the emergence of the Son gave way to cultural togetherness in the form of day-trips, picnics, sports and musical, and a stress on fund-raising and financial fraternity.[95] The charming depiction of a proud, patriotic, but serene people enjoying their Englishness together in largely serene ways does not tell the whole story. The anti-Irish sentiments that had fired up the OSStG in the first place and which had influenced St. George's Societies too during the 1870s and 1880s reemerged with even greater force as Irish Home Rule came closer to realization and when bloodshed and war stood between the Irish and their freedom. What shape that might take was not clear in 1919, when the OSStG founded the *English-Speaking World* newspaper to express not only its unionist philosophies but also those of, for example, the Ulster League of North America, whose connections to the unionist leader Edward Carson were regularly reported. By this time the OSStG had five hundred or more lodges and tens of thousands of members, and it had disbursed nearly a million dollars and eclipsed the St. George's Societies. It also had turned into a mass, public-friendly society, with its church parades and floats in hospital carnivals, and had lost the innate clandestine formulation of the 1870s. However, it had not abandoned that initial sectarian, anti-Irish, anti-Catholic ethos. Its rules still excluded non-Protestants. More important, it came to appear more like the Orange Order: sectarian, potentially paramilitary in its marches and parades, and strongly opinioned with respect to the Irish question.

Thus in the postwar period Mr. Brown, "supreme organizer" of the Order of the Sons of St. George and editor of its new newspaper, the *English-Speaking World,* reported a recruitment drive in 1920 and an upsurge in members. What caused this growth spurt in the wake of World War I? According to Brown, "there seems to be an awakening in the minds of the Englishmen and they realize what a great factor for good they can be, in the shop, store, factory or among their friends who are not of British origins, in offsetting the harmful and insidious work of the Sinn Feiners, pro-German or anti-British."[96] In keeping with the mood of the moment, the benevolent society remained an instrument of giving and helping; but its edges had been sharpened. In what were turbulent times of ethnic and racial conflict, immigration controls, and fear at the easing specters of communism and fascism, the OSStG's Anglo-Saxonism, which had initially fired it up against Irish Ribbon men, was once again coming more fully to the fore.

CONCLUSION

The potential strength of these various English societies was never fully capitalized on. While various attempts were made to unify the various English associations in order to maximize strength, clarity, and common purpose, these got no further than loose federation. The North America St. George's Union was an annual convention of St. George's Societies in the United States and Canada, which from the 1870s to the early 1900s represented a degree of federalism.[97] However, the two largest, popular English friendly societies—the OSStG in the United States and the Sons of England in Canada—considered mergers several times but could not agree on the terms. At the annual convention of the Sons of St. George convention at Scranton, Pennsylvania, in 1904 such a union was proposed between that society and the Canadian Sons of England, "since the former order was organized for the same purpose." The discussion went on: "The Sons of England is the younger order, and first made overtures to bring an amalgamation about. After the amalgamation both orders will probably be known as the Sons of St George."[98] Perhaps it was the prospect of losing their name that dampened the appeal to the Sons of England. Primarily, though, the Canadian Sons of England were concerned that the order in the United States allowed members who "exercise the privileges of full citizens of the Republic" to be members. Thus a "marked point of divergence" was "that of allegiance"—for the Sons, British citizenship was the key to full loyalty.[99] In the American Republic such a position simply could not be upheld. For these reasons, the merger did not happen, despite the fact that the Pennsylvania delegations apparently voted in favor of it.[100] In the end they got no further than a few joint meetings and invitations to each other's officers to attend functions.

Regardless of their failure to unite or federalize their operations, these societies remained broadly in union. Neither faction fighting nor warring has been uncovered. Other than their differing emphases on charity (St. George's) and collective self-help (OSStG), the societies had no differences of principle or expression. Patriotism to England remained a constant for both. Suspicion and fear surrounding the rise of Irish American power clearly also connected them; indeed this concern was shared with American Republicans too. This essay suggests that there were elements of English culture in the United States that contradicted ideas of easy assimilation. For too long scholars have assumed the synonymy of American and English cultures and the assimilation of immigrants into the host group. Yet there was an underlying tension for Englishmen. Even the wealthy and privileged felt something of it, as Henry E. Pellen, president of the New York St. George's Society, implied in 1875 when he wrote to Earl Dufferin, governor general of Canada, to invite him south for St. George's Day. Pellen touched on the balance of ethnic expression and assimilation affecting the English. "The English colony in New York," he told the governor general, "is not so influential as it ought to be: many men out here seem rather afraid of being known as Britons, while others marry into American families and become merged in the single genus."[101]

These were hardly the words of a universally dominant ethnic group. Moreover, for ordinary workers—as the rise of the OSStG clearly showed—the balance of integration, assimilation, and ethnic pillarization was delicate. The English could call upon Welsh and some American support but were hopelessly outnumbered by the Irish. The Irish, in turn, showed a superior drive to naturalization, concomitant votes, and local political influence, and they had an impressive communal coalescence shaped by economic hardship, anti-English/British feeling, and growing political nationalism. The English could not match this; but instead of disappearing into the mass of the host population—who in any case had their own reasons for hostility to the British Empire—they tried to counter Irish power and, in so doing, retained a clearly Protestant, English, sectarian ethnic identity that was remarkably durable across the decades.

NOTES

1. Bureau of the Census, *Population of the United States in 1860: Compiled from the Original Returns of the Eighth Census* (Washington, D.C.: U.S. Government Printers, 1864), "Introduction," xxii. At that point the Germans numbered 1.47 million.

2. Michael P. Weber, "Occupational Mobility of Ethnic Minorities in Nineteenth-Century Warren, Pennsylvania," in John E. Bodnar, *The Ethnic Experience in Pennsylvania* (Lewisburg, Pa.: Bucknell University Press, 1973), 26.

3. See Tanja Bueltmann, David T. Gleeson, and Donald M. MacRaild, "Invisible Diaspora? English Ethnicity in the United States before 1920," *Journal of American Ethnic History* 33, no. 4 (2014): 5–30, for a discussion of the limits of the historiography and counterarguments in favor of English ethnicity.

4. The term "invisible immigrants" is Charlotte Erickson's; see her *Invisible Immigrants: The Adaptation of English and Scottish Immigrants in Nineteenth-Century America* (Ithaca, N.Y.: Cornell University Press, 1992). Erickson included the Scots in this study. For Anglo-American culture, see W. E. Van Vugt, *British Immigration to the United States, 1776–1914* (London, Pickering & Chatto, 2009); C. Erickson, "English," in *Harvard Encyclopaedia of American Ethnic Groups*, ed. S. Thernstrom, A. Orlov, and O. Handlin (2nd ed., Cambridge, Mass., 1980). On countering the invisibility thesis, see David T. Gleeson, "Proving Their Loyalty to the Republic: English Immigrants and the American Civil War," in *The Civil War as Global Conflict: Transnational Meanings of the American Civil War*, ed. David T. Gleeson and Simon Lewis (Columbia: University of South Carolina Press, 2014).

5. Tanja Bueltmann and Donald M. MacRaild, *The English Diaspora in North America: Migration, Ethnicity and Association, 1730s–1950s* (Manchester: Manchester University Press, 2016), chap. 7, which compares the English with the Germans and Scots.

6. Data on the period 1899–1910: *Reports to the Immigration Commission*, 42 vols., *Statistical Review of Immigration, 1820–1910*, document 756, presented by W. P. Dillingham (Washington, D.C.: Government Printers, 1911), chap. 3, table 37, 359.

7. Wilbur S. Shepperson, Emigration and Disenchantment: Portraits of English Repatriated from the United States (University of Oklahoma Press, 1965). Wilbur S. Shepperson, *British Emigration to North America* (Oxford: Oxford University Press, 1956); Wilbur S. Shepperson, *Portraits of Englishmen Repatriated from the United States* (Norman: University of Oklahoma Press, 1965); Stephen Fender, *Sea Changes: British Emigration and American Literature* (Cambridge: Cambridge University Press, 1992).

8. David Fitzpatrick, "Exporting Brotherhood: Orangeism in South Australia," *Immigrants and Minorities* 23, nos. 2–3 (2005): 277.

9. Marcel van der Linden, ed., *Social Security Mutualism: The Comparative History of Mutual Benefit Societies* (New York: Peter Lang, 1996).

10. Alexis de Tocqueville, *Democracy in America*, 2 vols. (New York: Penguin, 2004), 1:10; 2:chap. 5.

11. Bruce Laurie, *Artisans into Workers: Labor in Nineteenth-Century America* (Urbana: University of Illinois Press, 1989), 43.

12. Donald M. MacRaild, *The Irish Diaspora in Britain, 1750–1939* (Basingstoke: Palgrave, 2010), chap. 7.

13. Robert Ernst, *Immigrant Life in New York, 1825–63* (Syracuse, N.Y.: Syracuse University Press, 1994), 168.

14. Charlotte Erickson, *American Industry and the European Immigrant, 1860–1885* (Cambridge, Mass.: Harvard University Press, 1958), 5.

15. A percipient new account from David Sim, *A Union Forever: The Irish Question and US Foreign Relations in the Victorian Age* (Ithaca, N.Y.: Cornell University Press, 2013), demonstrates that the political pressure applied to the American administration was generally not successful. For an excellent work on the broadest trajectories of Irish American power, see Niall Whelehan, *The Dynamiters: Irish Nationalism and Political Violence in the Wider World, 1867–1900* (New York: Cambridge University Press, 2012).

16. *Reports of the Immigration Commission, Immigrants in Industries,* part 17: *Copper Mining and Smelting,* William P. Dillingham (1911), table 74, 87; 88.

17. For an important discussion of Irish marriage patterns, see Hasia Diner, *Erin's Daughters in America: Irish Immigrant Women in the Nineteenth Century* (Baltimore, Md.: Johns Hopkins University Press, 1983), esp. chap. 3.

18. Reported in the *Nation,* November 14, 1846, cited in Graham Davis, "The Irish in Britain, 1815–1939," in *The Irish Diaspora,* ed. Andy Bielenberg (Harlow: Longman, 2000), 19.

19. MacRaild, *The Irish Diaspora,* chap. 2.

20. Bureau of the Census, *Population of the United States in 1860,* "Principal Cities and Towns; Native and Foreign Population," xxxi–xxxii.

21. The states are California, Connecticut, Delaware, Illinois, Iowa, Massachusetts, Michigan, Minnesota, New Jersey, New York, Rhode Island, and Wisconsin. See Bureau of the Census, *Population of the United States in 1860,* table, "Percentages of the Native, the English, and the Irish Population in each State and Territory in 1860," xxxi.

22. Department of the Interior, Census Office, *Statistics of the Population of the United States at the Tenth Census* (Washington, D.C.: U.S. Government Printers, 1882), table 16, "Foreign-born Population of Fifty Principal Cities," 538, 540.

23. E. P. Kraly and P. Vogelaar, "'Starting with Spoons': Refugee Migration and Resettlement Programs in Utica, New York," in *Race, Ethnicity, and Place in a Changing America,* ed. J. W. Frazier, E. L. Tetley-Fio, and N. F. Henry (Albany: State University of New York Press, 2011), 393.

24. William Davies to Rev. Ellis Evans, September 24, 1821, in Alan Conway, *The Welsh in America: Letters from the Immigrants* (St. Paul: University of Minnesota Press, 1961), 64–65 and passim for the Welsh in Utica.

25. Not that the ethnic history of the place recognizes the English in this way. James S. Pula, *Ethnic Utica* (Syracuse, N.Y.: Syracuse University Press, 2002), for example, contains no essay on the English.

26. Blewett, Mary H., 'USA: Shifting Landscapes of Class, Culture, Gender, Race and Protest in the American Northeast and South', in Lex Heerma van Voss, Els Hiemstra-Kuperus and Elise van Nederveen Meerkerk (eds), *The Ashgate Companion to the History of Textile Workers, 1650–2000* (London: Ashgate, 2010).

27. Ibid., 535.

28. B. C. Mitchell, *The Paddy Camps: The Irish of Lowell, 1821–61* (Urbana: University of Illinois Press, 2006).

29. William E. Van Vugt, "British (English, Scottish, Scots Irish, Welsh) and British Americans, 1870–1940," in *Immigrants in American History: Arrival, Adaptation, and Integration,* 4 [ed. Elliott R. Barkan (Santa Barbara, Calif.: ABC Clio, 2013), 2:237.

30. Mary Blewett, *Constant Turmoil: The Politics of Industrial Life in Nineteenth-Century New England* (Amherst: University of Massachusetts Press, 2000), 94.

31. Ibid. This classic work is run through with scores of examples of these immigrant labor activists.

32. Gary Gerstle, *American Crucible: Race and Nation in the Twentieth Century* (Princeton, N.J.: Princeton University Press, 2001), 50, 205, 256, 259, 266.

33. MacRaild, *The Irish Diaspora,* chap. 5; S. Fielding, *Class and Ethnicity: Irish Catholics in England, 1880–1939* (Buckingham: Open University Press, 1992), esp. intro. and chap. 1.

34. For the most thorough treatment, see Kevin Kenny, *Making Sense of the Molly Maguires* (New York: Oxford University Press, 1998), 14–34. An early work that differs in emphasis from Kenny's is J. Walter Coleman, *The Molly Maguire Riots: Industrial Conflict in the Pennsylvania Coal Region* (New York: Arno, 1969).

35. Mark Bulik, *The Sons of Molly Maguire: The Irish Roots of America's First Labor War* (New York: Fordham University Press, 2015).

36. R. C. Clipperton, HM's Consul, USA, 1886 (C. 4783), Commercial, No. 20 (1886), *Reports by Her Majesty's representatives abroad, on the system of co-operation in foreign countries,* p. 138.

37. D. Morris, "'Gone to Work to America': Irish Step-Migration through South Wales in the 1860s and 1870s," in *Immigrants and Minorities,* forthcoming 2016.

38. *Titusville Morning Herald,* March 22, 1875, 2; *Williamsport Daily Gazette and Bulletin,* March 22, 1875, 1.

39. *Fort Wayne Daily Sentinel,* March 31, 1875.

40. *Newport Daily News,* December 22, 1875.

41. Sim, *A Union Forever;* Whelehan, *The Dynamiters.*

42. Clipperton, *Reports by Her Majesty's Representatives,* 138.

43. *Canadian-American,* June 10, 1887; Rowland Tappan Berthoff, *British Immigrants in Industrial America, 1790–1950* (Cambridge, Mass.: Harvard University Press, 1953), 188. Whelehan, *The Dynamiters,* 86, however, pointed to Clipperton's use of paid informers and raised doubts about the veracity of his claims.

44. Kenny, *Making Sense of the Molly Maguires,* table 7.1, 188.

45. Ibid., 191.

46. Craig Phelan, *Grand Master Workman: Terence Powderly and the Knights of Labor* (Westport, Conn.: Greenwood Press, 2000), 27–28.

47. *Syracuse Sunday Herald,* October 1, 1897.

48. *Kane Daily Republican,* August 9, 1912.

49. The full roll included Thomas O. Jones, S. S. Bice, Richard Tyack, Joseph Davenport, William Maylin, George Allen, George Cooper, Edward C. Fletcher, Albert Roskelly, William Jarvis, H. S. Wyatt, and Thomas Atkins. See David Crafts, *History of*

Scranton, Penn: With Full Outline of the Natural Advantages, Accounts of the Indian Tribes, Early Settlements, Connecticut's Claim to the Wyoming Valley, the Trenton Decree, Down to the Present Time (Dayton, OH: H.W. Crew, 1891). 544.

50. *Syracuse Sunday Herald,* October 1, 1897.

51. "Knights of Labor," in *Ireland and the Americas: Culture, Politics, and History: A Multidisciplinary Encyclopedia,* ed. James P. Byrne, Philip Coleman, and Jason King (Santa Barbara, Calif.: ABC-CLIO, 2008), 2:506.

52. James Rodechko, "Irish-American Society in the Pennsylvania Anthracite Region: 1870–1880," in Bodnar, *The Ethnic Experience,* 26.

53. Joseph Gerteis, *Class and the Color Line: Interracial Class Coalition in the Knights of Labor* (Durham, N.C.: Duke University Press, 2007), 31; Mathew Hild, *Greenbackers, Knights of Labor, and Populists: Farmer-Labor Insurgency in the Late-Nineteenth-Century South* (Athens: University of Georgia Press, 2010), 47; Robert E. Weir, *Beyond Labor's Veil: The Culture of the Knights of Labor* (University Park: Pennsylvania State University Press, 2010), 10.

54. Kenny, *Making Sense of the Molly Maguires,* 187; Phelan, *Grand Master Workman,* 29.

55. Eric Foner, "The Land League and Irish America," in *Politics and Ideology in the Age of the Civil War* (New York: Oxford University Press, 1980), 170–74.

56. Phelan, *Grand Master Workman,* 70–71.

57. *Syracuse Sunday Herald,* October 1, 1897.

58. Ibid.

59. C. W. Heckethorn, *The Secret Societies of All Ages and Countries,* 2 vols. (London: George Redway, 1875), 2:275.

60. Paul Le Blanc, *Work and Struggle: Voices from US Labor Radicalism* (New York: Routledge, 2011), 126.

61. Clipperton, *Reports by Her Majesty's Representatives,* 138.

62. *Annual Reports of the St George's Society of New York for the Year 1884* (New York, 1884), 8.

63. *New York Times,* April 24, 1882.

64. This was noted in a retrospective piece many years later; see *Syracuse Sunday Herald,* October 1, 1897.

65. *Anglo-American Times,* June 27, 1884.

66. Ibid.

67. Hanael P. Bianchi, "St. George's Day: A Cultural History" (Ph.D. diss., Catholic University of America, 2011), 188.

68. *New Castle News,* July 6, 1892; *Boston Daily Globe,* August 29, 1893, May 12, 1896; *New York Times,* April 24, 1899.

69. *Chicago Daily Tribune,* April 22, 1895.

70. *Syracuse Daily Herald,* July 14, 1897. The same motto could be seen on the masthead of the *Sons of England Record,* the periodical of the OSStG's Canadian sibling organization.

71. *Frederick (Md.) News,* October 2, 1901, 1.

72. *Trenton Evening Standard,* August 30, 1907.

73. *Lowell Sun,* October 7, 1913.

74. Paul Hastings, "'Our glorious Anglo-Saxon race shall ever fill earth's highest place': The *Anglo-Saxon* and the Construction of Identity in Late-Nineteenth-Century Canada," in *Canada and the British World: Culture, Migration and Identity,* ed. R. Douglas Francis (Vancouver: University of British Columbia Press, 2006), 104–5.

75. In 1916 the society received a request for copies from Mr. C. W. Rowley of Winnipeg and agreed to send some. See TCA, StGST, series 1093, file 26, regular monthly meetings minutes, 1908–20, March 3, 1916, 84–85.

76. *English-Speaking World* 4, no. 1 (January 1919): 23.

77. Lesley Robinson, "English Associational Culture in Lancashire and Yorkshire, 1890s–c. 1930s," *Northern History* 51 (March 2014): 131–52; Bianchi, "St. George's Day," 213–14, 224–28.

78. *English-Speaking World* 3, no. 1 (January 1919): 16.

79. The Royal Society of St. George, *Annual Report and Year Book, 1904* (London, 1904), cited in Bianchi, "St. George's Day," 187.

80. George N. Fuller, *A History of the Upper Peninsula of Michigan,* 3 vols. (Dayton, Ohio: Lewis Publishing Company, 1926), 1: iii, 144, 195, 198, 202, 222, 230.

81. Kyle Hughes and Donald M. MacRaild, "Anti-Catholicism and Orangeism in Nineteenth-Century England and Scotland: Militant Loyalism in Action," in *Loyalism and the Formation of the British World,* ed. Allan Blackstock and Frank O'Gorman (Woodbridge: Boydell and Brewer, 2014), 45–68; Paul O'Leary, "When Was Anti-Catholicism? The Case of Nineteenth- and Twentieth-Century Wales," *Journal of Ecclesiastical History* 56 (April 2005): 308–25.

82. Conway, *The Welsh in America,* 62–63.

83. Quoted in Ernst, *Immigrant Life,* 168.

84. Ibid., 54, 105.

85. MDHS1881, minute books, 7 vols., 1866–1964, vol. 1, treasurer's report, January 19, 1874, Maryland Historical Society [hereafter MDHS], Baltimore, Maryland.

86. John Belchem, "'Freedom and Friendship to Ireland': Ribbonism in Early Nineteenth-Century Liverpool," *International Review of Social History* 39 (April 1994): 33–56.

87. David Emmons, *The Butte Irish: Class and Ethnicity in an American Mining Town, 1875–1925* (Urbana: University of Illinois Press, 1989), 293.

88. Ibid., 209.

89. David M. Emmons, "The Socialization of Uncertainty: The Ancient Order of Hibernians in Butte, Montana, 1880–1925," *Eire-Ireland* 29 (Autumn 1994): 74–92.

90. For reports of the church service, see MDHS1881, minute books, vol. 2, April 23, 1883, MDHS; *Baltimore American,* April 24, 1883.

91. T. H. Corfe, *Phoenix Murders: Conflict, Compromise and Tragedy in Ireland, 1879–1882* (London: Hodder and Stoughton, 1968).

92. K. R. M. Short, *Dynamite Wars: Irish American Bombers in Britain* (Dublin: Gill and Macmillan, 1979); Whelehan, *The Dynamiters.*

93. *Baltimore Sun,* April 24, 1883.

94. *New York Times,* April 24, 1883.

95. Clipperton, *Reports by Her Majesty's Representatives,* 138.

96. *English-Speaking World* 3, no. 7 (July 1920): 18.

97. Donald M. MacRaild, "Invisible Diaspora? English Associations in the Anglo-World, 1730–1945," in *Between Dispersion and Belonging: Recent Advances in Diaspora Studies,* ed. Amitava Chowdhury and Donald H. Akenson (Kingston, Ont.: McGill-Queens University Press, forthcoming 2016).

98. *Philadelphia Inquirer,* August 4, 1904.

99. *Sons of England Record* 3, no. 8 (November 1903): 5.

100. *Sons of England Record* 9, no. 6 (September 1904): 2.

101. Henry E. Pellen to The Right Honorable, The Earl of Dufferin, March 4, 1875, PRONI DIO71/H/B/P/155/4, Canada 1872–78, Public Record Office of Northern Ireland, Belfast.

Mutual, Ethnic, and Diasporic

The Sons of England in Canada, c. 1880 to 1910

n July 1910 several Winnipeg members of the Sons of England society left that city to join fellow society members in Montreal, there embarking on a month-long "home trip" to England. "A more enthusiastic body of excursionists," observed a reporter in a local newspaper, "could hardly be conceived, the east joining hands with the extreme west" as travelers made their way to the departure port from all over Canada.[1] A reported seven hundred excursionists thus left Canada on the steamer *Royal George* eagerly anticipating the specially arranged program of coach tours and cultural activities awaiting them in England, making it "the biggest excursion party ever taken out of Canada."[2] This was a remarkable instance of express loyalty extended to England by Canadians of English descent: they were traveling to what they regarded as "home," indulging in "old time greetings," and yet they were fully aware of their status as Canadians, with all "enthusiastic in their praise of the land of their adoption."[3] For these travelers, who hailed from all across Canada, it was their English culture that provided the critical communal glue, attesting to the pervasiveness of English ethnicity in the dominion. It is the subject of this essay to explore how that ethnicity and underpinning English culture—channeled through the Sons of England society—linked into wider Canadian society and impacted it.

THE SONS OF ENGLAND

The Sons of England Benevolent Society was formed in Toronto in late 1874, emerging from a feeling that even though the city's well-intentioned St. George's Society, which had been formed a good four decades earlier by well-to-do English migrants, doled out Christmas alms, its efforts were insufficient for the task of aiding Englishmen in need of support.[4] The very idea of charity was what concerned the founders of the Sons of England: "no man of fine feeling and high principle," the *Address to Englishmen* contained in the society's constitution asserted, "can receive charity without feeling humiliated."[5]As a result of this view, the principles of a friendly society lay at the heart of the operations of the Sons of England, with the association bringing together "Englishmen for their mutual benefit and support." This came in the form of "assistance to members when sick, or unable to follow their employment" and could extend to "supplying medical attendance and medicine to members, assuring lives of members on mutual principles, and assisting in defraying the funeral expenses of deceased members, members' deceased wives and children."[6] Membership was restricted to "Englishmen and their descendants,"[7] and this was closely adhered to—St. George's Societies in Canada and beyond could be more open in this respect, customarily accepting, certainly in the early years of their development, Welsh members.[8] The second core membership criterion for the Sons of England was religious denomination. Intrinsically entwined with loyalty to the Crown, the association firmly expressed that it "owes allegiance to God and the Protestant religion."[9] While sectarian divisions were in evidence elsewhere, the Sons of England was the only English ethnic association in Canada to enshrine religious criteria prominently in its rules, and thus Catholics were excluded.

This essay examines the history of the Sons of England from its foundation to 1910—the period of its greatest proliferation—through three distinct prisms to explore the wider role of the types of Englishness, English culture, and values in Canada that the organization promoted, assessing the impact of its activities on ordinary English migrants as well as within wider Canadian society. The first focus is on the core business pursued by lodges, the offer of mutual support, by shedding light on the mechanisms of sick benefit provision and the insurance systems that the Sons of England put in place. The second focus involves the recognition and examination of another tier of the organization's activities: the maintenance of English ethnicity. Like the St. George's Societies, the Sons of England too served as a locus of collective memory and sociability, aiding its members in keeping alive a connection with England, its culture, and its heritage. Maintaining such an orientation to the old homeland is a principal cornerstone that makes a diaspora, and the Sons of England utilized it for a wide variety of activities.[10] In so doing they acknowledged that they, while an English ethnic association based in Canada, were part of a wider English world, thus actively linking Canada to that world. This English world that connected the Sons of England with Canada but also England and locations throughout the empire was made tangible for English migrants and their descendants through gatherings on St. George's Day and similar cultural pursuits and celebrations. However, the Sons of England reconnected with the old homeland in an even more immediate way: by means of roots tourism, organizing large-scale temporary return visits to England. One such visit, held in 1910, is explored here as a concrete measure of diasporic connections maintained between England and Canada. Yet while this type of diasporic connection—a cultural one designed to allow English migrants to engage their roots in the old homeland—was fundamental to maintaining the Canadian English diaspora, the political arena offered another crucial outlet for a sense of diasporic consciousness, and thus provides the third and final prism through which the Sons of England's history is examined. While the Sons of England frequently stressed that the association was not a political organization, its very foundations—loyalty to the Crown and empire as well as Protestantism—often told a rather different story. In Canada the presence of French-speaking Canadians provided an important context, while the South African War set the scene for engagement in wider diaspora developments. Before discussion of the three prisms named here, it is important to consider the Sons of England's structure, activities, and presence in Canada.

STRUCTURE, ACTIVITIES, PRESENCE

Organized in a lodge system akin to that of associations such as the Orange Order, the Sons of England appeared more Masonic than St. George's Societies did but operated in a manner largely identical to that of the Order of the Sons of St. George, which is explored in another essay in this volume.[11] However, the Sons of England was not a secret society, or certainly not in the extreme—after all, the organization happily announced meetings in local papers, and reports of their activities circulated widely.[12] Members' Masonic behavior was largely ritualistic rather than clandestine, designed not for wont of secrecy or exclusion, except for non-English and Catholics, but rather to invite illusions of awe and an air of mystery. Another key development that set the Sons of England apart from the St. George's Society tradition was that the Sons of England also provided space to cater to women and juveniles, the former through a distinct association in its own right—the Daughters and Maids of England—and the latter through an associated juvenile lodge system. Providing associational space for the young was considered especially important, being a crucial means for forming the next generation of Sons of England members and leaders. In the spring of 1897 the supreme grand president thus stressed that "adult lodges" should take "a more active and live interest in" those of the young.[13] The Daughters and Maids of England Benevolent Society was organized on November 7, 1890, and was incorporated a good five years later, while juvenile lodges too began to spread in the early 1890s, with four having been established by 1896.[14]

The lodge system put in place by the Sons of England underscored that the association was markedly different in its structures from the many St. George's Societies that spanned the globe. While the latter had been collaborating closely in North America through the North America St. George's Union since the early 1870s, and while the London-based Royal Society of St. George eventually functioned as a global umbrella for many, St. George's Societies were neither governed as uniformly nor connected as closely through organizational structures as were the Sons of England.[15] The organization was comprised of the Supreme

Grand Lodge, Grand Lodges, and subordinate lodges, and presidents were at the helm of the day-to-day business, being supported by vice presidents, secretaries, treasurers, and committees. Subordinate lodges, which governed many of their affairs directly, normally met twice a month. In Moose Jaw, Saskatchewan, the local lodge decided to meet the second and fourth Saturdays of each month, renting the local Masonic hall, while farther west the meetings of Pride of the Island Lodge in Victoria, British Columbia, took place at St. George's Hall on the first and third Wednesdays of each month starting at 7:45 P.M.[16] Apart from these localized activities there were also district meetings in areas with larger numbers of lodges as well as annual—biannual from 1900—meetings of the Supreme Grand Lodge. Comprised of delegates from all lodges, the Supreme Grand Lodge conventions were sizable gatherings, each organized and hosted by a different lodge in a different location. This was critical to the internal organization and operations of the Sons of England, but Grand Lodge meetings also served as an important connector between lodge members across Canada. Moreover, through this joined-up oversight body members were able to lobby for particular causes or issues in a more effective way than individual lodges might have provided. This gave them critical standing in a wider society.

The 1902 Grand Lodge marked an important watershed: held in Winnipeg on August 12–15, this convention was the first to take place "beyond the confines of the Provinces of Ontario and Quebec."[17] This was a move designed to abolish the regional bias toward the eastern provinces, which for many new lodges in the west in particular was a principal concern.[18] This bias was not deliberate but rather a sign of the general settlement patterns within Canada: Ontario and the eastern provinces had been the main centers for new arrivals ever since Europeans had first made it to Canadian shores, with places such as Toronto and Montreal emerging as the key urban centers from the 1830s. At the same time, migrants made it to the Canadian prairie and the west in larger numbers only from the late nineteenth century.[19] This gave eastern lodges of the Sons of England an advantage in terms of membership numbers. Yet this very fact also meant that a meeting in a prairie state brought complications of its own, increasing travel costs for a large number of delegates as most hailed from the east. To facilitate attendance, therefore, the Sons of England negotiated reduced rail fares on the Grand Trunk Railway, the Canadian Pacific Railway, and the Intercolonial Railway.[20] The desired effect was achieved, with delegates beginning to arrive in Winnipeg around August 10, 1902, including "some thirty . . . by the lake route" and "a number arrived by way of Chicago" taking temporary residence in several of the city's hotels.[21] Consequently the Winnipeg convention was important not only because it generally was a success but also because it presented "a casting off of the last shreds of localism and provincialism" that the prior concentration of meetings in Ontario and Quebec had established.[22]

The Grand Lodge proceedings commenced with a welcome of delegates to Winnipeg by the city's mayor and continued with many sessions being held over the ensuing days. Issues ranged from the provision for subordinate lodges not to pay first-week sick pay to the agreement to devote $250 toward the endowment of a cot in Toronto's Sick Children's Hospital.[23] As had long been common at Grand Lodge meetings, the program of events also included social pursuits, for instance, "a trolley ride over the lines of the Winnipeg Electric Street railway" and a banquet in the Oddfellows' hall, "for which nearly 300 members of the society sat down" and where many a toast was cheered.[24] There was also an excursion in the form of a cruise on the Red River. More than "two hundred delegates and friends crowded the boat comfortably," and a visit was paid to St. Paul's Indian Industrial School.[25] This activity demonstrated awareness among the Sons of England of issues concerning Canada's native population. However, as the trip was largely about exploring how Indian children were trained in European ways by receiving a traditional European education, it reveals the degree to which the organization sought to promote in Canadian society a particular culture that was framed around English core values and whiteness.[26] There was no space for giving recognition to the distinctive cultures of different Indian tribes.

The move to diversify locations for meetings of the Grand Lodge was reflective of the general spread of the Sons of England throughout Canada—a spread that broadly followed the late nineteenth- and early twentieth-century migratory streams of the English, who moved into the prairie states and farther west into British Columbia.[27] Despite this geographical reach, Ontario, where the organization was born, remained its undisputed heartland when measured in its membership (see table 1). This was a direct result of the centrality of the eastern provinces to English settlement in Canada—provinces that also included Canada's urban population centers. It was in these centers that Canadian associational culture of all migrant groups took root and proliferated the most. The English were thus well in tune with general development.

TABLE 1. REGIONAL DISTRIBUTION OF SONS OF ENGLAND MEMBERS IN 1900

	1900	% of total membership
Alberta	145	1.05
Assiniboia (Saskatchewan)	95	0.7
British Columbia	453	3.3
Manitoba	700	5.1
New Brunswick	213	1.54
Newfoundland	337	2.44
Nova Scotia	346	2.51

Ontario	10,215	74.1
Prince Edward Island	122	0.88
Quebec	1,167	8.5
TOTAL MEMBERSHIP	13,793	

SOURCE: Based on statistics extracted from the *Sons of England Record*.

The total membership of 13,793 in 1900 was more than double that of a decade earlier, and by 1910 it had almost doubled again to 26,218, reflecting a trend that attests powerfully to the Sons of England's growing appeal.[28] This expansion—both numeric and geographic—is also clearly traceable in overall subordinate lodge numbers: while there were, for instance, two subordinate lodges in Assiniboia (later principally Saskatchewan) in 1901, by 1906 there were ten.[29] As English migrants were answering the call of the "best great west," the Sons of England increasingly took hold, "establishing itself," as a Quebec newspaper noted, "with increasing energy."[30] Alongside this growth of the male organization, the Daughters and Maids of England too expanded its membership, which in 1900 stood at 1,162.[31] Within this wider developmental context, the Sons of England's mutualism can be explored as it made the biggest impact not only for the Sons of England but also within the wider Canadian society.

MUTUALISM

Mutualism lay at the heart of the Sons of England's operations. Set up expressly to avoid the dispensation of charity in the tradition of St. George's Societies, the fundamental principles of the Sons of England were those of a friendly society, albeit one operating under a clear ethnic remit. Perpetrating the idea of collective self-help, the Sons of England sought to give its members the means to provide for themselves at times of distress rather than having to rely on the generosity of others.[32] In part this ideal was a reflection of the Sons of England's founders' backgrounds. St. George's Societies provided an associational outlet for the higher echelons of English immigrant society: from prominent businessmen to politicians, the motivation for engagement through English clubs and societies of these middle-class associational leaders rested on a profound sense of patrician benevolence—and one "founded on the principal belief that brotherly charity was necessary to solve prevailing social problems that were not sufficiently addressed by governments in the new places of settlement."[33] The founders of the Sons of England, by contrast, had a distinctly working-class background: they were bricklayers, coopers, and plasterers; some of the founders had even been unemployed at the time of the association's establishment.[34] These men had no desire to assert—and little use for—classic patrician benevolence; required was a systematic means of support that rested on the pillars of ethnicity and mutualism, a system that permitted them to look after themselves independently.[35] This was not a desire exclusive to the English as other migrant groups too utilized mutualism to cater for their needs—the Scots, for instance, established the Sons of Scotland at about the same time the English set up their group.

To achieve that goal all members had to pay a range of fees to be eligible for sick benefits. The Pride of the Island Lodge based in Victoria, British Columbia, which was instituted in mid-January 1891, for instance, levied an initiation fee based on age, ranging from $3.00 for those ages eighteen to thirty, to $40.00 for those between fifty-five and sixty. The lodge also required those seeking membership to pay $0.50 each for a compulsory medical examination and then uniform monthly dues of one dollar. Payment of these fees entitled members to sick leave benefits of $8.00 per week for thirteen weeks and $4.00 for the subsequent twenty-six weeks "at the expiration of twelve months from the date of their initiation," with a reduced payment made in cases of sickness prior to that date.[36] In addition to such local arrangements by means of bylaws, the Sons of England made benefits available to members through centrally administered schemes, most notably the Beneficiary Department scheme, which was designed to provide insurance in cases of death. Available to members between eighteen and forty-six years of age who were "in good standing in their respective lodges," the coverage available in 1897 ranged from $500.00 to $2,000.00, with contribution rates dependent on the desired coverage and a member's age. For a person age twenty-five, for instance, the contribution for coverage of $500.00 was $0.34 and $1.34 for coverage of $2,000.00; a member age forty, however, would have paid $0.47 and $1.88 respectively.[37]

Benefits thus dispensed were sizable and underscored the important place of the Sons of England within the English immigrant community. As statistics extracted from the *Sons of England Record* show, in 1897, $23,264.12 in sick benefits were dispensed and costs for medical services totaled $15,036.77; this was a phenomenal rise from the $1,150.00 and $894.94 respectively that were provided in 1881.[38] Reports from the superintendent of insurance of Ontario offer further substance. In 1907 the total membership of the Sons of England stood at 24,242 adults, and there were 1,167 juvenile members. That year the organization had 4,471 insurance contracts in force—not including sick and funeral benefits—that together amounted to an insurance coverage of $4,374,750.00. Moreover the association paid out $16,372.00 in funeral benefits for members and $5,200.00 in cases of deaths of members' wives. During the year 3,018 members received sick benefits, with $35,916.65 being paid out directly by subordinate lodges as they dealt with sick benefit provision locally and $458.34 by the juvenile branch. On top of these provisions subordinate lodges covered expenses of $27,356.32 for medical attendance, with juvenile branches spending $1,015.12. There were also significant assets—chiefly in real estate and cash deposits—of $99,920.40 for the

Supreme Lodge, $148,727.16 for subordinate lodges, and $5,730.70 for juvenile lodges.[39] Liabilities were, compared to the assets, negligible.

That same year the Daughters and Maids of England had a total membership of 1,489 and paid $540.00 in funeral benefits, while its subordinate branches paid $1,703.06 in sick benefits and 1,905.06 for medical attendance. The women's organization also had a juvenile branch, and this dispensed $39.42 in sick pay and $154.66 for medical attendance.[40] While these figures are clearly much lower than those of the Sons of England, they nonetheless emphasize the degree to which women could—and effectively did—make use of the same associational and friendly society structures as were available to men. After all, formed for "honorable and true Englishwomen," the Daughters and Maids of England had been established with the express purpose of educating members "in the true principles of womanhood," which was designed specifically to enable them to be self-reliant.[41] For working-class women too the emphasis lay on enabling independence rather than the provision of charity.[42]

Support by the Sons of England did not solely come in the form of benefit payments, however. At a meeting in early April 1906 Lodge Moose Jaw, Saskatchewan, agreed, for example, that it should "furnish a ward in the Moose Jaw Hospital" and that "a special assessment of $1.00 per member be made for the purpose of defraying the expense of furnishing such ward."[43] In Toronto there was a designated hospital committee that worked closely with local hospitals to care for patients who were members of the city's lodges. As the committee reported in 1901, of the thirty-five Toronto lodges represented, twenty-one supported patients in hospital care between January 1, 1899, and August 28, 1901, usually by means of direct coverage of expenses and lodge grants. Lodge Middlesex thus aided six of its members at a cost of $84.20 to the hospital committee and with a grant of $82.35 by the lodge.[44] In providing such service, the Sons of England worked with local authorities and hospitals, making critical contributions to the provision of sick care. In other cases the support received by Sons of England members was of a more practical nature. In Moose Jaw at a meeting of the lodge held in early May 1902 members agreed to order provisions for a sick member and immediately placed an order "at Kent + Brown's for $10.00 worth of provisions."[45] Farther west, in Calgary, a special "subscription was being taken up" for a Mrs. Osborne and family "to enable her to return to the old country."[46]

The Sons of England Record moreover told the stories of many other members for whom special appeals were made or who simply received a helping hand. These initiatives that went beyond the contractually enshrined provision of sick pay were valued immensely by members. As one member of Lodge Moose Jaw explained, he was delighted with the support received and was pleased to advise that he was doing well and "can get around fairly well without the use of crutches and I hope soon to be able to work again."[47] Yet not all benefit recipients dispensed praise; occasionally committees had to deal with complaints. These could include complaints by applicants whose membership had been rejected or the lodging of protests with respect to insurance claims, and in one case a member of Lodge Calgary "reported negligence of [the] Lodge surgeon in not attending him when called."[48]

To maintain the level of support offered, a variety of regulations were put in place to prevent abuse. Hence it was stipulated in the bylaws of the Pride of the Island Lodge that "any member receiving sick benefits from the Society shall not be allowed to do any kind of work whatever, neither frequent taverns or public houses," and a fine of fifty cents would be levied for such activities.[49] Lodge Moose Jaw further made provisions for the strict enforcement of regulations, with members being expelled for nonpayment of dues.[50] Ideally, of course, such issues would not occur in the first place given the vetting system in place for prospective members, which was designed not only to assess their health but also to establish their character. Customarily the vetting system rested on a number of principles, including the need for new members to be proposed and then investigated by the appropriate committee prior to initiation into a lodge. In November 1905 the relevant committee of Lodge Moose Jaw reported "favourable on characters" of several applicants for membership, who were then duly balloted for. Once the ballot had been concluded, "the initiation ceremony was then proceeded with."[51]

As these examples document, considerations relating to initiation processes and the charging of fees were of prime importance in the day-to-day operations of the Sons of England—a fact that explains too why good practice was shared among lodges. The *Sons of England Record* served an important function in this respect as the mouthpiece of the organization, but in addition lodges communicated directly with each other. Shortly after Lodge Moose Jaw had been established in late May 1904, for instance, the organizing committee decided to write to the lodges in Winnipeg and Regina to ask about "the course of procedure" they should adopt for the payment of fees and expenses, particularly with respect to the lodge physician.[52] The lodge system established by the Sons of England clearly provided a network—one that was actively used in written communications as well as through more immediate interactions. When Lodge Red Deer was formed, for example, Sons of England members from Edmonton, Strathcona, Wetaskiwin, Calgary, Medicine Hat, Lethbridge, and elsewhere journeyed to Red Deer to help the district deputy with the setting up of the lodge.[53] A direct request for help was issued in November 1904 by Lodge Moose Jaw, which sent a letter to the secretary of Regina Lodge "begging of him to make enquiries re Bro. Cassidy who is lying ill at the Regina Hospital."[54] In a less serious matter, the two lodges challenged each other on which lodge could initiate more members during a given time, with "the victorious lodge to receive a Past President

Jewel . . . from its 'opponent.'"[55] An element of friendly competitiveness was, it seems, considered a positive incentive in carrying forward the message of the Sons of England—so much so in fact that the Supreme Lodge began issuing prizes for the lodges, as well as individual members, who recruited the highest number of new members.[56]

Initiatives of intralodge networking were supported by visits from the head lodge, with supreme and past supreme grand presidents as well as other lodge officials frequently traveling throughout Canada to visit subordinate lodges. Moose Jaw thus saw the visit of Past Supreme President Bro. John Aldridge during his 1904 tour of western Canada and arranged several activities for him throughout his stay.[57] As the *Moose Jaw Signal* reported, Aldrige "complimented the lodge upon the way it discharged its duties and upon its great numerical strength for such a young lodge."[58]After his visit in Moose Jaw, Aldrige continued to travel farther west to visit other lodges, including Lodge Calgary, where an "enthusiastic celebration" was held.[59] On a smaller-scale level there is also clear evidence of visiting lodge members in attendance from other lodges.[60] A purely imagined diaspora this was not.[61]

ETHNIC CULTURE AND IDENTITY

As with the 1902 Grand Lodge meeting in Winnipeg, subordinate lodges too set great store by ensuring that there were outlets for social pursuits among members. Some of these activities operated on a small scale and were designed simply to provide entertainment. Smoke socials or smoking concerts were popular, at times intended too to bring together "eligible Englishmen . . . with the hope that they will eventually become members of the Society."[62] Many lodges, for instance Toronto-based Lodge Warwick, held annual excursions, with picnics often an integral part. These picnics and other outdoor activities were popular in Canada—this was a result in part of the good weather in the summer but also the fact that in winter outdoor pursuits were much more restricted: as many opportunities as possible were pursued in the summer months. In July 1896 lodge members thus left Yonge Street Wharf for Lake Island Park, Wilson, situated across Lake Ontario in the state of New York.[63]

Prominent larger-scale and public features of the Sons of England's annual events calendar were church parades, the first having been held as early as 1876.[64] Parades provided opportunities for the Sons of England to demonstrate visibly their presence in local communities large and small but also to cooperate with other associations in their places of residence. Church parades were frequently held on St. George's Day. In 1898, for example, members of various Toronto lodges and the Toronto St. George's Society, totaling about 250, came together on Elm Street to march to St. James' Cathedral.[65] While St. George's Day was the most significant outlet for English sentiment, other annual holidays such as Empire Day too saw many a parade.[66] For the Sons of England, these holidays and anniversary days provided a readily usable hook for the celebration of their English heritage. Compared to St. George's Societies both in Canada and around the world—which enshrined such celebrations as fundamental pillars for activities in its constitutions—the Sons of England did not formalize ethno-cultural pursuits in this way. This was a direct result of their focus on the provision of mutual aid, their primary concern, with social activities playing second fiddle. Still the organization certainly promoted them, seeking to be "united by the bond of that fair land which was 'home.'"[67]

Yet while such instances of ethnic identity expression by the Sons of England were important, members used their associational structures to maintain an even more tangible link with England: the organized return trip. From the late nineteenth century, a growing number of English residents abroad hailing from Australasia, South Africa, the Canadian prairies, or the American Midwest embarked on trips in search of the England they remembered from their childhood days, or the one they had been told about in stories by their parents and grandparents if they were born overseas. The growing popularity of such trips had much to do with the availability of better, faster, and cheaper modes of transport, but it also pointed to the impact of generational heritage and the desire of many a descendant of migrants to explore family roots in the old homeland. They traveled as roots tourists, exploring their ancestral history and culture. Roots tourism is a distinct form of the émigré return movement, albeit one that has been viewed primarily as a more modern phenomenon, having been explored by anthropologists as a facet of the growing popularity of genealogy as a pastime of next-generation descendants of migrants.[68] There is, however, clear evidence that that view is misleading as an abundance of earlier examples can be found: the roots of roots tourism lie in the late nineteenth and early twentieth centuries. While there were many motives for the temporary return of migrants, roots tourism offers an important perspective on the transnational connections maintained within a diaspora and is a topic that has not received much attention yet.[69]

Organized by Robert Verity, the Sons of England's 1910 trip referred to at the outset of this essay commenced in early July, when "five hundred sons and daughters of England gathered from various parts of Canada, [and] left by special train for Montreal."[70] All of them, the *Ottawa Citizen* was quick to point out, "are prosperous."[71] This was certainly a characteristic of early roots tourists, but return trips home nonetheless increased in popularity. An additional two hundred excursionists joined the group in Montreal, making it "the biggest excursion party ever taken out of Canada."[72] As one reporter observed, travelers were "all full of expectation of a delightful trip, and the renewal of old time associations. Long years have separated many from their friends and relatives, but the affection for the land of their birth still remains firmly rooted, not withstanding [sic] their loyalty to the land of their adoption. . . . [One of the travellers was] a well known Winnipeg merchant, who has been absent 43 years, and who is now retuning for his first visit, but with a return ticket in his pocket. So far as can be learned, this is the case with all the voyagers, whose principal desire is to cement the ties which bind Canada to the motherland."[73] The empire, of which Canada—as opposed to the United States—had remained a part, provided the critical connector here.

To facilitate the maintenance of these ties, a special program had been arranged for the entertainment of the group in England: there were special cars, coaching, and motor tours to allow travelers to get the most out of the tight itinerary, which included a tour of a little over two weeks that brought them from Bristol, via London, to Edinburgh, taking in cities that included Oxford, Stratford-upon-Avon, and Liverpool.[74] At the start of the tour in Bristol the city's lord mayor gave the Sons of England a cordial reception.[75] After stops en route in Cheddar and Bath, the party then made its way to London and spent five days in the capital. A large portion of the members went to visit the House of Commons, where, as was reported in the *Edmonton Capital,* "the members of Parliament were genuinely interested in them."[76] They clearly recognized the value of meeting with and talking to citizens of the empire. The *Ottawa Citizen* added that the travelers were "delighted with the metropolis and have seen all the sights that are historic and picturesque."[77]

Some of the Winnipeg members traveling home with the group were Mr. and Mrs. John Eddy, J. S. Nicholas, W. Walpole, and Mr. and Mrs. Jacob Freeman —all of whom had long since lived in Winnipeg and were well known in the city and among the Sons of England. Jacob Freeman, for instance, had been the lodge's district deputy for the Winnipeg district. It was in that role that in 1895 Freeman helped set up a new Winnipeg branch of the Sons of England to promote, as the local paper put it, benevolence and patriotism.[78] The return to the homeland in 1910 was Freeman's first visit to England after twenty-seven years in Canada and may well have been a long-awaited culmination of his patriotism—though one framed by the English patriotism promoted by the Sons of England.[79] Freeman certainly provided his local paper with an enthusiastic account of the trip, writing about the "warm reception" received.[80]

Freeman's account also reveals, however, that the trip was not simply serving the purpose of revisiting the old homeland; it was also an active attempt to entice new English migrants to Canada.[81] As the *Times* of London (UK) reported, in fact, "each member of the party will try to induce one resident of Great Britain to come to Canada"—an objective that needs to be seen, as Freeman's account highlighted, in the context of the settlement of the Canadian west.[82] In addition there was a second important factor. While not spelled out explicitly, it is likely that the growing number of migrants from southern and eastern Europe who made their way to Canada in the early twentieth century played a part in the thinking behind attracting new migrants from Britain. Perceived by many as a threat to the Canadian way of life, "mothercountry stock" from Britain was desired—a view also held, for instance, by Goldwin Smith, commentator and promoter of continental union with the United States, who argued that Canada was "deprived of a re-inforcement [sic]" from Britain and that the loss of these migrants was felt strongly when the country was grappling "with a vast influx of foreign emigration."[83]

The Sons of England's trip, therefore, brings to the fore three important points. First, despite still living within the British Empire, the organization was keen to offer members a tangible link to the old homeland, organizing return trips at reasonable rates to facilitate that connection. Second, and given the nature of the activities pursued in England, the trips were also designed to promote contact between people in England with members of the English diaspora in Canada, with a view to encouraging migration. This chimed well with politicians in Canada who in the early twentieth century were keen on promoting migration from England to counter the arrival of larger numbers of migrants from elsewhere. Such thinking was shaped by ideas of Anglo-Saxon superiority as well as the emergence of race as a critical criterion of differentiation between migrants of British stock and the mass of new arrivals from outside the British Isles.[84] Third, the desire of the Sons of England to promote new migration from England to Canada documented their allegiance to the new home as well as England—an allegiance perhaps suitably signaled on arrival "by [the] singing of the National Anthem and the Maple Leaf."[85] It is within the context of this dual allegiance—to Canada and England, and by extension to Britain and the empire —that the idea of a tangible English diaspora played a particularly important role in the late nineteenth and early twentieth centuries.

DIASPORA POLITICS

At their inception the exclusivist Protestant, English Sons of England were tainted by more than a whiff of anti-Irishness.[86] One particular episode, opposition to the lecturing tour through North America of William O'Brien, home-rule advocate and president of the Irish Land League, brought members wider attention in the press in the late 1880s.[87] Protesting against the Irish nationalist movement, the Sons of England organization was cast as an aggressive, conservative political bloc, being lumped together with the Orange Order and the local militia.[88] Even the suggestion that O'Brien should be protected by "the whole military force if necessary" seemed pointless, a newspaper report suggested, as "this is composed of every three out of five men who belong to the Orange [O] rder or to the Sons of England."[89] The Sons of England described here were overtly anti-Catholic, unionist, and belligerent. Yet members of the organization were always adamant that they were not political—a belief they later framed by casting the organization as an "independent entity": independent not only of particular political views but also of other associations and their activities. Still it is clear that the level of independence was limited given the members' loyalty to "the Protestant religion, to our Queen and country."[90] While there may not have been an overt political agenda, this framing of the organization reflected a particular mind-set that was not independent.

The Sons of England existed only in Canada and South Africa, in part as a result of members' express loyalty to the Crown and the empire, which would have been impossible to assert in a republican context. The history of British expansion in North America, as well as the emergence of the United States as a world power at a time when the British Empire was increasingly under pressure, therefore supplies an important context to explain how the Sons of England viewed the relationship between Canada and the United States. One member of the Sons of England, John Castell Hopkins, was particularly vocal on the subject, writing regularly in the *Record* about matters relating to the British Empire. Born in Dyersville, Iowa, Hopkins moved to Canada as a child when his parents relocated to Bowmanville in Ontario. As an adult he worked as a bank clerk but was known chiefly as an author and an imperialist, having been involved in the establishment of the Ontario branch of the Imperial Federation League.[91] Hopkins's fundamental assumption was that "British connection" had had "the greatest influence . . . in the development of Canadian institutions and the moulding of Canadian patriotism."[92] In his writings, therefore, he frequently criticized the present state in which, to his mind, Canada was becoming more removed from the motherland. This was all the more problematic given the "Americanization" of the world. "In the popular mind," Hopkins asserted, "'America' obscures 'Canada'":

> Under the former name is included the latter geographically, and as the people of the United States have arrogated to themselves the national use of the word "America," everything Canadian is naturally mixed up in the ideas of the masses with the concerns of the United States. Besides this fact, and contributing to enhance it, is the sending of cable news regarding Canada via New York, and it must be confessed that a further puzzling complication is given by Canadians themselves in the use of Provincial abbreviations, such as "Ont.," instead of writing in their business and other communications of Canada as a whole. The use of provincial hieroglyphics does serious harm in the present somewhat dazed state of geographical knowledge.[93]

To be able to progress, allowing the British Empire to stand strong against the United States, Canada would have to assert its position more vocally and in distinct separation from that of the United States. Only this could ensure that Canada would grow as an integral partner in an imperial federation with Britain rather than being overshadowed by its republican neighbor.

It was this thinking, Hopkins's "unqualified support" for any "imperial crusade," that pitted his views—and by extension the views of the Sons of England —against those of the famous businessman and philanthropist Andrew Carnegie, who became a frequent victim of attack in the *Record*.[94] While the Sons of England, writing in the context of William McKinley's presidential election, believed that "'our hatred of England,' has lost much of its old time power with the majority of the voters of the United States," Carnegie antagonized them greatly as he still represented that hatred in his criticism of the British Empire.[95] Hence even when Carnegie offered support to two Canadian cities through philanthropic contributions, there were voices of unease. A Sons of England member, William Robbins of Walkerville, Ontario, for instance, wrote a pamphlet stating that such gifts should not be accepted because of Carnegie's views. Robbins included extracts from Carnegie's writings in his pamphlet to trace where the problems lay, and they lay especially in Carnegie's dismissal of the queen.[96] Unsurprisingly this did not go down well with the Sons of England: to them it represented a "series of fabrications and insults" to the person they held most dear.[97] Sentiments heightened in the context of the question of an interimperial tariff. Carnegie did not support it and sent warning messages in the direction of Canada. For the Sons of England, such interference was unacceptable: "We beg Mr. Carnegie's pardon. He is not an American. He is a naturalized British subject . . . not all his lavish expenditure for college, hospitals and libraries in any part of the British Empire can hide the fact that Mr. Carnegie's real love is for the land where his dollars were made. . . . The fear which inspires his cry of warning is not that Canada may be tripped by the United States as she marches into an imperial preferential tariff, but that Canada may tread heavily on the corns of the Republic."[98]

The impact of economic considerations in the relationship between Canada and the United States was certainly not lost on the Sons of England, and Carnegie was not the only subject to rouse their sentiments. In "Keep the Flag Afloat," a piece published in the Record, the organization cautioned, for instance, that the supremacy of the empire was under threat "not by the fleets and armies of avowedly hostile nations, but by the financial machinations of the plutocracy of an alleged friendly power," the United States. It was "Yankee capitalists" who had helped establish "for the United States that shipping supremacy of the Atlantic which was first obtained by England," and therefore, "American money has dealt our Motherland a heavier blow than she ever received from foreign foe."[99]

It seemed clear to the Sons of England that republicanism had facilitated the development of a "despotic form of government," and in a "land where money is king and where that King both makes and administers the law," this could happen quickly.[100] The Sons of England thus cast having a monarch as head of state as a means to liberty. More practical solutions were required, however, and it was the Daughters of the Empire who "have shown the way" by pledging "to purchase and to induce others to purchase Canadian and other British goods in preference to those of foreign manufacture."[101]

There was a more practical side to Canadian-U.S. relations and the views of the Sons of England, one that was of more immediate relevance in the context of the status of the Yukon and Alaska. The Supreme Grand Executive at a meeting held in early April 1898 "proscribed for residence by members of the Order all that portion of North America lying north of the 60th parallel of north latitude, which embraces a portion of Alaska and the Yukon and adjacent territories. Notice is therefore hereby given that the Society will not be responsible for any benefits claimed on account of sickness or death happening on or by reason of residence within the district above named."[102] The Alaska boundary dispute was rearing its head.[103] Yet despite these issues that complicated the view held by the Sons of England regarding the United States, there were associational interactions that transcended them, speaking strongly to the strength of English diaspora connections across the globe.[104] Personal links played an important part in this, for instance through Sons of England members who had relocated to the United States but maintained contact.[105]

The complexities inherent in U.S.-Canadian relations seem small, however, when compared to Canada's internal dynamics in the relationship between English- and French-speaking Canadians. From the 1870s, as Canada was increasingly seeking its way as a nation in its own right after confederation in 1867, French Canadians had to find their place in the new constitutional setup.[106] For many contemporary observers this brought with it a series of problems. Goldwin Smith, for instance, saw the monarchism of French Canadians as a fundamental problem, noting that "French Canada is a relic of the historical past preserved in isolation, as Siberian mammoths are preserved in ice."[107] There were also growing concerns that French-speaking Canadians, at best, harbored divided loyalties to both the new dominion and the British Empire. Contributions in the *Sons of England Record* documented that the organization certainly viewed the latter possibility as problematic.

Many of those who contributed to debates about French-Canadians emphasized that they should not be automatically prejudiced against, and that only individuals for whom there was clear evidence of activity that did not show an adequate level of loyalty should be criticized. One such individual was Joseph Israel Tarte. Born in Lanoraie, Lower Canada, in January 1848, Tarte commenced his political career in the Conservative Party. This party had emerged from the coalition that had been formed in the 1850s to promote confederation and was largely comprised of moderates. Tarte was elected to the Quebec Legislative Assembly in 1877. However, given the Conservative Party's indifferent stance toward questions concerning French Canada, Tarte, who had since been elected to the Canadian House of Commons, eventually joined the Liberals and became minister of public works in the Laurier government in the summer of 1896.[108] While Tarte's views on French Canada were by no means unknown, in 1899 his pro-French statements caused the Sons of England to attack him openly. At the time Tarte was, as Canada's chief commissioner at the universal exposition, based in Paris, there choosing to "openly avow in effect that he is a Frenchman first and a British subject afterwards," as was observed in a *Record* report.[109] Therefore, and while "not animated by party feeling in one direction or the other," the Sons of England sought to "join forces . . . and insist upon the retirement from British official life of such variegated patriots as Monsieur Tarte."[110] It was not acceptable to the organization that a minister of the Canadian government, and thus by extension of Her Majesty's government, should express loyalty to another country as a result of his personal sentiments.

Almost a year later, with Tarte again in Paris, the Sons of England's attack resurfaced. While members expressed clearly that they "never had any sympathy with the cry of disloyalty hurled against the French-Canadian[s]," believing "them to be true British subjects with a natural feeling of affection for the land of their ancestors," Tarte's story remained a different one in their eyes as he was still "look[ing] to France." What made his new statements more problematic was that he actively "urged Frenchmen to emigrate [from France] to Canada." As Tarte was a minister of the British Crown, the Sons of England wondered what he meant when saying "We look to France. Englishmen can make their homes among us." For them the situation was clear: with loyalty to the Crown a central pillar, they said, "We know of no British colony that looks to a foreign power."[111] Critically, the Sons of England used their Englishness in addressing Tarte to make a case for Canada.

As in the examples regarding the relationship of Canada with the United States, the question of loyalty lay at the core of these concerns, but in the case of French Canadians it was overtly tied up with the issue of religion—a point of difference with Canadian St. George's Societies, which sought to remain politically neutral on such matters. For the Sons of England the situation was clear: given that the monarch made reference in the oath only to the Protestant faith, members had to follow that line. The Roman Catholic Church was "an organization seeking to exercise political power to the advancement of its own interests and the detriment of those of other creeds."[112] Whether through French-speaking patriots such as Tarte or Irish nationalists such as O'Brien, the prevention of such "detriment" was fundamental to the Sons of England's mind-set.[113]

Within both themes explored—U.S.-Canadian relations and the complexities of French Canada—one development amplified the situation: the Boer War. It was a time when some commentators began to wish "for the humiliation of the Anglo-Saxon race and the downfall of the British Empire," while pro-Boer sentiments, for instance as expressed by many a U.S. journalist, could keep alive "the insensate hatred of England . . . among a large class."[114] The Sons of England did, of course, agree that any war is best prevented, but with respect to the Boer War it was their firm belief that "it is not only the lesser of two evils, but it will be productive of much that will make for peace for years to come over a far wider area than South Africa."[115] Importantly there was also clear recognition of the wider relevance in terms of the English diaspora: the war was "a lesson in the solidarity . . . which England's covert enemies will not very soon forget," a solidarity shown by how quickly the English in Canada, and the Sons of England specifically, answered the empire's call.[116] This sense of imperial duty was important in Canada in particular, but the English in the republican United States too expressed sympathies with the British cause in Africa.

It was as a result of this solidarity—which extended from the Supreme Lodge to the subordinate-lodge level and was clearly strengthened by the fact that the Sons of England also existed in South Africa—that the war impacted Sons of England societies directly. News on the progression of the war, reports from South Africa, and commentaries on the situation appeared frequently on the pages of the *Record*. Through this communication a direct connection was facilitated. Moreover many a lodge expressed support. Lodge Commercial, for instance, passed a resolution at a meeting held on October 27, 1899, extending "to Englishmen, and Sons of England in particular, in South Africa, their deepest sympathy and good wishes for their complete success in the present struggle for the maintenance of the common rights and privileges of all free-born subjects of our Most Gracious Majesty the Queen."[117] Even more direct was the impact in those lodges that members had left to fight for the empire in the war. There was an immense pride in the contributions made by the Sons of England but also a profound sense of grief over those who did not return. Rolls of Honour were produced, and in those cases where members who had died were buried in Canada, members of the Sons of England were closely involved in the arrangements. In some cases lodges sought to support more actively those serving the empire; as an example, Commercial Lodge pledged "to keep in good standing on its books any member of this lodge who may go to South Africa with the Canadian Contingent until such time as he may be released from his term of active service in the Transvaal."[118] Moreover, and following in the footsteps of other ethnic associations, the Sons of England supported numerous relief funds. Calgary Lodge, for instance, gathered in November 1899 to collect money for the fund set up "for the relief of the widows and orphans of soldiers killed in the South African war," including for those resident in England.[119]

CONCLUSION

The formation of the Sons of England in the 1870s marked a key juncture in English ethnic associationalism in Canada. What had rested on the pillars of benevolence and charity, dispensed through many a St. George's Society, was being overtaken and eventually would be outdone in scale by ethnic mutualism. English cultural traditions and the desire to be sociable within a formalized group setting still played a role, but ultimately the Sons of England catered for a different cohort of English migrants both in terms of the timing of their arrival and in their socioeconomic background than did St. George's Societies, and it was this difference that translated into a distinct associational form. Moreover this distinct form was also set up in response to the lack of social security provisions made by the Canadian state, documenting the wider impact of the Sons of England's work within Canadian society.

Organized through a substantial lodge system that spanned the length of Canada, the Sons of England was an extremely well-connected organization that made the English diaspora tangible for its members not only through communication channels and the dissemination of news but also through organized return visits to England. Alongside these activities there was also a more political layer to the organization's sense of Englishness, one that occasionally gained the upper hand when members saw their identity—English, Protestant, and imperial, underpinned by a profound sense of loyalty to the Crown—threatened by the American Republic, French-speaking Canadians, and the Boer War. Within this wider context the case of the Sons of England highlights that English identity overseas channeled through associational culture was never one-dimensional or linear; it was always a directed response by English migrants, framed by the type of associational remit they had chosen for themselves.

NOTES

1. *Blairmore Enterprise,* July 21, 1910.
2. *Edmonton Capital,* July 9, 1910.
3. *Blairmore Enterprise,* July 21, 1910.
4. John S. King, *The Early History of the Sons of England Benevolent Society, Including Its Origins, Principles and Progress* (Toronto: Thomas Moore, 1891), 11. For details on St. George's Societies, including those in Toronto, see Tanja Bueltmann and Donald M. MacRaild, "Globalizing St George: English Associations in the Anglo-World to the 1930s," *Journal of Global History* 7, no. 1 (2012): 79–105.

5. *Constitution of the Sons of England Benevolent Society under the Supreme Jurisdiction of the Grand Lodge of Canada* (Bowmanville: M. A. James, 1888), 4.

6. This and the previous quotes are from ibid., 7.

7. Ibid., 8.

8. See, for instance, Baltimore St. George's Society Records, Minute Book, December 6, 1866, MS 1881, Maryland Historical Society.

9. *Sons of England Record* [hereafter *Record*] 1, no. 5 (October 15, 1896): 4.

10. See Tanja Bueltmann, Andrew Hinson, and Graeme Morton, eds., *The Scottish Diaspora* (Edinburgh: Edinburgh University Press, 2013), chap. 2, "Diaspora: Defining a Concept."

11. *Manitoba Free Press,* August 7, 1894.

12. A search of Peel's Prairie Provinces newspaper archive, hosted by University of Alberta Libraries and covering over one hundred newspapers from throughout the Canadian prairies, was indicative of the wide coverage of Sons of England activities. A search of the exact phrase "sons of England benefit society" alone yielded well over seven hundred results in the period from the group's establishment to World War II. While such a simple search does not fully capture the complexities of the Sons of England's activities or of mass-scale digital newspaper searching, it nonetheless is suggestive of the wider trends. For the archive, visit http://peel.library.ualberta.ca/newspapers/, accessed February 12, 2014.

13. *Record* 1, no. 11 (April 15, 1897): 1.

14. *Record* 1, no. 7 (December 15, 1896): 13.

15. See Bueltmann and MacRaild, "Globalizing St George," 95. For a detailed study of the role of the Royal Society of St. George, see Lesley C. Robinson, "Englishness in England and the 'Near Diaspora': Organisation, Influence and Expression, 1880s–1970s" (Ph.D. thesis, University of Ulster, 2014). See also Hanael Bianchi, "St. George's Day: A Cultural History" (Ph.D. diss., Catholic University of America, 2011).

16. Minute Book, 1904–7, May 28, 1904, Moose Jaw Sons of England Benefit Society foundations, MJ-6.001, Moose Jaw Public Library, Archives Department, Moose Jaw, Saskatchewan, Canada [hereafter MJPL]. The decision to meet at the local Masonic hall was made at a later date; see ibid., June 11, 1904. The hall was rented for sixty dollars per year, with the rent "to include light, use of furniture and a locker." See also *By-Laws of Pride of the Island Lodge, No. 131, Sons of England Benevolent Society* (Victoria: James A. Cohen, Printer, 1891), 4.

17. *Journal of Proceedings of the Twenty-Sixth Annual Session of the Supreme Lodge, Sons of England Benefit Society* (Toronto: Bryant Press, 1902).

18. *Record* 6, no. 12 (March 1902): 1.

19. Peter E. Pope, *Fish into Wine: The Newfoundland Plantation in the Seventeenth Century* (Chapel Hill: University of North Carolina Press, 2004); Dirk Hoerder, *Creating Societies: Immigrant Lives in Canada* (Kingston: McGill-Queens University Press, 1999).

20. *Record* 6, no. 12 (March 1902): 1.

21. *Manitoba Free Press,* August 1, 1902.

22. *Record* 7, no. 6 (September 1902): 1.

23. *Record* 7, no. 6 (September 1902): 2.

24. *Manitoba Free Press,* August 12, 1902; August 14, 1902.

25. Ibid., August 15, 1902. Photographs of the visit can be found in *Record* 7, no. 6 (September 1902): 4–5.

26. Jean Barman, Yvonne Hébert, and Don McCaskill, eds., *Indian Education in Canada: The Legacy* (Vancouver: University of British Columbia Press, 1986).

27. For further details, see, for example, Donald Kerr and Deryck W. Holdsworth, eds., *Historical Atlas of Canada: Addressing the Twentieth Century, 1891–1961* (Toronto: University of Toronto Press, 1990), esp. chap. 17ff; Barbara J. Messamore, ed., *Canadian Patterns: From Britain and North America* (Ottawa: University of Ottawa Press, 2004).

28. Ibid. Figures for 1900 were confirmed in *Report of the Inspector of Insurance and Registrar of Friendly Societies of Ontario 1900* (Toronto: L. K. Cameron by order of the Legislative Assembly of Ontario, 1900), C43. See also *Report of the Inspector of Insurance and Registrar of Friendly Societies of Ontario 1911* (Toronto: L. K. Cameron by order of the Legislative Assembly of Ontario, 1911), C26.

29. Based on statistics extracted from the *Record.*

30. See, for instance, R. Douglas Francies and Chris Kitzman, eds., *The Prairie West as Promised Land* (Calgary: University of Calgary Press, 2007); W. Peter Ward, "Population Growth in Western Canada, 1901–71," in *Developing the West,* ed. John E. Foster (Edmonton: University of Alberta Press, 1983), 157–78. See also *Quebec Saturday Budget,* April 28, 1906.

31. *Report of the Inspector of Insurance . . . 1900,* C82.

32. See, for instance, Simon Cordery, *British Friendly Societies, 1750–1914* (Houndmills and New York: Palgrave Macmillan, 2003).

33. Bueltmann and MacRaild, "Globalizing St George," 88.

34. King, *The Early History of the Sons of England,* 9ff.

35. See also Bruce S. Elliott, "The English," in *Encyclopedia of Canada's Peoples,* ed. Paul R. Magocsi (Toronto: University of Toronto Press, 1999), 483; Ross McCormack, "Cloth Caps and Jobs: The Ethnicity of English Immigrants in Canada 1900–14," in *Ethnicity, Power and Politics in Canada,* ed. Jorgen Dahlie and Tissa Fernando (Toronto: Methuen, 1981), the latter of which strongly argues for English ethnicity.

36. *By-Laws of Pride of the Island Lodge,* 5–6, quote on 6.

37. Figures and the previous quote are from *Record* 1, no. 8 (January 15, 1897): back of cover page.

38. Based on figures provided in various reports in *Record.*

39. *Report of the Inspector of Insurance and Registrar of Friendly Societies of Ontario 1908* (Toronto: L. K. Cameron by order of the Legislative Assembly of Ontario, 1908), C25ff.

40. Ibid., C203–4.

41. All quotes are from an information section in *Record* 1, no. 7 (December 15, 1896): n.p.

42. There is little scholarship on the associational activities of women. Some useful details are available in the context of female Orange lodges; see, for instance, Donald M. MacRaild and D. A. J. MacPherson, "Sisters of the Brotherhood: Female

Orangeism on Tyneside in the Late 19th and Early 20th Centuries," *Irish Historical Studies* 34 (May 2006): 40–60.

43. Minute Book, 1904–7, April 4, 1906, Moose Jaw Sons of England Benefit Society foundations, MJ-6.001, MJPL.

44. Toronto Hospital Committee, report of its work from January 1, 1899, to August 28, 1901, *Record* 6, no. 6 (September 1901): 6.

45. Minute Book, 1904–7, May 2, 1906, Moose Jaw Sons of England Benefit Society foundations, MJ-6.001, MJPL.

46. Minutes for Lodge Calgary, May 18, 1908, BD.I.U58A V.2, Glenbow Museum Archive, Calgary, Alberta, Canada (hereafter GMA).

47. Minute Book, 1904–7, September 10, 1904, Moose Jaw Sons of England Benefit Society foundations, MJ-6.001, MJPL.

48. Minutes for Lodge Calgary, February 3, 1908, BD.I.U58A V.2, GMA.

49. *By-Laws of Pride of the Island Lodge*, 8.

50. Minute Book, 1904–7, March 20, 1907, Moose Jaw Sons of England Benefit Society foundations, MJ-6.001, MJPL.

51. Ibid., November 11, 1905.

52. Ibid., May 28, 1904; June 11, 1904.

53. *Red Deer News*, April 13, 1910.

54. Minute Book, 1904–7, November 12, 1904, Moose Jaw Sons of England Benefit Society foundations, MJ-6.001, MJPL.

55. Ibid., November 26, 1904.

56. *Record* 2, no. 11 (April 15, 1898): 135.

57. Minute Book, 1904–7, October 8, 1904, Moose Jaw Sons of England Benefit Society foundations, MJ-6.001, MJPL.

58. *Moose Jaw Signal*, October 10, 1904, repr. in *Record* 9, no. 8 (November 1904): 2.

59. *Calgary Daily Herald*, October 19, 1904.

60. Ibid., July 8, 1905.

61. Framed in terms of the influential idea of an imagined community, cf. Benedict Anderson, *Imagined Communities: Reflections on the Origins and Spread of Nationalism* (London: Verso, 1983).

62. Minute Book, 1904–7, June 25, 1904, Moose Jaw Sons of England Benefit Society foundations, MJ-6.001, MJPL.

63. *Record* 1, no. 2 (July 15, 1896): 3.

64. *Record* 2, no. 7 (December 15, 1897): 78.

65. *Toronto Daily Mail and Empire*, April 25, 1898.

66. See, for instance, *Record* 6, no. 4 (July 1901): 3.

67. Toronto Daily Mail and Empire, April 25, 1898.

68. See, for example, Paul Basu, *Highland Homecomings: Genealogy and Heritage Tourism in the Scottish Diaspora* (London and New York: Routledge, 2007).

69. See also Tanja Bueltmann, "'Gentlemen, I am going to the Old Country': Scottish Roots-Tourists in the Late 19th and Early 20th Centuries," in *Back to Caledonia:*

Scottish Return Migration from the 16th Century to the Present, ed. Mario Varricchio (Edinburgh: John Donald, 2012).

70. *Toronto Globe,* July 6, 1910. Consecutive census records suggest that there was only one Robert Verity in Canada. In the 1911 census this Robert was listed as age fifty-four, born in England, a Methodist, and resident in Ward 6, Toronto. See Census of Canada, 1911, at https://www.bac-lac.gc.ca/eng/census/Pages/census.aspx, accessed March 15, 2014; *Ottawa Citizen,* July 7, 1910.

71. *Ottawa Citizen,* July 7, 1910.

72. *Edmonton Capital,* July 9, 1910. For the passengers' names, see In-Coming Passenger Manifest] port of Avonmouth, July 14, 1910.

73. *Blairmore Enterprise,* July 21, 1910.

74. *Manitoba Free Press,* July 4, 1910; this is also where the itinerary comes from.

75. Ibid., July 16, 1910.

76. *Edmonton Capital,* August 1, 1910.

77. *Ottawa Citizen,* July 22, 1910.

78. *Manitoba Free Press,* January 11, 1895.

79. Ibid., July 4, 1910.

80. Ibid., August 2, 1910.

81. Ibid.

82. *Times,* July 7, 1910.

83. Goldwin Smith, *The Schism in the Anglo-Saxon Race: An Address Delivered before the Canadian Club of New York* (New York: American News Company, 1887), 25.

84. Tanja Bueltmann, "Anglo-Saxonism and the Racialization of the English Diaspora," in *Locating the English Diaspora, 1500–2010,* ed. Tanja Bueltmann, David Gleeson, and Donald M. MacRaild (Liverpool: Liverpool University Press, 2012).

85. *Manitoba Free Press,* July 16, 1910.

86. *Freeman's Journal,* July 15, 1878; *Leeds Mercury,* July 20, 1878; *Lloyd's Weekly Register,* July 21, 1878.

87. See also Mark G. McGowan, *The Waning of the Green: Catholics, the Irish, and Identity in Toronto, 1887–1922* (Kingston and Montreal: McGill-Queen's University Press, 1999), 3; Gerald J. Stortz, "An Irish Radical in a Tory Town: William O'Brien in Toronto, 1887," *Eire-Ireland* 19 (Winter 1984): 35–58.

88. See, for instance, *Aberdeen Weekly Journal,* May 18, 1887.

89. *Elyria Daily Telephone,* May 15, 1887. The same account circulated more widely and was printed in several other papers either verbatim or in digested form.

90. *Record* 1, no. 5 (October 15, 1896): 4.

91. For details, see Jeffrey A. Keshen, "Hopkins, John Castell," in *Dictionary of Canadian Biography,* vol. 15, University of Toronto, http://www.biographi.ca/en/bio/hopkins_john_castell_15E.html, accessed March 13, 2014.

92. *Record* 4, no. 9 (December 13, 1899): 2.

93. Reprinted in *Record* 1, no. 3 (August 15, 1896): 2.

94. Keshen, "Hopkins."

95. *Record* 5, no. 8 (November 15, 1900): 6.

96. Andrew Carnegie, *Triumphant Democracy or Fifty Years' March of the Republic*

(London: Sampson Low, Marston, Searle & Rivington, 1886), 351. The stance was clear from the outset as Carnegie added an acknowledgment "to the beloved Republic under whose equal laws I am made the peer of any man, although denied political equality by my native land, I dedicate this book with an intensity of gratitude and admiration which the native-born citizen can neither feel nor understand." 97*Record* 6, no. 2 (May 1901): 2.

98. *Record* 8, no. 6 (September 1903): 4.

99. This and the previous quotes are from *Record* 7, no. 2 (May 1902): 1.

100. Ibid.

101. Ibid.

102. *Record* 2, no. 11 (April 15, 1898): 135.

103. See, for instance, Iestyn Adams, *Brothers across the Ocean: British Foreign Policy and the Origins of the 'Special Relationship' 1900–1905* (London: I. B. Tauris, 2005), esp. the section on America and Canada; F. M. Carroll, "Robert Lansing and the Alaskan Boundary Settlement," *International History Review* 9, no. 2 (1987): 271–90; Edward P. Kohn, *This Kindred People: Canadian-American Relations and the Anglo-Saxon Idea, 1895–1903* (Kingston and Montreal: McGill-Queen's University Press, 2004).

104. Particularly with respect to initiatives concerning the Order of the Sons of St. George based in the United States, see *Record* 8, no. 8 (November 1903): 4–5.

105. See, for example, *Record* 4, no. 12 (March 15, 1900): 3.

106. Phillip Buckner, "Introduction: Canada and the British Empire," in *Canada and the British Empire,* ed. Phillip Buckner (Oxford: Oxford University Press, 2008), 7.

107. Cited in Donal Lowry, "The Crown, Empire Loyalism and the Assimilation of Non-British White Subjects in the British World: An Argument against 'Ethnic Determinism,'" in *The British World: Diaspora, Culture and Identity,* ed. Carl Bridge and Kent Fedorowich (London: Frank Cass, 2003), 106.

108. Michèle Brassard and Jean Hamelin, "Tarte, Joseph Israel," in *Dictionary of Canadian Biography,* vol. 13, University of Toronto, http://www.biographi.ca/en/bio.php?id_nbr=7097, accessed March 20, 2014.

109. *Record* 4, no. 7 (October 16, 1899): 4.

110. *Record* 4, no. 7 (October 16, 1899): 5.

111. This and the previous quotes are from *Record* 5, no. 3 (June 15, 1900): 5.

112. *Record* 6, no. 2 (May 1901): 1.

113. See also *"England's Greatness": Anniversary Sermon Delivered to the Members of St George's Society of Ottawa and the Sons of England by Rev. Dr. Herridge* (Ottawa: Reynolds Print, 1899).

114. The first quote comes from *La Semaine Religieuse,* a Quebec-based journal that was vocal in its anti-Englishness; see *Record* 4, no. 11 (February 15, 1900): 5. The second quote is from *Record* 5, no. 7 (October 15, 1900): 5–6.

115. *Record* 4, no. 7 (October 16, 1899): 4.

116. Ibid.

117. *Record* 4, no. 8 (November 15, 1899): 7.

118. Ibid.

119. *Calgary Weekly Herald,* November 16, 1899.

KATHRYN G. LAMONTAGNE

"Lancashire in America"

The Culture of English Textile Mill Operatives in
Fall River, Massachusetts, 1875–1904

On June 24, 1911, at South Park in Fall River, Massachusetts, President William Howard Taft spoke to a crowd of thousands as part of the Cotton Centennial Exposition: "I congratulate you and your city of Fall River and the happiness you enjoy in the hum of your industry. You have men at the head of it, who, when that industry was threatened, gave their brains and energy for its welfare."[1] Horse shows, parades, amusements, a circus, and cultural exhibits filled the week's calendar. The Cotton Centennial joyously commemorated one hundred years of manufacturing might and dominance for Fall River in the global textile industry. However, by 1911 the city's fortunes were on the wane, and the Cotton Centennial may be remembered as a kind of Irish wake for both the textile industry in Fall River and the fortunes of the city. Drawing attention to this downturn, Taft stated that this "industry was threatened."[2] The president was not referring to the rising fortunes of King Cotton in the American South but rather to the "menace" of labor unions for instigating the economic decline and the slackening of the New England textile mill economy. This downturn was not unique; it was representative of dissonance in New and "old" England resulting from the demands of the mechanized workplace over the past century of urbanization and industrialization.

There were many strikes in Fall River throughout the nineteenth century as it became the greatest textile manufacturing location in the world, with over 100 mills and 3.3 million spindles.[3] Fall River, the "Spindle City," was the most ethnically diverse city in the United States at the turn of the century, but unionized textile workers from England played the most prominent role in the laboring community as it turned into a city that, according to some, was in "constant turmoil."[4]

Many scholars have studied the Fall River strikes of the nineteenth and early twentieth centuries. Among them, most notably, Mary Blewett, Charlotte Erickson, Rowland Berthoff, and Philip Silvia have provided a great breadth of research on the various roles of mass immigration, politics, and labor unionism in Fall River.[5] This essay focuses specifically on the social implications of Lancashire mill operatives and their leadership—the English Mule Spinners—on the culture of Fall River. Consequently examining perspectives of this often hidden diaspora, the working-class English, further suggests that the cultural baggage English immigrants brought with them to America had a major influence on the development of Fall River. Historians have largely overlooked ethnic markers of "Englishness," particularly in the case of working-class English immigrants in the United States.[6] However, the cultural capital of the English working classes in Fall River illustrates that at the time of the strikes, English culture and "Englishness" were understood as being particularly distinctive and furthermore that they remained a touchstone for the descendants of these immigrants in Fall River.

LABOR TRADITIONS—NEW ENGLAND AND "OLD" ENGLAND

Immigration to Fall River after the Civil War was quickly dominated by those from Lancashire and Ireland—those born in England and Irish people who had immigrated to Lancashire. Lancashire families who immigrated brought with them a long history of strike culture from Lancashire. As wages dropped and conditions became more difficult, these native women left the mills. Immigrants brought their skills as mule spinners, carders, and weavers from across the Atlantic to fill the gap. Lancastrian textile mill workers brought a tradition of reform, and they knew the effectiveness of mass demonstrations.

Emigrants from the north of England were not strangers to labor unionism in industry, nor were they strangers to the suffering that accompanied strikes. The famous Peterloo Massacre in Manchester in 1819 involved weavers and spinners who had gathered to campaign for universal suffrage. The Plug Plot of 1842 in Blackburn brought about riots in response to wage cuts.[7] Bread riots rocked Liverpool in 1855.[8] The men who immigrated to Fall River had been influenced by the Chartists and supporters of the Reform Acts and hoped to gain the same rights in their adopted nation. Chartists demanded rights such as universal manhood suffrage and secret ballots, which garnered vast support from the working classes. However, it was the Reform Acts of 1832, 1867, and 1884 that further extended suffrage in England to working-class men in agriculture and manufacturing. The working classes in England, unlike in America, had been successful in winning a ten-hour day, which Parliament adopted in 1847. The campaign for a ten-hour day was replicated in Fall River during the strike of 1873–74.

Despite small labor victories and the success of the Reform Acts, Chartism failed in the mid-1850s. For many, life was unbearable. From 1853 to 1854 a major strike in the cotton industry raged in Preston; Charles Dickens subsequently portrayed that strike in *Hard Times* (1854). The Preston strike was predicated on the reduction of mill operatives' pay by 10 percent in 1847, and it was never raised back to its preexisting levels. In *"Ten Percent and No Surrender": The Preston*

Strike, 1853–1854, the authors H. I. Dutton and J. E. King argued that this strike was integral in forming the basis of collective bargaining in the English psyche after the failure of Chartism.[9] Wage reductions of 10 percent became common grounds for strikes in Fall River over the nineteenth century as well. Mill operatives in Lancashire had long been involved with negotiating their wages and work hours, and they brought this propensity for collective bargaining with them to Fall River.

The next great difficulty for Lancashire textile workers was something completely out of their control, the Cotton Famine of the 1860s, when American cotton was not farmed due to the American Civil War. Edwin Waugh, a journalist from the *Manchester Examiner,* wrote an exposé of the effects of the Cotton Famine in Lancashire.[10] For his book *Home Life of the Lancashire Factory Folk during the Cotton Famine* (1867), Waugh stepped into the homes of those affected by the Cotton Famine. Waugh detailed how "the mill-yard . . . and the factory [were] still and silent" due to the Cotton Famine and wrote that "destitution may be found anywhere there just now, cowering in squalid corners."[11] The Cotton Famine taught Lancastrians to survive under extreme duress; they brought this knowledge with them to Fall River, which helped families survive during the Fall River strikes.[12] In England an escape from destitution was possible by mending roads, peat farming on the moors, or immigration to America.[13]

Fall River became the premier place of immigration for Lancashire workers during this time; called "Lancashire in America," it was synonymous with America. Benjamin Brierly related an experience of his voyage from Liverpool to Fall River in the 1880s:

"Wheere dun yo' come fro'?" I axt 'em
"Owdham an'Mossley," they said.
"Wheere yo' goin' to?" . . .
"To Fall River . . . we'n friends theere."[14]

Fall River proved an attractive destination because of the breadth of mill work and predominance of Lancastrians.[15] In fact, while in Fall River for Decoration Day celebrations, Brierly wrote that he "soon forget [sic] where I wur, an' fancied I're I'England."[16]

In the early days of the Fall River mills, factory owners recruited Lancashire men to bring their knowledge and skills to the city so that Fall River could compete with the English textile industry.[17] At the same time that Fall River's reputation grew, strikes became more frequent in Lancashire. Lancashire was expanding its role in working-class organizing, unknowingly nurturing the labor leaders who would immigrate to Fall River. As strikes grew more prevalent, blacklists were created in Lancashire to exclude union organizers from mill positions.

Those on the blacklists were unemployable but were still union members; thus they were a drain on union coffers. Unions and friendly societies offered to pay for packet transport to Fall River so that the blacklisted men could find permanent work. By supporting foreign immigration, unions reduced the number of laborers and preserved their own jobs.[18] This may have stemmed more from a self-protectionist mentality than any notions of creating transnational textile mill solidarity.[19]

Protectionist friendly societies, lodges, and unions functioned in England to support the working classes during times of financial need and as sources of leisure, benevolence, and conviviality. According to John T. Cumbler, "during the lean years, the operatives fell back upon the old clubs and societies which kept the union spirit alive."[20] Underpinning these clubs was a dedication to politics and more specifically organizing. Robert Howard, one of the most important labor leaders of the day, felt that these clubs were integral in forming protections for operatives during strikes. Upon their arrival in America, these men were "ready to convert the tranquil posture of a work force which had been composed largely of native Americans into an active, well-organized defensive stance on behalf of what they considered were right and just [labor] demands."[21]

LANCASHIRE LABOR LEADERS IN FALL RIVER

John Norris was one of the first notable labor leaders to emigrate from England to Fall River, and he led the strike of 1848 in Fall River as workers had done "in the old country."[22] Native workers were at first reticent to strike, but his moving speeches urging the power of group bargaining won them over, although many felt "no connection with striking immigrants."[23] The next strike, which lasted from 1850 to 1851, was led by the mule spinners, the laboring elite of the textile mills. A majority of the mule spinners were from the northwest part of England and were highly unionized. These men formed the backbone of worker-led agitation and subsequently worker-manufacturer animosity for the next sixty years.

Other important labor leaders continued to migrate from England in the late 1850s. Robert Howard was born in Cheshire, near Lancashire, and immigrated to Fall River in 1860. Howard first led the Spinners Association in 1880 and would hold that position until 1897.[24] In Stockport he had served as president of the local Stockport Mule Spinners' Union. Howard would go on to be elected to the Massachusetts House of Representatives as an Independent Labor Democrat for the Second Bristol District in 1881. As chair of the Labor Committee, he petitioned for and won the sixty-hour work week.[25] In *A Souvenir of Massachusetts Legislators from 1893*, put together by the *Boston Journal*, he stated that he "received his education, 'between the cotton-spinning mules.'"[26] His accomplishments were even more amazing when one considers that he, a manual laborer, served in the state senate alongside Henry Cabot Lodge. By 1893 Howard was considered the "senior member of that body [the Massachusetts State Senate] in point of service.'"[27] From 1881 to 1885 he was treasurer of the Federation of Trades and Labor Unions in North America.[28] From 1883 to 1893 he was twice secretary of the National Cotton Mule Spinners Association of America, which was more or less a Fall River/New England guild rather than "nationwide."[29] In 1887 he was district master workman of the Knights of Labor of Massachusetts.[30] While serving in the legislature he continued as secretary of the Fall River Spinners' Union.[31]

Howard felt that the basis of a strong union was money. With funding and organization, a union could gain clout on par with the mill owners, which under his leadership the mule spinners garnered.[32] Howard also believed that unions should act in accordance with market forces.[33] This meant that unions should act peacefully and demand higher wages only when the market was strong, leaving employers little choice but to capitulate to demands. His opposite in ideas of managing labor rights was George Gunton. Gunton, a weaver, moved to Rochdale in the 1860s for mill work.[34] He played an especially important role in the "Great Vacation of 1875," speaking at mass meetings, despite initial misgivings about the timing of the strike. He was editor of the Labor Standard and ran against Robert Howard for a legislative seat in 1880 but lost owing to his militancy. [35]

There were other important leaders with English connections. Patrick Delaney, born in Ashton-under-Lyme, immigrated to Fall River as a child in 1863 and worked in the mills. A Democrat, he served alongside Howard in the legislature as a state representative.[36] James Tansey, secretary of the carder's union in Fall River, carried on union involvement he had begun in Rochdale, Lancashire, in the 1904 strike.[37] John Golden, also a native of Lancashire, had been blacklisted there after campaigning for a nine-hour day before immigrating to Fall River and was vice-president of the United Textile Workers of America (UTWA) during the strike of 1904. James Langford, born in Heywood, Lancashire, entered the cotton mill industry in England and learned to spin. He worked at the Mechanics Mill in Fall River—the locus of some of the most contentious strikes—after he migrated; "he believed in unionism and served three years as president of the union of his craft and two years as its treasurer."[38] He was elected in 1880 to the Massachusetts state legislature. A true Englishman, he was also a member of the Fall River cricket club and the friendly societies of both the Unity Lodge of Odd Fellows and the U.S. Grant Lodge of the Sons of St. George. Thomas O'Donnell, who like Robert Howard served as secretary of the Spinners' Union, left Lancashire for Fall River in 1873. He was blacklisted after the strike of 1879 but eventually returned to Fall River.[39] Other Lancashire leaders from the 1904 strike included James Whitehead of the Fall River Weavers Progressive Association and Thomas Taylor of the Loom Fixers Union.

These men from Lancashire were well known, outspoken, and able to rouse thousands to strike. They formed the nucleus of the "agitating" community in Fall River, and without their presence non-English mill operatives may never have been compelled to strike. The influence of these labor leaders went beyond Fall River to the Massachusetts State House, where some served, and even back to England. Significantly, these labor leaders came predominantly from one profession: mule spinning.

LABOR'S ARISTOCRACY

Mule spinners were regarded in Fall River as the "labor aristocracy." The most skilled workers in England and America, they determined a crucial role in "the co-operative temper of labour relations in the mill."[40] This was because their job, to watch and fix breakages that occurred on the "mule" during yarn or thread spinning, necessitated physical strength, intelligence, and skill.[41] The elite of the mill crafts, the position of mule spinner was limited to those of English, Irish, and Scotch origins, as were the independent craft unions.[42] In England, "the unions of loomfixers, weavers, mule spinners, etc. . . . lay in protecting their own skilled group rather than in organizing the unskilled and semi-skilled throughout the industry."[43] The union of mule spinners was the most protectionist of all the unions and the most powerful by far, even to the extent of importing their own labor leaders. Lancashire unions operated the Fall River locals directly from Manchester.[44] This meant that it was in the best interest of other immigrant groups to follow the mule spinners' lead, as they did during the strikes of 1875 and 1904. This is an important point because it shows that despite the segregation of immigrants in Fall River in their neighborhoods and churches, they were able to strike together as a united front. The mule spinners were in charge of uniting this diverse group and did so during strikes from 1875 to 1904.

Mule spinners were the strongest agitators for working-class rights in New England during the Gilded Age, and they were the bane of the mill owners and the local government: "The mule spinners of Fall River are more numerous than the mule spinners of any other city in the country, because the warp and filling, both, in the mills, is spun on mules. That enables them to get together and form this strong organization. Then, besides, the rapid growth of Fall River called in a large foreign element. These people [the English] come in there with their strikes and strike notions, and incorporate them there . . . we are remedying them . . . labor agitators regard Fall River as the head centre from which they will start any movement of course."[45] Mule spinners combined elements of English labor militancy and craft unionism to achieve the rights of mill operatives. William Hartford has argued that these men successfully employed "conciliatory gestures, market-based economic demands, and [acted as] shop-floor militants" to achieve their objectives in Fall River.[46] One Blackburn newspaper wrote upon the formation of the Fall River Spinner's Union that "there would seem to be no reason why the Fall River Association should not be equally prosperous as its sister association of weavers in Blackburn," which they were.[47]

TRANSMISSION OF CULTURAL CAPITAL

The union work of the mule spinners in Fall River was underpinned by a shared working-class sentiment and ethnicity across the English-born population in the city. The cultural capital of the English immigrants was visible throughout Fall River and nearby New Bedford, Massachusetts, in both the landscape and leisure activities of the operatives. Besides unionism, other aspects of English daily life that migrated to Fall River were the friendly societies and lodges such as the Odd Fellows (Manchester Unity), which importantly answered directly to Manchester and not to the United States–based Odd Fellows; the Catholic Order of Foresters; and the Order of St. George, with no fewer than five lodges in 1905. New Bedford featured a stunning Odd Fellows Hall built in the Beaux-Arts style.[48] There were also groups and beneficial societies such as the British Club, the British Veteran Naval and Military Association, a Caledonian Ladies Society, the Daughters of St. George (two lodges), and the Royal Arcanum (which was linked to the Odd Fellows).[49] Many of these societies were located in downtown Fall River around South Main Street and close to City Hall and flats kept by single men workers in various purpose-built blocks. Leisure activities, which had newfound import in the industrialized world during the late Victorian era, traveled to America. Fall River had an active cricket league, horse racing, and a soccer league. One team, which won the American Football Association Cup in the later 1880s and early 1890s, was called the Rovers, after the Blackburn (Lancashire) Rovers.[50] From reports in government documents of a drinking culture, it seems that the local public house also became a center of leisure, conversation, and meeting in Fall River as in England. The transfer of these leisure activities and societies strengthened the bond of English mill employees and reinforced the hierarchical mill structure outside work hours.

Working-class immigrants of all levels were careful to hold on to the lexicon of the north and the English working classes and to re-create the cityscape of their homeland in many ways. Streets in Fall River were given names such as Albion, Weaver, and Manchester. In one neighborhood, "the Flint," the English were still an important part of the community in the 1950s, as "into the area came many from Great Britain, who established homes in the Flint and today are an integral part of the community."[51] Common names in Lancashire remained prominent in Fall River for much of the twentieth century, for example, Ratcliffe (rather than the more common Radcliffe), Jackson, Holt, and Sharples.

Generationally, use of the words "supper" and "parlour" were retained. Further dialectical comparisons would be helpful to explore when thinking of the cultural capital imparted from Lancashire to Fall River.

Foodways proved to be another way for immigrants to re-create Lancashire.[52] Beginning in 1902 Hartley's pork pies were made in the city following the English tradition. This is notable because these small, hand-held pastries were not customary and were made despite the prevalence of the Québécois traditional and readily available pork and pastry pie, the tourtière. A variation on the English sausage, which was closer in shape and size to the Irish banger, found its way into the Yankee clambake, demonstrating later levels of assimilation of foodways into regional culture. Likewise the widespread use of vinegar as a condiment on fried food, particularly "chips," became an ongoing part of the foodways of southeastern New England. A meal similar to Lancashire hot pot is still cooked by some families, with pork now substituted for lamb or beef.[53]

In addition to the lexicon, leisure, and foodways of northern England, families brought tangible memories of their lives there. One Preston man, a cotton grinder, left to his family in the United States a sampler created in 1854 in the north with a factory pictured at its center.[54] Samuel Watson, a Fall River spinner, returned to England at least three times from his home in the Flint, sometimes for as long as four years.[55] George Graham (b. Preston, 1857–1920), an electrician in the mills, would visit his family in the Plungington neighborhood often, bringing back to Fall River various members of his English family.[56] Reflecting religious pushes in the working-class communities of Fall River and England, one daughter, Elizabeth Graham, became a Hallelujah Lass in the northern United States; a son, George (b. Preston, 1885–1944), converted to Catholicism; and the family left behind in "Plungy" held closely to their Protestant faith.[57] As a single man George Graham, and later his sons, lived in purpose-built blocks of flats in the city center, within easy walking distance of his workplace. He did not reside in the more popular tenement or "triple-decker" apartments that are synonymous with New England mill housing. Unusually for this part of the country, Fall River did have some examples of row houses or terraced houses. However, these too were much larger than the Graham family homesteads in Preston that were "two-up and two-downs."[58] However, as they were in Preston, neighborhoods were populated by families, and George and his sons never lived far apart while in Fall River. In comparison, his daughter Elizabeth traveled widely through America as part of her mission with the Salvation Army.[59]

After World War I the elder George Graham left America for Preston in 1919 and then went to Glasgow.[60] Lacking further data, it is difficult to say how many other Lancastrians repatriated to Britain at the conclusion of their working careers and what their economic circumstances may have been at that time. What is especially compelling is that George Graham was married in Fall River in 1896 to Betsey Duncan, an English woman employed as a domestic, without divorcing his wife in Preston, Sarah Howard.[61] Upon his 1902 visit to Preston, Duncan traveled with him as they collected his sons William and George and his daughter Elizabeth from his mother's home, where the children had been residing, to take them to Fall River.[62] It could be inferred that his first wife was cognizant of his changed or dual marital position but did not seek immigration herself. Moreover, these kinds of kinship relationships pointed to overarching transnational links that were consistently reinforced across the Atlantic. Indeed it is not difficult to see why English operatives during the strike in the early months of 1875 that preceded the so-called "Great Vacation" strike remembered their connections with family in Fall River, despite their own hardships, and made "common cause with those striking here [in Fall River], and are sending them moneyed assistance to enable them to prosecute their cause."[63]

"THE GREAT VACATION OF 1875"

By the 1870s the similarities between work culture and leisure culture in both Fall River and Lancashire were profound. An economic depression haunted Fall River, as was the case in Lancashire. The Fall River Board of Trade, a coalition of Yankee textile mill owners, unilaterally made manufacturing decisions for all the mills.[64] The Fall River Board of Trade continuously reduced wages, as had happened in Lancashire, creating depressions and demands in the cheap print cloth market (calicos) and in turn an environment ripe for working-class anger due to the devaluation of skills.[65] This led to textile mill strikes annually throughout the 1870s but most notably in 1870, 1873, 1875, and 1879.

Late in 1874 three mills, Granite, Crescent, and Merchant's Mill, supported by the Fall River Board of Trade, reduced wages by 10 percent and reduced production by one-third to create a demand for calicos.[66] At this time union leaders—more specifically, the mule spinners—decided not to react to these reductions because the unions lacked funds to support the workers.[67] None of the operatives wanted to repeat the destitution of the eleven-month-long 1853–54 Preston strike, which had been undertaken without sufficient precautions for a lengthy term of unemployment.

Surprisingly it was the female operatives who demanded an immediate strike early in 1875 for fear that in delaying they would unwittingly give the Fall River Board of Trade "time to prepare counter-tactics."[68] With this declaration the other English-dominated textile unions—those for mule spinners, weavers, carding-room hands, slashers, and spoolers—quickly reversed their opposition to strike and took over the entire movement. However, the great majority of operatives were not organized at all.[69] The Englishmen George Gunton, Simon

Morgan, William Bence, William Sutcliffe, and Thomas Stevenson were the leaders of this strike, the first of 1875.[70]

The Fall River Board of Trade's other mills soon followed suit in shutting down when operatives struck to protest the proposed 10 percent wage reduction. Within days violence broke out when "knobsticks" were called in to replace the operatives.[71] Survival became increasingly difficult for the striking operatives during the cold days of winter without heat or food. Due to this, emigration began in earnest by some English. On February 2, 1875, the decision was made "to send 1,000 weavers back to England, managers of the strike thinking that it will be cheaper to send them to the old country than to maintain them here in idleness" during the strike.[72] In early March the Board of Trade offered a 3 percent wage reduction instead of 10 percent; this was grudgingly accepted by the various unions, and the operatives returned to work.[73]

During July the board reverted back to the 10 percent pay cut of January, negating the agreements of March to increase the profit margins for the mills while selling calico under market value.[74] Simultaneously the English unions in the city were participating in a summer organizing drive, which did not attract much funding but did attract an increase in worker solidarity before the declaration of another formal strike in July 1875. Robert Howard used this strike to reassert the moral power of the laborer over the owners and the desire for spinners to earn a living wage for their families.[75] However, because of the contracts signed to conclude the first strike of the year, future strikes were disallowed; therefore this strike was to be called a "stoppage" or "a vacation." The "vacation" would continue until there was assurance that the operatives' wages would not be reduced again.

As expected, the Board of Trade held firm and refused any pay increase, insisting that "the wages paid operatives in Fall River were considerably in excess of other manufacturing centers."[76] By August 3 the "strike" had spread to nearly all the mills, with fifteen thousand operatives off work.[77] The time that passed during the "strike" or "stoppage" or "lockout," as it was alternately called, was not spent just organizing. On August 16 roughly a thousand operatives gathered at Rocky Point, a seaside attraction in Rhode Island, to enjoy the day on rides, eat the famous clam chowder, and listen to speeches by labor leaders, such as George Gunton, advocating a ten-hour work day.[78] Despite the diversion of this summer day, not all striking operatives were enjoying their "vacation."

For some operatives this period was not a vacation at all, and "there was considerable suffering."[79] In September the twelve thousand to fifteen thousand who had struck sought a return to work.[80] The *New York Times* claimed that "the mass of the operatives are evidently anxious to return to work at the reduced rates, but are controlled by union men."[81] However, the Fall River Board of Trade promised to lock out their employees for another month in retaliation, which brought about rioting. The city was put under military control.[82] On September 28 a mob of five thousand marched through the city and joined ten thousand already gathered at a park to hear the Englishman Henry Sevey, the weekly *Labor Journal* editor, speak and hold a mass meeting.[83] The "mob" of workers then marched on the mayor's office, yelling "Bread! Bread!," waving sticks, throwing bricks at policemen, and demanding mayoral intervention to feed the starving and urge the Board of Trade to pay a living wage.[84] Bread revolts were a traditional form of English organized, ritualized protest used throughout the eighteenth and nineteenth centuries.[85] The governor of the labor reform council, E. M. Chamberlain, called a meeting in Boston to express his support of Fall River labor and regretted that police had been sent to Fall River to keep the peace.

While the populace supported the operatives, newspaper accounts of the strike said little about the presence of the English. However, the newspapers continuously reported that it was the "agitators" who had put these notions in the minds of the operatives, who would not have felt this way otherwise.[86] It would have been implicit that to be an "agitator" was to be English. For example, the *New York Times* on October 1, 1875 reported, "Much of the misery and mischief that have been wrought by the strikes is due to the insidious influence of the few adventurers, who, under the plea of befriending the working man, are really striving only to use him for their own advantage . . . this is the true state of affairs. The men are not masters of themselves. They allow themselves to be duped by designing agitators. . . . If they and their families suffer through their own misguided conduct, they should blame first the leaders who brought it upon them, and then themselves for their folly in listening to them."[87] Indirectly this passage referred to the mule spinners as the "designing agitators." The term "adventurers" could have referred to their foreign birthplace, but it also supported the argument that the other ethnicities were pushed into and/or intimidated into action by the mule spinners. Among the "leaders" may have been Henry Sevey, Simon Morgan, or Jonathan Biltcliffe, the men who orated at mass meetings.

By the beginning of October all the mills were working, staffed by a number of "knobsticks." In late October the labor leaders accepted the 10 percent wage reductions reluctantly. The Fall River Board of Trade created a blacklist to exclude men who were prone to strike: "The blacklist is directed mostly toward the members of the Mule Spinner's union, for they cause us the most trouble . . . it gave us the names and occupations of the most prominent in agitating strikes."[88] Yet a relentless cycle of wage cuts, strikes, reinstatements, and further cuts continued for the next twenty years.[89] One "Spinner" wrote to the *Fall River Herald* that the board during the aftermath of the Great Vacation of 1875 should remember that "they are dealing with men, who may not possess as much of the world's wealth as themselves, but who, nevertheless are men of thought and feeling, men who have their rights to defend, not 'dumb, driven cattle.'"[90]

CARROLL DAVIDSON WRIGHT AND THE FALL RIVER BOARD OF TRADE

In April 1881 a letter was sent to the Massachusetts Bureau of Statistics and Labor (MBSL) in Boston from a member of the Massachusetts House of Representatives asking, "Why is it that the working people of Fall River are in constant turmoil, when at Lowell and Lawrence they are quiet?"[91] In their annual report, the MBSL's chief, Carroll Davidson Wright, dedicated the entire 1882 volume to understanding just this question.[92] The most apparent reason for this "constant turmoil" was the presence of 20 percent more English in Fall River than in Lowell and Lawrence combined. Moreover these "agitating English" were all involved in Fall River's one industry, cotton textile manufacturing.

From June to November 1881 agents from the MBSL were sent to Fall River, Lowell, and Lawrence to investigate the source of such "constant turmoil" via a rather modern method of investigation that was similar in practice to a method popularized by reformers in Victorian England. Used by journalists and reformers, this process originated in the East End of London. In London investigators would enter the homes of the poor, interview them conversationally, and inspect their standards of living. Mirroring this, the MBSL's investigators scrutinized mill operatives in their homes and "asked [them] in general terms to give their reasons for being discontented."[93] Clearly the greater number of mill workers from Lancashire fostered the more radical environment in Fall River, which did not develop in Lowell or Lawrence; or, as one Lowell operative stated, "here we have but few English, while Fall River can be called a second England."[94] When a Fall River Englishman, "an agitator," traveled to these cities, he (whoever "he" was) was unfailingly credited with creating disorder, as one Lowell manufacturer stated to the MBSL investigator.

An examination of the table of respondents prompts further questioning of whether the source of the "constant turmoil" could ever have been uncovered in this study. From 1840 to 1870 Lowell's population grew much faster than did that of Fall River. Seemingly, Lowell should have been prone to more labor disputes.[95] But Lowell's industries were more diversified than Fall River's, with only twenty-four textile-mill-related industries in 1875 versus thirty-nine in Fall River.[96] In addition, with the English came strike culture, so consequently Fall River became synonymous with strikes.[97]

In reality, though, despite all this English activism, those employed in Fall River had a lower standard of living than those in Lowell did because Fall River was a cotton textile city producing just one cheap good, calico, throughout the entire city. The other cities had been able to diversify their economies and had operatives with a higher standard of living. Unfortunately the Lancastrians in Fall River knew only one business, the business of making fabric, and thus to Fall River they migrated. Mr. Baker, the treasurer of the Chace Mill in Fall River, in 1882 stated, "You compare the operatives of a strictly cotton manufacturing city with the operatives of a place like Lawrence [which produces a variety of work] . . . and they have a different class of operatives . . . because they require a higher grade of labor and they pay them more. And why? Because designers, engravers and machine printers receive much larger pay than spinners and carders and weavers."[98]

In its annual report the MBSL described the personalities and opinions of the Fall River operatives, stating that "the operatives [in Fall River] visited were all above the average intelligence of factory employés" and that they spoke "with discretion" but were "inclined to be radical . . . from early training and experience."[99] In addition in Fall River the workers seemed more tired than elsewhere. The "rowdy" habits of the English, such as heavy drinking, were blamed for exacerbating the tense labor atmosphere in Fall River.[100] An unnamed Fall River manufacturer articulated his exasperation with the Lancastrians: "We built many mills in 1871–72, and imported operatives rapidly. The whole trouble consists in the fact that they brought their habits with them. The men got drunk, the women were improvident, the children wretched and uneducated. The women don't know how to keep house, for they are always in the mill. The spinners are the best paid, but are the most poverty-stricken. They spend a great deal of their money for liquor. Fall River is the 'Manchester of America,' and the great depot for emigrant operatives. It is with this unassimilated material that all the trouble originates."[101]

The English in Fall River were also identified by their debt; many owed money to shop owners for daily goods and alcohol. With the switch to weekly rather than monthly wage payments, this situation did lessen to some degree, but many were often just subsisting and tending to "spend as they go."[102] Few owned their own homes.[103] According to the mill owners interviewed for the report, alcohol abuse was the cause of English problems rather than that they were underpaid, and that if the English saved rather than spending the money on drink, they would have no need to strike.

In contrast, one Fall River operative contended that "an Englishman tries to adopt the manners and customs of the country he lives in and is desirous of living in harmony with all."[104] Yet another stated, "The one great trouble with Fall River as compared with Lowell and Lawrence is the existence of so much English help. Fall River is the receiving depot to which they all come when they first land in this country and they come here with all of their old English ideas, which they had best leave behind them, for the American and English ideas clash. . . . The ideas that prevail here are English among the operatives, and American among the manufacturers. The people come to this country with no other idea than to improve their condition, and they are intelligent—that is, intelligent in all that pertains to millwork."[105]

Was it the Lancashire English who caused the "constant turmoil," as the manufacturers believed, or was it the Fall River Board of Trade's business choices that precipitated the "constant turmoil"? Carroll Wright's MBSL took a generally unfavorable view of the Fall River Board of Trade as the creator of class antagonisms and blamed it for developing ethnic rivalries and fostering a difficult work environment. The MBSL report sought to expose preconceived ideas about the English laborers, chastise the mill owners for their inequitable policies, and create a dialogue to improve the position of the working classes in Fall River. The MBSL concluded that the "constant turmoil" stemmed from the unjust actions of the Board of Trade.[106]

The Fall River Board of Trade published an anonymous, angry reply to the accusations of the MBSL in pamphlet form in 1882.[107] The author argued that the MBSL, and more specifically Carroll Wright, the compiler and author of the document and chief of the MBSL, was wrong in making assumptions about Fall River on "baseless gossip . . . [that was] filled with personal opinions and hearsay" rather than empirical information.[108] The author contended that the "valuable information" that the MBSL reported was actually the "noisy talk of professional agitators and labor reformers in and out of the city" and that the MBSL "has allowed every statement prejudicial to the interests of Fall River."[109] Furthermore he accused Wright of lending "his official position to give renewed publicity to the utterances of the worst class of labor agitators and demagogues in Massachusetts."[110]

WRIGHT'S RESPONSE

Remarkably the copy of the Fall River Board of Trade pamphlet at the Massachusetts State House Special Collections library was annotated in pencil on May 6, 1882 by, it is surmised, Carroll Wright.[111] Wright was clearly infuriated by the Board of Trade's pamphlet and dismissal of the poverty of mill operatives. In his annotations he wrote, "The spectacle of the Board of Trade of Fall River defending their operatives and applauding their thrifty lives and peaceful independent ways after one of its chief men had called them the scum of the English and Irish is certainly ample compensation for the [illegible] of the Bureau. If the B. has brought the F.R. Mfrs. to this happy position the public has reason to applaud—May 6, 1882."[112] Wright was angered at the audacity of the Board of Trade in daring to publish a document that denied its culpability in encouraging a strike culture. He felt that this was especially audacious given the poverty of the operatives in Fall River. On April 8, 1882, Wright met with a delegation from Fall River—Mayor Davenport and Treasurer Baker of the Chace Mill—at his office in Boston to dismiss their claim that he had misrepresented Fall River in the annual report. It seems as though Wright may have had a closer linkage with labor and the rights of labor than he admitted to the Fall River Board of Trade. He had, in fact, traveled throughout England and "defended Fall River all through Yorkshire in England, and through Lancashire . . . [and said that] it [Fall River] is remedying the troubles of its past, inherent troubles."[113] Soon thereafter Wright became the U.S. commissioner of labor, serving from 1885 to 1905.

Wright also responded to the accusations from the Board of Trade in an open letter to the people of Fall River, which is undated but presumably from 1882. He defended the MBSL's report and the commonwealth's "duty to hear the complaints of working men."[114] He stated, "The fact that England, for one hundred years, has had men in its government who would listen to the complaints and investigate the grievances of the humblest, has undoubtedly saved her from many social disturbances such as have troubled other European governments [and American government]."[115] Therefore, Wright felt that it was his duty, and the commonwealth's, to hear labor concerns and complaints. He emphatically concluded that the English "were steady-going, intelligent men and workers."[116]

THE STRIKE OF 1904

Most scholars have agreed that the primacy of the English in the city had been mitigated by 1904. However, it was not until the large-scale introduction of the automated Northrup loom to Fall River after 1904 that the mule spinners' authority was jeopardized, by making the mule spinners' profession obsolete. However, the Northrup loom was not introduced to "push" the "agitating" mule spinners out of Fall River. If this had been the case, the loom would have been introduced in 1874, when it was first available. This was not the case, and the English influence was still felt throughout Fall River in the early twentieth century.[117]

In 1902 a British author, T. M. Young, traveled to the United States and stated that neighboring New Bedford was "indebted to Lancashire for more than machinery . . . in nearly every mill one finds Englishmen in responsible positions —sometimes in supreme charge," which extended to the singing of "God Save the Queen" at the end of union meetings.[118] In 1903 an Englishman stated, "Fall River in the morning is but a gateway into workaday Lancashire. Fall River is Lancashire in epitome," proving that there was residual English influence if not a fully functioning English society there.[119]

The antecedents of the 1904 strike were, as in 1875, a proposed 10 percent wage reduction and work stoppages.[120] A wage reduction of 12.5 percent was then proposed, effective July 25, 1904, prompting the major craft unions, united under the banner of the United Textile Workers of America (UTWA), to vote 1,510 to 396 to strike on July 25, 1904.[121] John Golden, who had been blacklisted in Lancashire, was president of the UTW during the strike of 1904. A week before the strike was declared he stated, "I think it is nearly time that we pulled the lid off the industrial situation in Fall River. We have kept quiet for years, in order not to strain the relationship between capital and labor, believing that things would rectify themselves in time. Instead of such a thing taking place, it has gone from bad to worse."[122] Roughly 2,000 union men made the decision for the entire city to strike. In a city of 113,000 this was more evidence that the unions still held great sway over the majority of operatives. Unskilled laborers, many of whom were non-Anglophone, were excluded from union membership but were expected to and did act along with the unions. This resulted in the strike of 1904, which was at the time the largest strike in United States history at over 20,000 operatives strong. Fall River was the only city in America whose craft unions banded together to strike as a single, amalgamated group. This system, begun by the mule spinners, was called Fall River Trade Unionism.[123]

An estimated 26,000 workers did not show up for work at the textile mills on July 25, and those who did were beaten and stoned.[124] However, it should be noted that this violence was an exception to the general peacefulness of this strike, a tribute to the English ex-legislator Robert Howard's dedication to peaceful resistance.[125] The strike affected eighty-one mills, and nearly four million spindles were inoperable. The strike was supported by Samuel Gompers's American Federation of Labor (AFL), the Catholic Church, the laboring community in New England, and also throughout the city.[126] One grocer offered "food free to all children under ten years of age," and another "citizen donated 1000 loaves of bread."[127] The strike carried on for months, as neither side would budge from its position. The mule spinners' union was the only union able to pay full benefits to its members throughout the strike.[128] Union funds combined with charity money from the state coffers and the Catholic Church and friendly society stockpiles helped the operatives to survive, regardless if they were actual union members. As the situation worsened, many went without basic supplies; Bishop William Stang, of the newly created Diocese of Fall River, stated in October 1904, "I see every day from my windows men and women searching the woods and the fields for pieces of fuel, and on the streets I see the pinched faces of children who have not enough to eat. The priests tell me that the children and elder people as well, stay away from church and school. And when the reason is sought it is learned that they have no shoes and are ashamed of their ragged clothing."[129]

Governor John L. Bates, a Republican, who supported the wealthy Cotton Manufacturers Association, failed to intervene. Appearing in Fall River on

November 4, 1904, at a Republican rally, he was hissed and booed by operatives in the crowd.[130] Three days later, without a settlement, an announcement was made that the mills would reopen on November 14, 1904, with the 12.5 percent pay cut in force.[131] The mills did reopen but without operatives, proving the staying power of the English union leaders and the unity that went beyond ethnic cleavages in the city.[132] In January, Governor Bates was finally obliged to end the strike due to the extreme suffering in the city, and he upheld the reduction of wages by 12.5 percent.[133] After April 1, 1905, a sliding pay scale was introduced based on profit margins.[134]

There were lasting effects from the strike of 1904. Improved machinery, finally installed over the duration of the strike, meant that mule spinners' and weavers' crafts would be functionally obsolete in a short time.[135] Skilled workers were not needed to operate these improved devices, the automated Northrup looms. Consequently the traditional employment of the English in Fall River was made obsolete, and this stopped any further migrations from across the Atlantic. Their unions and, most notably, the strong leadership of the northern-born union men collapsed, hence leaving a lacuna in the political and economic landscape of Fall River. Since that time Fall River has been unable to regain any of its late nineteenth-century economic dominance.

CONCLUSION

Seven years after the 1904 strike, the Cotton Centennial took place in Fall River. The invitation to the celebration began, "One hundred years ago, to crude machines we owe a tribute grand./ Unfailing progress came, weaving both cloth and fame,/ wafting Fall River's name through every land."[136] Meant to celebrate one hundred years of the textile industry, the centennial instead celebrated the end of an era in Fall River. Technology had changed and consequently, with fewer mules, the mule spinners' union became subsumed under the UTWA until the craft disappeared completely.

The English spinners, however, had left an indelible mark on the city. Despite the textile mills closing in Fall River, the ethnic identity of the English working-class mill operatives continues to resonate through the city in its foodways, streets, and people. Fall Riverites of English extraction remain very much aware of their forbears and place in the history of the city. Many are also cognizant of places in England that their families have not seen for generations, such as Preston, Manchester, and Rochdale. Thus, while the English may be a hidden diaspora in many parts of the world, especially the working classes, their presence has been strongly felt and remains acknowledged in the case of Fall River, Massachusetts.

NOTES

1. Philip T. Silvia, ed., *Victorian Vistas: Fall River 1901–1911* (Fall River, Mass.: R. E. Smith Printing, 1992), 860–64.

2. Ibid.

3. Judith Boss, *Fall River: A Pictorial History* (Norfolk, Va.: Donning, 1982), 115.

4. Compiled from *Census of 1890*, Minor Civil Divisions, table 5, Population of States and Territories by Minor Civil Divisions: 1880 and 1890. Massachusetts and Statistics of Population: Country of Birth. The term "constant turmoil" was first used in a document from the *Massachusetts Bureau of Statistics: The Thirteenth Annual Report of the Massachusetts Bureau of Statistics of Labor, April, 1882* (Fall River, Mass.: Almy, Milne, 1882) to describe the intense labor situation in Fall River that was absent in Lawrence and Lowell. Neither of these cities experienced the yearly strikes that afflicted Fall River from 1870 to 1905. Mary H. Blewett later used the term in her book of the same name, *Constant Turmoil: The Politics of Industrial Life in Nineteenth Century New England* (Amherst: University of Massachusetts Press, 2000), to refer to labor issues throughout New England in the nineteenth and twentieth centuries.

5. Much is owed to the work of Blewett, who explored protest tradition in New England and the Fall River strike. Patterns of immigration by the British have been most notably traced in Rowland Berthoff's seminal work *British Immigrants in Industrial America, 1790–1950*. Berthoff treated the case of Fall River as exceptional from the generally "well-behaved British immigrant" construct. Seminally, Charlotte Erickson wrote in 1949 on the paid immigration of labor unionists to America by their unions in Lancashire throughout the middle of the nineteenth century. The labor historian John T. Cumbler argued in 1979 that Fall River was unique because its mills were located throughout the city (unlike in Lawrence and Lowell), which caused citywide ferment during strikes not due to the presence of the English. In 1990 Cumbler contributed an excellent chapter to *Labor Divided* on the Lancashire English and Irish in Fall River as well as cultural contributions. My essay builds upon and contributes new research and case studies to his arguments in that chapter, but in the context of the English diaspora. In the 1970s both Phillip T. Silvia Jr. and Anthony Coelho wrote their Ph.D. dissertations on the subject of Victorian Fall River. Silvia did not focus expressly on the English but offered a brilliant survey of Fall River at that time. Coelho studied changes in overall immigrant social activity and mobility empirically from 1850 to 1890. Coelho believed that working-class solidarity collapsed in 1884 after having been weakened irrevocably during the "Great Vacation" strike of 1875. See Blewett, *Constant Turmoil*; Rowland Tappan Berthoff, *British Immigrants in Industrial America, 1790–1850* (Cambridge, Mass.: Harvard University Press, 1953); Charlotte Erickson, "The Encouragement of Emigration by British Trade Unions, 1850–1900," *Population Studies* 3, no. 3 (December 1949): 248–73; John T. Cumbler, *Working-Class Communities in Industrial America* (Westport, Conn.: Greenwood Press, 1979), 1–2.; John T. Cumbler, "Immigration, Ethnicity and the American Working-Class Community: Fall River, 1850–1900," in *Labor Divided: Race and Ethnicity in United States*

Labor Struggles, 1835–1960, ed. Robert Asher and Charles Stephenson (Albany: State University of New York Press, 1990), 151–70; Jama Lazerow, "Spokesmen for the Working Class: Protestant Clergy and the Labor Movement in Antebellum New England," *Journal of the Early Republic* 13 (Fall 1993): 323–54.; Philip T. Silvia, "The Spindle City: Labor, Politics, and Religion, 1870–1905" (Ph.D. diss., Fordham University, 1973); Anthony Coelho, "A Row of Nationalities: Life in a Working Class Community: The Irish, English, and French Canadians of Fall River, Massachusetts, 1850–1890" (Ph.D. diss., Brown University, 1980).

6. Tanja Bueltmann, David T. Gleeson, and Donald M. MacRaild, *Locating the English Diaspora, 1500–2010* (Liverpool: Liverpool University Press, 2012).

7. "Alarming Riots in Manchester and the Neighbourhood," *Manchester Courier and Lancashire General Advertiser,* August 20, 1842.

8. "Bread Riots in Liverpool," *Manchester Courier and Lancashire General Advertiser,* February 24, 1855.

9. Duncan Bythell, review of H. I. Dutton and J. E. King, *"Ten Per Cent and No Surrender": The Preston Strike, 1853–1854,* in *English Historical Review* 99 (January 1984): 205–6.

10. This habit of government officials interviewing the poor in their homes was echoed again in 1875 by the Massachusetts Bureau of Statistics and Labor (MBSL). For more information on this practice in England, see Seth Koven, *Slumming: Sexual and Social Politics in Victorian London* (Cambridge: Cambridge University Press, 2004).

11. Edwin Waugh, *Home Life of the Lancashire Factory Folk during the Cotton Famine, 1867* (London: Simpkin, Marshall, 1867), 24–25.

12. Ibid., 42.

13. Ibid., 28, 156.

14. Benjamin Brierly, *AB-O'Th'-Yate in Yankeeland: The Results of Two Trips to America* (Manchester: Abel Heywood & Son, 1885), 19.

15. This a provocative contrast to Erickson's contention that, "in coming to America, they were usually unable to find work in their own trades exactly like that which they had done in the old country"; see Charlotte Erickson, *Invisible Immigrants* (Ithaca, N.Y.: Cornell University Press, 1990), 248.

16. Brierly, *AB-O'Th'-Yate in Yankeeland,* 140. Brierly later wrote that it was ironic as a Lancastrian to be mourning the military deaths of those lost in the American Civil War, as it precipitated "very nee th' ruin o' Lancashire" (ibid., 140).

17. Coelho, "A Row of Nationalities," 17.

18. Erickson, *Invisible Immigrants,* 248–73.

19. Ibid.

20. Cumbler, *Working-Class Communities,* 198.

21. Silvia, "Spindle City," 44.

22. Blewett, *Constant Turmoil,* 84.

23. Ibid., 87.

24. William H. Hartford, *Where Is Our Responsibility? Unions and Economic Change in the New England Textile Industry, 1870–1960* (Amherst: University of Massachusetts Press, 1996), 13.

25. Henry Fenner, *History of Fall River* (New York: F. T. Smiley, 1906), 141.

26. *A Souvenir of Massachusetts Legislators, 1892, Volume I* ([Brockton, Mass.]: A. M. Bridgman, 1892), 16.

27. *A Souvenir of Massachusetts Legislators, 1893, Volume II* (Brockton, Mass.: A. M. Bridgman, 1893), 118.

28. Ibid.

29. Ibid. The mule spinners, the few who were in the South, were not organized. For more information, see Herbert J. Lahne, *The Cotton Mill Worker* (New York: Farrar and Rinehart, 1944).

30. *Souvenir of Massachusetts Legislators, 1892,* 16.

31. Ibid.

32. Hartford, *Where Is Our Responsibility,* 15.

33. Ibid.

34. Blewett, *Constant Turmoil,* 131.

35. Hartford, *Where Is Our Responsibility,* 14.

36. *Souvenir of Massachusetts Legislators, 1892,* 48.

37. Arthur Sherman Phillips, *The Phillips History of Fall River* (Fall River, Mass.: Dover Press, 1944), 145–46. Tansey's work for labor rights earned him the honor of having an elementary school named after him in Fall River. The same honor was afforded to Samuel Watson, born in Newcastle, who was a mule spinner and later mill superintendent.

38. Fenner, *History of Fall River,* 243–44.

39. Cumbler, *Working-Class Communities,* 223.

40. Trevor Griffiths, *The Lancashire Working Classes: c. 1880–1930* (New York: Oxford University Press, 2001), 67.

41. Ibid., 24–25.

42. Lahne, *The Cotton Mill Worker,* 7.

43. Ibid.

44. Ibid., 176; Frank W. Hutt, *A History of Bristol County, Massachusetts* (New York, 1924), 116; Cumbler, *Working-Class Communities,* 200.

45. James P. Bacon, stenographer, Report of an interview between Carroll Wright and a delegation from Fall River (Mayor Davenport and Treasurer Baker of the Chace Mill), Office of the Bureau of Statistics, Boston, April 8, 1882, unpub. doc., Massachusetts State House Library Archives [State House], Special Collections, Ms. Coll., 78.

46. Hartford, *Where Is Our Responsibility,* 5.

47. Cumbler, *Working-Class Communities,* 223.

48. Alan Fowler and Terry Wyke have argued for the import of these buildings in creating an architectural history of labor unionism in Lancashire; see Fowler and Wyke, "Buildings in the Landscape," in *King Cotton,* ed. John F. Wilson (Lancaster: Crucible Books, 2009), 305–24.

49. See various *Fall River City Directories.*

50. Mills also had their own teams, or "sides," for example, the Conanicut Mill. See "Fall River Recognized as Nation's Soccer Center for Extended Period," *Herald News,* September 19, 1953.

51. "Flint Section of Area Almost City in Itself," *Herald News,* September 19, 1953.

52. See also Robert A. Orsi, *The Madonna of 115th Street,* 3rd ed. (New Haven, Conn.: Yale University Press, 2010), 53. Orsi has shown this style method of re-creating the home country via food in the case of Italian immigrants in Harlem.

53. Author's personal knowledge from living in Fall River.

54. Sampler in possession of the author.

55. Fenner, *History of Fall River,* 222–24.

56. Original 1887 arrival on the *Britannic.* For 1900 arrivals on the *Norseman,* see *Crew Lists of Vessels Arriving at Boston, Massachusetts, 1917–1943,* publication T938, roll 41, National Archives and Records Administration, Washington, D.C. For 1902 arrivals on the *Westernland,* Philadelphia, Pennsylvania, see *Passenger Lists of Vessels Arriving at Philadelphia, Pennsylvania, 1883–1945,* micropublication T840, RG085, rolls 1–181, National Archives, Washington, D.C. For 1907 arrivals on the *Ivernia,* see *Crew Lists of Vessels Arriving at Boston, Massachusetts, 1917–1943,* publication T938, roll 114, National Archives and Records Administration, Washington, D.C.

57. Service record of Elizabeth Ann Graham (1886–1930) courtesy of the Salvation Army Records Office, Denmark Hill, London.

58. Information was compiled from various *Fall River City Directories, 1888–1912.* Lancashire information was compiled from 1861, 1871, 1881, and 1891 *Census Returns of England and Wales.* See National Archives of the UK, Public Record Office, 1871–91, Kew, Surrey, England.

59. Service list for Elizabeth Anne Graham (b. 1886, Preston–d. approx. 1926, Chicago), information communicated via personal correspondence between Susan Mitchem, national archivist, Salvation Army National Archives, USA, and the author, June 27, 2011.

60. *The Statutory Registers of Births, Deaths and Marriages, 1930,* record for George Graham (statutory deaths 644/20 0056), National Records of Scotland, Edinburgh.

61. *Massachusetts Vital Records, 1840–1911,* New England Historic Genealogical Society, Boston, Massachusetts; *England and Wales Civil Registration Indexes,* marriage index for Preston, vol. 8e, 735, General Register Office, London, England.

62. *Commercial and Statistical Department and Successors: Outwards Passenger Lists,* BT27, Records of the Commercial, Companies, Labour, Railways and Statistics Departments, Records of the Board of Trade and of Successor and Related Bodies, National Archives of the UK, Public Record Office.

63. "Fall River Industries: Review of Labor Troubles in That City," *New York Times,* March 15, 1875.

64. There were only a few mills that did not join the Board of Trade. These were smaller mills, and work continued in them while strikes raged at other mills.

65. "Reduction of Time in the Mills," *Fall River Evening News,* September 24, 1874; "Fall River Industries: Review of Labor Troubles in That City," *New York Times,* March 15, 1875.

66. "The Cotton Manufacturing Interest," *Fall River Evening News,* September 26, 1874.

67. "The Fall River Mills," *New York Times,* January 13, 1875.

68. "The City Quiet," *New York Times*, September 29, 1875. It is unclear if these women were English, but the article stated that "the conduct of the female operatives since the strike has been disgusting; yesterday they were even more violent than the men, and to-day the language used by them on the streets is coarse and vulgar to indecency." See also Cumbler, *Working-Class Communities*, 226.

69. "The Fall River Mills," *New York Times*, January 10, 1875.

70. [Untitled], *Fall River Daily Evening News*, January 11, 1875.

71. [Various titles], *New York Times*, February 8–14, 1875. A "knobstick" is an English term for a strikebreaker or scab.

72. "Dissensions and Jealousies in the Ranks of the Operatives," *New York Times*, February 2, 1875. This was because funds had not been stockpiled before the strike began. See also "Anticipated Strike in Fall River Cotton Mills," *New York Times*, January 31, 1875.

73. "The Fall River Strike: Work to Be Resumed on Thursday," *New York Times*, March 17, 1875.

74. [Various titles], *New York Times*, July 18–30, 1875.

75. For further reading on the "moral right" argument by the English operatives, see Blewett, "Strikes in the Nineteenth-Century Cotton Textile Industry in the Northeast United States," in Aaron Brenner, Benjamin Day, and Immanuel Ness, *The Encyclopedia of Strikes in American History* (Armonk, N.Y.: M. E. Sharpe, 2009), 321. Blewett cited E. P. Thompson and William Reddy for the "moral economy" argument as underpinning the English operatives.

76. "Fall River Manufacturers," *New York Times*, July 19, 1875.

77. "The Strike at Fall River," *New York Times*, August 3, 1875.

78. "Ten Hours a Day: Meeting of Factory Operatives at Rocky Pt, RI.," *New York Times*, August 17, 1875.

79. "The Fall River Strike: The Operatives Suffering, and a Climax Approaching—What Their Organ Advises," *New York Times*, September 11, 1875.

80. "Fall River Troubles," *New York Times*, September 27, 1875.

81. "The Fall River Strike," *New York Times*, September 11, 1875. On September 25 the mills were reopened, but only for operatives who signed a guarantee that they would neither organize nor associate with strikers.

82. "The Fall River Strike," *New York Times*, September 25–28, 1875.

83. [Untitled], *Fall River Daily Evening News*, January 7, 1874. The weekly *Labor Journal*, whose words have largely been lost to history, was founded in January 1874 and sought to "elevate the working people of our community." There were labor journals in England as well. Nationally available were the *Bee-Hive* (1861–78) and the *Labour Standard* (1881–85). Local papers included the *Tamworth Miners' Examiner and Working Men's Journal* (1873–76), *Bradford's Labour Journal* (1892), and Manchester's *Cotton Factory Times* (1885–1937). According to "The Fall River Strike," *New York Times*, February 6, 1875, Sevey was a popular speaker at mass labor meetings and played a significant role in the Great Vacation of 1875 "strengthening the hearts of the strikers."

84. "The Fall River Strike," *New York Times*, September 28, 1875.

85. John Bohstedt, *The Politics of Provisions* (Burlington, Vt.: Ashgate, 2010), 2.

86. "Activity at Fall River," *New York Times*, November 26, 1875.

87. "The Fall River Rioters," *New York Times*, October 1, 1875.

88. MBSL, *Massachusetts Bureau of Statistics of Labor, Thirteenth Annual Report, Part III: Fall River, Lowell and Lawrence* (Boston: Rand, Avery, 1882), 347.

89. "Activity at Fall River," *New York Times*, November 26, 1875. For example, in November the Board of Trade again decided to reduce pay by 10 percent.

90. Blewett, *Constant Turmoil*, 270.

91. MBSL, *Massachusetts Bureau of Statistics of Labor, Thirteenth Annual Report*, 195.

92. Ibid., 195.

93. Ibid., 196.

94. Ibid., 201.

95. Ibid., 197.

96. Ibid., 200.

97. Ibid., 219.

98. Bacon, Report of an interview between Carroll Wright and a delegation from Fall River, 13–14.

99. MBSL, *Massachusetts Bureau of Statistics of Labor, Thirteenth Annual Report*, 201.

100. Ibid., 209. The Board of Trade criticized the English as alcoholics who fraudulently feigned overwork and exhaustion to conceal their excessive drinking.

101. Ibid., 201–2.

102. Ibid., 215.

103. Ibid.

104. Ibid., 205–6.

105. Ibid., 206.

106. Ibid.

107. [Attributed to Fall River Board of Trade], *Fall River versus the Massachusetts Bureau of Statistics: Reply of the Manufacturers' Board of Trade of Fall River, to Part III of the Thirteenth Annual Report of the Massachusetts Bureau of Statistics of Labor, April, 1882* (Fall River, Mass.: Almy, Milne, 1882).

108. Ibid., 1–6.

109. Ibid., 6.

110. Ibid., 7.

111. On the cover page there is a signature in pencil that appears to read, "Carroll D Wright—May 6, 1882." On the last page of the pamphlet, in the same hand, is this entry. The annotation clearly shows Wright's anger with the Fall River Board of Trade and their accusations against him and his office.

112. Copy annotated by Carroll Wright of *Fall River versus the Massachusetts Bureau of Statistics*, State House, Special Collections, Ms. Coll. 78.

113. Bacon, Report of an interview between Carroll Wright and a delegation from Fall River, 23.

114. Carroll Wright, Handwritten Letter to the People of Fall River, Boston, [1882?], State House, Special Collections, Ms. Coll. 78, 2.

115. Ibid., 3.

116. Ibid., 4.

117. T. W. Uttley, *Cotton Spinning and Manufacturing in the United States of America: A Report to the Electors to the Gartside Scholarships on the Results of a Tour of the American Cotton Manufacturing Centres Made in the Winter of 1903 and Spring of 1904* (Manchester: University Press, 1905), 4.

118. Daniel Georgianna, *The Strike of '28* (New Bedford, Mass.: Spinner Publications, 1993), 33.

119. T. M. Young, *The American Cotton Industry* (New York: Scribner, 1903), 1–2.

120. [Untitled], *New York Times*, June 12, 1904; "Textile Workers to Strike," *New York Times*, July 21, 1904.

121. MBSL, *Massachusetts Labor Bulletin, XXXIV* (December 1904), 322; "Textile Workers to Strike," *New York Times*, July 21, 1904.

122. Silvia, "Spindle City," 624.

123. Hartford, *Where Is Our Responsibility*, intro.

124. "Fall River Strike on in Full Force," *New York Times*, July 26, 1904.

125. Silvia, "Spindle City," 662–64.

126. The major Lancashire labor leaders over this time period, from the 1870s to 1910, were all Catholic: Robert Howard, Thomas O'Donnell, James Tansey, James Whitehead, and John Golden (Silvia, "Spindle City," 666). The preeminence of English Catholics is evident in their national parish, St. Mary's in Fall River, built in the English gothic revival style, which remained the cathedral for the Diocese of Fall River despite being much smaller than St. Anne's, the preeminent Québécois church.

127. "Fall River Strike on in Full Force," *New York Times*, July 26, 1904.

128. Silvia, "Spindle City," 626.

129. Ibid., 632.

130. "Hisses for Gov. Bates," *New York Times*, November 4, 1904.

131. "Textile Strike Continues," *New York Times*, November 8, 1904.

132. "Textile Strike Continues," *New York Times*, November 15, 1904; "Effort to End Strike Fails," *New York Times*, December 18, 1904; "Strikers Vote to Fight On," *New York Times*, December 31, 1904.

133. Silvia, "Spindle City," 643.

134. *Labor Bulletin of the Commonwealth of Massachusetts, 1906: Numbers 39–44* (Boston: Wright & Potter, 1897), 192.

135. "Reject Weaver's Demands," *New York Times*, March 30, 1905. The switch to the Northrup loom was not a deliberate attempt to put the mule spinners out of work but instead an attempt to keep the threat of King Cotton at bay. Northrup looms had actually been widely available for years before they were installed in Fall River.

136. J. Edmund Estes, "Invitation Ode" (1911), in Silvia, *Victorian Vistas*, frontispiece.

The Church of England and English Clergymen in the United States, 1783–1861

A merica's Anglican Church and its population of clergymen were among the major victims of the American Revolution. The church was commonly denounced as an accomplice of British monarchism and imperialism, and across the middle and northern colonies Anglican ministers were tarred, feathered, and beaten up.[1] By the time peace came in 1783 half of America's Anglican clergy had either died or fled. We know a good deal about the Anglican Church's role in the Loyalist cause and the subsequent Loyalist exodus; less well known is that Anglican clergymen would continue to migrate to America once hostilities were over.[2] One of the English-born clerical migrants was the Oxford graduate Thomas Ellison. Ellison was an unlikely candidate for the American ministry—contemporaries described him as "a genuine John Bull" and "of the true English school"—but he went on to enjoy a successful career as a teacher, intellectual, and minister in upstate New York; one of his protégés was the novelist James Fenimore Cooper.[3] How many members of the clergy followed in Ellison's footsteps is hard to judge as we do not have clergy lists for the entire Episcopal Church, but it is instructive that of the 512 clergymen who served in Maryland between 1793 and 1860, 76 had been born in Britain, Ireland, or the wider empire. Fourteen had been ordained in Britain, and 30 were English.[4]

That clerical migration started up quickly after the end of hostilities is not all that surprising: the new republic offered a free market in religion, and many different kinds of cultural and commercial exchange recommended between the former combatants after 1783.[5] It also is not surprising that the American branch of the Anglican Church—it was renamed the Protestant Episcopal Church in 1789 —would remain tied to the British "mother Church": American Anglicans had to get their first bishops consecrated in Britain, and the British Isles remained an important source of funding up to the mid-nineteenth century. Nevertheless historians have largely overlooked the contribution that these migrant clergymen made to the development of North American Anglicanism. This is partly because nineteenth-century American Anglicanism is so rarely studied. Major surveys have left the Episcopal Church out entirely, and when it is considered, the church usually emerges as a conservative and elitist organization that stood apart from the evangelical revivalism that dominated the nineteenth-century American religious scene.[6] The Episcopal Church's isolation was at least in part self-imposed. Memories of the political turmoil of the revolutionary period meant that Episcopalians, particularly High Churchmen who emphasized the church's independence, tried to keep well clear of the great political and social controversies that would tear the United States apart after midcentury.[7]

There are at least two reasons why the Episcopal Church and members of its English clergy warrant closer study. First, the church's English connections can shed new light on Englishness and the English in America. Recent research has challenged the old view that America's English communities had no positive sense of their own ethnicity; in addition scholarship has begun to revise—though not overthrow entirely—the notion that English immigrants slipped into American life more easily than did those from other linguistic and ethnic groups.[8] It is strange that Anglican clergymen have not been included in analyses of English assimilation, as in some senses migrant clergymen were the most English people in the United States. Members of the clergy were celebrated for their English learning, preaching, manners, and gentlemanliness, and both Americans and foreign visitors described their churches and colleges as the most English places in America.[9] The clerical careers sampled below show that for the most part clergymen did not encounter the kind of hostility faced by some of their compatriots; they also show that soon after the American Revolution, English clergymen were integrating themselves into American congregations and communities—indeed American congregations sometimes demanded English ministers. The Episcopal Church's growing Anglophilia therefore provides us with a useful lens through which to reconsider attitudes to the English and English culture in antebellum America.

Second, examining the foreign-born clergymen raises questions about how America's Episcopal Church wished to present and position itself in the new republic. The Episcopal Church spent much of the early nineteenth century wondering who it was and what its role in American society should be. Churchmen had to overcome accusations that their church was disloyal and, as one writer put it in the mid-1840s, antithetical to the American "characteristics of mind."[10] It is true that these accusations prompted some American churchmen to distance themselves from English Anglicanism. Americans adopted their own prayer book in 1789, and the vast majority of Episcopalian bishops were American born. But others wanted to cultivate an English outlook and aesthetic for their church. English clergymen were recruited; English church architecture was re-created;

and although it has not received any attention until now, a broad range of the Episcopalian clergy—and not just the English-born—stepped forward to lead English celebrations and benevolent societies for English immigrants.

The church's relationship with English associational life is particularly important as it raises larger questions about how conservative and elite groups adjusted to political change by acquiring new public roles and new kinds of social authority. Recent work on early nineteenth-century Philadelphia has, for example, shown how conservative Federalists responded to republican-ism's growing political strength by turning away from politics and cultivating a new kind of cultural authority. New forms of association—in early nineteenth-century Philadelphia there was a blossoming of private libraries, men's clubs, and philosophical and historical societies—allowed elite Federalists to present themselves as the leaders of a wider community.[11] Episcopalians were drawn to fraternal and benevolent associations because these gave churchmen the chance to broaden the church's popularity and leadership credentials.[12] The presence of Episcopalian clergymen in America's English benevolent societies—they were usually called St. George's Societies—indicate that some Episcopalians were seek-ing to carve out a public role for their church by presenting it as the spiritual representative of a broad, and vaguely defined, English community.[13] Just as the leaders of America's Catholic Church were trying to lead the Irish American community by attaching their church to an Irish identity, so Episcopalians tried something similar with their church and America's growing population of Eng-lish immigrants.[14]

This essay explores these issues through three sections. The first and second consider how the Episcopal Church meshed its English heritage with a new American identity. Section one shows that despite their adoption of a republican system of church government, Episcopalians continued to align themselves with the forces of privilege, conservatism, and aristocracy. The church's conservatism partly explains the clergy's Anglophile tendencies, but there were other forces that were drawing the branches of the church in America and Britain closer together. Section two focuses on the development of an international clerical profession and uses the careers of English-born migrant clergymen to shed light on the position of the English in America. The final section looks at how clerical migrants spearheaded the Episcopal Church's outreach work among America's English communities and associations. Here we interrogate what contemporaries meant when they used the term "English": the term was so imprecise and broad that when contemporaries spoke of an "English church," they were not talking about a church that served only the English-born. Episcopalian ambitions were instead directed toward serving a mixed ethnic community that was coming to be called "Anglo-Saxon." Surveying these areas shows that the Episcopal Church was always much more than an "English" or Anglophile institution. Evidence is drawn from across the United States, but the focus is on two areas, New York and Maryland, which retained particularly strong links to the "mother church."

THE EPISCOPAL CHURCH AND THE EARLY REPUBLIC

Three broad problems confronted America's Anglican population after 1783. First, churchmen had to prove that they were loyal to the new republic. Second, the church had to prevent its churchgoing community from joining non-Anglican denominations whose governing structures and social messages appeared to be more attuned to the dominant republican political culture.[15] Third, churchmen had to build an independent church that owned its own property and was capable of governing, funding, and staffing itself.[16] It would take Episcopalians most of the 1780s to work through these administrative problems; indeed for much of the decade it looked as though conflicts over church government, the status of bishops, and liturgical forms would drive Episcopalians apart. Nevertheless by 1789 a range of competing visions and parties had been brought together in what was now called the Protestant Episcopal Church. Unlike groups such as the Baptists, whose system of government was well suited to the republican environment, Episcopalians had to adapt, and this meant forming a new constitution that resembled the federal Constitution. Bishops would now be elected, and the government of the church would be vested in an interstate General Convention made up of elected clerical and lay delegates.

Episcopalians, however, were still confronted with the question of what the role of this new church would be in the early republic.[17] Clergymen also wondered how they could communicate their authority in a diverse and religiously pluralistic republic. The historian Robert Mullin has looked at the answers that were given to these questions by a group of High Church Episcopalians led by John Henry Hobart, bishop of New York from 1811 to 1830. For Hobart, the church's future growth was dependent on maintaining a distinctive identity and communicating its claim to be the modern representative of the primitive and universal church. For this to happen, Episcopalians had to separate themselves from politics and from other denominations. Hobartians refused to vote, refused to join with non-Episcopalians in philanthropic ventures, and wherever possible refused to associate with clubs, societies, and institutions that lay outside the church. Mullin maintained that the "Hobartian synthesis" played a critical role in shaping the outlooks of a great number of the clergymen ordained in the 1820s and 1830s.[18] Hobart's significance can, however, be pushed too far. Historians have so far overlooked the extent to which Episcopalian ministers were prominent and vocal players in the associations, festivals, and commemorations that shaped the political landscape and public culture of the early republic.[19] The focus on Hobart also fails to take into account those later Episcopalians who tried to work out a public role for their church by attaching it more closely to an English identity. This project opened up a role for the church in new kinds of associations and new kinds of patriotic displays.

Republicans thought that the Episcopal Church was allied to the conservative Federalist Party. Together the two formed an "Anglo-Federal" faction that, in Republican eyes, was trying to undermine the Constitution.[20] Much of this was fear-mongering, but Federalism and Episcopalianism were linked: the former's attachment to such old-world forms as monarchy, hierarchy, deference, and patronage marked its followers as accomplices of the denomination that seemed the most traditional, elitist, and British. A good proportion of the Episcopalian clergy identified as Federalists, and many were visible participants in the celebrations, festivals, and processions organized by Federalists in the 1790s and 1800s. Federalists used national events such as Washington's Birthday and the Fourth of July to articulate their vision of an aristocratic republic and a strong national government. Federalist observances of the Fourth of July, such as the one in Alexandria, Virginia, in 1798, were characterized by martial displays by voluntary militia, nonpartisan appeals to the American people, and toasts to the president, the Constitution, and the judiciary. Significantly, Alexandria's Federalists celebrated the Fourth in an Episcopal church where a "discourse suited to the occasion"—this was at the height of the so-called "Quasi War" with France—was delivered by the minister and Revolutionary War veteran Thomas Davis.[21] In 1800, the year of a runaway Republican presidential victory, a New Hampshire minister delivered a July Fourth sermon that extolled the virtues of a strong national government and castigated Republicans who wished "to throw their dearest rights on the turbulent ocean of Democracy."[22]

Of course not every Episcopalian was a Federalist. Republican organizations such as the Tammany Society and the Mechanics' Society celebrated the Fourth of July in Episcopal churches in New York and Philadelphia.[23] Yet the Episcopalian involvement in the politicization of the Republican community was dwarfed by the support that Episcopal ministers gave to the redefinition and revival of Federalist conservatism after the election of 1800. Episcopalians in the middle and northern states were prominent in the formation of party organizations—the most notable were the Washington Benevolent Societies—that aimed to revive and modernize the Federalist Party, spread conservative principles, and mobilize a new generation of Federalist voters.[24] The Washington Benevolent Society in Alexandria regularly met in Episcopal churches to celebrate the Fourth of July and commemorate George Washington, while in 1809 in Trenton, New Jersey, Federalists gathered in an Episcopal church to hear orations after attending a dinner where toasts to the "political death" of Jefferson and "French influence" were given.[25] The presence of Episcopalian ministers in these celebrations appears to bear out Simon Newman's assertion that Federalists sought a more

ordered and deferential form of "street politics" than did their Republican opponents.[26] Federalist partisanship continued into the War of 1812. Two hundred
members of Trenton's Washington Benevolent Society marched outside the Episcopal church in July 1812, and Episcopalian ministers, such as the Anglophile
Joseph Bend in Baltimore, became foci for Federalist opposition to the war—
although Bend and others found that they had to adopt patriotic stances once
war was declared.[27] Thereafter Federalism as a political force dwindled: the opening of Washington Hall in Philadelphia in 1816, an event attended by Bishop
William White of Pennsylvania, can be taken as the high-water mark of the
Federalist associations.[28]

The Episcopalian engagement with Federalist associations and festive culture
is an aspect of the church's adaptation to the new republic that until now has attracted little study.[29] Independence Day celebrations became more diverse in the
1820s and 1830s, when Episcopalian clergymen participated in many different
kinds of events: they offered prayers at Democratic and Whig gatherings; they
attended multidenominational Sunday school celebrations; and in southern
states ministers presented themselves at rallies for proslavery presidential can-
didates.[30] This public engagement set the scene for the church's growing involvement in English corporate behavior from the late 1830s on. For Anglophile
clergymen, a close involvement in English associations was a way to reconcile
the Episcopal Church's new American identity with the ecclesiastical, emotional,
and ethnic ties that linked it to England and America's growing English immigrant population. It was also another way for the church to resolve the crisis of
authority and identity described by Mullin. Essential to an examination of the
untold story of Episcopalianism and English associations is an understanding of
why the Episcopal Church—which has been called the "quintessential Anglo-
American institution"—was being drawn closer to the "Mother Church."[31]

THE EPISCOPAL CHURCH AND THE CHURCH OF ENGLAND IN BRITAIN

The letters that passed between bishops in Britain and those in America in
the early nineteenth century reveal just how little the former knew about the
American church. Richard Mant, Anglican bishop of Killaloe, Ireland, had to
ask Bishop James Kemp of Maryland for basic information about the church's
liturgy and government structures before he could write an 1823 article on the
American church.[32] By 1850 all this had changed. Members of the Anglican
clergy trafficked back and forth across the Atlantic; a growing genre of ecclesiastical travel literature shortened imaginative distances; and a new style of "rural
gothic"—brought to America in the 1830s by English architects—made Anglican
churches look the same the world over.[33] In the later 1840s clergymen began
to call for some kind of international synod that would allow British, colonial,

and American bishops to work out solutions to common problems. That these discussions were frequently colored by the rhetoric of Anglo-Saxon unity—one of the new breed of transatlantic Anglicans called the proposed gathering an "Anglo-Saxon synod"—is significant.[34] Anglican clergymen thought they had an important part to play in bringing the branches of an English-speaking or Anglo-Saxon race together in some kind of transatlantic and imperial union. Exactly who was included in this Anglo-Saxon community was never explicitly stated. The church may have sought to present itself in the ancient guise as the "Church of the English," but this was an institution inhabited by a multiethnic population of clergy and laity.

American churchmen had always celebrated their church's ties with the mother church, although not everyone agreed on what this "mother church" actually was. When Pennsylvania's Episcopalians met in convention in May 1784, they stipulated that in matters of doctrine and worship their church would remain as close as possible to the Church of England.[35] However, the church also had strong links to the tradition of nonjuring Episcopalianism that had taken root in Scotland after the Protestant succession in 1689. These links came about because America's first bishop, a former Loyalist named Samuel Seabury, had been consecrated in Aberdeen by Scottish bishops in 1784—the English bishops had refused to miter anyone who would not give the oath of loyalty to the British monarch. Seabury strengthened these Scottish ties when he got elements of the Scottish communion service into the 1789 American prayer book; he also accepted at least two Scottish-born ministers in the early years of his episcopate.[36]

Scottish connections were, however, controversial. Laymen, particularly in the middle and southern colonies, feared that Scotland provided American High Churchmen with a model of a strong episcopacy that was unsuitable for a republican environment. Others were nervous about attaching themselves to a Scottish church whose political loyalty was still in doubt. Even America's Scottish-born clergymen could feel this way: a Maryland cleric named Thomas Scot returned to Britain in 1811 but was reluctant to take up ministerial duties in Scottish parishes because he felt as if he were in an "enemy's country."[37] In spite of these concerns, connections between American and Scottish churchmen would persist into the nineteenth century. Scottish churchmen were drawn to the efforts that Bishop Hobart and others were making to build an idealized apostolic church in America, and there were Americans who continued to see Scotland as the "best source of our own Episcopacy."[38] The modern Episcopalian flag, with its mix of the cross of St. George and St. Andrew's saltire, is a reminder that the church cannot be treated simply as an English transplant.

There were many reasons why transatlantic ecclesiastical connections thickened in the nineteenth century. Bishop Hobart was appalled that American churchmen were dependent on a slothful English church for funds, but even he built contacts with English and Scottish High Churchmen during an 1823 visit. Hobart, like other educated American travelers, was moved by England's countryside and ecclesiastical architecture, but what struck him most about the mother country and its church was their history, not their dynamism or future potential. Anglophilia of this sort was not confined to High Churchmen. Manton Eastburn, the evangelical bishop of Massachusetts, went on a literary pilgrimage to his native England in 1840 and announced during the course of it that he would prefer to live under England's religious and political institutions.[39]

While Americans were drawn to England for emotional and intellectual reasons, English churchmen regarded the American church as something of a model. The success of America's voluntary churches showed that a church did not need a state to realize its spiritual mission. English High Churchmen also felt that America's Episcopal Church was closer to the Catholic and primitive ideal than their own established Church of England. This feeling became stronger during the English High Church revival of the mid-1830s; the revival, which became known as the Oxford Movement, emerged as a response to the church's loss of status during the 1832 Reform Act era. Prominent revival figures such as John Henry Newman believed that the American church had found a way to promote Catholic principles—such as the apostolic succession, baptismal regeneration, and the Real Presence in the Eucharist—within the kind of pluralistic, democratic, and antiestablishment environment that appeared to be creeping up on churchmen in post–Reform Act Britain. For the remainder of the century High Churchmen on both sides of the Atlantic worked together to develop a new spiritual identity for an independent Anglican Communion: American churchmen took inspiration from cathedral reform and England's gothic revival, and British churchmen looked to America for lessons on how the Anglican Church could maintain its identity amid democracy and secularization.[40] The freedom of the American church was clearly a major draw for English clergymen. A former British army officer named Marmaduke Dillon was one clergyman who felt this way: he told Bishop Whittingham of Maryland in 1856 that he had grown attached to the United States during earlier visits and that he preferred "many things in the constitution of the P. E. Church to my own dearly beloved Church of England."[41]

Dillon's journey to an American ministering post—he had previously served in Canada and the West Indies—shows that the development of the transatlantic "Anglo-American Church" was not just nourished by the back-and-forth movement of ideas and ecclesiastical travelers; also important were the clergymen who moved about the Atlantic world looking for work. Senior American churchmen felt that a more regular exchange of clergymen would encourage a "more ecclesiastical & formal & confessional mode of testifying & promoting all union & fellowship" between the British and American Episcopal Churches.[42] Some were, however, worried about becoming a colony of the mother church, and these concerns did lurk behind the canon stating that foreign clergymen had to have lived in America for one year before they could enter ecclesiastical posts.

Still it is striking how quickly British-born clergymen began to move into America after 1783. The compilation of Episcopal clergymen that the South Carolinian Andrew Fowler put together in the 1830s contained the names and biographies of twenty-three British-born clergymen who took American posts after the Revolutionary War. Some were curious choices for an infant church struggling in an inhospitable republican environment, but their presence makes sense when we remember that post-Revolution Episcopalianism suffered from a serious ministerial shortfall.[43] William Blackwall, a curate from Derbyshire who arrived in South Carolina in the early 1790s, was said to have been "remarkably fond of shew and parade, and generally walked or rode with two or three servants in his retinue." Fowler recorded that Blackwall was ousted from his position once his parishioners found out that his personal wealth had dried up. Fowler also commented on an Irish clerical migrant named George Wright who delivered a sermon that "exhibited the evidences of episcopacy" but "gave great offence to the non-Episcopalians of the city of New York." Wright left for Nova Scotia in 1789 when he found that "the religious discords of these states would not suit with his turn of mind."[44] Both did little to build an indigenous American church, but it is important to remember that both had been invited to minister by parish vestries.[45]

The arrival of these migrant clergymen shows that the new republic harbored large communities of Episcopalians and Loyalists who had not fled during the Revolutionary War era. The number of refugee clergymen who later returned to successful careers in America too points to the persistence of a strong Loyalist culture in the United States and also suggests that Loyalist communities were reintegrated into the new nation.[46] Even Thomas Bradbury Chandler, the most outspoken clerical Loyalist of the revolutionary period, was invited back in 1785—although apparently Chandler was subjected to "some insults" when he landed.[47] Another clerical refugee, a New York clergyman named John Doty, spent fifteen years ministering in Quebec before accepting an invitation from a church in Brooklyn in 1793. Although Doty hated the fact that the American church had altered the traditional English liturgy—so much so that he refused to read prayers during a trip to New York City in 1785—he had longed to return to his "relations and old connections" in America.[48] The welcome that these Loyalist clergymen received may be an example of a deep-seated American attachment to monarchy and ancien regime forms, which is a subject that has been explored by the historian Brendan McConville.[49] One clergyman who stayed on to minister in the new republic noted that former Loyalists had begun to "grow in popular esteem" by the mid-1790s.[50]

In addition to the Episcopal Church's problem of proving its acceptability to American society, clergymen who came from England or the British colonies had to show that they were compatible, but overall it seems that they, like other English professional groups, found assimilation straightforward.[51] Continuities in language and culture may have been a factor, and it is true that members of the clergy were trying to find a home in what was America's most Anglophile institution. Indeed it seems that the Anglophile tendencies of the church's high command were shared by many of the congregational rank and file. Clergymen had to be elected to parish rectories, and some parishes repeatedly selected English-born clergymen: for instance the first two rectors of St. Paul's in Flatbush, Long Island, were both English.[52] At least one English clergyman, the Staffordshire-born William Jackson, was treated to a hagiographic biography after serving in the dioceses of Maryland and Kentucky. The book hardly mentioned Jackson's English ethnicity; instead it focused on his identity as a "sound and decided *Churchman.*"[53] It is also notable that seven of the eight clergymen on the Maryland list who were ordained in England served an average of sixteen years each in the American church; the career of one man is unclear. Clearly not every English-born clergyman conformed to the image of the awkward alien that existing scholarship has tended to paint.[54]

Overall it appears that English clergymen were valued because they possessed particular skills. Delivering a good sermon or lecture was one; indeed newspaper reports suggest that several English clergymen achieved notoriety after successful sermon and lecture tours. The *New York Herald* reported in 1845 that the Englishman William Suddards was Philadelphia's "favourite preacher," and in the early 1870s the *New York Times* was worrying that all New York's notable pulpit orators were English and Scottish.[55] The number who took posts in America's burgeoning educational institutions indicates that members of the English clergy were valued for their academic qualifications. Three English clergymen ran academies in Maryland in the early years of the nineteenth century, and Charles Sawkins Williams, a Cambridge graduate and former Indian army officer, ditched a poorly paying Lincolnshire curacy to become president of the University of Maryland in 1825.[56] English clergymen with American teaching experience were common enough for Anthony Trollope to include a fictional one, the Reverend Peacocke, in his 1881 novel *Dr. Wortle's School,* although the fact that the character's American career was at the root of his later travails at an English school suggests that a stigma was attached to this kind of career move.[57]

English clergymen were so well regarded that fraudsters tried to make their livings out of impersonating them.[58] The picture is not entirely a positive one, though. The American church was a very different world from its English counterpart—the laity wielded far more authority in the former as opposed to the latter—and many of America's British clergymen did try to find opportunities in the British colonies.[59] American congregations could be suspicious, if not hostile, to English clergymen. One of Maryland's English clergymen teachers was so unpopular that local children reputedly rolled a stone over his grave to prevent him from tormenting them from the afterlife. A Philadelphia doctor who failed in getting Marmaduke Dillon appointed to his local church noted that it was the "peculiarity" of Dillon's "voice and manners" that prevented him from being elected to the post.[60] Dillon seems to have upset quite a few people during his American career, but whether this had anything to do with his ethnicity is not clear. A fellow English clergyman accused him of intemperance and lying; his Maryland parishioners complained about his overbearing authority; and the Union army described him as the "vilest of rebel sympathizers" when he prevented a provost marshal from gathering draftees. There is no conclusive evidence that Dillon was the victim of what Trollope called the "fretful anger against England" that boiled up in the northern states during the early stages of the Civil War, but it is notable that another English clergyman, David Christian Moore, had to leave Baltimore for an "abode somewhere on British ground" after falling out with his parishioners and fellow clergymen in 1861.[61]

To what extent does the experience of these English clergymen challenge or support existing narratives of English assimilation? Certainly Charlotte Erickson's description of the English as an "invisible" migrant community does not work when describing Anglican clergymen. When America's founders rejected Anglicanism as an established religion, they not only rendered Anglicans highly visible but also made sure that Anglicanism would not be one of those English institutions and tradition—such as the common law—that formed the basis of American culture. The evidence marshaled above might support the view proposed by William Van Vugt that English migrants found assimilation more straightforward than did migrants from other ethnic groups, but this kind of interpretation glosses over the fact that assimilation was fragile and that members of the clergy, like every other migrant community, had to prove their loyalty to their new home.[62] The career of Jonathan Mayhew Wainwright, the Liverpool-born bishop of New York, tells us that English-born clergymen could find the process difficult. Wainwright immigrated with his family when he was young and for most of his early life considered himself a naturalized American.[63] Wainwright's attachment to England became more pronounced after he visited his birthplace in 1836. American national celebrations started to become difficult events for Wainwright, particularly when they took place during moments of diplomatic tension with Britain. Wainwright was in New York in June 1839, a time when conflicts on the Maine border were threatening to boil over into war, and he told his brother that he wanted to "escape" both the visit of Democratic president Martin Van Buren and the upcoming Fourth of July celebrations.[64]

Wainwright's disquiet—he noted that his time in the city was "very uncomfortable" for him and his wife—is understandable in light of the fact that the loyalty of Episcopalians was called into question at moments of Anglo-American conflict.[65] The view that the English easily slipped on the garb of the dominant host community—that they were "already Americans," as Van Vugt put it—rather overlooks the point that groups that are accepted into host societies can quickly find themselves persecuted as political circumstances change.

These pieces of anecdotal evidence should not, however, draw attention away from the fact that the Episcopal Church did seek to cultivate an English aesthetic in the middle decades of the nineteenth century. This might have reflected the more harmonious Anglo-American relations of the later 1850s; it might also have been connected to the fact that new bogey figures were beginning to replace the English as the source of American anxiety: notably Irish Catholics, who came as a result of the famine; and Hispanics, who were absorbed as a result of American acquisitions during the Mexican War. The next section explores a previously understudied aspect of the strengthening ties between the Episcopal Church, America's English community, and the mother church: the connection that emerged between Episcopal clergymen and the English fraternal associations that sprouted up across North America in the early nineteenth century. The church's links with English associations were not all that they seemed, however. English corporate behavior did not mark the Episcopal Church as a minority or English institution; rather, English benevolent associations were cosmopolitan institutions that provided clergymen with an arena in which they could prove their compatibility with a multiethnic, pluralist, and "Anglo-Saxon" America.

THE EPISCOPAL CHURCH, ENGLISH IMMIGRANTS, AND ENGLISH ASSOCIATIONAL CULTURE

This essay has introduced us to the different visions that Episcopal clergymen had for their church. Hobartians wished to emphasize the universal character of their church, but others saw value in cultivating attachments to particular political groups or ethnic communities.[66] In the middle decades of the nineteenth century American churchmen made various attempts to reaffirm the links between the English church and the English people. In the mid-1850s English and American churchmen launched a cooperative venture called the Anglo-American Church Emigrants Aid Society, which was designed to keep English emigrants within a common church structure that stretched from the sending parish to the receiving one. In 1852 the British vice consul in New York, Robert Bunch, proposed a church in New York that would provide Anglican services and hospital beds for Protestant emigrants from England and the rest of Britain. For these purposes the Anglo-American Free Church of St. George the Martyr opened in 1860 with the help of private subscriptions and, after a struggle, a grant from the British-based Society for the Propagation of the Gospel.[67] Years earlier, in the 1830s, churchmen started to appear at moments of English corporate behavior, such as benevolent society gatherings, celebrations of the monarch's birthdays, and rituals associated with national saints' days. This phenomenon is important on two counts. First, it introduces us to another way that churchmen thought their church could position itself in American society. Second, it tells us something about how both Episcopalians and the English more generally were finding a place in the antebellum United States.

English corporate behavior was largely channeled through the national benevolent societies that cared for indigent immigrants. The first St. George's Societies had been founded in New York, Charleston, and Philadelphia in the colonial period, but by the 1850s there were branches across Canada and in most of the major American towns in the Midwest and the South. English associations were multifaceted and performed a number of roles.[68] St. George's Societies were primarily charitable organizations that doled out alms to hard-up immigrants, but they also offered convivial spaces where urban males could fraternize, celebrate common origins, and build up "social capital." These institutions were also attractive to Episcopal clergymen.

Anglican clergymen in British North America began to play visible roles in the Canadian St. George's Societies from the late 1830s on. This was the time when settler colonies across the British world were starting to replace their versions of the old "confessional state" with a new, liberal system of multiple Christian establishments. Churchmen railed against the loss of their political privileges, but most knew that to survive, their church had to provide religious leadership to English expatriates. This explains the Anglican interest in English cultural and ethnic behavior.[69] Links between the church and English corporate culture emerged around the same time in the United States, although what powered this development was not political change but rather the rising tide of English immigration; America's Anglican establishments had, after all, long since disintegrated. The early societies do not appear to have had chaplains, and their constitutions did not subject prospective members to religious tests; still, by the later 1830s Episcopalian ministers were starting to monopolize English corporate events.[70] Jonathan Wainwright—later bishop of New York—served as chaplain to the New York society in the early 1830s. His role was initially a minor one: all he did was say prayers before the society dinner. However, by 1848 society members were meeting to hear divine services and clerical orations in the gothic surroundings of Trinity Church.[71] Philadelphia's Society of the Sons of St. George did not meet in Episcopal churches, but it did count Episcopalian ministers among its founder members and had Episcopal chaplains as well. An Episcopal minister also helped set up Milwaukee's St. George's Society in 1857.[72] For some reason southern societies appear to have been immune to the Episcopal takeover, although occasionally demands for an Episcopalian monopoly were heard at English gatherings. For instance, at an anniversary meeting of the Charleston society in 1839, one of the members raised a volunteer toast to the "Church of England—True to the Throne."[73]

The conservatism of the liturgical content of the church gatherings—the 1848 New York meeting included prayers, lessons, and benedictions as prescribed by the Book of Common Prayer—showed that these were Anglican events and that the Anglican Church had a special claim to be a national and English institution. Although the Episcopalian contribution to the society fluctuated— in the early 1850s, for example, the society gathered for dinners but not divine services—it is notable that there were moments, such as in April 1858, when Episcopal churchmen were given free rein to shape impressive religious ceremonies that underscored the links between the church, the Crown, and the English people. In 1858, for instance, there were choir-sung anthems, a reading of the Prayer Book litany, and a prayer for Queen Victoria.[74]

In all, seventeen Episcopal clergymen were involved in Philadelphia's society between 1772 and 1872 either as members or as chaplains, and at least twenty-eight ministers and bishops were mentioned as playing some role in society events in New York.[75] The majority were, as might be expected, men of English birth or descent. Of the twenty-eight clergymen who were involved in the New York society before 1861, seven were English-born and one came from the West Indies. Most of them had migrated to America when they were young. One of them, Jonathan Wainwright, clearly looked on the saint's day as a time for renewing old ties and expressing corporate solidarity, as he frequently tried to get his wider family to attend.[76] These chaplains clung to their English identity and tried to cast themselves as guardians of the national character and national spirit. For example, James Stone, a chaplain who served the North America St. George's Union—an organization founded in the 1870s that brought together representatives from Canadian and American societies—published extensively on English history, customs, and landscapes.[77]

The St. George's events in New York were not, however, narrow and parochial events aimed at a small number of elite expatriates of English birth. The society tried to demonstrate its civic appeal through its day-to-day activities and in its annual celebrations: aid was given to a broad community of English, Scots, Welsh, Irish, and colonial-born; representatives of the German, Irish, Scottish, and Welsh national societies attended English events in New York in the 1840s and 1850s; and the branches of the society across America began a custom of toasting both the American president and the royal family at their annual saint's day dinners.[78] Then there was the fact that not all the clergymen who were involved were Englishmen: the twenty-eight members of the New York clergy included an Irishman and seven American-born clergymen.

It is possible that these men got involved only because they were ministers of the fashionable churches that hosted society events. Others tried to hide the fact that their churches had special relationships with English associations. In 1848, for instance, William Berrian of Trinity Church corrected a newspaper that had wrongly given the impression that the Easter services at his church had been specially put on for the society.[79] While Berrian was very much in the Hobartian mold, other clergymen wanted the public to know all about their involvement in associations and rituals that might have been branded as English, monarchical, and possibly disloyal. One way to stymie the critics was to deploy the language of Anglo-Saxonism and to play up racial continuities between Britons and Americans. Scholars have noted that the failure of the 1848 revolutions in France and southern Europe encouraged Britons and Americans to "believe ever more strongly in the superiority of Anglo-Saxons and Teutons," and it seems that the St. George's Societies and their chaplains helped popularize the Anglo-Saxon idea.[80] In 1849 Francis Vinton, rector of Trinity, told the society that the "experiments of abolitionists in this country, and socialists in Europe" brought the Anglo-Saxon tradition of "true liberty, equality and fraternity" into sharper focus. Like those of other clerical orators, Vinton's oration included a panegyric on British imperialism. Horatio Southgate, former bishop to the Ottoman Empire, said in 1859 that "in every department of national glory" England, or "Old England" as he put it, stood "preeminent" as a result of her "humane and magnanimous conduct" toward "her late rebellious subjects in India." For Southgate, British expansion in India and America's earlier imperialist forays in Mexico were both parts of a single Christian crusade. A year earlier, in 1858, William Ferdinand Morgan told the society that the recent deaths of the great imperial warriors Lord Raglan and Henry Havelock were reminders to both America and Britain that they were accountable to the Almighty and that providence had handed them the task of Christianizing the world.[81]

The society also helped turn other "great deaths" into transatlantic spectacles. In November 1852 Francis Hawks, a former chaplain of the St. George's Society, hosted a ceremony in honor of the Duke of Wellington that was attended by representatives of the national benevolent societies, Anglican clergymen from America and Canada, and a "respectable audience" of British subjects and American citizens. The oration that Vinton delivered at the ceremony tried to show that Wellington had appeal for a broad transatlantic community: not only could he claim an Anglo-Saxon lineage—Vinton said that Wellington was thirty-second in direct descent from Alfred—but he also resembled that other great warrior-politician George Washington. Both had supposedly nurtured a new kind of reformist conservatism, one founded on the principle that, as Vinton put it, "the wants of society are to overrule even pre-established system[s]."[82] Historians have seen the widespread mourning that accompanied Wellington's death as evidence of popular attachment to a sense of British nationality. The fact that sermons, orations, and memorial services also took place in America suggests two things: first, that expatriate clergymen were seeking to foster a national consciousness overseas; and second, that this national or "imagined community" was one to which American-born Anglophiles could claim access.[83]

It seems strange that image-conscious Episcopalian clergymen should attach themselves to events that reeked of British imperialism, monarchism, and conservatism. Indeed, Horatio Potter, bishop of New York, was castigated in the press for expressing proimperial sentiments at a church gathering in Canada in the mid-1850s, and members of the New York clergy were widely condemned for hosting the Prince of Wales at Trinity Church in 1860.[84] But the allusions that were made to a common Anglo-Saxon origin and civilization help explain why so many Anglican clerics were keen to attach themselves to the St. George's Societies. These events were opportunities for churchmen to remind everyone of their church's historic ties to a vaguely defined national or racial community that stretched far beyond England. The Church of England's claims to be a national church had taken a battering during the constitutional crises of the late 1820s and early 1830s, but the idea that the church could provide religious leadership for a diverse and pluralistic nation did not go away; indeed it was taking firmer hold in the 1840s and 1850s as a generation of "broad churchmen" began to write about a comprehensive church that could embody the nation and national spirit. For broad churchmen, the Church of England could continue to call itself a "national" church because it would present itself as a tolerant and pacific institution, one that was representative of the nation's great religious pluralism, and one that non-Anglicans would want to join.[85]

The church that exhibited itself at the St. George's Society gatherings in America and elsewhere was this broad and comprehensive church that claimed to represent and embody the nation, the national character, and the national spirit.[86] In 1848 the British consul referred to the English constitution and the English church as central to Englishness; he also described Trinity Church as "that noble monument of the Old Country." A year later Francis Vinton said that the Church of England lay at the root of the common customs, traditions, and political institutions that marked the English: for him, the church had made the English people happy as it upheld the English constitution and had spread feelings of "liberty, equality and fraternity."[87] The multiethnic and cosmopolitan St. George's Day gatherings gave the impression that a consensual, comprehensive, and popular church, one that provided religious leadership to a diverse nation or an "imagined community," could be realized.

What exactly was this "nation" and who belonged to it? Scholars of the mid-Victorian period have pointed out that the terms "Anglo-Saxon" and "English" were slippery and capacious categories: both could be used to refer to a broad community that was made up of different ethnic types. This was part of their attraction.[88] The crucial point is that the community who this national church claimed to represent, the "English," was ill-defined and potentially expansive. Matthew Grimley noted that in the early twentieth century the English were commonly viewed as a mixed "people" rather than as a "race," and while his comments referred to a later period, they do have relevance for the nineteenth century.[89] It was common for commentators, both within the church and outside it, to see the Church of England as the church of a widely scattered Anglo-Saxon community that had been made over centuries of migrations, exchanges, and absorptions. Indeed an article published in an American periodical in 1848 expressed the belief that a distinctively English church could be traced back to Anglo-Saxon times and that the key aspects of this church—the article focused on its upholding of the "democratic principle" and its missionary energy—had continued to shape the development of the "Anglo-Saxon race" up to the present day.[90] A Canadian clergyman writing in 1851 made a similar point when he argued that the church had played a formative role in "moulding the national character" of an expanding Anglo-Saxon race. According to this writer, the Anglo-Saxon race that inhabited the English-speaking world had been formed out of the "fusion" or amalgamation of various "nations" in two great epochs: the first had taken place centuries before in England; and the second was occurring in the present-day United States.[91] This idea that new arrivals would take on the character, customs, and manners of what was called the dominant race was, as Peter Mandler has shown, commonplace around the mid-1800s.[92] The national benevolent society gatherings, with their mix of representatives from the German, Irish, Scottish, and Welsh societies, seemed to illustrate this amalgamation as well as bear out the idea—strong from the late 1840s onward—that all these people, the Celts, Saxons, and Teutons, were Anglo-Saxons.[93]

Churchmen would have reacted positively to evidence that the Anglo-Saxon race was growing through processes of adoption, naturalization, and assimilation. After all, an Episcopalian church that mixed various Anglican liturgical traditions and was populated by a cosmopolitan community of English, Scottish, Irish, and American clergy seemed well placed to claim religious leadership of a far-flung and diverse Anglo-Saxon community. Hence clergymen appeared at later events that were designed to promote feelings of kinship between Britain and America. In 1887 members of the clergy gave thanksgiving prayers to commemorate Victoria's accession, and ten years later Episcopalians marked

Victoria's diamond jubilee by celebrating the "common language, literature, religion and lore" that were "imbedded in the English speaking people."[94]

These moments did not mean that a transatlantic "Anglo-Saxon" nation had come into existence or that the British Anglican Church had managed to "recolonize" the United States or its Episcopal Church.[95] The year 1897 marked Victoria's jubilee celebrations, but it was also when the dust settled on another Anglo-American boundary dispute: this time over Venezuela. The Anglo-American ecclesiastical union too was far from complete. One commentator writing in the 1860s said that Episcopalian clergymen were still finding that "Church folk" from Britain had no idea that "there is in these states the very same Church which they have had at home."[96] American clergymen traveling in England were often mistaken for Englishmen, but those who had been ordained in America still could not work there, as an 1840 parliamentary act designed to encourage mobility allowed American clergymen to conduct only occasional services in English churches.[97] Movements that looked as if they might draw churchmen closer together could also deepen divisions. Recent research has argued that the later, more Catholic, phase of the Oxford Movement brought into sharp focus the differences between English and American forms of High Churchmanship.[98] Even the Lambeth conferences, decennial gatherings of Anglican bishops that were supposed to signify a new age of Anglican internationalism, could leave American clergymen worrying about their church's diminishing independence.[99]

On the other side there were English clergymen—they were mostly extreme followers of the Oxford Movement—who wanted to resist any closer communion with a republican American church that had apparently "fallen back from the faith" when it omitted the Athanasian Creed from its prayer book in 1789.[100] Others worried that the church's republican governing structure damaged Episcopal authority and did nothing to shield clergymen from lay interference.[101] Perhaps the biggest sticking point, however, was slavery. Samuel Wilberforce apparently chose to edit out the material on the church's involvement with slavery when he published his—largely favorable—1844 *History of the Protestant Episcopal Church in America*. In private, however, he told American churchmen that he was angered by the Episcopal Church's unwillingness to condemn the entire "peculiar institution." The presence of slaveholding American clergymen damaged the image of the Episcopal Church and meant that the two churches had to look on while other denominations fed into, and gained strength from, a transatlantic abolitionist movement.[102]

CONCLUSION

This essay explores how the Episcopal Church and its English clergymen came to terms with a democratic and pluralistic United States. Different churchmen offered different models of adaptation: while Bishop Hobart thought that the church would have to retreat into a private realm, others made considerable use of the opportunities held out by America's rich and diverse associational culture. Fourth of July rituals broadcast the church's American credentials, but events that were coded as "English" offered different kinds of opportunities. On one level the St. George's Society gatherings were chances for Episcopalians to rediscover their church's ancient English origins. More importantly English associational activity gave clergymen the opportunity to think expansively. A church that had been facing ruin in the revolutionary period was by the mid-nineteenth century trying to claim religious leadership of a diverse Anglo-Saxon race and a far-flung "Greater Britain" or "British World"—names given to a transcontinental and transnational entity that could include the United States.[103] This was a church with a multiethnic and mobile clerical workforce, networks that embraced the whole of the Anglican world, and a liturgy that fused Scottish and English traditions with American innovations. In other words, the Episcopal Church—and the wider Anglican Communion of which it was part—stood as the institutional embodiment of Anglo-America and the supposed unity and connectedness of the Anglo-Saxon race.

So to what extent can America's Episcopal Church be described as an English institution? Certainly the church harbored numbers of English clergy, but it was also home to Scottish- and Irish-born clerics, and America's church—like other overseas branches of the Anglican Communion—built long-lasting links to Britain's other Anglican churches.[104] There are references from the 1870s to Episcopal churches demonstrating their Scottish roots by celebrating St. Andrew's Day, a practice that continues to this day.[105] It is also important to bear in mind that the majority of Episcopal clergymen were American-born and felt no affinity with English immigrants. The daughter of an English clergyman traveling in America in 1878 bumped into an Episcopalian clergyman who said "the most foolishly nasty things about England and our Queen." Three years earlier a clergyman named Richard T. Kerfoot complained that he was making little progress among the English immigrants who had been clustering around Evansville, Indiana, since the 1810s.[106] Kerfoot wanted to be transferred to a place where the population was "more mixed" as he felt that the English in Evansville disliked him. They were, he said, of the "cold blooded sort—unsympathetic & fishy." Tellingly he added that "it takes an Englishman to feel alright with certain classes of these old country folk."[107]

Yet despite its cosmopolitan character, the Episcopal Church played a vital role in forging and maintaining a distinct English diaspora in the United States, one made up of persons of English birth and descent. Other denominational groups made equally important contributions to the English expatriate life in North America: non-Anglican ministers were, for instance, much more likely to lead parties of migrants. What marks the Anglicans is that they felt that their church had a special duty to provide this diaspora with a national religion.[108] This vision of an Anglican Church providing religious leadership to a broad community of English migrants lay behind the foundation of the Church Emigrants Aid Society and the setting up of free churches for immigrants in New York. Moses Marcus, a clergyman who planned a free church for immigrants in New York in the mid-1840s, had initially wanted to provide immigrants with an English church with English forms of worship and an English prayer book. When the church was finally opened in 1860, it featured prayers for the queen and was described as "an Anglo-American Church."[109] The bishop of New York called the church "a kind of representative of the Anglican Church among us." Others, however, worried that the American church was becoming too closely associated with English Anglicanism and the English-born. Even the Anglophile *New York Albion* felt that members of the American clergy could not "accurately represent the national spirit" as they were too closely associated with England's clergy.[110] Complaints that America was becoming too dependent on English clergymen would reappear as emigration from England and the rest of Britain continued to rise in the later nineteenth century.[111] Clearly, then, it was not always the case that the overseas branches of the Anglican Church aligned themselves with new-world identities and cultural traditions once they separated themselves from the old English establishment.[112]

NOTES

I would like to thank the editor and the anonymous reviewer for their comments on earlier drafts of this article. Audience members at seminars and conferences hosted by the "Locating the Hidden Diaspora" project at Northumbria University too made useful suggestions. Mary Klein, archivist at the Episcopal Diocese of Maryland Archives, was enormously helpful.

1. Brendan McConville, *The King's Three Faces: The Rise & Fall of Royal America, 1688–1776* (Chapel Hill: University of North Carolina Press, 2006), 295–99. Farther south it was a different story, with Anglican clergymen usually appearing among the ranks of Patriots. For South Carolina, see Samuel C. Smith, *A Cautious Enthusiasm: Mystical Piety and Evangelicalism in Colonial South Carolina* (Columbia: University of South Carolina Press, 2013), 145.

2. Even some of the Loyalist clergymen who fled to Nova Scotia would return to the newly independent United States. Of the thirty-one Loyalist clergymen who were recorded as leaving during the Revolutionary War, six would return. See Arthur W. Eaton, *The Church of England in Nova Scotia and the Tory Clergy of the Revolution* (New York: Thomas Whittaker, 1891), 155–90.

3. Wayne Franklin, *James Fenimore Cooper: The Early Years* (New Haven, Conn.: Yale University Press, 2007), 44; Bruce Mullin, *Episcopal Vision/American Reality: High Church Theology and Social Thought in Evangelical America* (New Haven, Conn.: Yale

University Press, 1986), 8–9; Daniel W. Howe, *What Hath God Wrought: The Transformation of America, 1815–1848* (Oxford: Oxford University Press, 2007), 234.

4. Ethan Allen, *Clergy in Maryland of the Protestant Episcopal Church since the Independence of 1783* (Baltimore, Md.: James S. Waters, 1860).

5. James Belich, *Replenishing the Earth: The Settler Revolution and the Rise of the Anglo-World, 1783–1939* (Oxford: Oxford University Press, 2009), 50; Peter J. Marshall, *Remaking the British Atlantic: The United States and the British Empire after Independence* (Oxford: Oxford University Press, 2012).

6. The chapters on religion in Howe's *What Hath God Wrought* pay little or no attention to Episcopalians but have something to say about all other denominations.

7. Mullin, *Episcopal Vision/American Reality*, 86–91.

8. Tanja Bueltmann, Donald MacRaild, and David Gleeson, eds., *Locating the English Diaspora, 1500–2000* (Liverpool: Liverpool University Press, 2012), intro.

9. One commentator felt that English travelers would "feel at home" in American churches: see *Recent Recollections of the Anglo-American Church in the United States: by an English Layman, Five Year's Resident in That Republic* (London: Rivingtons, 1861), 28.

10. "Unitarian and Episcopal Affinities," *New Englander* 3 (1845): 556.

11. Albrecht Koschnik, *"Let a Common Interest Bind Us Together": Associations, Partisanship, and Culture in Philadelphia, 1775–1840* (Charlottesville: University Press of Virginia, 2007), chap. 5. Marshall Foletta, *Coming to Terms with Democracy: Federalist Intellectuals and the Shaping of an American Culture* (Charlottesville: University Press of Virginia, 2001), considered how later generations of Federalists carved out a public role for themselves in the fields of law, medicine, journalism, and education, but it mostly focuses on the Federalist construction of a new American literature.

12. Joseph Hardwick, *An Anglican British World: The Church of England and the Expansion of the Settler Empire, c. 1790–1860* (Manchester: Manchester University Press, 2014), chap. 6.

13. Imperial Anglicans tried to mesh their church with an English community and identity around the same time; see Hardwick, *An Anglican British World*, 205–15.

14. Howe, *What Hath God Wrought*, 197–200.

15. Jewel L. Spangler, *Virginians Reborn: Anglican Monopoly, Evangelical Dissent, and the Rise of the Baptists in the Late Eighteenth Century* (Charlottesville: University Press of Virginia, 2008), 214–18. Note that Spangler rarely mentioned the departure of Anglicans to Baptist churches in Virginia; indeed at 224–27 she noted that most Baptist converts after the Revolution were often related to or had close personal ties to existing Baptists.

16. Frederick V. Mills, *Bishops by Ballot: An Eighteenth-Century Ecclesiastical Revolution* (New York: Oxford University Press, 1971), 157–81.

17. Mullin, *Episcopal Vision/American Reality*, 5.

18. Ibid., 26–59, 85–89. For challenges to the "Hobartian synthesis," see 90–91, 95–96.

19. John L. Brooke, "Ancient Lodges and Self-Created Societies: Voluntary Associations and the Public Sphere in the Early Republic," in *Launching the Extended*

Republic: The Federalist Era, ed. Ronald Hoffman and Peter Albert (Charlottesville: University Press of Virginia, 1996), 273–377.

20. "Anglo-Federal Connections or Church and State," repr. from the *Aurora* in *New York American Citizen and General Advertizer,* September 1, 1800.

21. *Alexandria (Va.) Advertizer,* July 6, 1798.

22. Robert Fowle, *An Oration Delivered at Plymouth, in New Hampshire, on the Anniversary of the Independence of America, July 4th, 1800* (Concord, N.H.: George Hough, 1800), 9.

23. For Episcopalian links to Tammany, see Jason K. Duncan, *Citizens or Papists? The Politics of Anti-Catholicism in New York, 1685–1821* (New York: Fordham University Press, 2005), 85–86.

24. Koschnik, *"Let a Common Interest Bind Us Together,"* 77–82.

25. *Alexandria (Va.) Gazette,* June 27, 1803, and February 20, 1810; *Trenton Federalist,* July 10, 1809.

26. Simon Newman, *Parades and the Politics of the Street: Festive Culture in the Early Republic* (Philadelphia: University of Pennsylvania Press, 1997), 189.

27. *Trenton Federalist,* July 6, 1812. Bend made a show of attending a patriotic procession in Baltimore in July 1812, but he quickly sloped off; see Joseph Bend to Bishop James Kemp, July 6, 1812, Maryland Diocesan Archives, Baltimore, Maryland (hereafter MDA).

28. Koschnik, *"Let a Common Interest Bind Us Together,"* 89.

29. Jennifer Clark, "'Church of Our Fathers': The Development of the Protestant Episcopal Church within the Changing Post-revolutionary Anglo-American Relationship," *Journal of Religious History* 18, no. 1 (1994): 27–51.

30. Len Travers, *Celebrating the Fourth: Independence Day and the Rites of Nationalism in the Early Republic* (Amherst: University of Massachusetts Press, 1997), 221–27. For the Reverend Ransom Warner's presence at a Democratic Fourth of July meeting in Granby, Connecticut, see *Hartford Times,* July 7, 1838. For the Episcopal Church and southern Calhounite rallies, see *Richmond (Va.) Whig,* July 14, 1843. For Whig gatherings, see *Albany (N.Y.) Argus,* July 23, 1839. For Sunday schools, see *Daily National Intelligencer,* July 8, 1844.

31. Clark, "Church of Our Fathers," 28.

32. Bishop Mant to Kemp, February 21, 1819, MDA; "Episcopal Church in America," *British Critic* 20 (November 1823): 530–61.

33. Richard Upjohn, an English cabinetmaker who migrated to America in 1829, provided plans for gothic churches that were followed by church builders across America; see Joan R. Gutterson, "Rural Gothic: Episcopal Churches on the Minnesota Frontier," *Minnesota History* 50 (Fall 1987): 260–61.

34. Henry Caswall, *America, and the American Church,* 2nd ed. (London: John and Charles Mozley, 1851), 395.

35. Mills, *Bishops by Ballot,* 197; Clark, "Church of Our Fathers," 32, 41.

36. Mills, *Bishops by Ballot,* 225–26, 281; *A Reprint in Full of the Registry of Ordinations by Bishops Seabury and Jarvis, as Published in the Journal of A.D. 1882, by Order of*

the Convention (Hartford, Conn., 1882), available at http://anglicanhistory.org/usa/seabury/ordinations1882.html, accessed May 6, 2014.

37. Thomas Scot to Kemp, April 2, 1816, MDA.

38. William Berrian of New York was in contact with several Scottish bishops after he published a biography of Hobart in 1834. See Bishop Skinner of Aberdeen to Berrian, June 13, 1834, and Bishop Torry to Berrian, March 28, 1836, General Theological Seminary Library (hereafter GTSL), New York, Berrian Papers and Correspondence, MSS B458, case 2, folio pages. 148, 188. For the favorable view of Scottish episcopacy, see Benjamin Haight to Bishop William R. Whittingham, November 10, 1835, MDA.

39. Bishop Hobart to Kemp, September 17, 1824, MDA; Hobart to Jane Chandler Hobart, December 9, 1823, in William Berrian, Memoir of the Life of the Right Reverend John Henry Hobart, D.D. (New York: Swords, Stanford, 1833), 277–79; Manton Eastburn to Ward Eastburn and Neilson Eastburn, June 6, 1840, Yale University Special Collections, New Haven, Connecticut, Correspondence of Episcopal Bishops Collection, group 4, box 3, file 104.

40. Peter Nockles, "The Oxford Movement and the United States of America," in The Oxford Movement: Europe and the Wider World 1830–1930, ed. Stewart J. Brown and Peter Nockles (New York: Cambridge University Press, 2013), 133–52; Larry Crockett, "The Oxford Movement and the 19th Century Episcopal Church: Anglo-Catholic Ecclesiology and the American Experience," Quodlibet Online Journal of Christian Theology and Philosophy 1 (August 1999), available at www.quodlibet.net/articles/crockett-oxford.shtml, accessed May 7, 2014.

41. Marmaduke M. Dillon to Whittingham, May 3, 1856, MDA.

42. Bishop McIlvaine of Ohio to Whittingham, October 9, 1840, MDA.

43. Spangler, Virginians Reborn, 200.

44. Andrew Fowler, "Biographical Sketches of the Clergy of the Protestant Episcopal Church in the United States of America," New York Historical Society Library, MSS Collection, BV Fowler, vol. 4, folio pages. 781, 798.

45. For Wright's appointment, see St. Ann's Church (Brooklyn, New York) from the Year 1784 to the Year 1845, with a Memorial of the Sunday Schools (Brooklyn, N.Y.: F. G. Fish, 1845), 20–22, 124.

46. The return of Loyalist refugees has been briefly considered in Keith Mason, "Loyalism in British North America in the Age of Revolution, 1776–1812," in Loyalism and the Formation of the British World, 1775–1914, ed. Allan Blackstock and Frank O'Gorman (Woodbridge: Boydell, 2014), 170–71.

47. William B. Sprague, Annals of the American Pulpit; or Commemorative Notices of Distinguished American Clergymen of Various Denominations, 9 vols. (New York: Robert Carter & Brothers, 1859), 5:137–42; Mills, Bishops by Ballot, 204, 236.

48. John Doty to Reverend Morice (secretary to the United Society of the Propagation of the Gospel [hereafter SPG]), September 30, 1784, October 1, 1785, and October 14, 1793, SPG Archives, Rhodes House Library, Oxford, U.K. (hereafter RHL), C/CAN/PRE, folio pages 24, 28, 35.

49. McConville, The King's Three Faces, epilogue.

50. William Clark to Reverend Morice, September 30, 1796, SPG, RHL, C/AM/5, Massachusetts 1712–1812, folio page 78.

51. William Van Vugt, "The Hidden English Diaspora," in *Locating the English Diaspora, 1500–2000*, ed. Tanja Bueltmann, Donald MacRaild, and David Gleeson (Liverpool: Liverpool University Press, 2012), 83.

52. Thomas M. Strong, *The History of the Town of Flatbush, in Kings County, Long Island* (New York: Thomas R. Mercein, 1842), 106–7.

53. William M. Jackson, *The Remains of the Rev. William Jackson, Late Rector of St. Paul's Church, Louisville, Ky. with a Brief Sketch of His Life and Character* (New York: Stanford and Swords, 1847), 34.

54. Mullin, *Episcopal Vision/American Reality*, suggests that English clergy "could never serve as an adequate model of ministry for the young Episcopal Church" (9).

55. *New York Herald*, April 6, 1845; *New York Times*, April 28, 1872.

56. John Ireland was principal of an academy and rector in Harford County in the 1790s; George Ralph opened an academy in Baltimore County in 1809; and Francis Barclay was president of another academy in Easton from 1802. See *Archives of the General Convention*, vol. 1, *The Correspondence of John Henry Hobart, 1757–1797* (New York: Privately printed, 1911), 167, 227; *Archives of the General Convention*,vol. 6, 380.6.

57. Anthony Trollope, *Dr. Wortle's School* (New York: Oxford University Press, 1984), 13.

58. Newspapers carried warnings about such imposters, e.g., *Cincinnati Daily Gazette*, July 20, 1880.

59. Hardwick, *An Anglican British World*, 179.

60. For George Ralph's unpopularity, see *Archives of the General Convention*, vol. 1, 228; Caspar Morris to Whittingham, June 12, 1862, MDA.

61. Bishop Horatio Potter to Whittingham, February 25, 1864; Dillon to Whittingham, April 26, 1858, March 27, 1861, and May 3, 1864, MDA. For Moore, see Bishop Doane to Whittingham, May 10, 1861, and David Christian Moore to Whittingham, September 24 and October 23, 1861, MDA. For the awkward position occupied by the English during the Civil War period, see David T. Gleeson, "Proving Their Loyalty to the Republic: English Immigrants and the American Civil War," in *The Civil War as Global Conflict: Transnational Meanings of the America Civil War*, ed. David T. Gleeson and Simon Lewis (Columbia: University of South Carolina Press, 2013), 98–115; Anthony Trollope, *North America* (London: Chapman and Hall, 1862 [Penguin Books ed., 1968]), 137.

62. Gleeson, "Proving Their Loyalty," 111.

63. Jonathan Mayhew Wainwright to Peter Wainwright, August 12, 1814, Wainwright Family Papers, series 1, box 1, file 44, Manuscripts and Archives Division, New York Public Library, New York City (hereafter NYPL).

64. Wainwright to Peter Wainwright, June 12, 1839, Wainwright Family Papers, series 1, box 2, file 3, NYPL.

65. Episcopalianism was coupled with anti-Americanism around the time of the controversial Jay Treaty of 1794–95; see Donald H. Stewart, *The Opposition Press of the Federalist Era* (New York: State University of New York Press, 1969), 402.

66. John Henry Hobart, *The Origin, the General Character, and the Present Situation of the Protestant Episcopal Church, in the United States of America* (Philadelphia: Bradford and Inskeep, 1814), 8; Mullin, *Episcopal Vision/American Reality,* 87, 196–97.

67. *A Statement Respecting an Association for the Spiritual Aid of English Churchmen Emigrating to the United States of America* (London: W. Stevens, 1855). Details on the foundation of the Anglo-American Free Church and the SPG grant can be found in RHL, D-Series, D29, United States Letters & Papers. The SPG had committed five hundred pounds toward the project in 1852 but later doubted whether a church especially for emigrants was needed in the city.

68. Tanja Bueltmann and Donald M. MacRaild, "Globalizing St. George: English Associations in the Anglo-World to 1930," *Journal of Global History* 7 (March 2012): 79–105.

69. For more detail, see Hardwick, *An Anglican British World,* chap. 6.

70. Only rarely did ministers from other denominations show up at society gatherings: for instance, a Baptist minister, John Overton Choules, attended a celebration in New York in 1842 (*New York Albion,* April 30, 1842).

71. *New York Spectator,* May 8, 1832; *New York Herald,* April 25, 1848.

72. *Milwaukee Sentinel,* April 25, 1857.

73. The lack of an Anglican monopoly may have been because High Churchmen, who tended to dominate English corporate events in the north, were thin on the ground in southern states. For southern Low Churchmanship, see Elizabeth Fox-Genovese and Eugene D. Genovese, *The Mind of the Master Class: History and Faith in the Southern Slaveholders' Worldview* (Cambridge: Cambridge University Press, 2005), 429. The strong southern attachment to religious equality and toleration, discussed at 458–59, may also have been a factor. See also *Charleston (S.C.) Courier,* April 26, 1839.

74. *New York Herald,* April 24, 1858.

75. *An Historical Sketch of the Origin and Progress of the Society of the Sons of St. George* (Philadelphia, 1872), 81–90. The figure for New York was compiled from newspaper reports and the list of officers given in *A History of St. George's Society of New York, from 1770 to 1913* (New York: St. George's Society of New York, 1913), 211–33.

76. Jonathan M. Wainwright to Peter Wainwright, March 23, 1840, Wainwright Family Papers, series 1, box 2, file 159, NYPL.

77. James Stone, *The Heart of Merrie England* (Philadelphia: Porter & Coates, 1887); James Stone, *Woods and Dales of Derbyshire* (Philadelphia: George W. Jacobs & Co., 1894).

78. On the cosmopolitan nature of the recipients of society aid in New York, see *New York Albion,* May 1, 1852; and *New York Daily Times,* April 25, 1855.

79. Berrian to the Editors of the *New York Courier and Enquirer,* April 13, 1848, Berrian Papers, case 4, folio page 489, GTSL.

80. Fox-Genovese and Genovese, *The Mind of the Master Class,* 216; Peter Mandler, *The English National Character: The History of an Idea from Edmund Burke to Tony Blair* (New Haven, Conn.: Yale University Press, 2006), 86–100. For references to an

Anglo-Saxon "race," "family," or "stock," see *Albion: British, Colonial, and Foreign Weekly Gazette,* April 29, 1848, and April 27, 1850; *New York Weekly Herald,* April 28, 1849; *New York Daily Times,* April 25, 1855.

81. *Weekly New York Herald,* April 28, 1849; *New York Evening Post,* April 25, 1859; *New York Herald,* April 24, 1858.

82. *New York Times,* November 19, 1852. John Wolffe, *Great Deaths: Grieving, Religion, and Nationhood in Victorian and Edwardian Britain* (Oxford: Oxford University Press, 2000), suggests that while Wellington was cast as an "exemplar of Englishness," he was also presented as a symbol for a British national consciousness, the limits of which were unclear (51–53).

83. Wolffe, *Great Deaths,* 48. At page 68 Wolffe makes a brief and undeveloped comment on the inclusivity of the nation that came together to mourn the dead. For the imperial dimensions of Wellington's death, see Miles Taylor, "Wellington's World: The Duke of Wellington and the Making of the British Empire," Fifteenth Wellington Lecture, University of Southampton, 2003, 4–8.

84. *New Orleans Daily Picayune,* February 3, 1855; *New York Herald,* July 30, 1860.

85. Stewart J. Brown, "The Broad Church Movement, National Culture and the Established Churches of Great Britain, c. 1850–1900," in *Church and State in Old and New Worlds,* ed. Hilary Carey and John Gascoigne (Leiden: Brill, 2011), 99–130.

86. Hardwick, *An Anglican British World,* 214.

87. *New York Herald,* April 25, 1848; *New York Weekly Herald,* April 28, 1849.

88. Mandler, *The English National Character,* chap. 3. The slipperiness of the term "Anglo-Saxon" and the vagueness about who was included within it are attested to by the fact that during the Crimean War, a conflict in which Britain and France were on the same side, one society member could say that "Britons and Gauls are of the same blood" (*New York Daily Times,* April 25, 1854).

89. Matthew Grimley, "The Religion of Englishness: Puritanism, Providentialism, and 'National Character,'1918–1945," *Journal of British Studies* 46 (October 2007): 890.

90. "The Anglo-Saxon Race," *American Whig Review* 7 (January 1848): 30–31, 42–43.

91. [Rev. W. S. Darling], "The Anglo-Saxon Race on the Continent of America," *Church* [Cobourg, Ontario], April 10 and 24, 1851.

92. Mandler, *The English National Character,* 91.

93. Note that the president of New York's St. David's society raised a toast to "The Anglo-Saxon, the representative of the civilized races of the old and new World" in 1851 (*New York Weekly Herald,* May 3, 1851). This section draws upon Mandler, *The English National Character,* 86–100.

94. Printed circular from Bishop W. S. Perry of Iowa [1887], Benson Papers, vol. 48, folio page 150, Lambeth Palace Library, London; *New York Times,* June 28, 1897.

95. Belich, *Replenishing the Earth,* 479–82, uses the phrase to describe the processes by which British capital powered westward settlement in nineteenth-century America.

96. Bishop J. B. Kerfoot of Pittsburgh to Bishop Tait of London, May 21, 1869,Tait Papers, vol. 165, folio page 159, Lambeth Palace Library, London.

97. One clerical traveler said that he "got to be such a John Bull" that he struggled to convince polite society in Liverpool that he "was not either an Englishman or an Irishman" (Theodore B. Lyman to Whittingham, June 11, 1860, MDA).

98. Nockles, "The Oxford Movement and the United States."

99. Whittingham to the Archbishop of Canterbury, October 16, 1876, MDA.

100. Noted in Bishop Kerfoot to Whittingham, November 23, 1867, MDA.

101. Nockles, "The Oxford Movement and the United States."

102. R. King to Whittingham, November 16, 1846, MDA.

103. One might, then, take issue with Hilary Carey's decision to omit the United States from her recent study of the religious dimensions of the British world; see Hilary Carey, *God's Empire: Religion and Colonialism in the British World, c. 1801–1908* (Cambridge: Cambridge University Press, 2011).

104. Hardwick, *An Anglican British World,* chap. 4.

105. *New York Herald,* December 1, 1875. For a reference to modern celebrations, see "St. Andrew's Day in the USA," http://www.electricscotland.com/history/articles/atandrews.htm, accessed July 28, 2014.

106. For Indiana's English community, see the documents in William E. Van Vugt, ed., *British Immigration to the United States, 1776–1914,* vol. 1, *Building a Nation: 1776–1828* (London: Pickering & Chatto, 2009).

107. "Manuscript Diary of Mary Georgina Howson," entry for October 2, 1878, GTSL; Richard T. Kerfoot to Whittingham, August 9 and September 20, 1875, MDA.

108. A Methodist clergyman named Richard Wake helped build English settlements in Kansas beginning in the late 1860s; see William J. Chapman, *The Wakefield Colony: A Contribution to the Local History of Kansas* (Topeka: State Printing Office, 1908), 8–11, 17.

109. *New York Commercial Advertizer,* May 31, 1845; Robert Bunch to Ernest Hawkins (secretary of the SPG), May 6, 1861, SPG, D29, folio pages 2749–50, RHL.

110. Potter to Hawkins, May 16, 1861, SPG, D29, folio page 2772, RHL; *New York Albion,* March 20, 1869.

111. New Yorkers tried to use protectionist labor laws to block the appointment of an Englishman, the Reverend E. Walpole Warren, to Holy Trinity Church in the late 1880s (*New York Times,* April 24, 1888, and April 12, 1892).

112. See Grimley, "The Religion of Englishness," 892, for the idea that overseas Anglicans, as well as those in Ireland and Wales, sought to identify with the language and culture of their host community once disestablishment and separation from the mother church had taken place.

England and the
Antebellum South

L t. Col. Arthur Freemantle, a British army visitor to the Army of Northern Virginia in the summer of 1863, who was immortalized in his red uniform in the 1993 film *Gettysburg,* often noted in his journal the English connections Confederate officers boasted of among their ancestors. He thought that some, though born and raised in America, even spoke "English exactly like an English gentleman."[1] Virginians in particular seemed to be proud of their English ancestry, much to the chagrin of their more modest neighbors in North Carolina, one of whom complained of "our aristocrats of the Old Dominion, the hotbed of aristocracy of bloated pride."[2] Of course Virginia had been founded by Englishmen from the London Company who arrived in a place they named Jamestown for the king in 1607. The current monarch of the United Kingdom, Queen Elizabeth II, explicitly acknowledged as much by being sure to visit "historic Jamestown" at the 350th anniversary in 1947 and again at the 400th in 2007. In her 1957 speech on her official state visit to the United States as a reigning monarch, she remarked that "the great American nation was born at this place [Jamestown] 250 years ago. I cannot think of a more appropriate point for us to start our visit to the United States. The settlement in Jamestown was the beginning of a series of overseas settlements made throughout the world by British pioneers. Jamestown grew and became the United States. Those other settlements grew and became nations now united in our great commonwealth." She concluded that the founders of Jamestown were role models whose "faith and determination" made "us," Americans and British, proud of "our forefathers."[3]

These founders, though representing the first British king in James I, saw themselves as retaining the "rights and liberties" of Englishmen as expressly written into their 1606 charter.[4] Thus began the conflation of English with British that would dominate opinion in what would become the American South. Of course other colonies to the north of Virginia would represent English values in America too. The Pilgrims came to America in 1620 not just for religious freedom but also to preserve the English culture of their offspring. They had left the Netherlands, where their separation from the Church of England had not caused them any harm, for English and not Christian reasons. Their Puritan successors in Massachusetts Bay who would come almost ten years later were also English men and women. Yet both the Pilgrims and the Puritans saw themselves as creating something different from England, a new Jerusalem, a model of Christian charity and "a city upon a hill," as John Winthrop described it.[5] Virginia and the rest of the southern colonies apart from perhaps early Georgia would see themselves as extensions of England. Indeed, as Jack P. Greene has argued, rather than Massachusetts and the other New England colonies being the role models, the southern colonies were much more in the mainstream of the English and British colonial traditions than were those in the Northeast or those in the Middle Atlantic region—one of which, New York, had been originally founded by Dutch settlers, and the other, Pennsylvania, as a Quaker colony.[6]

This Englishness of the colonial era, then, was pronounced. The literary scholar Richard Gray has defined the raison d'être for Virginia to be "not merely helping to promote and extend a specifically English way of life" but also securing "its preservation, ensuring its survival." With its large amount of available land— to be taken from the natives of course—and the establishment of its church, laws, military organization, and eventually a replica of its political system through the revised charter of 1618, Virginia was to be more English than England itself. The English settlers of the seventeenth and early eighteenth centuries certainly saw it like that. The famous diarist William Byrd of Westover while exploring land to the west came to the fall line on the James River and named the spot Richmond because the bend in the river reminded him of Richmond-upon-Thames. Byrd had studied in England, and even after the foundation of the College of William and Mary in the 1690s, the best Virginia gentlemen often sent their sons to be educated at various English schools, universities, and the Inns of Court if one wished to study the law. They copied English cultural styles too, getting their representatives in London to purchase English books, journals, newspapers, clothes, and furniture. One contemporary historian of Virginia wrote, "The Habits, Life, customs, computations etc., of the Virginians are much the same as about London, which they esteem their home." Some longed to return to England with their newfound Virginia wealth to "breathe my native air" and "to enjoy the native soil."[7]

Carolina, especially the southern part around the settlement at Charles Town, too was Anglophilic. Complicating this love of all things English, however, was the large influx of settlers from the West Indies, who were English no doubt but influenced heavily by their sojourn in Barbados. In addition the large Huguenot influx, Calvinist refugees from France to Britain and Ireland and a bit later to North America complicated matters.[8] One South Carolina writer in 1859, William Henry Trescot, wrote that "Virginia was essentially an English settlement with old English prejudices, habits and institutions," but thanks to the Huguenots in South Carolina, there appeared a "combination" of English and

French, which "produced a third character, which differed widely from both its components, and developed a decided vigorous life of its own."[9] Yet these Huguenots had stopped speaking French and became Anglican and adapted quickly to the English laws and politics of South Carolina in order to, apart from their last names, become indistinguishable from their purely English neighbors.[10] However, one wonders how seamless this process was as the oldest St. George's Society was founded in Charles Town in 1733. If the place was so English, why was there a need to celebrate Englishness so separately and conspicuously? Charles Town was of course a cosmopolitan place with large numbers of other types of people, including Scots, Scots-Irish, Irish, and Germans, competing with the English and their descendants. There existed First (Scots) Presbyterian Church and Friendly Sons of St. Patrick with which to compete. Virginia lacked that urban center and so, despite an influx of Scots-Irish and German settlers to its backcountry in the 1700s, in the Tidewater areas the English ideal could be more purely preserved.[11]

Open Anglophilia, however, became unfashionable in the crises leading up to the American Revolution. Charles Town had a strong group of Sons of Liberty, who threatened anyone who was lukewarm to the Patriot cause. In Virginia, under the influence of another British tradition in America, that of the Scottish Common Sense enlightenment brought by Scottish and Scots-Irish teachers, men such as Thomas Jefferson and James Madison embraced a new independent world for America, rather than retaining the bond to the mother country. In the aftermath of the often bloody war for independence, particularly so in South Carolina, Charles Town became Charleston and its Anglican churches became Episcopal ones. Though Federalist in sympathy, Charles Town still had major protests against Jay's Treaty of 1794, which tied up some of the loose ends of the revolution not dealt with by the Treaty of Paris and which Thomas Jefferson had described as "a treaty of alliance between England and the Anglomen of this country." Of course in Virginia the Jeffersonian Republicans dominated to such an extent that they played a major role in driving George Washington out of politics and back to Mount Vernon.[12] The creation of the "Old Southwest" in Kentucky, Tennessee, Mississippi, and Alabama, settled primarily by Virginians and Carolinians, only exacerbated the Anglophobia. The area's great hero was Andrew Jackson, originally from South Carolina but the son of Scots-Irish immigrants, who was a despiser of England and the English.[13]

Yet despite a postcolonial desire to break away from the mother country's culture to define an American one in the South, southerners still looked back across the ocean to Europe for cultural inspiration. Even Jefferson continued to propagate the idea of the Anglo-Saxon tradition being the base of American and southern liberty. Britain had become corrupted under the Norman yoke when William the Conqueror came in 1066. In the South, even with its chattel slavery,

the belief in English liberty had been preserved.[14] The South's most famous antebellum writer, William Gilmore Simms, agreed. Born in Charleston, Simms, in
an oration titled "The Social Principle: The True Source of National Permanence"
delivered in 1843, claimed that English heritage accounted for the culture of
the South and indeed the United States. While in the Northeast of the United
States it was the Puritan variety of Englishness, in both Virginia and Carolina it
was the "cavalier" version. Simms was here echoing the growing popular idea
that the sections were in some ways different because different types of English
people had settled in each in the tumultuous period of the English civil war,
with the Royalist aristocratic supporters of King Charles I finding refuge in Virginia and the Roundhead supporters of Parliament dwelling in Massachusetts.[15]
Simms's ancestry on his mother's side had indeed come from Virginia, and so
he represented the "cavalier" myth in South Carolina. The one thing both types
of English Americans had, which made them different from the Spanish and
the French, was that they "came not for gold, for slaves or for conquest[;] the
English sought for nothing but a home."[16] Focusing on the South, Simms stated
that "the Cavaliers of Virginia and Carolina . . . despite being tainted with a
pernicious familiarity with the French and Italian customs of the sixteenth and
seventeenth century [sic] . . . never entirely surrendered the wholesome English
feeling, which in the word 'Home' finds another meaning for the word 'Comfort.'" These now American aristocrats "bore with them the household gods of
their ancestors—they set them up in the wilderness, and dignified the forests of
America with altars, in scrupulous imitation of those which they had left forever.
Their ambition," he concluded, "was to create a *New* England,—new homes
worthy of those they had abandoned, and in whose sweet similitude, the whole
aspect of their future world was drawn."[17]

Simms and modern-day scholars have agreed, then, that for many elite
Virginians and Carolinians, "the English ideal of the country gentleman seemed
the summum bonum ultimate importance."[18] As the decline of Virginia power
in the South as the focus of southern life shifted west to the cotton belt in the
nineteenth century, so too did a portion of Virginia's English, and the oldest
southern state "bequeathed to the rising planters of the cotton states much in
their style of living and even more in their own style of thinking."[19] The wider
South, then, retained a "style of thinking" still anchored in some ways in "old
England."

The South's Anglophilic tradition became strained, however, during the
Jacksonian era. Simms, for example, accepted that British politics had undermined many southerners' admiration for England if not English culture. In his
novel *Katherine Walton,* published in 1850, Simms described the politics of occupied Charleston and highlighted the oppressions of living there, including
preserving the tradition that his maternal grandfather Singleton could not resist

caricaturing Colonel Balfour, commander of the captured city, by costuming his pet baboon in the habiliments of that British officer. Balfour retaliated by including Singleton, though an old man, on the list of "treasonous prisoners" sent to St. Augustine.[20] Simms had described himself in 1839 by stating, "I am a Democrat of the Jackson school, a State rights man, opposed to Tariffs, Banks, Internal improvements, American systems, Fancy Rail Roads, Floats, Land Companies and every Humbug East or West, whether of cant or cunning. I believe in the people, and prefer trusting their impulses, than the craft, the cupidity, and the selfishness of trades and Whiggery."[21] But it was still "Anglo-Saxon instincts" that caused Americans in the South and the North to react strongly against King George III's trampling on their rights, particularly their right to be unmolested in their new homes because "the Englishman makes a castle wherever he plants a footstep" and thus the English influence was not "expelled from America." Instead George III's tyranny was driven out as "hostile to British liberty—and the expulsion of British arms from our soil was one of the noblest efforts of British freedom."[22] As the Anglo-Irish politician Edmund Burke had pointed out more than fifty years before, it was in defense of English liberty that the colonials had rebelled.[23]

Thus, Carolinians such as Simms could be American but also proud of their English heritage. Some took it to the extreme. According to the historian W. W. Freehling, "Carolinians thought themselves culturally special . . . because they outdid other Old South gentries in recreating [*sic*] Old English customs and politics." Thus, "they were allegedly truer English country gentlemen" than the "southwestern upstarts" in Alabama and Mississippi. Carolinians "loved English style racing. Fox-hunting was a favorite recreation. Race week in Charleston, like race week in London, was their supreme moment of sport." In another example, Freehling pointed out that in furniture making, "only Charleston craftsmen failed to make fully developed 'highboy[s],'" a type of chest of drawers, which were built on aspirational tall legs and which, in a republican sense, promoted "style without ostentation, power without heavy-handedness." "In America, only Charleston cabinetmakers turned out English styled 'tallboys,' the rich Englishmen's favourite chest[s]," which were "massive, heavy, imposing, meant to sink rectangularly, not soar curvaceously." These were the epitome of "aristocracy weightily commanding," Freehling concluded.[24] One English visitor to South Carolina in 1844 was impressed at those who considered themselves "*THE* [author's emphasis] *Gentlemen of America*," and "they were not without reason" for assuming this title. Their contempt for Jacksonian democracy and American politics in general reminded him of English conversations, so much so that if "a stranger dropped in amongst them from the clouds, [he] would hardly suppose himself among Americans."[25]

English visitors to the antebellum South did, in general, see it as a strange place, very unlike the England of the Victorian age. Charles Dickens, for example, in his 1842 tour of the United States, which produced two books on America, thought of going to Charleston and on to Columbia, South Carolina, but decided against it upon discovering the difficulty of traveling in the South and made it only as far as Washington and St. Louis. He was impressed with neither. Who knows what he might have thought of the deeper South, but others who did venture there before the Civil War were often particularly critical of the South for its "peculiar institution": slavery. The United Kingdom had ended slavery in its colonies in 1833, and many antebellum English visitors retained the belief that it was immoral. Visitors who wrote about America, such as Frances Trollope and especially Harriet Martineau, as well as residents such as the English actress Frances "Fanny" Kemble, wife of the planter Pierce Butler, were critical of slavery as well as its effects on the white populations.[26] These negative portrayals of the South emanating from England and the English were quite shocking to many southerners, including Simms. Simms wrote a harsh review of Martineau's *Society in America* in which he opined, "Truly the credulity of Miss Martineau on the subject of slave cruelty is perfectly English," by which he meant biased, exaggerated, and incorrect.[27] As a result, he said that "never was fanaticism more mad than on this subject of slavery, which was very good thing enough when 'England' and the 'North' sold slaves."[28] Simms was not alone is this view. The South became obsessed with the actions of British abolitionists, and many believed as Simms's fellow Carolinian Charles Drayton II did, that "the great slave question" had begun "in England" and as it crossed the Atlantic, "its whole evil will fall on the Southern Section."[29]

This seeming growing divide between England and the South over slavery was exacerbated by a potential clash over American annexation of Texas in the early 1840s, a pet project in particular of John C. Calhoun's. British abolitionists were angry when Calhoun in his brief sojourn as secretary of state raised the possibility of making the independent republic part of the United States. As a result, some prominent southerners began to denigrate England. James Henry Hammond of Aiken, South Carolina, a friend of Simms and part of what the historian Drew Faust has described as the "Sacred Circle" of antebellum southern intellectuals, had resurrected a moribund political career with his 1845 "Letters to Thomas Clarkson: The English Abolitionist," in which he defended southern slavery and condemned English justice. He charged that in England, "the poor and laboring classes of your own race and color, not just your fellow human beings, but your fellow citizens are more miserable and degraded, morally and physically, than our slaves; to be elevated to the actual condition of whom would be to these your fellow citizens a most glorious act of emancipation." He continued, "If a man steals a pig in England he is transported—torn from wife and family and sent to the Antipodes, infamous, and an outcast forever, though perhaps he took from the superabundance of his neighbor to save the lives of his famishing little ones. If one of our well-fed slaves steals, for the want of fresh meat, he perhaps gets 40 stripes."[30] Hammond came to despise the England of his age. After a visit there he stated, "I hate, I detest it. Everything is artificial in England—everything over wrought and over strained," and the English were "a people full of arrogance, humbuggery and frivolity."[31] John C. Calhoun, the emerging voice of the South and not just South Carolina, embraced his Irish background and declared to the Irish Emigrant Society that he was proud to be the son of an Irishman and agreed with a correspondent from Alabama in the middle of Ireland's potato famine that "the position of Ireland would be one of bliss compared to ours [within the Union]."[32]

From the early 1830s the South had begun to turn inward. While commentators such as Simms sought recognition abroad, including in England, many were content just to speak to each other and occasionally to their opponents in the North. The South would have to depend on itself and its own economic and intellectual prowess. The historian Michael O'Brien has shown in a study of the Charleston Library Society that its catalog from 1826 indicated it contained over 5,000 items purchased or donated since its founding. Of these, 4,737 had discernible places of publication: over 61 percent had been published in England, 26 percent in the United States, 6 percent in France, and 3 percent in Scotland. But when he examined the 1845 catalog of the 1,773 purchases since 1826, 78 percent were American and only 16 percent were English. Included in the American items were a number published in Charleston. The latter factor in particular he put down to the proliferation of political pamphlets being published in that city.[33]

This growing Anglophobia led to a rejection of even English origins. By the late 1850s some southern partisans were denying that their origins were Anglo-Saxon. There was a growing idea in some southern periodicals that southerners, though originating in England, were of Norman, that is French/Gallic, stock. Their ancestors had come to England and conquered it. They were a master race who had condemned the "boorish" Anglo-Saxons to villenage, that is slavery, and were just continuing this tradition in America, where the Yankee northeasterners preferred the drudgery of factories to the mastery of the plantation. William Falconer of Alabama wrote "The Differences of Race between the Northern and Southern People," which was published in the *Southern Literary Messenger* in 1860. In the article he stated that white southerners were Normans who were "warlike and fearless," the "race who have established law, order, and government over the earth." In contrast, northerners were "ancient Britons and Saxons" and the forebears of Puritans and "the present common people of England."[34]

This Gallic sympathy came full circle from Simms's description of the southern colonies as English to James Johnston Pettigrew's claim that the role model now for the South was not England but Spain. Pettigrew was a North Carolinian who had made his fortune in Charleston and would later become a prominent

Confederate general. In his book *Notes on Spain and the Spaniard,* published after secession in Charleston in 1861, he described "noble Romantic Spain," not England, as the preserver of civilization in the Middle Ages. Spain's combination of Gothic, Jewish, and Arab blood—all Caucasians according to Pettigrew—had produced a "fierce courage, valor, the sentiment of personal honor, the duel, the judgment of God and fidelity to his chief, poetry, grace, elegant horsemanship, skill in weapons, gallantry and mercy to the conquered." Ultimately this tradition created the concept of "chivalry," which "spread over Europe and from this came the seeds of civilization." The Spanish, according to Pettigrew, also had a strong commitment to the local, something long disdained in cosmopolitan England and northern cities such as New York. This love of home, which Simms had assigned to the English and which was key to "permanence," was now in Pettigrew's eyes Spanish. Thus he supported their claims on British-controlled Gibraltar and criticized the urge of "our [American] *soi-disant* cousins" to interfere constantly in others,' especially American, affairs.[35]

Pettigrew's claim linking Spanish culture to the South was pertinent because in 1861 eleven southern states had formed the Confederate States of America, which too was seeking permanence in the community of nations. The key element of that was foreign recognition and especially the recognition of the United Kingdom. Politicians such as James Henry Hammond believed that "King Cotton" would force Britain's hand. The new Confederate president, Jefferson Davis, focused on that issue as key to that recognition.[36] Economic pressure and not feelings of kinship would gain the Confederacy its rightful recognition. Robert Barnwell Rhett, proprietor of the *Charleston Mercury,* an advocate of secession from as early as the 1840s, and a man who worshipped his English ancestors—changing his name from Smith to Rhett in honor of his famous pirate-catcher ancestor from colonial Charleston—had no faith in the old mother country doing the right thing. In fact he had more faith in the poor Irish. His newspaper, under the editorship of his namesake son, editorialized that the greatest critics of the South in England were also the greatest condemners of the Irish. The *Mercury* explained this congruence: "The first and obvious [reason] is that the Irish, whether living in the North or the South, are, to a man, on the side of the constitution, and will always be found there, in peace or war." The editorial continued: "The spectacle of an Irish Abolitionist is a phenomenon not often beheld in this part of the world. The Irish have seen so much of real slavery in Ireland, that when an Englishman affects to sympathize with the woes of 'na-gurs,' Patrick, who knows by his own sad experience the hypocrisy and heartlessness of John Bull, only feels the most intense disgust and contempt." Contrary to English criticisms, the paper concluded, the Irish were not "indolent" but "industrious," and "their contributions to the labor of this country have given an irresistible impetus to all its great works of public improvement," implying that they would continue to do so for the new republic of South Carolina and any Confederacy it joined.[37]

In creating a cultural nationalism to back up this new nation-state's functioning government, judiciary, and military, however, Confederate writers looked to England for inspiration. They had to as their new nation had been formed in haste. The first great poem of the Confederacy, written by the Charlestonian Henry Timrod *"during the meeting of the first Southern Congress, at Montgomery February, 1861,"* as he put it, and titled "Ethnogenesis," proclaimed literally the birth of a new nation. Timrod began,

> Hath not the morning dawned with added light?
> And shall not evening call another star
> Out of the infinite regions of the night,
> To mark this day in Heaven? At last, we are
> A nation among nations; and the world
> Shall soon behold in many a distant port
> Another flag unfurled!

Acknowledging that the Confederacy would need more than the heavens to recognize this momentous event, he added, "Now, come what may, whose favor need we court?"/ The answer was, the whole world, which would come around because of "THE SNOW OF SOUTHERN SUMMERS! / Let the earth Rejoice! beneath those fleeces soft and warm Our happy land shall sleep"[38]

Cotton was king for sure for this Confederacy, and yet an examination of Confederate literature by Coleman Hutchison of the University of Texas described "Ethnogenesis" as an "ode which owes much to Tennyson and Coleridge." Douglas Southall Freeman, a biographer of Robert E. Lee, complained that in the Confederate search for originality as a new nation, "why did so many of them find no better way of expressing their poetic impulses than in palpable attempts to imitate Byron, Macaulay and lesser men?" Hutchison's response was that this copying of English tradition was natural because "cultural Euro and Anglophilia in fact helped to differentiate the new nation from its most relevant other. The United States might not deign to listen to the courtly muses of Europe, but the Confederate States was all ears."[39]

The English connection remained the most important because English was the language of the Confederacy and England's recognition both culturally and politically. Augusta Jane Evans of Mobile, who wrote the most popular Confederate novel of the Civil War, *Macaria: Or Altars of Sacrifice* (published in 1864), hoped that her and other Confederate works would spread "wherever the English language is spoken and read." She believed that Confederate works would have a particular resonance with the English elites because "next to the British aristocrat we know of no position in the world more desirable than that of the southern planter."[40] Paul Hamilton Hayne, another Charleston poet and a good friend of Henry Timrod, made allusions to Shakespeare in his poetry to give it credibility to foreign audiences. Indeed, Confederate writers emphasized the fact that their culture saw England as a model and would be one day as great. The Confederacy's effort to have its own literary but also popular periodical, akin to *Harper's* and *Frank Leslie's Illustrated News,* was the *Southern Illustrated News,* first published in September 1862 in Richmond. It was full of essays on Shakespeare, Milton, Shelley, Byron, and Tennyson with Burns, Walter Scott, and Thomas Moore thrown in from the Celtic fringe. Henry Hoetze, a Confederate agent in England working diligently to gain recognition for the new government in England, could safely claim, then, that Confederate literature was linked inextricably to English literature: "What is now written in the Confederate States, though necessarily hurried and imperfect, gives promise of a brilliant future, when the people of the Confederate States will have a literature worthy of the glory in arms *and of their descent.*" The greatness of the Confederacy, then, was its "glory in arms," that is its armed forces, and its "descent" from England.[41]

England was back in favor in the Confederate States of America. When Queen Victoria granted belligerent status to the Confederacy in May 1861 on behalf of her government, much to the chagrin of Abraham Lincoln and his secretary of state, William Henry Seward, this favorable view increased further. After the U.S. Navy seized the Confederate envoys James Mason and John Slidell on board the *RMS Trent* at the end of the year, which almost brought Britain and the United States to war, Confederate excitement about an alliance with "England" increased. Even the compromise of early 1862 that avoided conflict impressed them as the release of Mason and Slidell by the U.S. government brought "humiliation" to their enemies.[42] With this "humiliation" along with the fact that the Confederacy was allowed to purchase and refit blockade-running and blockade-breaking ships such as the *CSS Atlanta* or construct ships such as the *CSS Alabama* from and in British shipyards, many Confederates felt sure that Britain would recognize their new country and join the conflict on their side. Disillusionment set in quickly, however. Some began to lose patience with the former mother country. A correspondent to the *Memphis Daily Appeal* wrote;

> England! See our sacrifice
> See the Cotton blaze! God of nations! Now to thee, Southrons
>   bend th' imploring knee; 'Tis our country's hour of need
> Hear the multitudes intercede
> Hear the little children plead."[43]

For some, pleading turned to anger. In 1862 Maria Clopton of a planter family just east of Richmond, Virginia, facing the attacks of George McClellan's Union Army of the Potomac, wrote, "If I could control markets I would burn every blade of tobacco and every bale of cotton but what would be necessary for our own clothing, and England would feel in their own homes all the destruction and death they have caused us. England is a wicked nation but I suppose the cup of her wickedness is not yet run over and the Lord suffers here to go on producing misery wherever she thinks she can ensnare and control for her own aggrandizement, but she and the United States will yet mutually destroy each other for their unholy alliance against us."[44] England was becoming an enemy, not a potential friend. By 1863 the diplomatic situation had gotten worse, and President Davis apparently entered the new year "giving up on receiving help from the European powers," especially Britain.[45]

The literature became more pessimistic too. Along with odes to Shakespeare and Milton, there was criticism of British government policy. William Thompson wrote a piece especially for the *Southern Illustrated News* in August 1863 and titled it "England's Neutrality," conflating Britain with England. It began, "Who dream that England soon will drop her long miscalled neutrality / And give us, with hearty shake, the hand of nationality?" Thompson answered,

> Not yet, not yet to interfere does England see occasion
> But treats our Good commissioners with nothing but evasion
> Such coolness in the premises that really t'is refrigerant
> To think that two long years ago, she called us a belligerent.

Lord Palmerston, the prime minister, was partly to blame:

> But further Downing Street is dumb, the Premier deaf to reason
> As deaf as in the *Morning Post* both in and out of season
> The working men of Lancashire are all reduced to beggary
> And yet they will not listen unto [John Arthur] Roebuck or
>   [Lord William] Gregory.

Pro-Union men such as John Bright, the radical Liberal member of Parliament for Birmingham, were more evil: "'Why let em fight,' he exclaims, 'these Southerners, I hate em / And hope the black Republicans will soon exterminate em. / If freedom [Emancipation] can't rebellion crush, pray tell me what's the use of her' / and so he chuckles over the fray as gleefully as Lucifer." Thompson was stunned that England would not stand by her American cousins in the South: "Of course we claim the fame of glorious Stonewall Jackson [who had been killed the previous May] / Who typifies the English race, a sterling Anglo-Saxon." The poem ended pessimistically, seeing England ultimately desiring the destruction of the South. But defiantly Thompson concluded,

> And so we turn again to fight the Yankee bandit
> Convinced that we shall fairly win at last our nationality
> Without the help of Britain's arm
> *In spite of* her neutrality.[46]

This change in tone to one of bitterness had major implications for English immigrants in the Confederacy, especially those not in the armed forces. Queen Victoria's declaration of neutrality had included an express forbidding of any British subject to join any American army, but the Confederate authorities and many natives disliked this immensely. One British consul based in Mobile noted in 1863 that in the Confederacy, "the hatred publicly expressed against England makes it far from pleasant to be known here as a British subject and in some instances no language or threats seem sufficient to express the growing enmity." In Confederate eyes, English was British. In Charleston too there was increasing hostility toward the "English" government and its citizens. The consul there, H. P. Walker, who was a prominent member of the St. George's Society, noted that British subjects who were not in the armed services were being dismissed from their jobs and forced into the military. Those who refused to enter found themselves thrown into the city jail.[47]

The finale came in October 1863, when Confederate secretary of state Judah P. Benjamin, ironically himself a British subject due to his birth in the West Indies, ordered the "expulsion" of two British consuls in the Confederacy, one of whom was Walker, and withdrew recognition of the others. They would no longer have the recognized power of representing or defending the rights of British subjects in the Confederate States of America.[48] In an era when military service was closely linked to citizenship, or as the legal historian Christian Samito put it, one "became American under fire," the English would have been seen not as long-lost cousins but as shirking foreigners. Thus, Irish nationalists in the Confederacy such as John Mitchel, who despised the British government and the "British spirit of the age," though ironically was a product of it himself, could publish numerous anti-English articles in the Richmond newspapers. His rhetoric began to pay off when newspapers such as the *Charleston Mercury* began to propagate in opposition to emancipation the idea that only "the Yankee and the Englishman have imagined the negro to be equal to the Caucasian."[49]

This equating of England with the "Yankees" and emancipation was embraced in the North, especially by English immigrants there. The various St. George's Societies in New York, Philadelphia, and Cleveland celebrated the fact that the United States had declared emancipation just as England had done thirty years earlier. The Cleveland group felt in 1863 that England's example had finally been taken up by the United States. "Greater than the victories of Waterloo and Trafalgar," one speaker noted, "were those victories over selfishness and oppression, the emancipation of her slaves." He then linked the greatness of England to the growing greatness of America: "The highest and proudest boast that England could possibly make is that the shackles fall from the slave whenever he touches British soil." He reminded America, "Let a nation boast of its greatness and power, but let that greatness and power be tempered with liberty and justice."[50] Native abolitionists too recognized the link. Frederick Douglass admired England from his visits there and told Americans that he had had "to seek a refuge in monarchical England from the dangers of republican slavery." He became so enamored of England that, according to one scholar, he accepted the idea of Anglo-Saxon superiority leading the world out of the darkness of bondage and into the light of freedom. "She [England] is still the mother country and the mother too, of our abolition movement," he stated. Indeed, he continued, "England can take no step forward in the pathway of a higher civilization without drawing us in the same direction."[51]

Thus the estrangement between England and the antebellum South was complete as Britain seemed to reject what it stood for and what it was fighting for. Yet the cultural attachment never went away. It was the politics that had interfered. Nathaniel Hawthorne believed that in mid-nineteenth-century America there was "still an unspeakable yearning toward England"; here he was speaking of his native Northeast, but this could have equally applied to the South. He continued, "Even so late as these days [more than seventy years after the break], they [ancestral roots] remain entangled in our heartstrings, and might have often influenced our national cause like the tiller-ropes of a ship," but, and this is key, "the rough gripe of England had been capable of managing." In other words, if England's, that is Britain's, political relations with America had been better, then the connection, "like the tiller-ropes of a ship," would have been stronger. What then does this dual opinion of England in America mean for those interested in the story of England, the English, and the Confederacy? Ultimately it tells us of the ethnicity of the English in America. Being Anglo-American provided certain cultural advantages but also meant that one carried baggage similar to that of other immigrants, even in the American South. In the South, for an English immigrant, Anglo cultural heritage, Anglo-Saxon roots, and Protestantism—one historian has described the region as the "WASP nest"—did not necessarily guarantee easy integration into the host society.[52] The English immigrant too would have to become American and, after 1861, Confederate. Ultimately, even in the region often proudest of its English roots, the English immigrants were an ethnic minority. Many English in the region explicitly acknowledged this by joining their own English societies. This discussion of the ethnicity of the English in the South continues the process of revising the idea of the Old South as a white, Anglo-Saxon, Protestant nest, especially since some of those WASPs were also at times, it seems, "aliens."

NOTES

1. Arthur Lyon Freemantle, *Three Months in the Southern States, April—June 1863* (New York: John Bradburn, 1864), 140, 172; *Gettysburg*, dir. Ron Maxwell (Turner Pictures, 1993).

2. James Norcom, quoted in Elizabeth Fox-Genovese and Eugene D. Genovese, *The Mind of the Master Class: History and Faith in the Southern Slaveholder's Worldview* (Cambridge: Cambridge University Press, 2005), 116.

3. "Queen Elizabeth, Phillip, Welcomed in Virginia," transcribed from *Richmond Times Despatch,* October 6, 1957, http://www.lva.virginia.gov/queen/transcriptions .htm, accessed September 30, 2014.

4. "The First Charter of Virginia, April 10, 1606," http://avalon.law.yale.edu/ 17th_century/va01.asp, accessed August 1, 2015.

5. Francis J. Bremer, *John Winthrop: America's Forgotten Founding Father* (New York: Oxford University Press, 2003), 179–81.

6. Jack P. Greene, *Pursuits of Happiness: The Social Development of Early Modern British Colonies and the Formation of American Culture* (Chapel Hill: University of North Carolina Press, 1988), 165–66; David Hackett Fisher in *Albion's Seed: Four British Folkways in America* (New York: Oxford University Press, 1989), sees the roots of this difference and others in the regional cultures that British settlers brought with them to America. This view has been challenged. See, for example, David D. Hall, review of *Albion's Seed,* in *New England Quarterly* 63 (December 1990): 657–61.

7. Richard Gray, *Writing the South: Ideas of the American South* (Baton Rouge: Louisiana State University Press, 1997), 1, 5, 17, quotes on 1, 17.

8. Greene, *Pursuits of Happiness,* 141–51; R. C. Nash, "Huguenot Merchants and the Development of South Carolina's Slave-Plantation and Atlantic Trading Economy, 1660–1775," in *Memory and Identity: The Huguenots in France and the Atlantic Diaspora,* ed. Bertrand Van Ruymbeke and Randy J. Sparks (Columbia: University of South Carolina Press, 2003), 208–40.

9. Quoted in Michael O'Brien, *Conjectures of Order: An Intellectual History of the Old South,* 2 vols. (Chapel Hill: University of North Carolina Press, 2002), 1:291.

10. For a description of Huguenot assimilation, see Bertrand Van Ruymbeke, *From Babylon to New Eden: The Huguenots and Their Migration to Colonial South Carolina* (Columbia: University of South Carolina Press, 2006).

11. Charleston was the first city in what became the United States to have a St. George's Society, founded in 1733. See St. George's Society Collection, South Carolina Historical Society, Charleston, South Carolina.

12. Gordon S. Wood, *Empire of Liberty: A History of the Early Republic, 1789–1815* (New York: Oxford University Press, 2009), 197–99, 206, Jefferson quote on 198–99.

13. Quoted in Jon Meachem, *American Lion: Andrew Jackson in the White House* (New York: Random House, 2009), 11.

14. See, for example, Christopher Michael Curtis, *Jefferson's Freeholders and the Politics of Ownership in the Old Dominion* (New York: Cambridge University Press, 2012), 22–24, 52.

15. For more on this myth, see William Taylor, *Cavalier and Yankee: The Old South and American National Character* (New York: Oxford University Press, 1993).

16. William Gilmore Simms, *The Social Principle: The True Source of National Permanence* (Tuscaloosa: Erosophic Society of the University of Alabama, 1843), 8.

17. Ibid., 11.

18. Richard Beale Davis, *Intellectual Life in Jefferson's Virginia, 1790–1830* (Knoxville: University of Tennessee Press, 1972), 5–6.

19. Fox-Genovese and Genovese, *The Mind of the Master Class*, 115–16.

20. Mary C. Simms Oliphant, Alfred Taylor Odell, and T. C. Duncan Eaves, *The Letters of William Gilmore Simms*, 6 vols. (Columbia: University of South Carolina Press, 2012), 1:lix–lx.

21. Ibid., 1:167.

22. Simms, *The Social Principle*, 16–17.

23. Drew Maciag, *Edmund Burke in America: The Contested Career of the Father of Modern Conservatism* (Ithaca, N.Y.: Cornell University Press, 2013), 9–10.

24. W. W. Freehling, *The Road to Disunion: Secessionists at Bay, 1776–1854* (New York: Oxford University Press, 1991), 218–19, 229–30.

25. George William Featherstonhaugh, *Excursion through the Slave States*, 2 vols. (London: John Murray, 1844), 2:332–33, 340.

26. Frances Trollope, *Domestic Manners of the Americans* (London: Whitaker, Teacher, 1832); Harriet Martineau, *Society in America* (repr., New York: Cambridge University Press, 2009); Frances Anne Kemble, *Journal of a Residence on a Georgian Plantation in 1838–1839* (New York: Harper, 1864).

27. [William Gilmore Simms], *Slavery in America: Being a Brief Review of Miss Martineau on That Subject by a South Carolinian* (Richmond, Va.: Thomas W. White, 1838), 29.

28. Ibid., 72.

29. Quoted in Brian Schoen, *The Fragile Fabric of Union: Cotton, Federal Politics and the Origins of the Civil War* (Baltimore, Md.: Johns Hopkins University Press, 2009), 162. Schoen gave good coverage and analysis of this obsession; see esp. 161–73.

30. James Henry Hammond, *Gov. [James Henry] Hammond's Letters on Southern Slavery: Addressed to Thomas Clarkson, the English Abolitionist* (Charleston, S.C.: Walker and Burke, 1845), 14, 16; Drew Gilpin Faust, *A Sacred Circle: The Dilemma of the Intellectual in the Old South* (Philadelphia: University of Pennsylvania Press, 1986).

31. Quoted in O'Brien, *Conjectures of Order*, 1:109.

32. John C. Calhoun to "Secretary of the Irish Emigrant Society" [Gilbert C. Rice], September 13, 1841, in John C. Calhoun, *The Papers of John C. Calhoun*, 28 vols., ed. Clyde N. Wilson (Columbia: University of South Carolina Press, 1984); 15:774; John C. Calhoun to Chas. Jas. Faulkner, August 1, 1847, in ibid., 24:481; Joseph W. Lesesne to John C. Calhoun, September, 12, 1847, in ibid., 24:552–53.

33. O'Brien, *Conjectures of Order*, 1:495–97.

34. Quoted in ibid., 1:250–51.

35. Quoted in ibid., 2:1174–75; J[ames] J[ohnston] P[ettigrew], *Notes on Spain and the Spaniards in the Summer of 1859 with a Glance at Sardinia: By a Carolinian* (Charleston, S.C.: Evans and Cogswell, 1861), 426–27.

36. Brian Schoen has highlighted well how much cotton played in developing a sense of southern identity in *Fragile Fabric of Union*. See also Howard Jones, *Blue and Gray Diplomacy: A History of Confederate and Union Foreign Relations* (Chapel Hill: University of North Carolina Press, 2010), 13.

37. *Charleston (S.C.) Mercury*, November 9, 17, December 29, 1860, quotation in January 5, 1861. For information on Rhett and the call for secession in 1844, see William C. Davis, *Rhett: The Turbulent Life and Times of a Fire-Eater* (Columbia: University of South Carolina Press, 2001), 199–201. For non-Irish, see Stephanie McCurry, *Masters of Small Worlds: Yeoman Households, Gender Relations and the Political Culture of the Antebellum South Carolina Low Country* (New York: Oxford University Press, 1995), 277–304.

38. Quoted in Paul Hamilton Hayne, ed., *The Poems of Henry Timrod* (New York: E. J. Hale and Son, 1872), 100–101.

39. Coleman Hutchison, *Apples and Ashes: Literature, Nationalism and the Confederate States of America* (Athens: University of Georgia Press, 2012), 12.

40. Quoted in ibid., 73–75.

41. Quoted in ibid., 194.

42. *Charleston Mercury*, November 19, 29, December 31, 1861; January 9, 1862.

43. Quoted in Christopher Hanlon, *America's England: Antebellum Literature and Atlantic Sectionalism* (New York: Oxford University Press, 2013), 184.

44. Maria Clopton to Joyce, March 5, 1862, Clopton Family Papers, David M. Rubenstein Rare Book and Manuscript Library, Duke University, Durham, North Carolina.

45. Jones, *Blue and Gray Diplomacy*, 293.

46. *Richmond Southern Illustrated News*, August 8, 1863. I am grateful to Coleman Hutchison for this reference.

47. Frederick Cridland, quoted in Eugene H. Berwanger, *The British Foreign Service and the American Civil War* (Lexington: University Press of Kentucky, 1994), 111.

48. Ibid., 114–20.

49. Christian G. Samito, *Becoming American under Fire: Irish Americans, African Americans and the Politics of Citizenship in the Civil War Era* (Ithaca, N.Y.: Cornell University Press, 2009); *Daily Richmond Examiner*, January 15, August 13, 1864; *Charleston Mercury*, January 15, April 5, 1864.

50. *Daily Cleveland Herald*, April 24, 1863.

51. Quoted in Eliza Tamarkin, *Anglophilia: Deference, Devotion, and Antebellum America* (Chicago: University of Chicago Press, 2008), 194, 241.

52. Dennis C. Rousey, "Aliens in the WASP's Nest: Ethnocultural Diversity in the Antebellum Urban South," *Journal of American History* 79 (June 1992): 152–64.

"Time and circumstance work great changes in public sentiment"

Royal Statues and Monuments in the United States of America, 1770–2010

A t a banquet to celebrate Queen Victoria's birthday held at London's Hotel Cecil on May 25, 1899, the guest of honor, former British prime minister Lord Rosebery, described the "many members of the American Society in London" in attendance, including the U.S. consul general, as "representing a great commonwealth of states once part of the British empire, but [now] nearer than any country except the colonies." In response to this declaration of transatlantic friendship, an American, one Colonel Taylor, responded on behalf of the society by paying tribute to the queen and reading out a cablegram that he had recently received from Tampa, Florida, where a number of Royal Navy men-of-war were then visiting: "The Floridians salute you, assembled here in thousands, with the invited British warships uniting with us in celebrating Queen Victoria's birthday. Let Americans honor the British queen by erecting a statue of her majesty in the United States paid for by Americans. Will the London Americans inaugurate the movement? Their brothers on this side will do the rest." The London gathering responded with a "storm of cheers" and in turn sent a message to Tampa stating that "Americans now at the banquet with their English brothers . . . cordially endorse the proposed honor to her majesty."[1]

The late 1890s were the high point of transatlantic Anglo-Saxonism, an ideology that "helped shape the anglophilia of important policy makers" in America while "undermining the anglophobia" of others.[2] However, away from the bonhomie of the Hotel Cecil, some American commentators looked rather more coolly on the proposal from Florida. Indeed, while the *Washington Post* conceded that "time and circumstance had worked great changes in public sentiment," it nonetheless recalled that the "last British monarch who adorned a public place in this country was so little esteemed by Americans that his counterfeit was considered useful only as material for casting bullets to be shot at his scarlet-coated minions." This reflection on the fate of colonial New York's equestrian statue of George III—unveiled in 1770 only to be ritually destroyed six years later by soldiers of George Washington's Continental army—prompted the newspaper to conclude that "while the reconciliation of the branches of the English-speaking race gives cause for sincere congratulation," this rapprochement ought, nonetheless, to "be symbolized in a more appropriate manner than that proposed by the jolly banqueters at Tampa."[3]

The lukewarm response of the diners at the Hotel Cecil helped to dampen enthusiasm for the project in 1899, but the idea put forward by the Floridians was not so far-fetched. After all, on the same day as it had been made, President William McKinley had sent Queen Victoria a message of congratulation on her eightieth birthday, while in Albany, Gov. Theodore Roosevelt had unveiled a painting of the queen at the New York state capitol building, at which "two marines, English and American, standing on either side of the portrait, [had] clasped each other's hands" to symbolize Anglo-American amity.[4] Indeed the idea of erecting a statue of Queen Victoria in the United States in 1899 was by no means the first and was far from the last such proposal.

Yet, as this essay demonstrates, the cold water poured on the proposal by the *Washington Post* was indicative of a consistent strand of American opinion that could celebrate improved Anglo-American relations, and even appreciate the benefits of transatlantic cultural diplomacy, while at the same time seeing little benefit in the erection of statues to English queens and kings on American soil. That so many statues of and monuments to English crowned heads of one kind or another were nevertheless erected in the United States of America in the half-century or so after 1899 is the central phenomenon explored here.[5]

The earliest recorded monumental tribute to a European crowned head to be erected in North America was not New York's statue of George III but instead a bust of France's Louis XIV in Quebec City almost a century earlier. In 1686 the attendant of New France, Jean Bochart de Champigny, had arranged for a bronze bust of the king to be erected in the newly named Place Royale.[6] Quebec's royal square was rather modest when compared to some of the *place royales* of France, where the term had come to mean "a particular type of public space created to glorify the reigning monarch," in which "a statue of the king [was situated] amid buildings of uniform and ennobling design."[7] Even if New York's statue of George III was not the first monument to a European crowned head on the continent, it was the first in what was shortly to become the United States, and it was arguably the most impressive.

Scholars have been rather more interested in the destruction of New York's royal monument than its erection, but the story of how it came about is nonetheless a fascinating one. This emphasis reflects the fact that the statue has often been presented by scholars as having been merely "an after-thought."[8] Originally, it seems, it was William Pitt, the "Champion of the American cause in Parliament and his efforts for the repeal of the Stamp Act" in 1766, whom "the Colonists desired mostly to honor."[9] It was only some months after the original proposal for a statue of Pitt had been made that the assembly of the colony of New York contemplated the idea of erecting a statue of George III, prompted apparently by the fact that it was deemed "imprudent and inopportune to erect a statue of the king's minister . . . in a city where there was as yet no publicly standing monument to the king himself."[10] As a consequence, the assembly resolved in June 1766 that "this House will make Provision for an Equestrian Statue of His Present Majesty . . . to be erected in the City of New York, to perpetuate to the latest posterity, the deep Sense this Colony has, of the eminent and singular Blessings derived from him, during His most auspicious Reign."[11]

In fact concern about royal sensitivities was arguably only one of several reasons behind the assembly's decision to erect a royal statue. After all, although royal emblems and symbols were "very numerous in all the Colonies anterior to the American Revolution," royal statues were not a feature of this colonial landscape before 1770.[12] Excepting prints, cheap portraits, coins, and glassware—which formed part of what the historian Brendan McConville has termed "the royalization of the household" in the American colonies—the only other figurative likenesses of any of the Georgian kings known to have existed in America before the Revolutionary War were wax figurines of the kind then also circulating in Britain.[13] That this was the case was probably a matter of American aesthetic preferences, the dearth of local talent, and the realities of transatlantic logistics, although it almost certainly also reflected prevailing tastes in Britain. While statues of George I and II were erected at various locations in the British Isles during the respective reigns of the first two Hanoverian kings, these were not commissioned by the House of Hanover.[14] Indeed both George I and George II had something of an "aversion" to erecting statues of themselves, a reflection of the fact that for much of the eighteenth century the Crown "made little consistent endeavour to foster a popular cult of the monarchy."[15] As a result royal statues were invariably commissioned in Britain and Ireland only by "a corporation, institution or great magnate" with the financial means to do so.[16] As such, they must be seen not only as assertions of royal power but also as expressions of civic pride, personal allegiance, and corporate loyalty.[17]

It is in this context that the commission for an equestrian statue, awarded by the assembly of New York to the English sculptor Joseph Wilton, should be understood. George III's accession marked the beginning of "a process of royal resurgence in the second half of the eighteenth century," and New York's equestrian statue can be understood as part of this revival.[18] Wilton had been appointed sculptor in ordinary to George III in 1761 and over the next decade received a number of commissions for royal monuments from distinguished individuals and institutions: a statue of George III for the Corporation of London in 1764; a bust of George III for Montreal in 1766; a statue of George II for Cambridge University in 1766; and an equestrian statue of George III for London's Berkeley Square in 1772.[19] In commissioning Wilton, then, the representatives of New York were making a public statement about the status and ambition of the colony within the broader context of the first British Empire.

This expression of New York's civic pride was clearly manifested in the nature of the statue, its location, and the ceremonial surrounding its erection. The statue was expensive and of a conventional type: the king was depicted as a Roman emperor on horseback, rendered in gilded lead, one-third larger than life, and mounted on a pedestal eighteen feet high.[20] Just as the statue was the product of neoclassical metropolitan artistic preferences, so too—when it finally arrived in New York on June 4, 1770—the siting of the statue reflected sensitivity to Georgian tastes. That the city's Bowling Green had been the location of the Stamp Act Riot in 1765 may well have been a consideration, freighted as that site was with colonial meaning, but arguably as important was the fact that the setting most closely conformed to European notions about the appropriate location for royal statuary. Not only was Bowling Green "the most prominent open space in the city," but it was also located in front of Fort George, surrounded by "several churches and other Elegant buildings," and situated at the top of the city's principal street.[21] In addition its unveiling on August 16, 1770, was framed very much in terms that would have been immediately recognized by a British audience: members of the council and assembly, senior officers, magistrates, clergymen, and leading residents attended the acting governor at the fort, where loyal toasts were drunk and a 32-gun salute fired before the assembly processed to and around the statue.[22] Employing language customary for such an occasion, the lieutenant governor of New York afterward reported to the secretary of state for the colonies that "the Spectators expressed their Joy" and demonstrated their "great cheerfulness and good humor" on the occasion.[23]

Once erected, New York's royal statue became, as in Britain and Ireland, the focus of ritualized demonstrations of loyalty. However, as the erection of a fence around the statue in 1771 suggests, it also became the target, as was the case in various locations in eighteenth-century Europe, of acts of iconoclasm.[24] Such attacks prefigured the ultimate act of desecration only six years after the statue had been unveiled, when it was ritually destroyed. The immediate context of this "king killing ritual" was the reading of the Declaration of Independence by George Washington to his troops on July 9, 1776, and the anticipated arrival of British forces in New York Harbor.[25] That evening soldiers of Washington's Continental army along with local citizens clambered over the fence and used ropes to topple the statue, whereupon its assailants sought to decapitate the king's head, in the course of which George III's face was badly disfigured.[26] The ritualized destruction of the statue was not yet complete. As one contemporary reported, "The

Lead, we hear, is to be run up into Musquet [*sic*] balls for the use of the Yankies, when it is hoped that the Emanations of the Leaden George will make . . . deep impressions in the Bodies of some of his red Coated & Torie Subjects."[27] Indeed 42,088 bullets were reportedly produced from the melted-down monument.

The destruction of New York's statue of George III formed part of the wider "orgy of iconoclastic violence" that gradually spread across colonial America between 1774 and 1776.[28] Although other communities engaged in acts of "symbolic regicide," the ritualized destruction of handmade effigies of America's last king—such as in Huntingdon, Long Island, and in Baltimore—ultimately underscored the fact that New York's equestrian royal statue was, as a material object, unique.[29] As a consequence the New York episode came to be seen as an important moment in America's revolutionary "foundation myth," immortalized in many popular prints and "numerous national histories" in the decades that followed.[30] Indeed its power as an enduring cultural reference is evident in the fact that the *Washington Post* invoked the events of 1776 in 1899 when the "jolly banqueters at Tampa" proposed a statue of George III's granddaughter, Queen Victoria.

In April 1839 the *New York Morning Herald* reported in effusive terms on the recent exhibition of a "sublime work" of statuary depicting the "perfect representation of a beautiful American female, young, animated, and full of life and sensibility —with every soft limb and swelling lineament half developed through the gossamer but classic drapery floating around her." The figure depicted by the artist James V. Stout, who was described by the press as "a youthful American— a native of New York—a republican," was not, however, simply an idealized vision of American womanhood, as the press implied. Rather, Stout's statue was indicative of what Mary Loeffelholz has identified as the "American . . . use . . . of queens . . . to define antebellum American womanhood," since the subject was none other than the "pretty, graceful, modest, and benevolent looking young Queen of old England."[31] Indeed other press commentators expressed their admiration for the beauty of the statue, with special attention paid to praise for the statue's striking likeness to the sovereign, as confirmed by the Countess of Westmoreland, then sojourning in New York.[32]

The praise lavished on Stout's statue of Victoria, especially with regard to the "fetishism of the queen's person," was characteristic of the interest in and enthusiasm for Victoria's coronation manifested the previous year by many New Yorkers. Indeed, New York, where Victoria's grandfather's statue had been toppled only sixty-two years earlier, was described at the time as having gone "queen mad."[33] Such "Victoria fever" and "Queen mania" did not, however, prevent the plaster-of-paris statue of the queen from suffering the same fate as had the monument to her grandfather, although rather than the result of a deliberate act of iconoclasm, as in 1776, the destruction of the queen's statue came about by accident while it was being transported to Boston for exhibition.[34]

Although the early decades of Victoria's reign were "not good years for Anglo-American relations," with ongoing territorial disputes and continuing American anxiety about British overseas ambitions, many citizens of the new republic were nonetheless curious about Britain's queen.[35] If her longevity meant that by the latter part of her reign American parlors were "just as likely" to feature color lithographs of Victoria as they were depictions of American presidents, "advancing technology, the greater availability of manufactured goods, and widening prosperity on both sides of the Atlantic" meant that even in the more difficult years of the midcentury, examples of Victoriana still reached American shores.[36] In 1838 full-sized paintings of the new queen had successfully toured a number of East Coast cities, while prints of Victoria had also sold well.[37] In particular, technical and commercial developments in ceramic production—which had resulted in America becoming the "most important trading destination for English pottery"—meant that the figurative representations of Victoria that came to "grace . . . mantles [sic] from Dublin to Durban" as the century progressed were also imported into the United States.[38] Thus in 1838 one visitor to Philadelphia reported seeing a "bust of Her Majesty" on a local mantelpiece.[39] In the following decades there were reports of small parian, a type of bisque porcelain, busts of her in locations as far afield as New Orleans and Illinois and of manufacturers, for example the New England Glass Company, producing items for the American market such as paperweights bearing Victoria's image.[40]

However, while "emergent discourses of racial 'Anglo-Saxonism'" in midcentury tied the prehistory of the United States to England's ancient past, Victoria found "no necessary place in the chain of vigorous Anglo-Saxon masculinity" that characterized American understandings of its distant political history.[41] As such, the "cult of Queen Victoria" was slow to take hold in the United States. Although dolls of Prince Albert, the future King Edward VII, were available to purchase in New York on the occasion of his visit to America in 1860, the bronze bust of his mother obtained by his hosts in Boston was only for the purposes of making him feel comfortable, placed as it was in his private apartments.[42] Had Victoria visited America during her lifetime, it is quite possible that a statue of her might well have been erected, as was the case in various parts of Britain and Ireland after she made official visits there.[43]

That she did not visit the United States meant that the first definite proposal to erect a permanent statue to a British monarch since the Revolutionary War occurred in 1886, when "80 natives or descendants of natives of Great Britain and Ireland"—including representatives of the Canadian Club, St. George's Society, the British Benevolent Society, the Sons of St. George, and St. Andrew's Society—gathered in mid-November in New York to organize celebrations to mark Victoria's golden jubilee. A resolution was reportedly adopted at the meeting in favor of a "permanent memorial" to Victoria, to take the form of a statue at Fort Wadsworth, Staten Island. That the memorial was to be "at least 100 feet higher than Bartholdi's" statue suggests that a certain amount of Anglo-French rivalry colored these efforts; it indicates that New York's British population was partly motivated by irritation over the unveiling of France's monumental gift to America: the Statue of Liberty on Bedloe's, renamed Liberty, Island earlier the same year.[44] However, within a fortnight there were signs that the committee appointed at the inaugural meeting regarded the proposal as both "impracticable and impolitic," not least because of "the [local] hostility which such a move . . . would create."[45] Whether the opposition to the jubilee mounted by Irish Americans, such as in Boston, played a part is unknown, but the proposal for a 250-foot statue of Victoria overlooking New York Bay was quietly shelved, with attention focusing by January 1887 on more modest plans for a parade.[46]

Notwithstanding the embarrassment caused by the zeal of some of New York's British residents in 1886–87, the idea of a permanent memorial to Victoria on American soil did not go away. Indeed, Anglo-American rapprochement from the 1890s on seems to have breathed new life into the idea. In addition to the 1899 Tampa proposal, the most sustained pressure for such a monument came in the decade or so after the queen's death. Within a matter of days of Victoria's passing on January 22, 1901, what the press termed "representative British-Americans"—although in fact most of them were Englishmen—in Chicago announced plans for a "permanent Victorian memorial" in the city, to take the form of a "statue, arch, or an endowment."[47] The committee appointed for this purpose was apparently divided between those who favored donating a number of hospital beds, as had apparently been done in 1897 to mark the queen's diamond jubilee in Chicago, and those who "believe[d] a monument to the Queen would be more fitting and a more lasting testimonial to her goodness."[48] By early February it was clear that the former section had won the debate, to the benefit of Chicago's St. Luke's hospital, with the minority promising that a "separate organization" would nonetheless be "formed later" to advance the erection of a statue, although this never transpired.[49]

In contrast to the proposals for a statue of Victoria on American soil that emanated from émigré Britons resident within the United States between the 1880s and the 1900s, the schemes advanced thereafter were more clearly part of a process of Anglo-American cultural diplomacy, which reflected the sea change in transatlantic relations after 1897. Indicative of this improved relationship was the proposal made by the committed Anglo-Saxonist and noted Anglophile Joseph Choate, American ambassador to Britain (1899–1905), at an Independence Day banquet hosted by the American Society in London in July 1903. Choate declared that "all the talk of Anglo-American unity ought to be more than talk"; to this end he proposed that a statue of George Washington be erected in London and a statue of Queen Victoria be erected in the American capital, owing to the fact that "at a critical moment she absolutely saved us from conflict with Europe'"[50]

This was a reference to what has been described as the "canonical moment for [Victoria's] . . . reputation in the United States," the so-called "Trent affair," an international incident that had involved the removal of two Confederate diplomats from a British ship by the Union navy in late 1861. Victoria and a dying Prince Albert were widely credited with modifying the British government's initially hostile response and thereby averting a potential conflict. In referring to the affair, Choate was far from unusual among American commentators, although he was the only one to use the event as the pretext for the erection of a monument to Victoria.[51]

Whereas a committee of the Pilgrims Society, the English-American association established the previous year to promote transatlantic goodwill, met the same month and quickly secured a site for Washington's statue in St. Paul's Cathedral, Choate's proposal for a statue of the queen in the American capital met with little enthusiasm. While one American commentator judged that the idea would probably find favor with "American women," reflecting Victoria's transatlantic reputation as a "role model for women of her race and nation," others downplayed the whole scheme as deliberately "facetious" and "semi-humorous." This may have reflected the fact that Canadian feathers seem to have been ruffled by the idea of a statue of Washington in London.[52] Yet others, while regarding the case for such a statue in London as "undeniable," felt that a statue of "Queen Vic" did "not so strongly commend itself"; after all, at least one observer asked if the royal family might not object to the proposal, in light of the fate of the last monarchical statue in America, that of 1770.[53]

Evidently even after her death many Americans found it difficult to see Victoria as a meaningful symbol of the recent Anglo-American rapprochement; they certainly seem not—in contrast to Choate—to have valued her role as a peacemaker between Washington and London during the Civil War sufficiently to regard the erection of a permanent monument as a priority.[54] Nonetheless the desire to give the growing ties between the two countries some form of monumental expression continued to animate some diplomats and politicians on both sides of the Atlantic. Indeed a number of the same elements circulating in 1903 resurfaced a decade later as part of the Anglo-American movement to celebrate the century of peace since the Treaty of Ghent in 1814, which had brought the Anglo-American War of 1812 to a close. Although he had retired as ambassador to London in 1905, Choate was one of the honorary chairmen of the American National Committee for the Celebration of the One Hundredth Anniversary of Peace among English-Speaking Peoples, set up in 1911.[55] As in America, the semiofficial committees established in Canada and Britain in the months that followed were animated by a shared commitment to Anglo-Saxonism and the merits of arbitration in the interests of international peace. Various commemorative activities were originally planned: monuments of different kinds; a memorial bridge on the Niagara frontier between America and Canada; and ceremonies in Britain, America, Canada, and Belgium.[56]

As a result of the various national committees meeting together in New York in May 1913, it was provisionally agreed that, among other things, the Washington family's former English home in Northamptonshire, Sulgrave Manor, would be purchased and renovated. Subsequently, at the behest of the Sub-Executive Committee of the International Peace Celebration Committee, of which Choate was a member, it was decided that a statue of President Abraham Lincoln would be erected in London and that, in turn, a statue of Queen Victoria would go up in Washington, D.C.[57] As in 1903, it was suggested that American women would take a particular interest in Victoria's statue, and indeed Mrs. John Miller Horton, a resident of Buffalo and a senior figure in the Daughters of the American Revolution, took the lead, declaring that "a statue to the good Queen Victoria would prove an effective means of arousing the patriotic interest of the women of the United States."[58] Horton subsequently reported that the women's "patriotic societies" she had consulted on the matter had been "strongly in favor of such a memorial," and so she formed part of a delegation that lobbied Congress in December 1913 to provide sufficient financial support for the American celebrations as a whole—the cost for the Victoria statue being estimated at five hundred thousand dollars.[59]

By no means all Americans were so enthusiastic about the idea, however. Although former president Theodore Roosevelt was chairman of the American committee, he described the international body overseeing the centenary as "preposterous" and regarded as ridiculous the proposal to erect a statue of Victoria in New York's Central Park, since it would furnish "a steady occupation for the police force in protecting it from celtic [sic] enthusiasts whose life ambition it would be to blow it up."[60] By the following year it was clear that American enthusiasm for the statue more generally was waning, with the congressional appropriation bill still not passed and the sum sought having been reduced to just twenty-five thousand dollars.[61] In February 1914 Horton reported that the memorial to Victoria might "not take the form of a statue" but instead would be some other kind of "lasting memorial" that might be erected in Buffalo rather than Washington, D.C. or New York.[62] Even this, however, was optimistic, since with the outbreak of World War I in August 1914, the planned celebrations were mothballed.

Although participation in World War I helped to "sober" some of the more unrealistic expectations surrounding Anglo-American cultural diplomacy before 1914, elements of it nonetheless survived the conflict.[63] While the proposal for a statue of Victoria was dropped—Choate's death in 1917 being perhaps significant in this regard—several of the presidential statues proposed for London before the war were eventually completed: Lincoln's statue was erected in 1921; and even the abortive 1903 proposal to erect a statue of Washington was finally realized in 1924.[64] In the years since, this monumental traffic has by no means been all one-way: busts and statues of numerous distinguished British political, artistic, and legal figures—including at least one woman—have been erected in various parts of the United States of America.[65] Yet Britain's longest-serving queen at the time remains unmemorialized in America.[66]

Notwithstanding the rapprochement in Anglo-American relations in the decade after 1897, declarations of transatlantic Anglo-Saxon affinity were by themselves never enough to galvanize support for the erection of a statue of Queen Victoria on American soil, despite the fact that toward the end of her reign she came to be seen by some in the United States as the "'race mother' of Anglo-Saxondom."[67] Nevertheless, if Americans could not see their way to putting up a statue to Victoria, they proved more willing during the five decades following the end of her reign to erect monuments of various types to other, earlier English crowned heads.

Perhaps the first instance of this came in the year that Queen Victoria died. Before her death she had expressed approval for efforts to mark the one-thousandth anniversary of the death of King Alfred, the centerpiece of which was to be a statue of the Saxon king in Winchester. Drawing on the long-established English "cult" of Alfred, the town of Winchester's millenary celebrations in 1901 presented him as the originator of public education, national defense, imperial endeavor, and constitutional government in the English-speaking world.[68] Indeed the latter item was the dominant motif in the celebration's discourse, with Alfred represented "as the first chapter in a national narrative of gradual constitutional progress . . . [which claimed] that he had instituted the earliest British parliament, to become the country's first limited monarch."[69]

Given that a sense of shared Anglo-Saxon heritage was a prominent component of the rapprochement in Anglo-American relations that characterized the early years of the twentieth century, it is not surprising that Americans played a prominent part in the 1901 celebrations.[70] Indeed the organizers of the millenary were especially keen to attract the support of the western branch of the "English-speaking race." To this end, the letter sent by the mayor of Winchester, Alfred Bowker, to the American press appealing for donations toward the erection of a statue of Alfred deliberately presented the Anglo-Saxon king as the "Great Forerunner of Washington."[71]

In some quarters this approach was met with a degree of suspicion. At least one American newspaper wondered whether the compliment might "not . . . merely be a bit of sweetmeat to win financial approval," given that it had been reported earlier that the organizers were short of funds. After all, it reasoned, "the English have never been known to love [George Washington]."[72] In fact throughout the War of Independence, British commentators had consistently portrayed Washington as a "gentlemanly citizen soldier," and this image continued into the nineteenth century, with Victorian Britons—including the noted Anglo-Saxon scholar E. A. Freeman—drawing favorable comparisons between America's first president and King Alfred.[73] Nor was Mayor Bowker alone among the sponsors of the 1901 celebrations in making the comparison. Distinguished British Anglo-Saxonists such as James Bryce, the future ambassador to America (1907–13), and the author Arthur Conan Doyle went out of their way to emphasize the similarities between the two men.[74] Likewise on his anniversary lecture tour of America in 1901, the British jurist and historian Frederic Harrison also compared Alfred and Washington.[75] Such sympathy helps to explain why Edwardian British Anglo-Saxonists were so ready to welcome the erection of a statue of Washington in London.

That Americans accepted the British comparison of Alfred with Washington in 1901, notwithstanding reservations in some quarters, reflected less their susceptibility to flattery and more their particular understanding of Anglo-Saxon history. Amid the wooly, if enthusiastic, rhetoric of Anglo-Saxondom, the anniversary's organizers seem not to have been aware of "America's native cult of Alfred."[76] The facts that American commemorative activity in 1901 centered on the Episcopalian (Anglican) St. Paul's chapel in New York, where, as president, Washington had worshipped, and that American commentators made glowing comparisons between "the great Alfred and the great Washington" reflected more than millenary hyperbole. After all, Americans celebrated Alfred as more than just "England's hero king"; they also had a strong sense of Alfred as part of America's unique constitutional story.[77]

The stance of the American popular historian John Fiske, who was invited to give a public lecture during the Winchester millenary but died shortly before the event, is suggestive in this respect. In various publications during the 1890s, Fiske argued that the Norman conquest had "transformed the Old-English thanehood [the collective term for the free retainers of Anglo-Saxon lords] into the finest middle-class of rural gentry and yeomanry that has ever existed in any country" and that this was "a point of especial interest to Americans" because "it was this stratum of society [from which the] . . . most powerful streams of English migration to America . . . ha[d] their source."[78] This, in turn, was significant because it reflected elements of the Jeffersonian tradition that "Americans were the most distinguished descendants of the Anglo-Saxons" and that it was only through the revolution of the late eighteenth century that ancient "English" rights, liberties, and free institutions that had been lost with the conquest and the resulting "Norman Yoke" had ultimately been restored.[79]

In contrast to Fiske's interpretation of Anglo-Saxon progress in America, the Winchester millenary celebrations were informed by arguments advanced by English Whig historians, such as William Stubbs and E. A. Freeman, whose research since the 1870s had worked toward what Clare Simmons has termed the "reversal of the Conquest."[80] In contrast to older notions of the "Norman Yoke" that continued to inform some American perspectives, Stubbs in particular argued that after 1066 Anglo-Saxon protodemocracy and local government had gradually been fused with the Norman genius for centralized administration and strong kingship; Alfredianists such as Lord Rosebery, who unveiled Winchester's statue of the king in 1901, were thereby able to argue that through the Norman Conquest "iron [had] enter[ed] the English soul—not to slay, but to strengthen, to introduce, indeed, the last element wanted to compose the Imperial race."[81] This stance also found scholarly and popular adherents in America in the final decades of the century, before it was overtaken by the ideas advanced by a new generation of professional scholars such as George Burton Adams and Charles Homer Haskins in America and John Horace Round in England, who argued from the 1890s on that "the Normans were far more important than the Anglo-Saxons in forging the institutional foundations of Anglo-American law and government."[82]

Notwithstanding this new orthodoxy, the older Whiggish view of Alfred and the Anglo-Saxons continued to have some purchase on both sides of the Atlantic.[83] One reflection of this is the fact that in 1900 a statue of Alfred, symbolizing Anglo-Saxon law, was unveiled on the grounds of the New York State Supreme Court building on the corner of East 25th Street and Madison Avenue—alongside statues of other ancient lawgivers whose reforms had contributed to forging the American legal system. A decade later another statue of Alfred, this time as a symbol of the English common law, was commissioned for the exterior of the new Cuyahoga County Courthouse in Cleveland, Ohio—once again accompanied by representations of other notable figures in Western constitutional history.

Alongside Alfred's contribution to English law, his religious legacy too was celebrated in the years before 1914. In 1907 the bishop of London, Arthur Winnington-Ingram, representing the archbishop of Canterbury at the stone-laying ceremony for the new National Cathedral in Washington, D.C., celebrated the British and American shared tradition of religious liberty by presenting the "Canterbury ambon," or pulpit, to the dean and chapter.[84] In this example of religio-cultural diplomacy, Alfred featured among the carvings on the pulpit in recognition of his translation of the Psalms into Anglo-Saxon in A.D. 871. In this case, however, Alfred was not the main focus of the sculpture, since the central bas relief depicted Stephen Langton, archbishop of Canterbury (c. 1150–1228), acting in concert with the barons to secure the grant of the Magna Carta from

King John in 1215. While the gift of the ambon, with its representations of other key church figures such as Bede, Tyndal, and Wycliffe, was meant to signify both the ancient heritage of Anglicanism and the extension of this tradition to America—the tercentenary of whose church fell in 1907—its emphasis on 1215 can be viewed as indicative of the increasing prominence given to the Norman Conquest in America as the century progressed. It was during these years that, along with the Normanization of historical studies on both sides of the Atlantic, the foundation of the International Magna Charta Day Association in Minnesota in 1907 and the seven-hundredth anniversary celebrations of the granting of the Magna Carta in 1915 took place.[85]

While statues and sculptures of Anglo-Saxon kings did not disappear, representations of Anglo-Norman monarchs became more numerous in "the architecture of government" in the first half of the twentieth century.[86] Thus, while the south facade of the Nebraska State Capitol, built between 1922 and 1934, featured among its depictions of the Western legal tradition King Ethelbert of Kent, symbolizing the codification of Anglo-Saxon law in c. A.D. 600, it also featured a relief carving of King John conceding the Magna Carta. Moreover, among the eight canonical scenes in the evolution of Western law rendered in relief on the massive bronze doors of the Supreme Court building in Washington, D.C. in 1935 was one—described recently by a scholar as "balletic, a graceful pas de deux"—that depicted King John being forced to concede the Magna Carta.[87] Within the courtroom the friezes of the "Great Lawgivers of History" that decorate the walls include a stone figure "clothed in chain-mail armor and clutching a copy of Magna Carta," which is customarily described as King John, although it seems more likely that it is one of the barons.[88] The statue symbolizing the achievement of 1215 at the Los Angeles Superior Court building, opened in 1956, is certainly a depiction of a thirteenth-century knight. That no such figurative representations of kings or knights are featured on the American Bar Association's stone memorial erected in 1957 at Runnymede suggests that such tropes were already passing out of fashion by that time.

While King John features as an antihero in the various figurative representations of the Magna Carta created in mid-twentieth-century America, Edward I, his grandson, was portrayed much more positively in several American public settings. A marble statue of Edward features among the various historic lawgivers mounted on top of the Cuyahoga County Courthouse in Cleveland, Ohio, alongside statues of Archbishop Stephen Langton signifying the Magna Carta and Simon de Montfort signifying the development of English law. As in Ohio, Edward I's depiction on the bronze doors of the U.S. Supreme Court and the relief portrait of him installed above the gallery doors of the House Chamber in the U.S. Capitol (1949–50) reflect the significance attached to his enactment of the Statute of Westminster in 1275.

The prominence given to various Anglo-Saxon and Anglo-Norman kings in the ornamentation of so many American public buildings erected in the years between c. 1900 and 1960 reflected the construction of a teleology of constitutional progress as American lawyers, historians, and politicians sought ideologically to buttress their system in "an age of dictators" and the cold war that followed.[89] The only exception to this succession of medieval English kings is James I, who —like King John—appears on the doors of the Supreme Court as a tyrant, juxtaposed against Edward Coke, the seventeenth-century "advocate, judge, councilor, and parliamentarian" who resisted "arbitrary Stuart government" in favor of "mixed monarchy" in the 1620s, invoking the ancient constitution and the Magna Carta in support of his cause.[90]

This is not to say that statues and sculptures of other English—and indeed British—kings and queens do not exist in America. Indeed, although the enthusiasm of American politicians and lawyers for the Norman Conquest abated somewhat several decades ago, royal statues have continued to find a home in the United States. They tend, however, to sit outside the constitutional narrative articulated through the decoration of postwar America's "halls of justice and 'temples of sovereignty.'"[91] The University of Notre Dame's statue of King Edward the Confessor is, for example, one of a number of statues of the saint-king—not only in Indiana but also Massachusetts and Florida—associated with religious and educational institutions. Statues of another saintly king, Charles I, feature in Episcopalian churches in Maryland and Pennsylvania associated with the American branch of the Anglo-Catholic Society of King Charles the Martyr. Although less well known than the statue of Norborne Berkeley, colonial governor of Virginia between 1768 and 1770, statues of William III and Queen Mary have adorned the college in Virginia that bears their name since the 1920s.[92] Elsewhere statues of another queen have been erected: the city of Charlotte in North Carolina possesses two late twentieth-century statues of its namesake, Queen Charlotte, the last queen of America and Queen Victoria's grandmother.[93]

Some statues hark back to the early twentieth-century tradition of cultural diplomacy. One such example is the first public royal statue to be erected in America since 1770, which was unveiled in Jamestown, Virginia, in May 1962. Like the statue of King George erected in New York 192 years earlier, the statue of Queen Elizabeth I (1962) unveiled in Virginia had been made in Britain; and also like the 1770 monument, the fortunes of the 1962 statue reveal something about how Americans at the time saw themselves in relation to "England."

Whereas New York's royal statue was an expression of the city's civic pride and imperial ambition, the one in Virginia was positioned very much in terms of America's colonial heritage. On Elizabeth II's first overseas trip as queen in 1957, she and Prince Philip had visited the Jamestown Festival Park to commemorate the 350th anniversary of the first permanent English settlement in America.

The 1957 commemoration was framed in terms of the "expansion overseas of the English speaking peoples," with the Public Record Office at Kew lending the festival its 1297 copy of the Magna Carta, thereby "affirm[ing] the two nations' common heritage of religion, justice, government, learning, and liberty," as one contemporary commentator put it.[94] Although Jamestown already possessed a number of monuments to historical figures associated with the early history of the colony, such as John Smith, Pocahontas, and Sir Walter Raleigh, there seems to have been no suggestion that the queen's visit should be the occasion for the unveiling of any new statuary. Indeed when a new royal statue was added five years later, it was in rather different circumstances.

In fairness, the atmosphere surrounding the erection in 1962 of a statue of the English "Virgin queen" certainly echoed elements of the proceedings of five years earlier. The statue was made in England by a sculptor recommended by the British government and was based on what was thought to be one of only two representations of Elizabeth I produced in her lifetime—the original standing in London's Fleet Street.[95] It was erected at the entrance of the park, the so-called "Court of Welcome," where Elizabeth II had delivered her first public address on American soil in 1957.[96] Although her presence was not expected in 1962, the organizers hoped that she might send her official "Greetings" on the day of the ceremony, at which time it was also anticipated that the British ambassador to the United States would be in attendance.[97]

All that said, the occasion for the unveiling of the statue was nonetheless a rather different affair from Elizabeth II's visit in 1957, since the statue was actually the centerpiece of a "Tobacco Pageant" held at colonial Jamestown and sponsored by the Tobacco Institute of America to celebrate 350 years since the first export shipment of Virginian tobacco to England.[98] Thus, rather than the rhetoric of Anglo-American amity of 1957, the emphasis of the three-day festival was firmly on "The Beginning of US Commerce and Industry, 1612–1962." Perhaps because of this, the hoped-for message of goodwill from Elizabeth II was not forthcoming, and it was the British commercial attaché, not the ambassador, who attended.[99] The organizers also sent invitations to President John F. Kennedy and his wife, but these too were declined.

The erection of the "first [statue] in the Old Dominion honoring the Queen" in 1962 did not ultimately capture the imagination of the American public or the governing elite on either side of the Atlantic; the postwar Anglo-American "special relationship" was not then articulated through royal statuary of queens or kings, living or dead. For mid-twentieth-century Americans, particularly those who went to the cinema, Elizabeth I, like her royal successor Queen Victoria, certainly meant something, but she seems to have embodied neither the spirit of "constant enterprise and vision" of the early colonists—and by implication their descendants—nor the human-interest story of the "first contact" between natives and settlers that occurred at Jamestown.[100] For these things, the statues of Raleigh, Smith, and Pocahontas served much more effectively.

Indeed, despite the claim that a statue of Elizabeth I had "been much wanted by the Jamestown Foundation for some time," its subsequent fortunes in Virginia are more suggestive of ambivalence than amity or goodwill.[101] Several decades after its erection, the statue was removed from its original site, and only in 2006 did it reappear, albeit much transformed. In a fascinating shift from its original commemorative purpose, the bronze figure was "retrofitted" by being covered in a reversible plastic to mimic the stone of the London statue in Fleet Street; it was then mounted in a niche above a reconstruction of a late sixteenth-century London street scene that featured in the new museum built for the four-hundredth anniversary of the Jamestown settlement in 2007. Queen Elizabeth II may well have seen it that year when she visited Jamestown for the second time during her reign.

The fortunes of the Jamestown statue can be usefully contrasted with those of the only other modern public sculpture of an English monarch to be erected in America. This statue of Elizabeth I is located near the site of an unsuccessful Elizabethan colony in the 1580s on Roanoke Island, off the coast of North Carolina. Today the island features Fort Raleigh National Historic Site, in which the "Elizabethan Gardens" are located. Like Jamestown, the gardens can once again clearly be seen in terms of mid-century efforts to reinforce the "special relationship," since they were the suggestion of Sir Evelyn Wrench and his wife. Wrench was the founder of the English-Speaking Union, an educational organization created in 1918 to promote closer ties between English-speaking peoples around the world. He suggested the idea of a garden attached to the heritage site as a means of commemorating the Elizabethan colony.[102] Work commenced on June 2, 1953, the date of Queen Elizabeth II's coronation, and the gardens were formally opened in 1960. In the years since then, the current British royal family has developed a relationship with the gardens, as it has with Jamestown; Princess Anne visited Roanoke in 1984.[103] As was the statue in Jamestown, the bronze statue of Elizabeth I at Roanoke Island was a later addition, with the latter being the gift of a private individual in 2006 in honor of his wife. Unlike Jamestown's statue of Elizabeth I, Roanoke's, which depicts the queen picking roses, is arguably more successful, if only because it seems not to have been freighted with more than ornamental and decorative significance. It is the gardens, not the monuments that ornament them, that symbolize the linkage between America and Britain.

Whereas New York's statue of George III was famously destroyed in 1776, the statue originally commissioned as its companion, a monument to the memory of William Pitt the Elder, experienced a rather different fate. Rendered in marble and depicting Pitt as a Roman senator carrying a scroll with the inscription "Articuli Magna Charta," it was unveiled with much less ceremonial fanfare than was the king's statue on September 7, 1770. Indeed its more humble location, on Wall Street, further underlined its more modest status in the eyes of New York's colonial governors. Nonetheless the statue was reportedly unveiled "amidst the Acclamations of a great Number of Inhabitants." Although it apparently suffered some damage in the early 1770s, it was—in what may have been a response to the events of July 1776—British soldiers who decapitated Pitt's statue after Crown forces occupied New York in September 1776. Otherwise, like the statue of Pitt erected in Charleston, South Carolina, in 1770, it might well have survived to the modern day—notwithstanding Pitt's ultimate opposition to American independence.[104] New York's headless statue survived the Revolutionary War and remained in situ until it was taken down and put in storage in 1788. It remained hidden until it surfaced in the 1860s as one of the exhibits in a "museum hotel," after which it was purchased and donated to the New York Historical Society in 1864.[105]

The contrasting fortunes of New York's statues of George III and William Pitt highlight the more general point this essay has sought to make: that from 1770 on Americans have consistently struggled to accept the idea that statues of English and British kings and queens could symbolize Anglo-American fraternity in an authentic or meaningful way. The statues of Anglo-Saxon and Anglo-Norman kings erected on or near public buildings in the first half of the twentieth century were acceptable precisely because they were intended not to embody transatlantic amity but rather to signify America's manifest destiny. Successive British governments and indeed the British monarchy seem to have long since grasped this reality. As a result, while North America's landscape above the 49th parallel is likely to continue to feature monuments to kings and queens, the monumental tradition begun in 1770 in what was shortly to become the United States of America is likely now concluded.

NOTES

The author would like to thank Michael Patrick Cullinane of Northumbria University for his valuable comments on an earlier draft of this chapter.

1. "Rampant Anglomania," *Irish World and American Industrial Liberator*, June 3, 1899, p. 1.

2. Edward P. Kohn, *The Kindred People: Canadian-American Relations and the Anglo-Saxon Idea, 1895–1903* (Montreal: McGill-Queen's University Press, 2005), 164.

3. "A Changed Public Sentiment," *Washington Post*, June 4, 1899, 6.

4. "Britons at Tampa," *Los Angeles Herald*, May 25, 1899, 2.

5. This essay does not consider statues of British monarchs in Canada.

6. Richard L. Cleary, *The Place Royale and Urban Design in the Ancien Regime* (Cambridge: Cambridge University Press, 1999), 245–46.

7. Ibid., 4. On the fortunes of Quebec's Place Royale, see Richard Handler, *Nationalism and the Politics of Culture in Quebec* (Madison: University of Wisconsin Press, 1988), 140–58.

8. Alexander J. Wall, *The Equestrian Statue of George III*. (New York: New York Historical Society, 1920), 37; Arthur S. Marks, "The Statue of King George III in New York and the Iconology of Regicide," *American Art Journal* 13 (Summer 1981): 61; Holger Hoock, *Empire of the Imagination: Politics, War, and the Arts in the British World, 1750–1850* (London: Profile Books, 2010), 49.

9. Wall, *The Equestrian Statue of George III*, 42.

10. Marks, "The Statue of King George III," 61.

11. Wall, *The Equestrian Statue of George III*, 0.

12. Brendan McConville, *The King's Three Faces: The Rise and Fall of Royal America, 1688–1776* (Chapel Hill: University of North Carolina Press, 2006), 128–31; Edmund G. Slafter, "Royal Memorials and Emblems in Use in the Colonies before the Revolution," *Proceedings of the Massachusetts Historical Society* 2, no. 4 (1887–89): 252.

13. McConville, *The King's Three Faces*, 127–28, 136; Marks, "The Statue of King George III," 61; Hannah Smith, *Georgian Monarchy: Politics and Culture, 1714–1760* (Cambridge: Cambridge University Press, 2006), 142; Wayne Craven, *Sculpture in America* (New York: Cornwall Books, 1968), 26. There is an uncorroborated report of statues of George III and Queen Charlotte being seen in New York in 1781 in the King's Head Tavern on the visit of Prince William. See Elisa Tamarkin, *Anglophilia: Deference, Devotion, and Antebellum America* (Chicago: University of Chicago Press, 2007), 123. Wax figurines of the royal family continued to be displayed in New York into the 1790s. See Craven, *Sculpture in America*, 29.

14. Joan Coutu, *Persuasion and Propaganda: Monuments and the Eighteenth-Century British Empire* (Montreal: McGill-Queen's University Press, 2006), 367n21.

15. Smith, *Georgian Monarchy*, 79; Linda Colley, *Britons: Forging the Nation, 1707–1837* (New Haven, Conn., and London: Yale University Press, 1992), 201.

16. Smith, *Georgian Monarchy*, 140.

17. Charlotte Chastel-Rousseaum, "Introduction," in *Reading the Royal Monument in Eighteenth-Century Europe,* ed. Charlotte Chastel-Rousseaum (Farnham: Ashgate, 2011), 4.

18. Colley, *Britons*, 207.

19. Joan Coutu, "Wilton, Joseph (1722–1803)," *Oxford Dictionary of National Biography,* Oxford University Press, 2004, online ed., January 2008, http://www.oxford dnb.com/view/article/29706, accessed April 6, 2014.

20. Marks, "The Statue of King George III," 61.

21. Hoock, *Empire of the Imagination,* 49; Coutu, *Persuasion and Propaganda,* 223; Wall, *The Equestrian Statue of George III,* 49.

22. For example, see Philip McEvansoneya, "Royal Monuments and Civil Ritual in Eighteenth-Century Dublin," in *Reading the Royal Monument in Eighteenth-Century Europe,* ed. Charlotte Chastel-Rousseaum (Cambridge: Cambridge University Press, 2011), 181.

23. Wall, *The Equestrian Statue of George III,* 46.

24. Ibid., 47; Chastel-Rousseaum, "Introduction," 7.

25. David Waldstreicher, "Rites of Rebellion, Rites of Assent: Celebrations, Print Culture, and the Origins of American Nationalism," *Journal of American History* 82, no. 1 (June 1995): 47; McConville, *The King's Three Faces,* 309.

26. Hoock, *Empire of the Imagination,* 51.

27. Wall, *The Equestrian Statue of George III,* 50.

28. McConville, *The King's Three Faces,* 306.

29. Hoock, *Empire of the Imagination,* 52–53.

30. Frank Prochaska, *The Eagle and the Crown: Americans and the British Monarchy* (New Haven, Conn.: Yale University Press, 2008), 4; Marks, "The Statue of King George III," 74, 78.

31. "Stout's Statue of Queen," *New York Morning Herald,* April 20, 1839, 2; Mary Loeffelholz, "Crossing the Atlantic with Victoria: American Receptions, 1837–1901," in *Remaking Queen Victoria,* ed. Margaret Homans and Adrienne Munich (Cambridge: Cambridge University Press, 1997), 38.

32. "Statue of Victoria," *New York Mirror,* April 13, 1839, 335; "The Countess of Westmoreland," New York Morning Herald, July 19, 1839, 2.

33. Tamarkin, *Anglophilia,* 30.

34. Prochaska, *The Eagle and the Crown,* 48; *Boston Courier,* August 1, 1839.

35. Tamarkin, *Anglophilia,* 58.

36. Margaret Homans and Adrienne Munich, "Introduction," in *Remaking Queen Victoria,* ed. Margaret Homans and Adrienne Munich (Cambridge: Cambridge University Press, 1997), 3; Prochaska, *The Eagle and the Crown,* 44.

37. Tamarkin, *Anglophilia,* 58.

38. Homans and Munich, "Introduction," 3.

39. "The Victoria Fever," *United States Magazine and Democratic Review,* 6 (July 1839), 76.

40. Eliza Ripley, *Social Life in Old New Orleans* (New York: D. Appleton, 1912), 103; Betsy B. Kitch, *Pike to Durham: An American Farmer's Journal* (Bloomington, Ind.: Authorhouse, 2010), xiv; Prochaska, *The Eagle and the Crown,* plate 6.

41. Loeffelholz, "Crossing the Atlantic with Victoria," 37–38.

42. Prochaska, *The Eagle and the Crown,* 69; *New York Times,* October 20, 1860.

43. Hazel Conway and David Lambert, "Buildings and Monuments," in *The Regeneration of Public Parks,* ed. Jan Woudstra and Ken Fieldhouse (London: Palgrave Macmillan, 2000), 53.

44. "Queen Victoria's Jubilee," *New York Times,* November 14, 1886, 7.

45. "Victoria's Anniversary," *New York Times,* December 2, 1886, 8.

46. Loeffelholz, "Crossing the Atlantic with Victoria," 48; "The Queen's Jubilee in New York," *New York Times,* January 22, 1887, 8.

47. "To Perpetuate Queen's Memory," *Chicago Daily Tribune,* January 25, 1901, 2.

48. "Service for Queen," *Chicago Daily Tribune,* January 26, 1901, 3; "Services in Chicago, " *New York Times,* February 25, 1901, 2.

49. "Meeting Today at Auditorium," *Chicago Daily Tribune,* February 3, 1901, 4.

50. "Americans Abroad Celebrate the Fourth," *New York Times,* July 5, 1903., 4.

51. Loeffelholz, "Crossing the Atlantic with Victoria," 33–36.

52. "Art Notes," *New York Times,* July 9, 1903, 5; "Topics of the Times, August 29, 1903, 6; Alison Booth, "Illustrious Company: Victoria among Other Women in Anglo-American Role Model Anthologies," in *Remaking Queen Victoria,* ed. Margaret Homans and Adrienne Munich (Cambridge: Cambridge University Press, 1997), 61.

53. "For Mutual Admiration," *Minneapolis Journal,* July 17, 1903, 4.

54. Ibid.

55. T. G. Otte, "'The Shrine of Sulgrave': The Preservation of the Washington Ancestral Home as an 'English Mount Vernon' and Transatlantic Relations," in *Towards World Heritage: International Origins of the Preservation Movement, 1870–1930,* ed. Melanie Hall (Farnham: Ashgate, 2011), 114.

56. Ibid., 115; "A Hundred Years of Peace," *New York Tribune,* May 5, 1913, 6.

57. "Statue of Victoria for Washington," *New York Times,* May 24, 1913, 13.

58. "Asks Shaft to Queen," *Washington Post,* February 3, 1914, 4.

59. Ibid.; "Ask Congress to Aid Peace Celebration," *New York Times,* December 6, 1913, 13.

60. "Theodore Roosevelt to Arthur Hamilton Lee," July 7, 1913, in Etting E. Morison, ed., *The Day of Armageddon, 1909–1914: The Letters of Theodore Roosevelt* (Cambridge, Mass.: Harvard University Press, 1954), 738–39.

61. Otte, "The Shrine of Sulgrave," 132.

62. "Asks Shaft to Queen," *Washington Post,* February 3, 1914, 4.

63. Richard A. Cosgrove, *Our Lady the Common Law: An Anglo-American Legal Community, 1870–1930* (New York: New York University Press, 1987), 75.

64. "Lincoln's Statue for London," *London Times,* September 24, 1917, 7; "Washington Statue for London," February 12, 1921, 9. For a more detailed discussion of Anglo-American cultural diplomacy after World War I, see Michael Patrick Cullinane, "London's Curious Public Memorials to Abe and George in the Tense 1920s," paper presented at British Association of American Studies, University of Central Lancashire, Preston, U.K., April 14–17, 2011.

65. The list includes but is probably not limited to statues of Charles Dickens in Philadelphia (1891); Edmund Burke in Washington, D.C. (1922); Sir William Blackstone in Washington, D.C. (1943); Winston Churchill in Washington, D.C. (1966) and in Fulton, Missouri (1969); William Shakespeare in New York (1864), Chicago (1888), Washington, D.C. (1896), and Montgomery, Alabama (1986); Sir Walter Raleigh in Raleigh, North Carolina (1976); and Margaret Thatcher in Michigan (2008).

66. See "Burke Statue for Washington," London *Times,* February 11, 1922, 9; "Statues for America," March 28, 1922, 15; "Lord Chief Justice to Visit U.S.," August 27, 19548; "Churchill's Statue Unveiled in U.S.," April 11, 1966, 7.

67. Stuart Anderson, *Race and Rapprochement: Anglo-Saxonism and Anglo-American Relations, 1895–1904* (Rutherford, N.J.: Fairleigh Dickinson University Press, 1981); Loeffelholz, "Crossing the Atlantic with Victoria," 49.

68. Joanne M. Parker, "The Day of a Thousand Years: Winchester's 1901 Commemoration of Alfred the Great," in *Studies in Medievalism: Film and Fiction; Reviewing the Middle Ages,* ed. Tom Shippey (Cambridge: Cambridge University Press, 2003), xii, 113.

69. Joanne Parker, *"England's Darling": The Victorian Cult of Alfred the Great* (Manchester: Manchester University Press, 2007), 117.

70. Ibid., 154.

71. "For Alfred the Great," *Washington Post,* July 28, 1901, 22.

72. Ibid.

73. Troy O. Bickham, "Sympathizing with Sedition? George Washington, the British Press, and British Attitudes during the American War of Independence," *William and Mary Quarterly* 59, no. 1 (January 2002): 102, 122; Robert Huish, *The History of the Life and Reign of William IV* (London: W. Emans, 1837), 107; Edward Augustus Freeman, *The History of the Norman Conquest of England,* 6 vols. (Oxford: Oxford University Press, 1867–79), 2:162.

74. Parker, *"England's Darling,"* 155.

75. Frederic Harrison, *George Washington and Other American Addresses* (New York: Macmillan, 1901), 3, 4, 26.

76. Ibid., 157.

77. Ibid., 157–58; Edwin D. Mead, "The King Alfred Millenial," *Proceedings of the American Antiquarian Society* 15 (April 1902): 88.

78. John Fiske, *The Beginnings of New England, or the Puritan Theocracy in Its Relations to Civil and Religious Liberty* (Boston and New York: Houghton, Mifflin, 1900), 30.

79. Reginald Horsman, *Race and Manifest Destiny: The Origins of American Racial Anglo-Saxonism* (Cambridge, Mass.: Harvard University Press, 1981), 18–23, 81.

80. Clare A. Simmons, Reversing the Conquest: History and Myth in Nineteenth-Century British Literature (New Brunswick, NJ, 1990). 191.

81. Marjorie Chibnall, *The Debate on the Norman Conquest* (Manchester: Manchester University Press, 1999), 37, 42, 47; Anthony Brundage and Richard A. Cosgrove, *The Great Tradition: Constitutional History and National Identity in Britain and the United States, 1870–1960* (Stanford, Calif.: Stanford University Press, 2007), chaps. 2, 3.

82. Brundage and Cosgrove, *The Great Tradition,* 52, 73, 86, 143, 152; James K. Hosmer, *A Short History of Anglo-Saxon Freedom* (New York: Scribner, 1890); Chibnall, *The Debate on the Norman Conquest,* 61–62.

83. Brundage and Cosgrove, *The Great Tradition,* 137.

84. "Foundation Stone Laid," *Shreveport Caucasian,* October 1, 1907, 2.

85. Brundage and Cosgrove, *The Great Tradition,* 86; Stephen Bowman, Sylvia Ellis, and Donald M. MacRaild, "Interdependence Day and the Magna Charta: James Hamilton's Public Diplomacy in the Anglo-World, 1907–1940s," *Journal of Transatlantic Studies* 12, no. 2 (2014): 126–48.

86. Peter Linebaugh, *The Magna Carta Manifesto: Liberties and Commons for All* (Berkeley: University of California Press, 2008), 208. Also see 193–98 for a discussion of Magna Carta murals.

87. Ibid., 205.

88. For the King John attribution, see ibid., 206; Sandra Day O'Connor, *The Majesty of the Law: Reflections of a Supreme Court Judge* (New York: Random House, 2004), 33.

89. Linebaugh, *The Magna Carta Manifesto,* 206, 211.

90. Allan D. Boyer, *Shaping the Common Law: From Glanville to Hale, 1188–1688* (Stanford, Calif.: Stanford University Press, 2008), 27–28.

91. Linebaugh, *The Magna Carta Manifesto*, 208.

92. Chris Dickon, *The College of William and Mary* (Mount Pleasant, S.C.: Arcadia, 2007), 21.

93. *"Sculptor's Ideas Define Freestyle,"* Pittsburgh Post-Gazette, January 28, 1989; *"Queen Charlotte Departs from Airport Terminal,"* Charlotte Business Journal, January 25, 2011.

94. "Virginia's Tribute to First British Settlers," *London Times,* March 29, April 2, 1957, 8; *Rotarian,* October 1957, 36. > *Times,* March 29, April 2, 1957; *Rotarian,* October 1957, 36.

95. "Queen's Statue Leaves for U.S.," *Washington Post,* April 12, 1962.

96. Press release, March 4, 1962, Papers of the Tobacco Institute of America (hereafter PTIA), Legacy Tobacco Documents Library (hereafter LTDL), http://legacy.library .ucsf.edu/tid/bjy56b00/pdf, accessed June 2, 2014; Draft Memorandum, October 25, 1961, PTIA, LTDL, http://legacy.library.ucsf.edu/tid/ozjo9b00/pdf, accessed June 2, 2014.

97. Tentative Schedule of Events for Williamsburg Meeting, May 16–19, March 6, 1962, PTIA, LTDL, http://legacy.library.ucsf.edu/tid/wvr18b00/pdf, accessed June 2, 2014.

98. "Virginia Marks Tobacco Anniversary", *New York Times,* May 6, 1962, 412.

99. Press release, May 15, 1962, PTIA, LTDL, http://legacy.library.ucsf.edu/tid/pgh7 6a00/pdf, accessed June 2, 2014.

100. Press release, March 4, 1962, PTIA, LTDL. For a discussion of Elizabeth and Hollywood, see Elizabeth A. Ford and Deborah C. Mitchell, *Royal Portraits in Hollywood: Filming the Lives of Queens* (Lexington: University Press of Kentucky, 2009), chap. 7; Bethany Latham, *Elizabeth I in Film and Television: A Study of the Major Portrayals* (Jefferson, N.C.: McFarland, 2011).

101. Draft memorandum, October 25, 1961, PTIA, LTDL.

102. Albert Coates, *By Her Own Bootstraps: A Saga of Women in North Carolina* (Raleigh, N.C.: Albert Coates, 1975), 86.

103. "Princess to Visit 'Lost Colony' Site," *London Times,* July 13, 1984, 6.

104. Jeremy Black, *Pitt the Elder* (Cambridge: Cambridge University Press, 1992), 296–97. On the history of the Charleston statue, see Jonathan H. Poston, "Statue of William Pitt, Earl of Chatham," in *In Pursuit of Refinement: Charlestonians Abroad, 1740–1860,* ed. Maurie D. McInnis and Angela D. Mack (Columbia: University of South Carolina Press, 1999).

105. On New York's statue of Pitt, see Wall, *The Equestrian Statue of George III,* passim.

DEAN ALLEN

"The Game of the English"

Cricket and the Spread of English Culture in
North America, 1830–1900

A s in England, sport in North America evolved from an essentially unorga-
nized activity to a highly structured and organized phenomenon during
the mid to late nineteenth century. Alongside mass immigration, the
advent of industrialization, new technology, and the decline of religious opposition to recreation and leisure activities, sport evolved in a manner that mirrored
its development in the British Isles. Indeed, as it had done throughout the British Empire during this period, an English middle-class influence had strongly
affected Americans' attitudes toward sport and at times and to varying degrees
created the popularity of boating, horse racing, cricket, field hockey, tennis, and
track and field, among other recreational activities, in the United States.

The power of English sport at this time was similar to that of the nobility,
which, as T. F. Dale described it at the beginning of the twentieth century, was
"entirely unsupported by force; it is all so intangible and made up of so many
threads that it is almost impossible to define."[1] Despite the failure of concerted
efforts by British cultural imperialists to convince the American people to submit
to the superiority of British culture and sport, members of the English diaspora in
America continued to express their "Englishness" through a rich variety of sporting clubs and societies. This essay explores the significance of sport to both English and American society throughout selected regions of North America from
the 1830s, when English immigrants brought cricket to Philadelphia, to the 1870s
and 1880s with the introduction of other "English" sports such as rugby and
the foundation of the American Football (soccer) Association, respectively. A variety of sources are used to examine specifically the role and meaning of cricket,
that quintessential "English sport," in areas such as New York, Massachusetts,
and Pennsylvania.

Steven A. Riess explained that "outside of the Indian game of lacrosse, cricket
was the first major team sport and the first organized team sport in America."[2]
By the mid-eighteenth century the game had spread from Georgia to Maryland,
and in 1751 a match between colonists and a team of Londoners resulted in what
some believe to have been the "first American international sporting event."[3]

Cricket was played informally in urban areas during the colonial era, the 1830s, and in the decades that followed there was an expansion of organized cricket in the larger East Coast cities such as New York, Boston, and Philadelphia. Many middle-class antebellum English and American Victorian sportsmen found that cricket provided a vehicle for social interaction and advancement in healthy and pleasant outdoor settings. This was an ethos that had been transferred from across the Atlantic.

THE ENGLISHMAN'S GAME

"Cricket, a sturdy plant indigenous to England; let us prove that it can be successfully transplanted to American soil," announced Robert Waller in 1843 following a match between his Philadelphia Union Club and the St. George's Club of New York.[4] Waller, a merchant operating out of America's Northeast, believed, as did most English gentlemen of his era, that cricket was a great educational medium and the perfect sporting expression of English culture and values. At a time when Queen Victoria was expanding her empire in other parts of the globe, cricket came to symbolize the civilizing mission of the Englishman abroad. For Britons such as Waller, the game epitomized the spread of English influence throughout the United States while representing a tangible link with home.

Reflecting on cricket's place in the social history of England, J. A. Mangan has suggested how the game "held up a mirror to society; it reflected its essential inequalities, snobberies and its essential harmony: but it did more, it successfully sustained all three."[5] The attraction to cricket by the expatriate English based in North America came in the game's exclusiveness, its codes of practice, and an ethos that made it distinctly "English." With its trappings of "white flannels, lush green lawns, scheduled tea breaks, and three-day matches," cricket's wide appeal in nineteenth-century America has been described J. Thomas Jable and other U.S. historians.[6] Cricket was a product of England, and its customs and traditions had been shaped in the mother country; as such, the English diaspora saw it as a reflection of the enlightened "superiority" of Anglo-Saxon culture. Cricket thus played a key role in defining English ethnicity among other immigrant cultures in America. As such, this group increasingly viewed the game as an expression of their moral worth.

Back home the English had transformed cricket into more than a game. For Keith Sandiford, the social centrality of Victorian cricket was fostered, nurtured, and maintained by key institutions and agencies such as England's public schools and churches, which regarded the game as a major cultural virtue and therefore worth promoting within society.[7] By the mid-1800s cricket had spread to all societies across the Anglo world where organized games were played. The game's influence was spread throughout large parts of the British Empire, with people in

India, the Caribbean, Australasia, and Southern Africa all playing and emulating a game that had its origins in rural England. There it had been developed from a simple, pastoral game into a powerful and symbolic force representing all that was deemed by the ruling classes to be worthy in the Anglo-Saxon character.

"In a fiercely nationalistic era Englishmen regarded cricket, an exclusively English creation unsullied by outside influence, as proof of their cultural supremacy."[8] In 1877 Charles Box produced *The English Game of Cricket*, in which he explained to the "outside world" how that "manly and noble game" is "a perfect physical discipline, an admirable moral training. It is food to the patriotic conviction, and fire to the patriotic soul. . . . Even down to the minutest point it is in harmony with those conservative tendencies and habits which are as eminently English as the warm love of freedom is English."[9] It was a message that had been readily adopted by English communities in North America with the game already established around this time.

Cricket was useful in the area of moral training as the Victorians back in England and those promoting the game in America had become obsessed with the concept of "character."[10] In fact the newly formed Cricket Association of the United States, founded and based in Philadelphia, reflected this ideology in its motto: "No selfish, conceited, lazy, or irritable man can be a first-class cricketer."[11] Tremendous significance was attached to the fact that cricket involved strict adherence to explicit rules and implicit conventions. For the English, cricket was about self-discipline. It was a game that meant accepting the umpire's verdict without question and thus developing a healthy stoicism. It meant contributing to a larger cause, that of team and country, without focusing too narrowly on the needs of oneself. The game, after all, was supposed to build character and produce other benefits that were highly valued by English communities. Despite its essential exclusivity, cricket and its ethos were encouraged throughout all levels of society, and even if access to the game was not always available, its lessons in morality were apparent to all.

The English in America were influenced by the preaching of cricket's protagonists back in the old country who argued for the sport's central role in improving the morals of society. Rev. James Pycroft was known for extolling how "games of some kind men must have, and it is no small praise of cricket that it occupies the place of less innocent sports. Drinking, gambling, and cudgel playing, insensibly disappear before a manly recreation, which draws the labourer from the dark haunts of vice and misery to the open common."[12] For men such as Pycroft, the game could confer untold benefits upon Englishmen throughout the globe. As a distraction from vice, "a cricket-field is a sphere of wholesome discipline in obedience and good order," he proclaimed, "not to mention that manly spirit which faces danger without shrinking, and bears disappointment with good-nature."[13]

More than any other sport, cricket engendered a deep sense of white, elite, and distinctively masculine Englishness and was seen to be beyond the conception of those foreign to English tradition and culture. This appealed to the English diaspora in settings such as the United States, where the game not only represented a tangible link with home but also provided a distinct and separate activity for a group looking to preserve their own ethnic identity. Literature at this time helped to promote the idea that cricket was unique to the English. Neville Cardus, a renowned writer on the subject of cricket, once reflected how "cricket somehow holds up the mirror to the English nature."[14] The novelist E. W. Hornung, a product of the Victorian age, declared in *Kenyon's Innings*, "My dear fellow, it [cricket] was only a game—yet it was life."[15] "In the late Victorian period and for at least the first half of the twentieth century, cricket," explained Jack Williams, "was taken to encapsulate the essence of England and had a key role in how the English, particularly the economically privileged, imagined their national identity."[16] For men such as Richard Waller, now based in America and the founder of several cricket clubs there, this was profoundly important.

EARLY AMERICAN CRICKET

Although a few cricket clubs were organized in the British colonies and during the early period following independence,the significant era of the sport in America really began in the 1830s. "For almost one hundred years the game of cricket was a distinctive element in the social life of Philadelphia," wrote John Lester.[17] J. Thomas Jable recorded that English residents of Philadelphia were indeed playing cricket there as early as 1831, with the game spreading to nearby Haverford College five years later.[18] Farther north in New York several groups in Albany played formal matches, and the St. George Cricket Club (SGCC) of Manhattan, founded in 1838, laid claim to being the first regular club governed by rules and regulations.[19] One quarter of SGCC members belonged to the prestigious St. George's Society, the leading English voluntary association in the metropolis. Richard Waller was instrumental in the formation of the St. George Cricket Club in New York City and the Union Cricket Club founded in Philadelphia in 1842.

In the spring of 1844 the SGCC found itself with a new rival in the field, the New York Cricket Club (NYCC). Founded by John Richards, the English-born publisher of the *Spirit of the Times*, the NYCC quickly established itself among the city's literary and artistic communities at a time when notable Englishmen controlled cricket within the region.[20] With its home ground near Hoboken's Elysian Fields in New Jersey, the club's membership swelled as English merchants and the American professional classes were drawn to the exclusive nature of this English-styled institution. Throughout the 1840s the *Spirit* published English and

New York cricket scores and promoted a healthy competition in the city between the rival clubs.[21]

While the game appeared to be thriving, George Kirsch analyzed cricket's development in America during the two decades that preceded the Civil War and argued that it is necessary to focus on five key factors shaping the sport at this time. The first, he suggested, is "geographical mobility and the willingness of the English immigrants to teach cricket to younger and older Americans." The second is "the New York City sporting journals and the local dailies" that offered valuable print space to cricket and reported on the game throughout the Northeast. Third is "intercity competition," which spread the game's influence during this time between the major cities alongside the fourth factor, "the New York City cricket conventions," which were aimed at "centralizing the game" throughout the country. The fifth factor, Kirsch suggested, is the "special all-star and international matches" that helped raise the profile of the sport in America on the eve of the country's greatest conflict.[22]

Although Americans did play alongside English cricketers during this period, they did not take part in the sport in significant numbers until later in the 1840s.[23] The historian Melvin Adelmen has agreed with the view that ball playing was not a main American sport prior to this time. He pointed to the weakness of the kind of "ritualistic, deferential, traditional, and communal society" that had fostered ball playing in the "Old World." He also noted the absence of a landed gentry and a feudal shire system throughout America, which in his view promoted and maintained sports such as cricket back in England.[24]

Puritanical views of sport and recreation still persisted along stretches of America's East Coast, and these had to be overcome before many locals could take part in English-styled sports. As late as the 1850s, for example, some American churches still disciplined their members for participating in ball games. In 1859 as George Parr's England team was touring America, a Maryland congregation expelled several young men for playing cricket and warned others not to follow their example.[25] To win over the dominant Protestant middle class to the new attitudes regarding games, the approval of the clergy was thus fundamental. While some pastors remained skeptical, many used their pens and pulpits to preach the new gospel of "muscular Christianity" that had been imported by the English and maintained by an active diaspora. According to Kirsch, the most famous religious convert to the sporting creed was Thomas W. Higginson, a Harvard graduate, minister, renowned abolitionist, and president of the Lincoln Cricket Club in Worcester, Massachusetts.[26] In 1858 he published the influential article "Saints and Their Bodies" in the *Atlantic Monthly,* in which he extolled the virtues of exercise and "manly" sports such as cricket.[27]

Propagandists for the new philosophy of sport in America aimed their message at children and women as well as men. The *Brooklyn Eagle* declared that "it would be an addition to every school that would lead to great advantages to mental and bodily health, if each had a cricket or ball club attached to it, as in England."[28] Despite inherent chauvinism, the Americans were in fact ahead of the English in their notion that sport could benefit women as well as men. In 1859 the *New York Clipper* praised those of the "fairer sex" who took part in graceful exercise as they "would be much better fitted to become mothers of American children. . . . If the children are born of puny mothers, the race degenerates, mentally and physically . . . whatever then will tend to render the mothers of future generations robust and hearty, will conduce immensely to the wellbeing of the race."[29] Unlike the English, who vehemently maintained that cricket should remain a manly preserve, the *Clipper* went so far as to suggest that "a day's exercise on the cricket field would not be such a breach of manners . . . even for ladies . . . such amusement . . . will be found quite as salutary in its results, as a night's frolic in a ball-room."[30]

With both writers and the clergy now supporting the notion of cricket in Philadelphia, the person credited with introducing Americans to the sport in the city was William Wister, who had observed the game being played among English textile workers during his teenage years. A fascination for cricket led Wister and his brother John to form a junior club in their Germantown neighborhood and at the University of Pennsylvania. Although there were no restrictions regarding ancestry or place of birth, Wister later wrote that "all the members were to the manner born."[31] The students employed the services of William Bradshaw, an English immigrant, as their instructor and had access to Richard Waller's Union Cricket Club facilities. Although Waller would return to New York, in 1854 the Wisters founded the Philadelphia Cricket Club (PCC), which "encouraged English residents to join with native Philadelphians to promote and to preserve cricket" in the city.[32]

In the next few years "a cricket mania swept Philadelphia,"[33] and by 1859 the PCC had acquired a membership of over a hundred and was playing a ten-match season that included opponents from New Jersey, New York, Maryland, and the District of Columbia. The nearby Germantown Cricket Club (GCC) too was flourishing, and although its membership was bolstered by a group of Nottinghamshire weavers, Jable claimed that it was "thoroughly American in spirit" and was the first club to field an "all-native American eleven."[34] There was clearly a drive to contest English domination of cricket in Philadelphia at this time, and the founding of the Young America Cricket Club (YACC) in 1855 was built on the premise that the game would be learned at this club "without the aid of the English residents."[35]

Cricket among the English community was still revered at this time, however, and a highlight in Philadelphia's social and sporting calendar was the annual English versus American matches held at Camden every July during the

Independence Day festivities. Initiated in 1856, these matches were attracting in access of seven thousand spectators by the time the Americans won their first contest in 1860. This victory prompted the *New York Clipper* to call upon the Americans to challenge a British team from England.[36] The previous year a team of professionals from England had been brought to America by Robert Waller and had easily defeated teams in Montreal, New York, Philadelphia, Rochester, and Hamilton (Ontario).[37] The Philadelphians had been the only side to emerge with any credit, losing by seven wickets but showing a vast improvement in play compared to the other regions. Fred Lillywhite, who had led the All-England team along with George Parr, proclaimed that "cricket in Philadelphia has every prospect of becoming the national game."[38]

Cricket was flourishing on both sides of the Atlantic at this time. As early as 1840 Lord William Lennox had referred to cricket in England as the "national game" that "preserves the manly character of the Briton, and has been truly characterized as a healthful, manly recreation giving strength to the body and cheerfulness to the mind."[39] In America on the eve of the Civil War, Thomas Dodsworth proclaimed at the SGCC anniversary dinner that "the time will come when every nook and corner of the continent, where the English language is spoken, will have its cricket club; when the lovers of the game will be numbered by tens of thousands."[40] The English communities throughout the United States as well as American sportsmen were drawn to a game that brought with it respect and potential social elevation. According to the *New York Clipper,* cricket "afforded a convenient excuse for partially demolishing social barriers and for permitting a friendly reunion of Britons of every stripe—mechanics, small tradesmen and artisans—proving they could scientifically wield the will or deliver a true blow."[41] As E. W. Hornung reflected some years later, cricket was now more than a game; it had become "the quintessence and epitome of life."[42]

By the mid-1800s cricket implied wealth, exclusivity, and an aura of "good form." High standards of honor, loyalty, and morality were expected from its players and those who supported the game, and as *the* game of virtue, cricket's association with "Englishness" had already been cemented. For the English in America, cricket was a virtuous pursuit, free from the vices that threatened the ever-expanding immigrant society on that side of the Atlantic. American administrators and cricketers alike imbued their game with a sense of moral worth, claiming that it could bring out the best in those involved. The famous English amateur C. B. Fry, for one, exclaimed later that "there is something in the game that smothers pretence and affectation, and gives air to character." To Fry, cricket was a "form of recreation free from all tendency to degrade either those who play or those who pay."[43]

The game provided a cultural barrier for an English diaspora who feared losing identity among the more "visible" cultures of Irish and European immigrants.[44] Within America cricket was played and enjoyed by groups of English due to the complex rules and exclusive nature of the sport. For many, the appeal came in creating a haven of superiority that was beyond the comprehension of noncricketing nations and groups. While Americans in places such as Philadelphia and New York successfully adopted the game during its infancy, no one could deny that the sport carried a real essence of England in the way it was played and organized.

The "Englishness" of cricket was deep-rooted, wrote Pycroft in 1882: "The game is essentially Anglo-Saxon. Foreigners have rarely, very rarely imitated us. . . . The English settlers and residents everywhere play at cricket; but of no single club have we ever heard dieted either with frogs, sour-krout, or macaroni," he declared disparagingly.[45] Xenophobia was rife in English society. In 1877 a journalist of the *Sporting Review* wrote how cricket's "very associations are English. Who could, for instance, picture to the imagination the phlegmatic Dutchman, with his capacious round stern, chasing or sending the ball through the air like a canon shot, and getting a run with the speed of a roebuck. The idea even appears beyond the pale of conception. The effeminate inhabitants of cloudless Italy, Spain and Portugal would sooner face a solid square of British infantry than an approaching ball from the sinewy arm of a first class bowler. Instead of the bat, their backs would be turned for the purpose of stopping it . . . foreigners, as a rule, are likewise slow in attempting to unravel the mysteries of the game."[46] Although Americans had adopted the game, the English were successful in keeping the "Englishness" of cricket distinct in the eyes of other Europeans. For the German Rudolph Kircher, writing in 1928, cricket had always been "preeminently English. . . . A phase of English mentality, a key to the Englishman's soul, a product of English temperament[,]" and "the most typical of all English games."[47] Fundamentally, in the eyes of the world the game was an expression of a distinctly English sense of moral worth. Fearing the prospect of losing identity, America's English societies became preoccupied with aggrandizing those institutions that were considered part of Anglicized culture and heritage. As the "Englishman's game," cricket became an important part of this process throughout the United States.

While the turmoil created by the American Civil War hindered the spread of cricket beyond the country's eastern states, the game survived and continued to flourish in Philadelphia. Despite the threat posed by the emergence of baseball, a second English tour arrived in 1868, and four years later cricket in America received the ultimate accolade as W. G. Grace, the most famous cricketer of his generation, came to lead the next touring team from England. The nineteenth-century sports writer Henry Chadwick declared that the contest that followed between the English and Americans was the "finest exhibition of cricket in America," and despite a close victory for the English eleven against the local twenty-two, the "superlative play," according to Jable, "inspired native Americans to work harder at learning the English game."[48]

When Grace and his England team were touring America, the English diaspora based in the United States remained determined to preserve cricket as a distinctly English pursuit. In their opinion, the game was not a thing to be shared freely with other communities. Indeed research by Jable suggested that cricket club membership at this time was strictly divided between English- and American-controlled clubs. American-run clubs in Philadelphia—for example the GCC, PCC, and YACC—continued to strive for sporting independence, while "English residents . . . found more comfort in joining cricket clubs organised by fellow Englishmen."[49] Cricket's elitist character, however, was a factor shared by both groups as the entire cricket club membership in the city was made up largely of the professional classes, which in turn limited the spread of the game elsewhere.[50]

THE IMPACT OF URBANIZATION

The English in America had appropriated cricket in the same way that the game was being remodeled back in the old country. Assumptions about the English nature of cricket and of the morality of the game within America were linked with perceptions of cricket as essentially a sport of the English countryside.[51] True, the game had originated in the rural areas such as the Sussex Weald and adjoining counties, but it was the Victorian writers on cricket who were responsible for portraying village cricket as the epitome of English life. In fact, despite such notions of rural tranquillity, it was during the final decades of the industrial revolution when cricket most fully rose to prominence in England. Between 1840 and 1860 the number of county clubs almost doubled; the number of county games tripled between 1836 and 1863 and then in the next thirty years tripled again; and between 1869 and 1896 the Marylebone Cricket Club quadrupled its match load.[52] At the same time, in Philadelphia alone five major clubs were established, each with memberships of five hundred to thirteen hundred.[53] Elaborate clubhouses on expensive city plots had elevated cricket's position in some of America's leading cities.

Cities such as Philadelphia changed dramatically during the third quarter of the nineteenth century. Consolidation with Philadelphia County in 1854 increased the city's territory from 2 to 130 square miles, and this was coupled with a twofold rise in population from 408,000 in 1850 to nearly 841,000 by 1880.[54] English immigrants, along with other migrants from Europe, made up a significant part of this number, and cricket as a result was affected. As with American urbanization, the migration of workers into English cities and the final rounds of the enclosure movement during the industrial revolution back in Britain meant that sport was promoted and that cricket's popularity grew among all classes as a compensation for "space" lost elsewhere:[55] As Ian Baucom wrote, "Deprived of the land itself, England's labouring classes, one might say, were offered the cricket field as a substitute common."[56]

This change in taste for sporting activity had resulted in the development of sophisticated team games with rules and codes of practice that were far removed from the disorganized "mob" sports that preceded them. The first industrial revolution had produced a more urbanized and disciplined society, and because of the consequent need for exercise and relaxation within confined limits of space and time for leisure, "rational recreation" had replaced the bloodier and rowdier sports of the previous age.[57] The emergence of Victorianism and its associated "moral revolution" had created a more orderly, civilized society, and cricket with its perceived codes and ethics fit this new model perfectly.[58] Cricket as a simple pastoral game would be transformed during the Victorian age within England and throughout the world.

In America, as the sport historian George Kirsch explained, people in the middle decades of the nineteenth century also "witnessed a series of revolutions in industry, transportation, communication, urban life, and values. These innovations provided the preconditions that made modern cricket possible in the United States. Men and women who lived through these developments at first tried to maintain their traditional patterns of play and leisure. Yet the changes in most areas of their lives forced them to abandon their older practices or adapt them to new circumstances. Americans transformed traditional recreation or invented new forms to suit their needs. Their desire to play remained strong, but it was expressed in new contexts and in new ways."[59] Both Kirsch and fellow sport historian Steven Reiss have examined the influence of urbanization on the development of sport in America during this time.[60] As in Britain, the social organization of newly expanded cities in the United States created the dynamic in which modern forms of sport would emerge. "As native and European migrants [English included] flooded into Brooklyn, New York City, Newark, Boston, Philadelphia, and other places," Kirsch explained, "these metropolitan centres grew more diverse in race, religion, and ethnicity. Communities became fragmented as social and class relations were strained. Many urbanites sought a sense of identity and fellowship in voluntary associations for political, religious, cultural, or sporting purposes."[61] Cricket, with its exclusive reputation, became an ideal vehicle through which to achieve this retention of old connections.

It was the Victorians back in England who bestowed upon cricket this aristocratic air. In previous times the game was far from a pursuit of the bourgeoisie. According to Keith Sandiford, "It was the hired hand who, in the service of the great patron, made the more telling contribution to the evolution of Georgian cricket."[62] Only after 1850, at the same time that organized sport was taking off in parts of America, did a spectacular increase in sport and leisure take place back in Britain.[63] Industrialization had transformed Victorian society with gradual improvement in the standards of living, the steady reduction of working hours, and the impact of muscular Christianity, meaning that many societies and clubs were formed during this period and would influence the structure of British and American sport in the years to come.

So despite cricket's pastoral image, the game in both England and America was transformed by the ongoing process of urbanization. By the 1850s New York City had become the largest metropolis in the United States, and other sizable urban areas were expanding in Boston, Philadelphia, Baltimore, New Orleans, and St. Louis around this time. Back in Britain, between 1871 and 1901 the percentage of the English population living in urban centers increased from 61 to 77 percent, thereby producing a larger audience for commercialized sport. Real wages too increased by an estimated 60 percent during the last three decades of the nineteenth century and thus allowed the British working classes greater opportunities for attending sporting events.[64] The same dynamic was thus taking place on both sides of the Atlantic.

In addition, as in Britain, the pattern of participation in sports such as cricket throughout America was dictated by social class within these new urban settings. In the post–Civil War era the middle classes enjoyed an enormous resurgence in sport, primarily because of their belief in the positive sports creed that justified recreation as time well spent away from the workplace. In addition middle-income people had sufficient money and discretionary time to join clubs and to have access to parks and facilities within the new towns and cities. The different social classes intermingled as little as possible, however, in their sporting pleasures. Reiss reported, "Until the 1920s they often would not, or could not, attend the same spectator sports; if they did, they would sit in separate sections, determined by the price of tickets."[65] Organized team sports, such as cricket, were often arranged by status-orientated voluntary sports associations that promoted competition by establishing eligibility rules, sponsoring contests, and securing playing sites.

CRICKET AND ETHNICITY

Middle- and upper-income cricket clubs with restricted memberships were located in prime locations compared to other working-class sports clubs, which were often based in the slum areas among people from the same ethnic backgrounds. While members of the first generation of immigrants were unfamiliar with American sports, baseball in particular started to attract a healthy following among those of the next generation. Despite the efforts of ethnic sports clubs to pass on traditional pastimes and to slow the pace of acculturation and structural assimilation, American games began encroaching on traditional ethnic sports within these areas. For cricket to survive in America it therefore had to adapt.

Just as the Scottish, Irish, and German immigrants came to America with a strong sporting tradition, the English arrived with an athletic heritage that became a focal point for the formation of distinct ethnic communities within an expanding urban landscape. Moreover, "English immigrants encountered relatively little cultural shock in American cities, and because they spoke English and were literate and skilled, they fared well financially and faced little discrimination in comparison to other newcomers."[66] Nevertheless those in the English diaspora were quick to form cultural and sporting organizations, along with other ethnic societies, to sustain their identity and to promote their own sense of community. Reiss has asserted that "the most important English sports clubs sponsored cricket—a uniquely English sport that was manly, complex, competitive, and required considerable skill."[67] As a result, throughout the mid-nineteenth century groups of English living within the U.S. Northeast established cricket in cities such as Boston, Brooklyn, Lawrence, Lowell, New York, and Newark. Similar to the pattern in England, most games were scheduled for Saturdays, decades before the Saturday half-day holiday became the norm for American workers.[68]

The original English-styled cricket clubs in places such as New York were still largely governed by the professional classes going into the second half of the nineteenth century. In Manhattan, for example, managers, merchants, as well as other professionals made up almost 95 percent of the membership of the prestigious SGCC.[69] However, while well-to-do men of commerce and finance joined cricket clubs to demonstrate their social status in the established centers, at the same time working-class English immigrants were dominating the sport in up-and-coming industrial cities such as Newark. In the late 1850s nearly 85 percent of Newark's cricketers were manual workers; most, 77 percent, were artisans, primarily metal or clothing workers, and just 7 percent were semiskilled or unskilled workers. Riess explained: "Working-class cricket players in Newark were far more prosperous than the city's average residents, and many could afford to live in its inner- and outer-ring middle-class neighbourhoods. They did not have the time to play the standard two innings that could go on for days [and] instead played for a fixed time limit. Sometimes they played weekday pickup games in the street during lunchbreak or after work. To promote loyalty to the firm, some bosses gave employees time off to practice, especially if the company sponsored the team."[70]

Cultural pursuits such as cricket could transcend all classes and encourage a prosperous and productive society. The English therefore considered themselves to be superior in the virtuous use of sport throughout America. As early as the 1850s, the Bostonian physician Dr. Oliver Wendell Holmes recognized this and found it necessary to chastise "the vegetative life of the American" in comparison to the robust life of the English gentry. He anticipated the impending decline of the race, certain that "such a set of back-coated, stiff-jointed, soft-muscled, paste-complexioned youth as we can boast in our Atlantic cities never before sprang from loins of Anglo-Saxon lineage."[71] Beyond physical strength, "the development of a sports creed from England that justified and encouraged participation in clean outdoor sport that was not merely pleasurable but also built character, improved morals, and enhanced personal and community health dramatically changed middle-class attitudes and behaviour."[72] This tied in perfectly with the masculine sporting ethos of cricket that was readily transferred, along with other virtues, from across the Atlantic: "The positive role models of English, Scottish, and German sporting cultures proved athletics could provide the stoop-shouldered office worker with a moral equivalent of the healthful work habits of the yeoman farmer, a real man who earned his keep by the sweat of his brow. Respectable young urbanites enthusiastically participated in many newly developing sports—especially team games, because they enjoyed the camaraderie, excitement, and competition of group contests which, although not yet congruent with the independent nature of middle-class work in the antebellum era, seemed to superbly embody the spirit of the new sporting ideology."[73]

One sport that gained popularity as a result of the new enthusiasm for team games before the Civil War was baseball. It was a game that had evolved from a simple, informal children's pastime into an organized team sport of considerable sophistication, and significantly, in the late 1850s it was to replace cricket as the leading team sport in America. Different forms of "baseball" were played in the antebellum era, but the one that eventually triumphed was known as the "New York Game" and was developed by the Knickerbocker Club, founded in 1845. Compared to cricket and other elitist sports, the mixing of classes was relatively common in baseball, so despite the fact that the Knickerbocker Club was originally founded as an upper-middle-class New York organization, its social prestige never came close to that of the SGCC or the city's Yacht Club and various jockey clubs—all of which were frequented by the English gentry.[74]

POSTWAR REVIVAL AND DECLINE

The end of the Civil War in April 1865 meant that normal sporting pastimes could resume throughout America. Unfortunately the prospects for cricket in the United States in the postwar period were not nearly as bright as those for baseball. War-time disruptions had inflicted more damage on the English sport, while America's new national ball game had already surpassed cricket in popularity in all regions of the country. However, despite the commonly held notion that cricket in America faded completely during this period, both Lester and

Kirsch have shown that the 1870s and 1880s in fact experienced a renaissance in the game's fortunes.[75]

Both British- and American-born sportsmen kept cricket alive at this time and contributed to its "golden era," which stretched from the 1880s to the first decade of the twentieth century.[76] White-collar professionals and blue-collar artisans and workers competed in cities and in factory towns in New England, the Middle Atlantic region, the South, the Midwest, and along the Pacific coast. The continuing migration of English officials, businessmen, and skilled craftsmen to the United States after the war prevented cricket from dying out in areas where clubs had existed before 1861. According to Kirsch, "Fresh blood from England reinvigorated both white- and blue-collar organisations. In San Francisco the California Cricket Club, founded in 1867, met in the same rooms as the British Benevolent Society, and its president was the British consul, William Lane Booker. In Trenton, New Jersey, potters from Staffordshire, England, were prominent in that city's industrial and recreational life. They formed lodges affiliated with the sons of St. George and organised cricket clubs to secure and strengthen their ethnic identity."[77]

English cricket in America was again given a boost by the visit of the all-England teams in 1868 and 1872. The first team, a squad of professionals led by Edgar Willsher of Kent, competed against clubs along the East Coast at both cricket and baseball. Four years later a select amateur team captained by R. A. Fitzgerald and including the world-famous W. G. Grace, arrived to give the game a further lift in the face of increased competition from local sports. While the international contests greatly encouraged the leading cricketers in the East, in reality the two visits did little to popularize cricket among baseball players or the American masses. Fitzgerald doubted that the English tour "advanced the cause of cricket as against baseball," but the English captain did believe "that a great stir was made by our advent, and that many returned to cricket who had abandoned it, and that some will take it up who have never tried it."[78]

While the English visits did lay the foundation for the more frequent cricket contests between England and America during the late nineteenth and early twentieth centuries, English residents and American enthusiasts were not always able to maintain prewar levels of interest in the game. With the growing popularity of English-style country clubs, these institutions adopted other British sports such as tennis and golf, which became more popular than cricket to a large number of English expatriates. As the elites abandoned the game, the English working-class immigrants were unable by themselves to sustain the previous standing of the sport.

Later that century cricket also received further competition from another locally created game in the shape of American football. While native Americans and English villagers had played forms of football in previous centuries, this distinct handling game evolved during the late 1800s. Constructed upon the same lines as British sports in terms of masculinity and character building, football gave players opportunities to display the virtues of endurance, bravery, and strength of character in a totally different and more physically robust sporting form.[79] As Riess highlighted, "most elite opinion makers in the late nineteenth century, like Theodore Roosevelt, Woodrow Wilson, and Casper Whitney, had great respect for the game [football], which epitomised social Darwinism and inculcated, in the words of Brahmin Charles K. Adams, president of the University of Wisconsin, 'those characteristics that have made the Anglo-Saxon race preeminent in history.'"[80] If American football was going to replace ball games such as cricket for the nation's favor, then it was apt that the first off-campus football game between Yale and Princeton in 1878 was played in front of two thousand spectators at Hoboken's St. George Cricket Grounds.

Despite the optimism of Jerome Flannery, editor of the *American Cricket Annual* in 1897, that the "ultimate success [of cricket] as the leading amateur summer pastime is assured," in reality at the dawn of the twentieth century cricket had been surpassed by American sports in many parts of the country. While it was still played in exclusive neighborhoods of Philadelphia and New York, its wider appeal had faded.[81] A few American college and private English clubs kept the sport alive for a time, but ultimately cricket's status in America now depended on East and West Indian newcomers whose countries were part of the British Empire. Cricket had been an important part of America's sporting history, but by the early 1900s its "golden age" was at an end.

CONCLUSION

Cricket's emergence in 1830s America occurred at a time when the response to the rapid urbanization and the hegemony of the sporting fraternity was the development of a positive sports creed that addressed many of the social issues generated by the changing landscape. Sports such as cricket, introduced and played by English communities throughout America, were promoted at this time in order to raise morality, build character, and improve health. John Lucas and Ronald Smith suggested that "the fever of reform and the romantic evangelical spirit of American religious life during the 1830s acted as an incubator for personal and community health concerns and for the expansion of spectator and participatory sporting amusements."[82] As a result cricket, with its moral lessons and codes of conduct imported from England, flourished during this period.

On both sides of the Atlantic there existed the "widely-held belief that moral, social and vocational values could be developed through cricket."[83] In America the game was an English import played mainly by groups of English keen at this time to maintain a distinct cultural and ethnic identity separate from an expanding immigrant population. Ultimately "nationality was a more important factor in the formation of early American cricket clubs. . . . English immigrants, who introduced cricket into America, constituted the core of that sport's leading clubs."[84] A closer scrutiny of cricket also reveals its role in the formation, maintenance, and differentiation of social classes within the English communities as well as the local population. As in England, the process of urbanization and industrialization in America produced a new social class built upon newly acquired wealth. This nouveau riche group of merchants, manufacturers, and company executives in places such as Boston, New York, and Philadelphia formed a new business class that looked to English-styled institutions, such as cricket, to differentiate themselves from the masses.

Within a decade after English immigrants had first brought cricket to Philadelphia, local cricket clubs began to take shape to provide an arena in which both Americans and English could practice the "empire game."[85] In keeping with the early practice of workmen and gentlemen playing together, several gentlemen —both native-born and English—organized the Union Cricket Club and "tried to make the game popular with all classes."[86] This the Americans achieved themselves. In mid-Victorian Philadelphia, as Jable explained, "university players were largely middle and upper class, whereas in the neighbourhoods, cricketers came from all classes and virtually all sectors of the population including African Americans who organised no less [sic] than three cricket clubs in the mid-1860s."[87] The sport, however, still took its lead on race and gender issues from the British, and despite some encouragement for women's cricket in America, the game did not transcend racial barriers. There are no records of black cricketers playing for or against white clubs during this period.[88]

As in other parts of the former empire, the power of the English game in the United States was key to the retention of a sense of connection to the former metropole. "Proper Philadelphians, caught up in Anglophilia, moved cricket closer to their British traditions with stately club-houses, proper attire and deportment, and strict adherence to British rules."[89] These trends, however, ultimately made it difficult for those without sufficient wealth or leisure to play the game. Although members of all social classes did play cricket together in nineteenth-century America, there is little evidence that these interclass games extended beyond the cricket grounds. Certainly toward the end of the century, as cricket became even more exclusive, Philadelphia's and New York's aristocracies kept class boundaries intact.

While other immigrant groups to America such as the Scots and the Irish displayed and shared distinct expressions of their cultural identity, the more subtle impact of the English should not be underestimated. "The English," according to Lucas and Smith, "were a pervasive influence in the change of American attitudes toward sport, and they did much to stimulate organised sport in America in the latter half of the nineteenth century."[90] The ideology of athleticism encouraged the growth of elite and middle-class sports associations and clubs by rationalizing the social value of physical culture throughout America. These clubs arranged competition and built facilities for communities of people with similar ethnic and social backgrounds and thus enabled members to sustain a particular culture. Via cricket members of the English diaspora within America were thus able to promote and maintain a sense of authentic English culture in a distant and foreign environment, a sense of English culture that many native-born Americans too endorsed.

With the increased influence of baseball and other American sports, interest in cricket began to decline toward the end of the nineteenth century. Even in the Philadelphia region, with its strong cricket heritage, the dilution of a distinct and separate English culture led to a reduction in the number of cricket clubs in the region, prompting a writer at the time to note that only "a languid interest in the game is maintained."[91] While cricket and baseball shared many characteristics, they differed markedly in their respective degrees of popularity and modernization. According to Kirsch, "Social forces combined with the unique qualities of each to determine their respective fates in nineteenth-century America."[92] The dominant sporting culture in the United States would move away from an English influence and instead head toward the twentieth century and the "holy trinity" of baseball, football, and basketball.[93]

Henry Chadwick, writing in 1868, perhaps best summed up the eventual decline of cricket in the country: "Every game or pastime of a nation possesses in part the peculiar characteristics of the people with whom it is a favourite, and probably, in no instance is this fact more strikingly illustrated than in the case of the English national game of cricket. We, fast people of America," he added, "call cricket slow and tedious; while the leisurely, take-your-time-my-boy-people of England think our game of base ball too fast. Each game, however, just suits the people of the two nations."[94] By the turn of the century cricket had been replaced as the national sport in America, but its influence would continue beyond these shores as diasporas around the world continued to play and celebrate this most "English" of games.

NOTES

1. Thomas F. Dale, *The Eighth Duke of Beaufort and the Badminton Hunt* (London: Archibald Constable, 1901), 137, quoted in Ying Wu, "The Pilgrims Come to America: A Failed Mission of British Cultural Imperialism," *Sport History Review* 29 (November 1998): 212–24.

2. Steven A. Reiss, *City Games: The Evolution of American Urban Society and the Rise of Sports* (Urbana: University of Illinois Press, 1989), 33.

3. See John A. Lucas and Ronald A. Smith, *Saga of American Sport* (Philadelphia: Lea & Fobiger, 1978), 48.

4. William Rotch Wister, *Some Reminiscences of Cricket in Philadelphia before 1861* (Philadelphia: Allen, Lane & Scott, 1904), 142.

5. James A. Mangan, "Series Editor's Forward," in Jack Williams, *Cricket and England: A Cultural and Social History of the Inter-War Years* (London: Routledge 1999), xi.

6. J. Thomas Jable, "Social Class and the Sport of Cricket in Philadelphia, 1850–1880," *Journal of Sport History* 18 (Summer 1991): 205. For example, also see George B. Kirsch, *The Creation of American Team Sports: Baseball and Cricket, 1838–72* (Urbana: University of Illinois Press, 1989); Reiss, *City Games;* David K. Wiggins, ed., *Sport in America: From Wicked Amusement to National Obsession* (Champaign, Ill.: Human Kinetics, 1995).

7. Keith A. P. Sandiford, "England," in *The Imperial Game,* ed. Brian Stoddart and Keith A. P. Sandiford (Manchester: Manchester University Press, 1998), 11.

8. Ibid., 9.

9. Charles Box, *The English Game of Cricket* (London: Field Office, 1877), 12.

10. The publication of Charles Darwin's *On the Origin of Species* in 1859 had a marked impact on the Victorians. David Brown, for one, has shown how "Social Darwinism" infiltrated Victorian sport and affected how it was both perceived and played: "Moral earnestness and compassionate gentility symbolized ideal qualities which it was deemed necessary for men to possess if they were to be perceived as 'men of character' and 'decent' members of society." Through cricket this could be enacted. See David W. Brown, "Social Darwinism, Private Schooling and Sport in Victorian and Edwardian Canada," in *Pleasure, Profit, Proselytism: British Culture and Sport at Home and Abroad,* ed. James A. Mangan (London: Frank Cass, 1988), 216.

11. John A. Lester, *Century of Philadelphia Cricket* (Philadelphia: University of Pennsylvania Press, 1951), 136.

12. Rev. James Pycroft, *The Cricket-Field* (London: Cricket Press, 1882), 34. According to the National Book League, Pycroft was indeed the pioneer of all cricket historians and had also been a cricketer of some note. At Oxford he had been largely responsible for reinstating the varsity match as an annual event. See National Book League, *Cricket* (London: Cambridge University Press, 1950), 25.

13. Pycroft, *The Cricket-Field,* 41.

14. Neville Cardus, *English Cricket* (London: Collins, 1945), 9.

15. Quoted in Malcolm Tozer, "Cricket, School and Empire: E. W. Hornung and His Young Guard," *International Journal of the History of Sport* 6, no. 2 (1989): 159.

16. Jack Williams, *Cricket and Race* (Oxford: Berg, 2001), 1.

17. *Wilkes' Spirit of the Times,* December 5, 1863, recorded how, for example, in 1809 the Boston Cricket Club had a membership of thirty, played once a week, charged fees, but did not engage in interclub competition; the quote is from Lester, *Century of Philadelphia Cricket,* xi.

18. J. Thomas Jable, "Latter-Day Cultural Imperialists: The British Influence on the Establishment of Cricket in Philadelphia, 1842–1872," in *Pleasure, Profit, Proselytism: British Culture and Sport at Home and Abroad,* ed. J. A. Mangan (London: Frank Cass, 1988), 176.

19. George Kirsch recorded how "during the fall of 1838, several sides of Englishmen resident in New York and Brooklyn played two matches that led to the founding of the St. George Club. On September 20, former residents of Nottingham and Sheffield contested at Brooklyn for a stake of $100; on October 22 and 23, eleven cricketers from the New York Cricket Club traveled to Brooklyn to play eleven Long Islanders and won $500" (Kirsch, *The Creation of American Team Sports*, 21).

20. Ibid., 122.

21. See ibid., 27.

22. Ibid., 24–29.

23. Wister, *Some Reminiscences of Cricket*.

24. Melvin Adelman, *A Sporting Time: New York City and the Rise of Modern Athletics* (Urbana: University of Illinois Press, 1986), 97–100.

25. *New York Clipper* 7 (December 3, 1859): 258.

26. See Kirsch, *The Creation of American Team Sports*, 13.

27. Thomas W. Higginson, "Saints and Their Bodies," *Atlantic Monthly* 1 (March 1858): 582–95.

28. Quoted in *Spirit of the Times* 28 (March 27, 1858): 78.

29. *New York Clipper* 7 (November 19, 1859): 242.

30. *New York Clipper* 5 (October 31, 1857): 220.

31. Quoted in Jable, "Social Class," 214.

32. Jable, "Latter-Day Cultural Imperialists," 176.

33. Kirsch, *The Creation of American Team Sports*, 16.

34. Jable, "Latter-Day Cultural Imperialists," 177.

35. Ibid., 178.

36. *New York Clipper* 8 (July 14, 1860): 98.

37. Cricket was also established in parts of Canada among English communities during this time. In 1840 the inaugural Canada versus America cricket contest took place with English immigrants representing both sides. See Kirsch, *The Creation of American Team Sports*, 34.

38. Jable, "Latter-Day Cultural Imperialists," 179.

39. Box, *The English Game of Cricket*, 75.

40. *Porter's Spirit* 6 (April 9, 1859): 84.

41. *New York Clipper* 16 (October 17, 1868): 220.

42. E. W. Hornung, *Mr. Justice Raffles* (London: Thomas Nelson, 1909), 122.

43. Cited in R. H. Lyttelton, *Giants of the Game* (Newton Abbott: Reader's Union, 1974), 117–18.

44. For rivalry between Irish and English in America, see the essay in this book by Donald M. MacRaild, "Ethnic Conflict and English Associational Culture in America."

45. Pycroft, *The Cricket-Field*, 24.

46. Cited in Box, *The English Game of Cricket*, 78.

47. Rudolph Kircher, *Fair Play: The Games of Merrie England* (London: Collins, 1928), 57, 61.

48. Henry Chadwick, *Chadwick's American Cricket Manual* (New York, 1873), 95; Jable, "Latter-Day Cultural Imperialists," 190.

49. Jable, "Latter-Day Cultural Imperialists," 184.

50. Ibid.

51. Williams, *Cricket and Race*, 15–16.

52. Keith A. P. Sandiford, *Cricket and the Victorians* (Aldershot: Scolar Press, 1994), 53.

53. Reiss, *City Games*, 58.

54. Theodore Hershberg, Alan N. Burstein, Eugene P. Erickson, Stephanie Greenberg, and William L. Yancey, "A Tale of Three Cities: Blacks, Immigrants, and Opportunity in Philadelphia, 1850–1880, 1930, 1970," in *Philadelphia, Work, Space, Family, and Group Experience in the 19th Century*, ed. T. Hershberg (New York: Oxford University Press, 1981), 472.

55. See Baucom, *Out of Place* (Princeton, N.J.: Princeton University Press, 1999). Cricket became as popular in the cities as elsewhere. Albert Knight recorded how "of the 450 cricket pitches provided in public parks by the London County Council in 1905, no less [sic] than 1568 clubs made application"; see Albert E. Knight, *The Complete Cricketer* (London: Methuen, 1906), 325.

56. Baucom, *Out of Place*, 150.

57. Richard Holt, *Sport and the British* (Oxford: Oxford University Press, 1989), 136.

58. See Harold Perkin, "Teaching the Nations How to Play," in *The Cultural Bond: Sport, Empire, Society*, ed. James A. Mangan (London: Frank Cass, 1992). Birley has suggested that cricket was attractive to the Victorians because of its exclusive "code of honour": "part of the punditry of cricket is that it has laws, not mere rules like lesser games. The high code assumes unquestioned adherence to these laws, written and unwritten, to the letter and the spirit"; see Derek Birley, *The Willow Wand* (London: Aurum, 2000), 20.

59. Kirsch, *The Creation of American Team Sports*, 5.

60. Ibid.; Reiss, *City Games*.

61. Kirsch, *The Creation of American Team Sports*, 9.

62. Sandiford, *Cricket and the Victorians*, 25.

63. Ibid., 34.

64. Ibid., 54.

65. Reiss, *City Games*, 5.

66. Ibid., 21.

67. Ibid.

68. Rowland Tappan Berthoff, *British Immigrants in Industrial America, 1790–1950* (Cambridge, Mass.: Harvard University Press, 1953), 149.

69. Reiss, *City Games*, 33.

70. Ibid., .34. See also Berthoff, *British Immigrants in Industrial America*, 149.

71. Reiss, *City Games*, 27.

72. Ibid., 30.

73. Ibid., 31.

74. Reiss, City Games, 34.

75. Lester, *Century of Philadelphia Cricket*; Kirsch, *The Creation of American Team Sports*.

76. Kirsch, *The Creation of American Team Sports,* 213.

77. Ibid., 214.

78. Fitzgerald quoted in ibid., 220.

79. See Nancy L. Struna, *People of Prowess: Sport, Leisure and Labor in Early Anglo-America* (Chicago: University of Illinois Press, 1996), 74.

80. Reiss, *City Games,* 56.

81. Jerome Flannery, "Introduction," in *American Cricket Annual,* ed. Jerome Flannery. (New York: Jerome Flannery, 1897), 1.

82. Lucas and Smith, *Saga of American Sport,* 84–85.

83. Jable, "Social Class," 205.

84. Kirsch, *The Creation of American Team Sports,* 148.

85. For a discussion of cricket as the "empire game," see Dean Allen, "South African Cricket and the Expansion of Empire," in *Cricket: International and Interdisciplinary Perspectives,* ed. Dominic. Malcolm et al. (London: Routledge, 2009); Dean Allen, "England's 'Golden Age': Imperial Cricket and Late Victorian Society," *Sport in Society* 15 (March 2012): 209–26.

86. Wister, *Some Reminiscences of Cricket,* 9.

87. Jable, "Social Class," 215–14.

88. See *Philadelphia Tribune,* May 3, 1913.

89. Jable, "Social Class," 218. Anglophilia was also apparent through Philadelphians' proclivity for English art, literature, and educational practices. See Berthoff, *British Immigrants in Industrial America,* 131.

90. Lucas and Smith, *Saga of American Sport,* 137.

91. A. M. F. Davis, "College Athletics," *Atlantic Monthly* 51 (1883): 679.

92. Kirsch, *The Creation of American Team Sports,* 17.

93. Struna, *People of Prowess,* 193.

94. Henry Chadwick, *American Chronicle of Sports and Pastimes* 1 (February 13, 1868): 52.

Reviving English Folk Customs in America in the Early Twentieth Century

Toward the end of the nineteenth century and into the early twentieth, there was an explosion of interest in folk culture in Britain and the United States, with enthusiasts on both sides of the Atlantic not only collecting and recording but also reviving and promoting traditional pastimes, which in many areas were disappearing.[1] The initial stirrings of this interest can be traced back to the early students of English folklore, such as Joseph Strutt, whose *Sports and Pastimes of the People of England* was first published in 1801 and was frequently reprinted.[2] The romanticizing authors of the first half of the nineteenth century, including Sir Walter Scott; Alfred, Lord Tennyson; Washington Irving; and Nathaniel Hawthorne, helped to popularize the topic further through their writing.[3] In the 1840s the interest in folk culture progressed from antiquarian recording and describing to practical engagement when a handful of local worthies in Britain began organizing festivals that involved customs associated with "Merrie England," for example, sack racing, dancing around the Maypole, drinking tea, and eating cakes.[4] The fashion spread in the 1880s, and the organization of the events passed on from prominent individuals to committees and institutions, among them Whitelands College in Chelsea, which, inspired by John Ruskin, instituted its May Festival in 1881. Besides food, drink, and Maypole dancing, festivals of this period also came to include such activities as crowning the May Queen, processions, and pageants.[5]

In the following years the folk revival movement gained momentum, taking hold on both sides of the Atlantic. It was expressed in a variety of formats: collections and publications of traditional songs and dances; folk dancing and games among grown-ups and children; May festivals; and pageants that involved dressing up in folk costumes and re-creating scenes of rural life. In the area of folk dance, the key British revivalist, Cecil Sharp (also a song collector), Maud Karpeles, Mary Neal, Florence Warren, and A. Claud Wright started their activities in Britain and then extended them to the United States. In America their ideas were quickly taken up and further developed by local enthusiasts, most notably

Elizabeth Burchenal and Luther Halsey Gulick.[6] Similarly, the earliest revivals in the field of pageantry occurred in Britain, where Louis Napoleon Parker, inspired by the arts and crafts movement, staged his first historical pageant in Sherborne, Dorset, in 1905 and followed it with similar productions in Warwick (1906), Bury St. Edmunds (1907), Dover (1908), and York and Colchester (1909).[7] The news of those English pageants aroused the interest of like-minded American intellectuals, and in 1908 the first events of this type were organized in Boston; Springfield, Massachusetts; Hartford, Connecticut; and Philadelphia.[8] In the following two decades, historical pageantry gained immense popularity in the United States, with hundreds of events occurring across the nation.[9] In 1913 the American Pageant Association was established, and it published bulletins, ran courses, and certified pageant masters to ensure high artistic quality.[10] Thus, the folk revival movement in its different manifestations quickly pervaded the United States, reaching its peak there in the second decade of the twentieth century.

Much of the turn-of-the-century folk revival on both sides of the Atlantic focused on English traditions. This is not surprising in the context of England, given that many of the early activists hailed from there and it was where the movement gradually acquired a nationalistic flavor.[11] However, the corresponding interest in English culture and customs in the United States raises interesting questions. Were American folk revivalists Anglophiles? Did they identify with some vision of Englishness that they wanted to cultivate? Did they look for the roots of American culture in the English heritage? This essay addresses these questions by examining the opinions and practices of the American folk revivalists at the beginning of the twentieth century.

POLITICS OF THE FOLK REVIVAL MOVEMENT

What the promoters of different strands of folk revival—dances, songs, festivals, and pageants—had in common was their attitude to the past and its importance for the present. They felt that old, traditional customs had fallen into disuse and that they urgently needed to be revived in order to address current social problems. These problems, which in both Britain and America stemmed from rapid industrialization and urbanization, included mechanical factory work replacing earlier rural and artisanal modes of employment; appalling living conditions of the working classes in overcrowded cities; and, particularly in the United States, increased immigration. Commentators of the time believed that these factors caused not only poverty and physical disease but also alienation, severing of previous community ties, crime, drunkenness, and dissolution of morals. They saw a return to an idealized bygone age, symbolized by "wholesome" folk customs, as the solution to those problems.[12] On both sides of the Atlantic, social reformers advocated resurrecting traditional games, dances, and songs as a way of reconnecting with an allegedly healthier past. Thus in 1906 an anonymous author in the British periodical *Review of Reviews* enthused about "a sane and sensible revival of the sports and pastimes of Merrie England" that was being undertaken at the time. He announced, "All that is beautiful and inspiring in Pagan myth or mediæval legend, all that is glorious in the storied annals of our race, all that is uplifting in the rites of all religions, and all that is joyous and gladsome in the sports and pastimes of all ages, are once more to be pressed into the Service of Man."[13] Similarly, in the United States an article about the revival of folk customs in the *Craftsman* proclaimed, "It is the sign of a return to more wholesome things that we are at last beginning to realize how much we are missing that is worth while [*sic*], and most encouraging that this realization has become vivid enough to crystallize into a definite movement toward the restoration of more normal social conditions."[14]

Social reformers of the period saw folk pastimes not only as "joyous" and "wholesome" but also as the expressions of better, "more normal" ways of life that "our race" had allegedly once enjoyed.[15] Thus, they attempted to reconstruct an idyllic past in order to shape present-day society. Subsequent criticism has further analyzed the political motivations and implications of such reconstructions. The historian Eric Hobsbawm applied the term "invented tradition" to denote "a set of practices, normally governed by overtly or tacitly accepted rules and of a ritual or symbolic nature, which seek to inculcate certain values and norms of behaviour by repetition, which automatically implies continuity with the past." He suggested that these practices are in fact "responses to novel situations which take the form of reference to old situations, or which establish their own past by quasi-obligatory repetition."[16] The dance historian Allison Thompson warned that this should not, however, lead us to assume "that before there were invented traditions there were real ones—however one would identify or measure these—that were not invented, and that these would *ipso facto* be better." Nonetheless, she argued, this formulation by Hobsbawm and his associates is still useful, "in that it allows us to step away from the activity itself to examine the motives and feelings of its sponsors and participants."[17] In other words, their formulation helps us to analyze the politics of the uses of tradition.

When applying the concept of "invented tradition" to the folk-culture revivalists at the turn of the twentieth century, it can be argued that they were attempting to resurrect a "traditional" way of life of an imagined past in response to the rapid technological and social changes of their own time. As the cultural historian David Glassberg argued in relation to the United States, "the 'romanticized' history prevalent at the turn of the twentieth century was not a 'misty-eyed' escape from industrial civilization and mass culture but rather an aggressive attempt to use the past to shape that culture."[18] Thus, what may at first sight look like nostalgic antiquarianism in the United States was in reality a political intervention into the present. This hypothesis is confirmed by the fact that the folk-revival activists, in the United States in particular, not only operated on the level of clubs and voluntary organizations but also made efforts to introduce folk customs, especially dancing, into the school curricula of various cities and states throughout America.[19]

What vision of the past did the turn-of-the-century folk revivalists promote as their model of an ideal society? It was a vision of a "Merrie England" that possessed the following attributes: "a contented, revelling peasantry and a hierarchical order in which each one happily accepted his place and where the feast in the baronial hall symbolised the ideal social relationship."[20] Furthermore, intellectuals of the time responded to their fear and loathing of the contemporary "masses" by developing the "cult of the peasant," identifying the Elizabethan period as the best historical era in which to locate the perfect past they wished to emulate.[21] Thus, the turn-of-the-century folk enthusiasts attempted to resurrect a past that was distant enough to acquire not only historical authority but also a slight flavor of myth. Moreover, that past was ideologically conservative, marked by an orderly social hierarchy that, allegedly, everybody—including those on the bottom of the social ladder—willingly embraced. In the midst of an unprecedented industrialization, urbanization, and mechanization of life, folk revivalists were longing for what Michael Dobson has described as "the restoration of the organic society, the return to an imagined collective artisan life of unalienated labour."[22] However, can this ideal society be seen as embodying concepts of "Englishness"? If so, how did these concepts travel across the Atlantic?

FOLK REVIVAL AND ENGLISHNESS

The social and cultural historian Daniel J. Walkowitz postulated that the folk revival in western Europe and the United States at the turn of the twentieth century developed "alongside a tide of nationalism" and became "an instrument of a project that was nationalist, imperialist, and, at home, a form of domestic colonialism." He argued that in Britain "the folk revival in dance centered on the English folk tradition as a native source of Englishness, in which dancers would embody the 'peasant' folk as the bedrock of pure, natural, 'primitive' roots unsullied by the 'modern,' urban, and industrial."[23] The folk-revival activist Cecil Sharp, in particular, "led the fight to have the folk repertoire made a permanent part of the school curriculum as an expression of the redemptive power of essential Englishness."[24] Indeed, Sharp claimed, "The careful preservation of its folkmusic is to a nation a matter of the highest import," lamenting what he saw as the degeneration of music in England after the Restoration, when it "became divorced from the national tradition."[25] He advocated the introduction of English songs and dances into schools in order "to refine and strengthen the national character," predicting that this would "arouse that love of country and pride of race, the absence of which we now deplore."[26] Thus to the most influential folk revivalist of the period, the movement had a distinct patriotic slant, promoting a recovery of a lost English national character and heritage.

A number of critics have extended this interpretation of the turn-of-the-century folk revival to its American counterpart, viewing it as an attempt by the established U.S. elites to impose their own, Anglo-Saxon heritage on the newer immigrants to the country. Thus, Glassberg has seen the revival of Elizabethan holiday customs in the United States as an attempt to "bolster the genteel elite's confidence in the vitality and picturesqueness of their own Anglo-American Protestant history and customs" and to disseminate those customs to the immigrant masses, thus "reinforcing social order and the nation's Anglo-American identity."[27] Similarly, Thompson argued that the Protestant Progressives who introduced May Day activities in the United States were "determined to Anglo-Saxonize" the "masses of poor Catholic or Jewish immigrants" and to "inculcate [poor, urban, mostly immigrant children] with Anglo-American values and prepare them for citizenship in a democracy."[28] The literary critics Thomas Cartelli and Coppélia Kahn, when discussing the 1916 masque *Caliban by the Yellow Sands*, which included an English folk interlude choreographed by Cecil Sharp, placed it within "the anxieties . . . regarding how best to 'Americanize' the newly arrived masses of immigrants and introduce them to the standards and obligations of Anglo-Saxon culture," seeing the event as "coher[ing] all too well with the Anglo-Saxon vision of America into which many reformers expected immigrants to blend."[29]

This view of the American folk revival as the established elites' attempt to disseminate "Anglo-Saxon" or "Anglo-American" values to the newly arrived immigrants has become something of a critical orthodoxy. Thus, at the beginning of his study of English folk dances in the United States, Walkowitz argued,

> Sharp, who founded the American Branch of the English Folk Dance Society, advanced the dances as nominally about Englishness; but he and his Anglo-American followers appreciated that the dance tradition was equally about Americanism. As arbiters of American culture, East Coast WASP Brahmins, whose ancestors came from the British Isles, celebrated English Country Dance as part of an Anglo-American dance tradition and as the root of "American" contra and square dance. Progressive Era social reformers committed to Americanization saw these English dances as "respectable" and healthy alternatives to the sultry tango and wild, vertiginous spinning of the waltz and polka popular among immigrants.[30]

Nevertheless, contrary to Sharp's emphasis on "pure" English dances, some American folk revivalists had rather different ideas: while supporting Americanization, they believed that English folk culture was only one strand among many that contributed to American culture.[31] Walkowitz singled out Elizabeth Burchenal, a leading American folk-dance activist, as the person who "had thrown down the folk gauntlet" to Sharp, challenging his Anglo-centric views: "while Sharp applauded English folk dancing as 'probably the best and certainly, technically, the most accurate and definite' folk dance tradition and expected it would dominate over other forms, Elizabeth Burchenal averred to him that 'all things *good* in dancing are in the folk traditions of all countries'."[32]

FOLK REVIVAL AND AMERICANIZATION

There can be little doubt that the Americanization of newly arrived immigrants was high on the agenda of the promoters of folk revival in the United States at the turn of the century. Together with other Progressive reformers, they saw their work as an important social mission aimed at improving the lot of the poor, mostly immigrant urban masses, through education and increased integration into American society. They considered "wholesome" recreation—including folk games and customs—to be an important factor in shaping future citizens, a belief encapsulated in the title of a 1907 article, "Play as a School of the Citizen," by Joseph Lee, who was to become president of the National Recreation Association from 1910 until 1937.[33] Elsewhere, Lee explicitly spelled out the patriotic implications of this citizen schooling: "Let us give our children the ideal of making themselves the sort of men and women the country needs, the sort of stone of which our temple can be built. Behind the idea of standard, we must put the patriotic motive. There is hardly anything such a standard cannot accomplish. *Do it for America!* That is the motive we have got to put into the mind of every boy and girl."[34] Similarly, Burchenal believed that folk customs could serve the purposes of Americanization and wished to stress folk dancing's "possibilities as a Democratic Socializing Agent, and its value as a form of *real* Americanization."[35] Therefore, as Walkowitz pointed out, to the U.S. folk revivalists, "folk dance was social dance, but it was also an orderly form of sociability," which could inculcate American democratic values and thus "transform foreigners into Americans, albeit hyphenated ones."[36]

What is much less clear is the extent to which these folk activists equated "American values" with "Englishness" or "Anglo-Saxon" heritage. In 1917 Charles Mills Gayley, professor of English language and literature at the University of California, proclaimed that Americans had always been "essentially at one with Englishmen . . . in everything that counts," and he enthusiastically extolled the two nations' common "heritage of language and literature, of race, of custom, of law."[37] However, Gayley was not a folk revivalist, and the word "custom" as he repeatedly used it did not refer to folk customs with which the dance, song, and festival activists were concerned. Instead, his book discussed the customs of the English common law and liberal political thought, "the institutions, the law and the liberty," that in his view had been taken across the Atlantic by the liberals who had left England under James I and on which American democracy had been built.[38] Thus, while believing in America's "Anglo-Saxon heritage," Gayley was not looking for the expressions of this heritage in folk customs.[39]

The folk revivalists at the turn of the twentieth century were less unequivocal than Gayley in emphasizing American culture's English features or Anglo-Saxon roots. It is true that English folk customs, particularly variations on the May Day festival, provided a large part of their repertory. However, their Englishness did not tend to be singled out as the key feature in the Americanization process. In fact, when Englishness did get mentioned, it was with interesting qualifications that made a straightforward "Anglo-Saxon heritage" reading of the American folk revival movement problematic. In one such reading, for example, Glassberg used Lee's article "Restoring Their Play Inheritance to Our City Children" as evidence that "recreation workers . . . believed that 'Elizabethan' play reinforced Anglo-American identity, the 'stock' at the base of America's 'melting pot.'"[40] To back up this interpretation, he quoted Lee's statements that "our first playgrounds are an inheritance from the England of the Elizabethan age" and that the "ancient games" were currently threatened by "the crowding of the city, the loneliness of the country, and unlimited alien immigration."[41] However, while Lee indeed located the origins of American playgrounds in "the old town commons, an English institution planted in America in the early part of the seventeenth century," and lamented the decrease of traditional pastimes caused by urbanization, rural depopulation, and immigration, a careful reading of his article reveals a more complex attitude to the "Englishness" of American folk games.[42] After stating that "one great stream of play and song we get from old England, and it is a stream that ought to be preserved," Lee unexpectedly added, "This play tradition from old England is really not English but European."[43] He developed this insight further, claiming that "Hop Scotch seems to be a nearly universal game, its range being from England to Hindustan" and that "Jackstones seem to be of Japanese origin, but have put a circle around the earth, until America has received the tradition from both East and West."[44] This indicates a more open attitude than an unqualified privileging of Anglo-Americanism: old English traditions are appreciated, but they emerge as one strand, by no means unique, among many influences.

While Lee appreciated non-English elements contributing to American folk customs, he could still be accused of downplaying the contribution and cultural value of newly arrived immigrants. He argued that immigration "has hitherto had a curiously sterilizing effect" on the nation's "recreational life," claiming that "the immigrant has not brought his own games with him, and except for baseball, crap shooting and marbles, seems to absorb very little of our American tradition."[45] Other advocates of folk revival, however, went much further in recognizing and embracing customs other than those of English origin. Thus, Burchenal stated, "It is quite proper that we should use the folk dances of Europe,—we should keep them alive with the people who come to swell our population."[46] Elsewhere she argued, "Surely, the folk-dances and music of all the nationalities which make up the people of our country may be considered ours just as these people are our people, and every effort should be made to encourage, preserve, and assimilate this dancing and music, so that we may not only have these added resources for social enjoyment and recreation; but that our national life may be enriched with beauty and color and joy of living which may become the foundation of a yet undreamed-of development of art in this country."[47] Rather than proposing to impose Anglo-American customs on new immigrants, Burchenal was in fact advocating an increased recognition and appreciation of diverse national traditions in order to enrich American culture.

Similarly, the author of "Teaching American Children to Play" did not seem to equate teaching immigrants the values of "good citizenship" with the privileging of one, English, ethnic strand. On the contrary, the article boasted of the Playground Association's success "in making the national and folk dances of different countries a distinct feature of the physical training of children in the public schools in New York, particularly those which are situated in the congested districts of the East Side, where the majority of the children are either foreign-born or the American-born children of foreign parents."[48] The writer went on to identify the key problems faced by those who tried to teach citizenship to such children. The first was the "racial antagonism" between immigrants coming from different national groups, which "soon vanishes when all share in the dances and games at the playground."[49] The second issue is particularly interesting for a discussion of Americanization and its alleged Anglo-Saxon bias:

> Another element of discord is the inevitable result of the newly acquired American "smartness" which makes [the children of immigrants] ashamed of the old fashioned foreign speech and ways of their parents, and anxious to forget, as soon as possible, the customs of the old country. As the denial of loyalty to the traditions of their native land is hardly the best foundation upon which to build a sound and loyal citizenship in this country, it was considered advisable to try to keep alive in the hearts of the children a kindly memory of the land of their forefathers, as well as genuine interest and respect for the customs and speech of their parents and grandparents, by reviving the traditional

games and dances that are a part of the national life of almost every people but our own.[50]

The article did not dismiss new immigrants' native traditions or propose to replace them with English ones. Instead, it made respecting them a key factor in fostering "sound and loyal" American citizenship. The *"real* Americanization" that the Progressive folk revivalists advocated thus emerges as more multicultural than the model of Anglo-American acculturation advocated by current criticism.[51] Moreover, there are indications of some awareness that it was not just the new immigrants who could learn from the longer-established American citizens; the reverse was also true. As Burchenal argued, "The folk-dancing of a people expresses their spirit and character as no words could, and in such a vivid, human and universally comprehensible way that it has an educative value for the general public, whose knowledge of the newer Americans is woefully meagre and whose horizon would be broadened by cultural advantages acquired through contact with people of other countries."[52] Consequently, the educational project advocated by the American folk revivalists does not seem to have been just a paternalistic, top-down inculcation of Anglo-Saxon values into new immigrants but rather was an attempt at a more reciprocal improvement of the entire society.

AMERICAN CULTURE: ANGLO-SAXONISM OR TRANSNATIONALISM?

The proponents of folk revival in the United States were "deeply concerned with tradition," and the English tradition of the early American settlers was certainly one in which they were interested.[53] However, their attitude to that tradition and to the place it should be accorded in modern American culture seems to have been less exclusive, elitist, and conservative than much current criticism has maintained. In fact, some of their pronouncements on Americanization came closer to those of the radical thinker Randolph S. Bourne as expressed in his 1916 article "Trans-National America" than to those of the Anglophile Charles Mills Gayley. Unlike Gayley, Bourne did not believe that Americans were "essentially at one" with the English, and he strenuously objected to those who "insist that the alien shall be forcibly assimilated to that Anglo-Saxon tradition which they unquestioningly label 'American.'"[54] Far from equating Anglo-Saxonism with Americanism, Bourne claimed that "the distinctively American spirit—pioneer, as distinguished from the reminiscently English— . . . has had to exist on sufferance alongside of this other cult, unconsciously belittled by our cultural makers of opinion."[55] He considered those coming from the "British stocks" to be simply "the first permanent immigrants," who established themselves as "a ruling class" in America.[56] He deplored the fact that this ruling class came to equate "Americanizing" with "Anglo-Saxonizing" and argued that "the Anglo-Saxon element is guilty of just what every dominant race is guilty of in every European country: the imposition of its own culture upon the minority peoples."[57] Bourne claimed that the idea of the melting pot, which he equated with this kind of "Anglo-Saxonizing" Americanization, had failed but that this failure did not constitute "the failure of Americanization" or "the failure of democracy." Instead, he proposed that it should "urge us to an investigation of what Americanism may rightly mean."[58]

To replace what Bourne saw as a narrow-minded model of Americanism, he developed an idea of a society in which new immigrants "are no longer masses of aliens, waiting to be 'assimilated,' waiting to be melted down into the indistinguishable dough of Anglo-Saxonism. They are rather threads of living and potent cultures, blindly striving to weave themselves into a novel international nation, the first the world has seen."[59] Bourne called this new model "trans-nationalism," explaining, "America is coming to be, not a nationality but a trans-nationality, a weaving back and forth, with the other lands, of many threads of all sizes and colors. Any movement which attempts to thwart this weaving, or to dye the fabric any one color, or disentangle the threads of the strands, is false to this cosmopolitan vision."[60]

Even though they did not use the term "trans-nationalism," the American folk revivalists echoed some of Bourne's ideas. While Bourne declared, "We are all foreign-born or the descendants of foreign-born, and if distinctions are to be made between us they should rightly be on some other ground than indigenousness," Burchenal wrote, "America has been colonized, peopled and developed by emigrants of practically all the nations and races of the world. We are an immigrant nation," and she decried the fact that many of the immigrant peoples' contributions have been "overlooked and lost."[61] While Bourne advocated the "weaving" together of different cultural strands instead of "melting" new immigrants to fit into a preexisting tradition, the author of "Teaching American Children to Play" spoke of "training the children who will one day help to make up our composite nation to meet together on a common ground of social enjoyment and to move rhythmically side by side in the spirited and picturesque figures of the folk dances" of different nations.[62] These pronouncements point to recognition of a more inclusive, "composite" Americanism than the theory that old elites were forcing Anglo-Saxon norms on new immigrants allows.

Of course one cannot rely entirely on what the folk revivalists explicitly said. It is possible that their practice went against those inclusive statements and in fact promoted Anglo-American heritage as the preferred model. For instance, it is true that "Merrie England" or "England of the Elizabethan age" was among the most popular images they called upon and attempted to resurrect.[63] The titles of several pageants indicated their focus on this image, among them *Old English Pageant* (Rock Hill, South Carolina, 1913); *An Elizabethan Pageant (Masque)*

(Tennessee College, Murfreesboro, Tennessee, 1914); "Merrie England" (Glouces-
ter, Massachusetts, 1915); *An Old English May Day Festival* (Greenville, Mississippi,
1916); and *An Old English May Day* (Fort Hays, Kansas, 1916).[64] Many other pageants and masques included scenes re-creating "Merrie England."[65] Nonetheless,
there were also events that focused on international themes, such as *A Parade of
Nations* (Springfield, Massachusetts, 1908); *The Pageant of the Italian Renaissance*
(Chicago, Illinois, 1910); *The Irish Pageant* (New York, 1913); *The Pageant of the
Nations* (Newburyport, Massachusetts, 1913); *Greek Festival at Nashville* (Nashville,
Tennessee, 1913); *A Pageant of Nations* (New York City, 1914); *Greek Games* (Bar-
nard College, Columbia University, New York, 1914); and *A Pageant of World Peace*
(Somerville, Massachusetts, 1915).[66]

Moreover, even the reconstructions of customs associated with Englishness,
such as Maypole dancing, became highly hybridized in America, including elements of other national traditions. Thus, Jennette Lincoln's *The Festival Book:
May-Day Pastime and the May-Pole* opened with a promise that the participants
in May Day festivities would be "drinking in new life in high glee as in the
old days of 'Merrie England.'"[67] Lincoln, however, did not limit herself to the
dances of English origin. Instead, she introduced "The May-Pole Waltz," "The
May-Pole-ka," "Dutch Windmill Dance," "Japanese Dance," as well as a whole
section of "Selected National Dances Adapted for May-Pole Festivals," which
included Swedish, Scottish, American, English, and ancient Roman pieces.[68]
Glassberg argued that this demonstrates that "despite the reformers' professed
cosmopolitan stance, their Maypole festivals tended to assimilate immigrants
into Anglo-American tradition and American nationality. . . . They incorporated
various ethnic dances into the Maypole form, just as various nationalities would
become 'American' in a white, Anglo-Saxon, Protestant nation."[69] This is certainly one plausible interpretation. However, Lincoln did not seem to privilege
customs of English origin in her discussion of "a successful May-Day pageant,"
describing instead "groups of various national dancers in the characteristic costume of their countries."[70] Moreover, when she talked about "drinking in new
life in high glee *as in* the old days of 'Merrie England' [emphasis added]," she
seems to have been aware of the fact that she was describing an imitation or a
reconstruction—and a reconstruction of something that in itself was semificti-
tious, as the scare quotes around "Merrie England" indicate—rather than an
authentic immersion in a living tradition. After all, the American folk revivalists
were not trying to maintain a set of customs current in their time; rather they
sought to restore traditions they saw as having dwindled "almost to the point
of disappearance."[71] The fact that these activists were consciously engaged in a
reconstruction perhaps gave them a chance to work out a flexible model, allowing for "a sympathetic bond between old and new; . . . new-old material bringing
the inspiration of freshness and simplicity."[72] This model had the potential to

be more culturally inclusive than the prescriptive idea of acculturating new immigrants into one, prescriptive, "Anglo-Saxon" mold.

CONCLUSION

An examination of the writings of early twentieth-century American folk revivalists suggests that current criticism has overstated their commitment to the enforcement of "Anglo-Saxon" norms and traditions on the newly arriving immigrants and their children. This is not to say that these activists were entirely free from prejudice or were egalitarian. There were many problematic areas in these folk revivalists' practices, not the least being the fact that their "privileging of European folk dancing denied and left unrecognized the presence and cultural practices of African Americans, long resident in the land. It left unremarked as well the more recent flows of Asian immigrants to the West Coast."[73] Moreover, the place they accorded to the customs of new immigrants requires further investigation in order to test fully Glassberg's hypothesis that those customs were assimilated or incorporated into the dominant, Anglo-Saxon tradition.[74] Such an investigation would require a detailed analysis of the ways that dances, tunes, and festival practices were selected and combined, with particular attention to the specific modifications introduced into non-English immigrant customs. This brief foray into the thinking of the early twentieth-century American folk revivalists suggests, though, that their attitudes to the place of Englishness in American culture and their definitions of American culture were more complex and more radical than they were previously thought to be.

NOTES

1. See Roy Judge, "May Day and Merrie England," *Folklore* 102, no. 2 (1991): 131–48; Allison Thompson, *May Day Festivals in America, 1830 to the Present* (Jefferson, N.C., and London: McFarland, 2009); Daniel J. Walkowitz, *City Folk: English Country Dance and the Politics of the Folk in Modern America* (New York: New York University Press, 2010); and Peter Burke's comprehensive discussion of the beginnings of interest in folklore across Europe in his *Popular Culture in Early Modern Europe* (1978; rev. repr., Aldershot: Scolar Press, 1994), 1–87.

2. Other early publications on the topic include John Brady, *Clavis Calendaria; or a Compendious Analysis of the Calendar* (1812); William Hone, *The Every-Day Book, or The Guide to the Year, Relating the Popular Amusements, Sports, Ceremonies, Manners, Customs, and Events, Incident to 365 Days in Past and Present Times* (1825); Horatio Smith, *Festivals, Games and Amusements, Ancient and Modern* (1831); and William Howitt, *The Rural Life of England* (1838). See Judge, "May Day and Merrie England," 132.

3. See Thompson, *May Day Festivals in America*, esp. 1–31.

4. The early organizers included Rev. J. F. Russell, a clergyman from Enfield; Viscount and Viscountess Campden of Barnham Court in Kent; and Rowland Eyles

Egerton-Warburton, the owner of Arley Hall in Cheshire. See Judge, "May Day and Merrie England," 134–36.

5. Ibid., 136–40; Thompson, *May Day Festivals in America*, 32–37.

6. See Walkowitz, *City Folk*, 15–157. It must be noted that American interest in folk dance had been developing before the British revivalists arrived in the United States (Neal and Warren in 1910, Wright in 1913 and 1914, and Sharp several times between 1914 and 1918). The American folk-dance specialist Elizabeth Burchenal traveled widely in Europe (including England, Ireland, Scandinavia, Germany, France, and Spain) collecting folk dances, from as early as 1904. See Walkowitz, *City Folk*, 68; Linda J. Tomko, *Dancing Class: Gender, Ethnicity, and Social Divides in American Dance, 1890–1920* (Bloomington: Indiana University Press, 1999), 192–93.

7. See David Glassberg, *American Historical Pageantry: The Uses of Tradition in the Early Twentieth Century* (Chapel Hill: University of North Carolina Press, 1990), 43–44.

8. Naima Prevots, *American Pageantry: A Movement for Art and Democracy* (Ann Arbor: University of Michigan Research Press, 1990), 177.

9. For an extensive list of events put on between 1908 and 1917, see Prevots, *American Pageantry*, 177–99.

10. Glassberg, *American Historical Pageantry*, 107–13.

11. Judge, "May Day and Merrie England," pointed out that around the turn of the century, "the idea of May Day in Merrie England . . . gathered a strong element of patriotic Englishness" (140). In a wider context, encompassing German romantic writers and the "Celtic revival," the folklorist Margaret Dean-Smith has made a case that "'the predisposition to folkery' is inextricably entwined with national feeling"; see Margaret Dean-Smith, "The Pre-Disposition to Folkery," *Folklore* 79, no. 3 (Autumn 1968): 161–75, quote on 175. Similarly, Burke, *Popular Culture in Early Modern Europe*, argued that "the discovery of popular culture was closely associated with the rise of nationalism" (11).

12. See Thompson, *May Day Festivals in America*, 58–66; Walkowitz, *City Folk*, 20–27.

13. "The Revival of Merrie England," *Review of Reviews* 33, no. 198 (June 1906): 594–95, quote on 594.

14. "Teaching American Children to Play: Significance of the Revival of Folk Dances, Games and Festivals by the Playground Association," *Craftsman* 15, no. 2 (November 1908): 192–99, quote on 192. Thompson, *May Day Festivals in America*, 62; and Tomko, *Dancing Class*, 204, attributed this article to Luther Halsey Gulick, possibly because it opened with a quote from Gulick, but the magazine did not specify the author's name.

15. The word "race" at the time was often used to denote "nationality" or "ethnicity," as seems to have been the case in "The Revival of Merrie England." See Thompson, *May Day Festivals in America*, 78. However, during this period discourses associated with racialism and racism as they are understood now developed, and some areas of folk revival can be seen as implicated in these discourses. See, among others, Matthew Pratt Guterl, *The Color of Race in America, 1900–1940* (Cambridge, Mass.: Harvard University Press, 2001); John Higham, *Strangers in the Land: Patterns of American*

Nativism 1860–1925 (New York: Atheneum, 1955; repr., 1963); Matthew Frye Jacobson, *Whiteness of a Different Color: European Immigrants and the Alchemy of Race* (Cambridge, Mass.: Harvard University Press, 1998).

16. Eric Hobsbawm, "Introduction: Inventing Traditions," in *The Invention of Tradition*, ed. Eric Hobsbawm and Terence Ranger (Cambridge: Cambridge University Press, 1983), 1–14, quote on 1–2.

17. Thompson, *May Day Festivals in America*, 5.

18. David Glassberg, "Restoring a 'Forgotten Childhood': American Play and the Progressive Era's Elizabethan Past," *American Quarterly* 32, no. 4 (Autumn 1980): 351–68, quote on 367.

19. Walkowitz, *City Folk*, 1–2, 73–74, 64–65, 79–80.

20. Keith Thomas, *The Perception of the Past in Early Modern England: The Creighton Trust Lecture 1983* (London: University of London, 1983), 22; also quoted in Judge, "May Day and Merrie England," 131. Thomas traced the nostalgia for such an ideal as far back as the Tudor and early Stuart periods.

21. John Carey, *The Intellectuals and the Masses: Pride and Prejudice among the Literary Intelligentsia, 1880–1939* (London: Faber and Faber, 1992); Glassberg, *American Historical Pageantry*, 35–37; "Restoring a 'Forgotten Childhood,'" passim.

22. Michael Dobson, *Shakespeare and Amateur Performance: A Cultural History* (Cambridge: Cambridge University Press, 2011), 101.

23. Walkowitz, *City Folk*, 6. Walkowitz focused on country dances in particular, but his insights can be applied to the period's revival of other folk forms, such as song, games, and festivals.

24. Ibid.

25. Cecil J. Sharp, ed., *One Hundred English Folksongs* (Boston: Oliver Ditson; New York: Chas. H. Ditson; Chicago: Lyon & Healy, 1916), xiv.

26. Sharp's lecture before the Small Queen's Hall, April 3, 1906, quoted in Walkowitz, *City Folk*, 74.

27. Glassberg, *American Historical Pageantry*, 34–37.

28. Thompson, *May Day Festivals in America*, 7–8.

29. Thomas Cartelli, *Repositioning Shakespeare: National Formations, Postcolonial Appropriations* (London: Routledge, 1999), 63; Coppélia Kahn, "Caliban at the Stadium: Shakespeare and the Making of Americans," *Massachusetts Review* 41, no. 2 (2000): 256–84, quote on 270.

30. Walkowitz, *City Folk*, 6–7.

31. Ibid., 118, 188–89.

32. Ibid., 118.

33. Joseph Lee, "Play as a School of the Citizen," *Charities and the Commons* 18 (August 3, 1907): 486–91. Similarly the Playground Association of America saw its task as "the training of our future citizens by means of organized play, which at all times has been practically synonymous with mental and moral as well as physical development" ("Teaching American Children to Play," 195).

34. Joseph Lee, "Restoring Their Play Inheritance to Our City Children," *Craftsman* 25, no. 6 (March 1914): 545–55, quote on 555, emphasis in the original.

35. Elizabeth Burchenal, "Folk-Dancing as a Social Recreation for Adults," *Playground* (October 1920): 9–12, quoted in Walkowitz, *City Folk*, 66, emphasis Burchenal's.

36. Walkowitz, *City Folk*, 65.

37. Charles Mills Gayley, *Shakespeare and the Founders of Liberty in America* (New York: Macmillan, 1917), v–vi. It should be noted that Gayley's outpouring of pro-English sentiment came during World War I and that Gayley strongly supported the United States' entry into the conflict on the side of Britain.

38. Ibid., v.

39. Ibid., 218.

40. Glassberg, "Restoring a 'Forgotten Childhood,'" 357.

41. Lee, "Restoring Their Play Inheritance," 545, 553; Glassberg, "Restoring a 'Forgotten Childhood,'" 357.

42. Lee, "Restoring Their Play Inheritance," 545.

43. Ibid., 546.

44. Ibid.

45. Ibid., 553.

46. Elizabeth Burchenal, "The Nature and Function of Folk Dancing," *Playground* 10 (1916): 434–38, quote on 435.

47. Elizabeth Burchenal, ed., *American Country Dances*, vol. 1: *Twenty-Eight Contra-Dances, Largely from the New England States* (New York: G. Schirmer, 1918), v.

48. "Teaching American Children to Play," 195.

49. Ibid.

50. Ibid.

51. Burchenal, "Folk-Dancing as a Social Recreation for Adults," quoted in Walkowitz, *City Folk*, 66, emphasis Burchenal's.

52. Elizabeth Burchenal, *Folk-Dancing as a Popular Recreation: A Handbook* (New York: G. Schirmer, 1922), 2.

53. Glassberg, "Restoring a 'Forgotten Childhood,'" 351.

54. Gayley, *Shakespeare and the Founders of Liberty in America*, v; Randolph S. Bourne, "Trans-National America," *Atlantic Monthly* 118, no. 1 (July 1916): 86–97, quote on 86.

55. Bourne, "Trans-National America," 88.

56. Ibid., 87.

57. Ibid., 89. It should be noted that Bourne did not belong to the "new immigration" and that in this article he explicitly said, "I speak as an Anglo-Saxon" (90).

58. Ibid., 86.

59. Ibid., 95.

60. Ibid., 96.

61. Ibid., 87; Burchenal, *Folk-Dancing as a Popular Recreation*, 1.

62. "Teaching American Children to Play," 198.

63. Also see, for example, Percival Chubb et al., *Festivals and Plays in Schools and Elsewhere* (New York and London: Harper, 1912), xvi; Jennette Emeline Carpenter Lincoln, *The Festival Book: May-Day Pastime and the May-Pole; Dances, Revels and Musical*

Games for the Playground, School and College (New York: S. A. Barnes, 1912), vii; Lee, "Restoring Their Play Inheritance," 545–46.

64. See Prevots, *American Pageantry*, 181, 183, 192, 193, 195.

65. See Glassberg, "Restoring a 'Forgotten Childhood,'" 362–65.

66. See Prevots, *American Pageantry*, 177, 181, 182, 184, 187, 191.

67. Lincoln, *The Festival Book*, vii.

68. Ibid., 23–24, 28–30, 44–45, 47–64. Interestingly, Lincoln incorporated into her May Day festival the waltz and polka, two of the dances that, according to Walkowitz, *City Folk*, 6–7, the Progressive social reformers wanted to expurgate and replace with English country dancing. Also see my discussion above.

69. Glassberg, "Restoring a 'Forgotten Childhood,'" 359.

70. Lincoln, *The Festival Book*, 10.

71. Lee, "Restoring Their Play Inheritance," 553.

72. Mari Ruef Hofer, speaking at the first Congress of the Playground Association, quoted in "Teaching American Children to Play," 197.

73. Tomko, *Dancing Class*, 205.

74. A good starting point was offered by Tomko, *Dancing Class*, who in her discussion of the practices of the Girls' Branch of Public Schools Athletic League postulated, "Rather than simply assimilating European materials to an American tradition or dancing urtext, Girls' Branch folk dancing may be seen as making an urtext—the making of Americans, as Gertrude Stein might have put it" (205).

The Morris Diaspora

*Transplanting an Old English Tradition or
Inventing a New American One?*

The history of any leisure pursuit may illuminate changing patterns of sociability in the wider community, as happened, for example, with Robert Putnam's *Bowling Alone: The Collapse and Revival of American Community.*[1] America's morris dance groups seem as worthy of study as her bowling leagues, and an activity with such deep English roots and extensive American branches surely deserves its niche in the diaspora project. This brief study cannot offer a comprehensive history of American morris.[2] Its more limited aim is to reveal how the ethos and techniques of morris reached America and what became of them there. Its conclusions rest on the analysis of primary and secondary sources, on responses to a lengthy questionnaire, and on participant observations with American morris clubs, or "sides" ["Side" is the standard term for a group of Morris dancers who practice and perform regularly, and have designated officers such as a secretary, treasurer, etc].

Most traditional dances are either social or ceremonial. Social dances usually involve equal numbers of men and women, are often associated with courtship or flirtation, and are generally performed throughout the year in everyday dress. Ceremonial dances often celebrate specific seasons—sometimes particular days—and frequently involve single-gender groups wearing distinctive costumes. Morris is England's ceremonial dance. For centuries it offered villagers occasional respite from their annual round of drudgery and deference, but as their material circumstances altered, their recreations changed. In the early 1900s, when morris had almost disappeared, folklorists attempted to document and conserve what remained. They secured a niche for it in England and introduced it to North America despite the absence of a vernacular morris tradition there.

Much cultural baggage carried by English-speaking migrants survived the Atlantic crossing. Robin Hood ballads circulated alongside tributes to Jesse James, while English country dances remained popular—even if the folk dance Sir Roger de Coverley was rebranded as the Virginia reel.[3] Sir Humphrey Gilbert's 1583 expedition allegedly brought "Musike in good variety not omitting the least toyes, as Morris dancers, Hobby horses, and Maylike conceits to delight the Savage people."[4] Yet morris never took root; though a few nineteenth-century American publications mentioned it briefly as a novelty item in theatrical productions.[5] Twentieth-century English visitors launched what some call the American morris revival, although one participant firmly rejected that label, stating that "the vast majority of these men and women now dancing in the US have never been to England to watch Morris dancing. They do it because it seems to fill a place in their lives rather than because it comes from England. *They are not reviving anything* [emphasis added]."[6]

But if not a "revival," what is it? Any definition raises difficulties since the term "morris" is an umbrella covering numerous activities and controversies. For the moment, therefore, internal differences will be disregarded while an attempt is made to locate the movement on a wider historical canvas. In many cultures people wearing unusual costumes occasionally invade public spaces to indulge in exuberant behavior.[7] Events such as the Rio Carnival or the New Orleans Mardi Gras are familiar to global audiences.[8] Others, for example the Palio in Siena or Bonfire Night in Lewes, arouse intense passions locally while remaining relatively unknown elsewhere.[9] It seems that their roots reach far into our collective past. Written and pictorial sources covering a considerable span of time and space recorded festivities or rituals in which humans wore animal masks, skins, or horns.[10] Such behavior seems to have been common throughout medieval Europe, and despite hostility from the clergy, it continued into the modern era.[11]

The blurring of boundaries between animal and humankind occurs in carnival costumes worldwide, while Dick Whittington's cat and Idle Jack's cow still feature in Britain's Christmas pantomimes alongside the "Dame" and her foolish son, who preserve parallel traditions of festive transgression.[12] Beyond our theater walls, civic spaces become playgrounds for eccentrically dressed revelers celebrating "stag" (bachelor) and "hen"(bachelorette) nights. Also visible there are morris dancers, often accompanied by a hobbyhorse or similar man-animal figure. "Horse-play" has been a term for disorderly behavior since 1590.[13] Such activities appear to express a fundamental need. The Dutch historian Johan Huizinga suggested that we should call our species *homo ludens,* or the animal that plays, and described dancing as "pure play, the most perfect form of play that exists."[14] More recently Barbara Ehrenreich argued, "To submit, bodily, to the music through dance is to be incorporated into the community in a way far deeper than shared myth or common custom."[15] The archaeologist Steven Mithen claimed that dancing contributed significantly to our ancestors' mental and social development after they adopted bipedalism.[16] It is against this background that the history of morris should be examined.

THE RISE AND FALL OF MORRIS:
FROM THE MIDDLE AGES TO THE GREAT WAR

In 1448 London's Company of Goldsmiths paid "moryssh daunsers" to entertain at their feast. Although no earlier references survive, this was probably not the debut performance of England's first morris side. Similarly a will dated 1458 mentioned a silver cup decorated with a "moreys daunce," but the cup has been lost, and we have no idea when it was made.[17] The earliest sources did not describe the dance. A stained-glass window, probably made after 1550, is informative about costume—the bells are clearly visible—but reveals little about choreography. A painting from around 1620 is more helpful but leaves some questions unanswered.[18] The origins of morris therefore remain obscure. Some thought that this English dance copied older Spanish ones featuring mock combats between Christians and Moors, perhaps arriving via Italy, France, the Netherlands, or Germany, where variants—Moresca, Mourisque, Moresk, Mohrentanz, respectively—were known. Others have argued that an indigenous English dance became known as "Moorish" because its performers sometimes disguised their faces with soot or ash.[19]

Contemporaries would have been sensitive to this resemblance. Until the mid-1600s Corsairs frequently raided English coastal villages and carried off residents to slavery in North Africa.[20] However, although actors representing Moors appeared in court masques, they seem to have had no direct link with morris.[21] The "blacking up" revived by some modern morris sides may be a nineteenth-century addition, borrowed from the May Day dances of English chimney sweeps or from American minstrel troupes. Some early twentieth-century folklorists believed that morris was a vestige of an ancient pagan rite; this thesis has been demolished by recent scholarship, although it is still popular with modern pagans.[22] It is probably safest to say that while most cultures have niches where people can fool about in fancy dress, we have no idea why the English chose morris dancing to occupy theirs.

Whatever its origins, the dance was often performed before Henry VII and Henry VIII between the 1490s and the 1520s. Thereafter it lost favor at court but still appeared in civic pageants and entertainments at wealthy households.[23] By the 1590s it was a feature of village festivities, and authors of Shakespeare's era associated it with rustic merrymaking.[24] The dancers often had one or more eccentric companions, such as a clown (the 'Fool'), a hobbyhorse, or a man in woman's clothing, all of whom featured in other seasonal festive customs involving role reversal and "misrule."[25] Puritans condemned such activities as disorderly and ungodly, suppressing them wherever they could.[26] When the "Merry

Monarch" Charles II returned to England in May 1660, Maypoles and morris dancing were prominent in the celebrations.[27]

English laborers performed morris dances throughout the eighteenth and nineteenth centuries. Several regional variants appeared, including the hand-kerchief-waving and stick-clashing dances of the South Midlands (Cotswold Morris); the processional and garland dances of Lancashire and Cheshire (North-West Morris); the "Bedlam" dances of Shropshire, Herefordshire, and Worcester-shire (Border Morris); and the "Molly" dances of East Anglia. The sword dances of Northumberland, Durham, and North Yorkshire are generally included in the morris family, for though their origins may be different, the cultural niche they occupy is similar. The more recent "Carnival" morris dances of North West England too are regarded by some as a valid offshoot of the tradition, while oddi-ties such as the Abbots Bromley Horn Dance from Staffordshire and the wood-gathering dance of Groveley Forest in Wiltshire are usually lumped with morris. Together they form a complex and occasionally contentious family.[28]

These dances were frequently associated with specific festivals such as New Year, Plough Monday, May Day, or Whitsun but might have been performed to earn money whenever paid work was scarce. They disappeared from many communities between 1850 and 1900, as rural depopulation reduced the pool of potential dancers while clergy and magistrates condemned the drinking and disorderly behavior that often accompanied the dancing.[29] Twentieth-century enthusiasts began collecting and performing the surviving dances, and in 1911 they acquired an institutional base when Cecil Sharp founded the English Folk Dance Society (EFDS).[30] Morris was featured in celebrations for the coronation of George V and in Stratford-upon-Avon on Shakespeare's birthday.[31] By 1914 it was also, rather surprisingly, gaining support in America.

"HERITAGE": ITS USES AND ABUSES

The creation of the United States of America left a legacy of resentment. Thou-sands of colonists who had supported the losing side escaped reprisals by fleeing to Canada, along with ex-slaves who had fought against their former masters.[32] Long after the War of 1812, expansionists saw annexing Canada as part of the "manifest destiny" of the United States, and anti-English sentiments were further amplified by Irish immigrants who fled the famine.[33] Hostility toward the British state and English culture persisted in twentieth-century America.[34] Nevertheless many English national icons—from Jane Austen to Monty Python and from Gilbert and Sullivan to the Beatles—have gained substantial followings there.[35] Devotees often progress from admiration to imitation; for example American Sherlock Holmes enthusiasts convene in period dress to reenact episodes from

Conan Doyle's tales, and Doctor Who fans hold well-attended gatherings in bizarre costumes.[36]

Such apparently trivial activities may have wider significance. The historians Eric Hobsbawm and Terence Ranger noted the role of "invented traditions" in the creation of collective identities, while Benedict Anderson's ideas about "imagined communities" threw further light on this issue.[37] The folklorists Ronald Hutton and Roy Judge have shown that some "ancient" English customs have comparatively recent origins, while radical critics such as Dave Harker and Georgina Boyes have dismissed much of the folk revival's output as "fakesong" or expressions of bourgeois nostalgia for an "imagined village."[38] For communities in crisis, this issue has serious implications. Michael Ignatieff highlighted the impact of fictionalized traditions on interethnic strife in the Balkans: "Kitsch is the natural aesthetic of an ethnic 'cleanser.' There is no killer on either side of the checkpoints who will not pause, between firing at his enemies, to sing a nostalgic song, or even recite the lines of some ethnic epic."[39]

In the United States historical narratives carry political weight and heritage-based activities impact on the cultural and physical landscapes.[40] Americans who are not content with purchasing a commodified "heritage experience" spend their leisure performing elaborate historical reenactments.[41] Such events have a long pedigree. On May Day in 1627 Thomas Morton, a Massachusetts trader, organized "revels and merriment after the old English custom." Having brewed "a barrel of excellent beer" and provided "other good cheer, for all comers of that day" the revelers erected their Maypole, "a goodly pine tree of 80 foot long." This infuriated local Puritans, who "termed it an Idol; yea, they called it the Calf of Horeb and stood in defiance at the place, naming it Mount Dagon."[42] Morton claimed that the community's elites wanted a pretext to monopolize the fur trade for themselves, but whatever their motives, they expelled him from the colony and destroyed his Maypole.[43] Despite this inauspicious precedent, historical pageants and reenactments have remained popular in America.

Medieval tournaments, Renaissance fairs, Jane Austen–themed formal balls, and Dickensian Christmas feasts now form a significant sector of the American leisure industry.[44] Thousands of summer soldiers have spent their holidays wielding blunted swords and firing blank cartridges.[45] The Society for Creative Anachronism (SCA), founded in 1966 by Berkeley students, has around thirty thousand members who have celebrated medieval and Renaissance European culture.[46] A much wider range has been covered by members of the Period Events and Entertainments Re-creation Society (PEERS).[47] Such occasions have often featured morris dancing. Several groups contacted during this research have supported reenactments; one was started by SCA members.[48] Before a consideration of how creative or anachronistic their performances have been, an overview of recent morris history is necessary.

TWENTIETH-CENTURY MORRIS: REVIVAL OR REINVENTION?

Authenticity is a problematic concept in folklore studies. Scholars sometimes complain that recent changes have spoiled a traditional custom, while local people protest that they are entitled to change it if they wish.[49] Similar arguments have afflicted the morris community. Cecil Sharp and his followers noted down the dances of the few surviving village sides and attempted to reconstruct the repertoires of defunct ones from the recollections of elderly survivors.[50] They embedded this canon of dances in a system of examinations and certificates designed "to conserve the Morris Dance in all its traditional purity; and . . . to teach it as accurately as possible to those who desire to become dancers themselves or professed teachers of it."[51] World War I interrupted their project, but after 1918 a few traditional village sides resumed dancing and revivalists started others. The EFDS, which merged with the Folk Song Society to form the EFDSS in 1932, continued promoting the dances, but they remained a minority interest.

Sharp's disciples insisted on preserving the distinctive repertoire and style, the "tradition," of each source village. The only loophole for innovation was the reconstruction of dances from communities where sides had once existed but where little information about them survived.[52] The EFDSS, and from 1934 the more specialized Morris Ring, maintained this policy for decades. However, an alternative morris methodology had been championed by Mary Neal, then Sharp's rival for leadership of the revival.[53] Neal was a volunteer social worker who was battling to improve employment, educational, and social opportunities for working-class girls in Edwardian London. Sharp's publications inspired her to introduce folk songs and dances to the Espérance Girls Club, which she helped to run—but while Sharp's priority was excellence, Neal's was inclusiveness. She believed that the dances "are not an entertainment given by a few highly trained exhibitors while the rest stand around and stare."[54]

Despite Sharp's dismissal of their "hoydenish gambols," Neal's Espérance girls won considerable acclaim.[55] Some became respected dance teachers, particularly Florrie Warren, who visited the United States with Neal in the winter of 1910–11. Florrie married an American and quit dancing, while Neal abandoned the folklore movement for other forms of social activism after 1914.[56] Sharp's more rigorous approach prevailed. It was transmitted in the United States by teachers such as May Gadd, "a wonderfully buoyant and crusty old English-woman. . . . A product of EFDSS, she was very insistent that the style of dancing, both Morris and English country, be as she knew it to be correct."[57]

Like its English equivalent, the U.S Country Dance, later Country Dance and Song, Society encouraged schools and colleges to bring folk dancing into the physical education curriculum.[58] It also invaded the distinctively American environment of the summer camp, notably at Pinewoods in Massachusetts, where English-trained teachers such as Gadd and Sidney "Nibs" Matthews, subsequently EFDSS artistic director, ran morris workshops using the approved repertoire.[59] The Pinewoods Morris Men were formally instituted as a side in 1964, although they were not yet "a team as we think of a team now. . . . Members lived all over the world and got together only at Camp and for an occasional tour."[60] In 1967, however, some Pinewoods alumni formed the Village Morris Men in New York City, and soon locally grounded sides appeared across the United States and Canada.[61] Several adopted an innovative approach that was closer to Neal's than to Sharp's.

English morris underwent a similar shake-up. In the early 1970s electric folk groups such as Steeleye Span and the Albion Band brought morris tunes and dances to a wider audience.[62] Meanwhile two previously neglected traditions were revived: the "Border Morris" of Shropshire, Herefordshire, and Worcestershire; and the "Molly" dances of East Anglia. Since they were poorly documented, any reconstructions were conjectural.[63] Even so, young dancers eagerly adopted and augmented them, creating colorful displays of street theater.[64] On both sides of the Atlantic some people felt that these innovations preserved the spirit of the morris tradition, while others feared they were debasing it.[65]

Meanwhile there was an equally controversial invasion of the morris scene by a wave of female dancers. England's Morris Ring, despite historical evidence to the contrary, regarded the dances as a "men-only" tradition.[66] This sentiment was not shared by Sharp's first morris informant, the Oxfordshire bricklayer William Kimber, who told a Morris Ring meeting, "Why shouldn't they dance? . . . they dances a damn sight neater than 'alf of you do."[67] The Morris Ring's exclusion of women was bypassed in 1975 by the formation of the Women's Morris Federation, now simply the Morris Federation.[68] Parallel disputes in America were vividly recalled in responses to the questionnaire circulated for this project and are considered below. The first task of the survey, however, was to discover how many American morris sides existed and what they danced.

DEVELOPMENT OF AN AMERICAN "TRADITION"

In 2012 online reference sources yielded a list of around 150 North American morris sides.[69] Further inquiries revealed that some had disappeared entirely and others were currently inactive. Eventually a questionnaire went to 99 U.S. and Canadian sides with locatable e-mail addresses. Twenty-nine cooperated fully, and 12 others volunteered some information without completing the questionnaire. Of the 29 responding sides, 14 reported performing only Cotswold dances. Nine others performed Cotswold plus subsidiary traditions. Two sides listed Border as their sole tradition, while 7 more combined it with others, mostly Cotswold. Three sides specialized in Rapper sword dances, two of which also danced Longsword. Two Cotswold sides as well danced Rapper. One side performed North West Garland dances. No Molly sides responded. How far this reflects the relative popularity of these disciplines is unclear. Information from correspondents and fieldwork by the present author suggest that while Cotswold Morris is widespread in America, Border, Molly and sword dancing are more popular than the survey indicated.

In the context of the English diaspora project at Northumbria University, it seemed relevant to discover whether American sides that had received instruction from English or English-trained dance teachers were less innovative than sides that had not been so instructed. Accordingly an attempt was made to trace their teaching lineages.[70] Of the 29 sides that completed the questionnaire, 16 cited no direct English influences; 8 of them had created new dances. The remaining 13 sides had had significant input from English dancers or from Americans who had danced in England; only 5 of them had invented new dances. No firm conclusions can be drawn from this exercise, not only because the data set was small but also because the concept of innovation is problematic.

Some sides invented new dances in the style of a recognized tradition. Others preserved the traditional repertoire but made stylistic changes. Some changed both style and repertoire. Many responses described evolutionary rather than revolutionary changes. The leader of Ramsay's Braggarts in Minnesota, founded in 1988, remarked, "Small stylistic changes come about over the course of each year's practice, as we collectively work on individual movements and steps that we incorporate into the team's style. This is in part a spontaneous thing, but it gets discussed and tested and hammered out and then collectively decided on."[71] Although the current repertoire of Ramsay's Braggarts derives from several sources, their dances are performed in the style of a single Cotswold village, Bledington. However, they insist that this is "very much *our* version of Bledington."[72]

Wake Robin Morris, Massachusetts, founded in 1981, underwent a similar process while learning dances from the village of Field Town: "The Fieldtown that we danced was particularly our own because of the way we learned. . . . Since we had a variety of teachers we had the challenge to coalesce what we'd been taught into a cohesive whole."[73] Other sides were more radical. Rich Holmes recalled that Salt Springs Morris New York, founded in 1996, started with Cotswold dances in traditional style but from 1999 on chose to do "'our own tradition'—or, if you prefer, not to do a tradition at all . . . we began developing our own set of figures, steps, hand motions, and dances."[74] In contrast, Hart's Brook Garland Women, Massachusetts, founded in 1991, moved cautiously toward independence. Beginning with a repertoire of two traditional dances from North West England, they added on average only one per year, but now "we do feel less bound to the book . . . and more free to adapt material to suit us."[75] Sometimes adaptation was unavoidable; limited numbers drove Heartwood Morris, New York, founded in the late 1990s, to invent dances for three or four people.[76]

Some changes were more dramatic. Forest City Morris Ontario, founded in 1978, originally performed dances from several Cotswold traditions but were slipping into an increasingly homogenized style until they attended a gathering in Vermont: "what a revelation that was! All of these different teams, many doing 'our' dances—but in such different ways. Barely recognizable. . . . The following year, Alistair went to English week at Pinewoods Camp and returned practically speaking in tongues: . . . in 1980, a few of us Forest City types went to Pinewoods. In retrospect this was, as they say, a turning point."[77]

In 1981 several dancers left Forest City to found Thames Valley International. They limited themselves to dances from a single Cotswold village, Field Town, and strove to reproduce their idiosyncrasies faithfully. However, Paul Handford recalled, "Though I *was* thinking about coherence, the decisions about how to achieve it were sometimes arrived at after much experimentation . . . at this time I was thinking about dancing a lot, and found myself convinced that almost every tune that I liked was just tailormade for an F.T. [Field Town] dance. So eventually I looked at inventing one."[78]

Thames Valley International now does several original dances in the Field Town style. Eventually their former colleagues limited their repertoire to a single, adapted Cotswold tradition: "Forest City draws inspiration for its dances from the village of Kirtlington, but most of what we do is as much Forest City as it is Kirtlington."[79] This Kirtlington "tradition" was reconstructed by Paul Davenport, based on what little was known about a side defunct for a century.[80] Other resurrected Cotswold "traditions" have taken root in America. The Oxfordshire village of Duns Tew had morris men, but their dances were never collected. Tim Radford, an Englishman who taught at Pinewoods, blended elements of dances from three neighboring villages with ideas of his own to synthesize a "Duns Tew tradition."[81] While visiting England in 1986, Jocelyn Reynolds encountered it at Sidmouth Folk Week:

> I brought what I had learned in a 20-minute teaching session, and the dances [sic] notes they gave me, back to the USA. 10 years later I founded Goat Hill [in California], and decided to use that tradition for our repertoire. The notes were not very detailed, so we didn't get everything right. . . . We have continued to dance Duns Tew throughout. The style in which we do it has evolved over time, as we refined it. The dance notes had very little indication of style in them, so I (and later we) worked out the details as we went along . . . [repertoire] changes occurred organically as team members wrote dances and brought them to

the team. . . . We have also "stolen" a few dances from other Cotswold traditions and modified them to work within our tradition.[82]

Bessels Leigh is another "lost" village tradition, reconstructed from hints and fragments.[83] Berkeley Morris, California, founded in 1977, adopted it, altering some figures and adding others.[84] As one member observed, "West Coast Morris takes dances and even bits from anywhere, makes significant changes to existing dances and writes new dances on [a] fairly frequent basis."[85] Members of Berkeley Morris perform several dances from two other Cotswold villages, Bledington and Field Town, in a manner sufficiently traditional for the present author to participate in them during a recent visit. In addition they have created new dances in the Bledington and Field Town styles that are too complex for visitors to join in immediately, although they can be learned with sufficient application.[86]

In a similar spirit, members of Ladies of the Rolling Pin, Rhode Island, founded in 1998, said, "We either make up our own dances or base our dances on ones another side has taught us and add our own figures."[87] They have learned dances from English sides via YouTube but have had no direct tuition from English dancers. Neither has Duck or Grouse Rapper Sword Minnesota, founded in 2006, although a significant part of their repertoire too came from YouTube videos, including several by English sword dancers. They recalled, "Our first dance was based on traditional figures but from the start we choreographed our own dances and developed our own 'tradition.'"[88] However, a new tradition may involve more than innovations in repertoire or style. Changes in group ethos are equally significant.

AMERICAN MORRIS SIDES AS COMMUNITIES

Morris sides generally practice one evening a week and "dance out" when opportunities arise, but they often meet on other occasions. The questionnaire asked whether sides socialised outside their routine meetings for practice and performance, and whether they organised any events which were primarily social in nature. Of the twenty-nine responding sides, only nine said they did not socialize regularly. Ramsay's Braggarts in Minnesota declared, "You couldn't possibly reply with a more emphatic YES to this question."[89] Marlboro Morris Men in Vermont hold parties for "opening and closing of the season . . . and watching the Super Bowl."[90] Members of Greenwood Morris, Florida, founded in 1997, enjoy "movie days/nights, Happy Hour, and . . . canoeing and bicycling together."[91] Pokingbrook Morris, New York, members have "an annual banquet in the fall, a winter feast (potluck), a video night, a gathering in a member's yard for July 4th Fireworks, and often a summer picnic."[92]

Half Moon Sword, New York, too has a busy calendar: "Several musicians are in the same contra dance bands. Several of us participant [sic] in the same social dance and singing events. We have a traditional dinner and wine tasting evening, in preparation for the Sword Dance Festival."[93] Sometimes there are stronger bonds of solidarity. Juggler Meadow members make up an all-male Massachusetts side that is closely linked with its neighbors Harts Brook Garland Women. As well as gathering at a pub after practice and holding regular potluck suppers, members of both sides help each other with "moving, car repairs, child care, convalescence (and hospice), home improvement, etc."[94]

In this context, a significant development over the past half-century has been a shift in the gender balance of the morris world. This clearly relates to much larger social changes associated with the ongoing struggle for equality.[95] However, the focus here is on how these changes impacted the morris ethos. Of the twenty-nine responding sides, fourteen included men and women, nine were men only, and six were women only—although some women-only dance sides had male musicians and vice versa. This diversity is now generally accepted, but Cynthia Wheare of Muddy River Morris Massachusetts, founded in 1975, recalled that "the early women's sides were definitely an expression and reflection of the turbulent issues of the 70s. . . . 30 years ago women performing Morris was A BIG DEAL. There were strong emotions and extreme behaviors about it."[96]

Rock Creek Women, Washington, D.C., founded in 1979, grew out of an existing side, Foggy Bottom Morris, founded in 1977, in which men and women performed Cotswold dances but in separate sets. Their instructor was an Englishman who "did not believe in mixed sets. Indeed, many women felt that his attitude toward women dancing was archaic. In the context of Morris Ring of the time, he could be regarded as a moderate on the issue. But not in the Washington of 1978. . . . As in many separate-but-equal arrangements, one side felt distinctly unequal. . . . The discussion was fervent, but the outcome was foreordained: Divorce. Foggy Bottom became a men's team in reality, as it had begun in spirit. The women went on to form Rock Creek, a team with quite different traditions. The split, I think it safe to say, benefited us all."[97]

Similar issues were involved in the split in Forest City Morris (Ontario), whose members were then "mixed in gender . . . [and] . . . mixed in attitude and point of view about what we were doing and how (and why) we were doing it." In 1981 some male dancers left to form Thames Valley International, which has described itself as "a men's team, though with a few invited female individuals, some of long-standing."[98] Forest City shed its remaining male dancers in 1989, which some members felt improved their performances: "When you get a group of women doing it there's a common thing, and they dance the same, just the same as a group of men will dance roughly the same. I think [Forest City becoming all-female dancers] has been a really good move because it's all of a sudden starting to look like something again instead of a sloppy mess, which is what I really think that last couple of years have been."[99] Anthony Barrand made a similar point: "The morris is at its best when the individual members of the set are lost in the greater unit of the whole. Men dancing opposite women will not draw upon and emphasize the similarities between each other nor be seen as doing so by an audience as readily as when women dance with women, and men dance with men. . . . There are historical instances of men and women dancing in the same morris sides . . . I started my team in this way when we did not have enough men or women for separate sides. . . . If asked though, I would discourage people from dancing 'mixed' morris."[100] Nevertheless some Forest City women enjoy the "masculine" aspects of Morris: "When you get a women's team together, we can't look like a bunch of ballerinas. We have to dance strong and we have to almost forget about our [femininity], especially with the clashing stick dances. . . . It's a great outlet for stress, the stick dances. I just whack the hell out of them, you know. You feel better and better after you've danced those stick dances for a while. You think, hey gees, I feel a lot better, when you go home."[101]

These opinions are not surprising. Morris is transgressive, celebrating the crossing of boundaries—between the seasons or between the old year and the new, for instance—by symbolically breaking barriers. In morris performances ambiguous creatures such as the hobbyhorse blur the line between humanity and animals or the man-woman mocks gender conventions. The killing and resurrection of a hero figure in the mumming play—integral to some dance traditions—confronts the boundary between life and death. American and Canadian women in breeches whacking at each other with sticks are ultimately upholding the morris tradition, not subverting it.

Today male, female, and mixed sides as well as gay and lesbian ones flourish in America.[102] A respondent from Vermont's Marlboro Morris Men (founded in 1974 as Marlboro Morris and Sword, but re-founded and renamed in 1986), concluded, "Gender is fast becoming irrelevant in the community. There is at least one 'Men's Side' that includes women dancers and I suspect that more currently single-sex teams will become 'coed' in the next few years. I think most new sides are 'sexless.'"[103] At a California morris gathering in 2013, this author observed numerous mixed-gender West Coast sides and danced as a guest with several of them. Throughout the weekend all-male, all-female, and mixed groups shared the stage at public venues with mutual respect and good humor. In private gatherings individuals mingled amicably, acquiring new skills in workshops or dancing informally in "scratch" sets.

This experience corroborated the impression conveyed by several survey responses, that "the Morris community" is more than an abstract concept or a pious aspiration. Several survey responses echoed that of Berkeley Morris in California: "We are sort of an extended family."[104] While each side is a community in its own way, however, most are linked in a wider network that helps them resist what historians—in a different context—call "the tyranny of distance."[105]

THE AMERICAN MORRIS NETWORK AS A COMMUNITY

Morris sides exist from Alaska to Florida, but their distribution is uneven. Of the ninety-nine approached in this survey, fifty-one hailed from just four states: twenty-two in Massachusetts; eleven in California; and nine each in Minnesota and New York. Of the twenty-nine responders, over half were in those same four states: five each from New York and Massachusetts; four from California; and three from Minnesota. Interestingly, those four morris-friendly states all supported the Democratic candidate in the 2012 presidential election. No morris sides are listed in Alabama, Arkansas, the Dakotas, Georgia, Idaho, Kansas, Louisiana, Mississippi, Montana, Oklahoma, South Carolina, or Wyoming—all Republican territory in 2016. However, these figures do not necessarily indicate a link between morris dancing and political affiliation.[106] They may simply reflect the fact that morris sides often spring up around universities; Oxford had its Dancing Dons as early as 1913.[107]

Regardless of politics, geography has affected the development of morris sides. Pre-1900 village sides generally walked to practices and performances. English revival sides perform further afield but still reach some engagements on foot or by public transport. Where this is impracticable, carpooling reduces costs and encourages conviviality. In America, however, sides routinely fly to out-of-state events, and some dancers have a solitary fifty-mile drive to their weekly practices.[108] Greenwood Morris Florida is an extreme case: members' nearest neighbors are in Kentucky: "I think our side had harder beginnings than other teams. I started the team, but knew nothing about morris dancing. My learning came from 1) a book and music tape, 'Welcome In The Spring' by Paul Kerlee; 2) Bruce Brandt, who taught me the difference between Paul Kerlee's written dance description and the real thing; and 3) the CDSS morris dance videos by Tony Barrand, which I rented and avidly studied. I do wish there had been/are other teams close to us in North Florida with whom we could get together from time to time! Much of the confusion of our first couple of years of dancing would have been eliminated."[109]

Members of Two Rivers Morris, Oregon, founded in 2010, were slightly more fortunate. They were launched at a workshop sponsored by the Eugene Folklore Society, with an instructor from Massachusetts. Since then they have been self-taught, apart from occasional meetings with sides from Portland, a hundred miles away. "Our teacher Barbara Boylan had no Morris dance experience prior to the workshop. She learns dances at workshops and from videos and info posted on the internet."[110] In such circumstances networking can be crucial, although some sides relished a degree of isolation, as Ramsay's Braggarts in Minnesota indicated: "yes, there has [sic] been influences from the outside but our distance from the east coast, mainstream Morris community has allowed us to be creative, self-confident, and determined to maintain our regional feel. . . . The area has produced some quirks of style do [sic] to its original remote detachment from the rest of the continent's Morris community when it launched in the late 1960s and early '70s and it takes pride in maintaining some of those idiosyncrasies as local dialects."[111]

In Britain, collaboration has been fostered by the EFDSS, the Morris Ring, and more recently by the Morris Federation and Open Morris, but in the United States the creation of a coordinating body was rejected at a meeting held during the first "Marlboro Ale." (English village ales were traditionally held around Whitsuntide to raise money for repairing the church or assisting the local poor. Morris dancing was often part of the entertainment, and rival sides sometimes competed for prizes.[112] In the twentieth century, England's Morris Ring began calling its own convivial gatherings "ales", and Marlboro Morris and Sword (Vermont) introduced the custom to the USA in 1976.) The Marboro Ale became an annual event—a weekend of dancing and socialising, but also an important channel of communication.[113] When it could no longer accommodate the growing number of North American sides, other gatherings—including the California, Mid-Western, and Toronto Ales - emerged.[114] Of the twenty-nine sides completing the survey, twenty-five mentioned attending or hosting ales. Most expressed enthusiasm for them, and some identified specific ales as turning points in their development.

Along with the tyranny of distance, American sides have struggled with the tyranny of time. Of the twenty-nine responding sides, one was founded in the 1960s, eight in the 1970s, eight in the 1980s, eight in the 1990s, but only four after 2000. Several described themselves as an aging population. Mary Chor of Rock Creek Morris Women, Washington, D.C., founded in 1979, noted, "Next generation dancers have joined but recruitment is less than optimal."[115] Dick Bagwell of Deer Creek Morris in California, founded in 1986, wrote, "Been some years since we've had any beginners. . . . All Bay Area sides really need more members. Several sides have gone under in recent memory, in both Northern and Southern California."[116] Kalia Kliban of Apple Tree Morris in California, founded in 1998, was equally pessimistic: "My perception is that the Cotswold morris community on the West Coast is aging and the teams are dwindling. . . . The East Coast seems to have a large group of young dancers coming into the tradition, but that hasn't happened out here yet."[117]

Maintaining a sustainable morris culture may require long-term planning. Tom Kruskal of Pinewoods Morris Men started two mixed youth teams, which "have served as a sort of 'farm system' that feeds many teams in the Boston area and (as members go off to college) beyond."[118] Sometimes, however, the culture seems to emerge spontaneously if a critical mass is attained. Laura Friedman-Shedlov of Duck or Grouse Rapper Sword in Minnesota, founded in 2006, observed, "We have an unusually vibrant Morris dance community here in the Twin Cities. There are currently six active Cotswold Morris groups, as well as two Border Morris groups (three if you count one based just outside the Twin Cities area in western Wisconsin). In addition there is one other rapper sword group, a longsword group, and an English clogging group."[119] Advancing years have often reduced the quality of dancing as well as the number of dancers. Some, such as Oak Apple Morris in Wisconsin, founded in 1978, carry on regardless: "I would guess that the early members were in their 20s and 30s. Today, half the team is over 60. . . . In the beginning, I understand that the side was very precise, and we aren't any more. The focus now is on having fun and preserving our knees. The side was also larger in the beginning and people had to be 'certified' on dances before they could dance them in public. Today we just struggle to get up a side and feel successful if we get through the dance."[120]

Others, such as Jim Brickwedde of Ramsay's Braggarts, preferred to quit when the flesh weakened, even if the spirit remained willing: "Damaged discs in my lower spine precludes [sic] doing full capers. My bones remember a very athletic style of Morris. . . . To do less then [sic] that would not satisfy my soul. Pedestrian Morris is not my style."[121] Nevertheless some sides have resisted decline. Jerry Callen of Pinewoods Morris Men, Massachusetts, founded in 1964, stated, "We are multi-generational, with several father/son pairs on the team."[122] Deirdre Bialo-Padin of Half Moon Sword in New York too was fairly optimistic: "Many of us have been on the team for a long time. That means we started in our 20's, and many of us are in our 50's. We have some younger dancers. In recent years, daughters of team members have joined us. Because New York City is an expensive place to live, our younger team members often move away to work or go to school. By the same token, younger dancers have joined us after having danced with teams in the Boston and Washington DC area."[123]

Another positive response came from Renegade Morris, Pennsylvania, founded in 2007: "Even in our first year, we had members in every decade of age —from teens to 70s. We celebrate that inter-generational aspect of our group. . . . The last two years we have been able to field a side with father, daughter, and grandson dancing together!"[124] Maroon Bells, Colorado, founded in 1982, has been similarly fortunate: "We've been around long enough to have kids of members form a kid's [sic] side. . . . They've been dancing for about 12 years. The original kids are now in and out of college. They've danced with the adult team once they are ready."[125] In general, it appears that a culture of renewal is easier to foster when sides meet socially and families become involved. The family atmosphere is particularly visible in Berkeley Morris. One senior member noted that six couples currently dancing with the side met their partners there.[126]

THE AMERICANIZATION OF MORRIS:
HAS THE DIASPORA BECOME NATURALIZED?

In 1973 Roger Cartwright, who started several sides and inspired many dancers, circulated a letter about the future of American morris, and it was quoted in an address at his funeral: "I sense it is time for the Morris to grow on its own; to begin experimenting with developing a folk base. Not as a 'cute' imitation of old village life, but in ways which seem genuine and consistent to our present lives."[127] Anthony Barrand urged morris sides to find niches in their local communities' calendars. This, he argued, need not take long. A custom "becomes traditional when people can't remember what life was like without it."[128] Several respondents have pursued similar goals. In Wisconsin, Oak Apple Morris has supported a wide range of events and places, including "May Day, Beltane for a Wiccan group, Mai Fest for a German restaurant, Finnish mid-summer festival, Farmers' Markets, Art Festivals, Folk Festivals, Community Festivals, nursing homes, weddings and anniversaries (and once for a funeral)."[129]

In Minneapolis, Ramsay's Braggarts have danced at parks, pubs, riverfront restaurants, and the annual community festivals. "Our goal is to get out into the neighborhoods of the Twin Cities on a weekly basis, bringing music and dance and a sense of place to the residents," several members reported.[130] In California, Berkeley Morris dance at venues ranging from the Solano Avenue Stroll, a street festival attracting 250,000 visitors, to sidewalks outside tiny cafés and bars.[131] The Bay Area abounds with professional street entertainers, so to hold an audience, Berkeley's dancers have to put on shows. An accomplished band has provided musical support, the Fool's comic patter was delivered with theatrical panache, and even walking on and off have been choreographed. Meanwhile their mascot Lucy, modeled on California's state emblem, the Golden Bear, has delighted small children with her antics.[132]

Regardless of these show-business trappings, Berkeley's dancers have been firmly committed to performing the dances accurately and vigorously. A similar intensity of engagement has prevailed in most of the American sides observed by the present author. Some have argued that since morris has no traditional place in their culture, it needs to be pitched energetically to audiences. John Shewmaker of Capering Roisterers Missouri, founded in 1984, remarked that "if you are going to do silly things in public, it is best to do them well, with great precision and verve."[133] This positive attitude agrees with the totemic American virtues of get-up-and-go and the can-do spirit. Indeed the prevalence of that ethos—rather than accumulating variations in style and repertoire—may be the clearest indicator of an emerging American morris "tradition."

Steve Howe of Marlboro Morris Men recalled changes in both repertoire and attitude: "We tended to stick to Bacon [the English Morris Ring's handbook] until the mid '80s when more invention and borrowing was in style. Now we don't remember if the dance is 'traditional' or made up (unless it is really new)."[134] Jerry Callan of Pinewoods Morris Men felt that independence has now been achieved: "I think I can safely say than none of us think of ourselves as part of an 'English Diaspora.' We are grateful for the gift of Morris, but Morris dance in the U.S. has developed a distinctly American style and 'feel.' The young adults in the North American Morris community . . . are taking their dancing in new and exciting (to me) directions that are very different from what I think of as 'traditional' Morris."[135]

Nevertheless a simplistic narrative in which Americans boldly dance as no one has danced before while English traditionalists remain unenterprisingly earthbound will not withstand scrutiny. Anthony Barrand recalled that at the first Marlboro ale all but one of the dances performed were officially "traditional," whereas thirty years later the balance was about 50–50, with many of the new dances being American creations. However, he also noted that imported ideas contributed significantly to these developments: "The films of performances I took [in England] in the summer of 1979, and that Rhett Krause gathered during his year in England (1982), revolutionized my teaching and my approach to shaping the Marlboro team's dancing."[136]

American morris sides now learn English dances via YouTube and vice versa. But when sides or individuals cross the Atlantic, the experiences of dancing with their hosts reaffirm that both communities share a common heritage. Maple Morris is a group of youngsters from the United States and Canada who usually perform with their hometown sides but convene occasionally for tours.[137] While visiting England in 2011 they joined a local youth group, Morris Offspring, to create an ambitious theatrical presentation.[138] At that year's Sidmouth Folk Week, the present author met members of Maple Morris and—as a member of Hexham Morrismen—participated with them in a joint display. Their dancing was exciting and distinctive, but its English roots were still clearly recognizable.[139] In a workshop at the 2013 California Ale, thirty experienced American dancers were introduced by the present author to a dance from a rarely seen Cotswold tradition, Wheatley, and within an hour were performing it creditably.[140] Similar exchanges continue.[141] Despite their diverse dialects, British and American morris dancers share a common language of dance but in a partnership rather than a master-apprentice relationship. The diaspora has generated a dialogue.

NOTES

I thank colleagues at Northumbria University for their support and the Arts and Humanities Research Council of Great Britain for a travel grant. I am grateful to all the American and English dancers who kindly shared their knowledge, especially Berkeley Morris and the SCA (Society for Creative Anachronism) Historic Dance Group in San José. I thank Karen and Chaz, who put me up (and put up with me) for two delightful weeks in California. Finally, I thank Philippa for her assistance and encouragement throughout this project.

1. Robert D. Putnam, *Bowling Alone: The Collapse and Revival of American Community* (New York: Simon & Schuster, 2000); compare Margaret Talbot, "Who Wants to Be a Legionnaire?, *New York Times*, June 25, 2000, http://www.nytimes.com/books/00/06/25/reviews/000625.25talbott.html, accessed September 7, 2014.

2. For example, there is no space to consider the morrislike dances taught by the Spanish to Native Americans, discussed in John Forrest, *Morris and Matachin, a Study in Comparative Choreography* (Sheffield: CECTAL Publications, 1984), 42–49.

3. See Tristram Potter Coffin and Roger deV. Renwick, *The British Traditional Ballad in North America* (Austin: University of Texas Press, 2014); Kate Van Winkle Keller, *Dance and Its Music in America, 1528–1789* (Hillsdale, N.Y.: Pendragon, 2007).

4. Edward Haies, "Narrative of Sir Humphrey Gilbert's Last Expedition," reproduced in David B. Quinn, *The Voyages and Colonizing Enterprises of Sir Humphrey Gilbert*, 2 vols. (London: Hakluyt Society, 1940), 1:385–423.

5. In 1839 at New York's Broadway Circus, a blackface burlesque called *The Dying Moor's Defense of His Flag* was accompanied by a "Comic Morris Dance by the whole company"; see Dale Cockrell, *Demons of Disorder: Early Blackface Minstrels and Their World* (Cambridge: Cambridge University Press, 1997), 52. See also Rhett Krause, "Morris Dancing and America prior to 1913," *American Morris Newsletter* 25 (December 2005), http://www.americanmorrisnews.org/pastissues/dec2005v25n4/current_issue/rhettkrausev25n4morrisdancingandamerica.html, accessed April 10, 2014. For contrast, see Roy Judge, "'The Old English Morris Dance': Theatrical Morris 1801–1880," *Folk Music Journal* 7, no. 3 (1997): 311–50.

6. Anthony G. Barrand, Six Fools and a Dancer: The Timeless Way of the Morris (Plainfield, Vt.: Northern Harmony, 1991), 41.

7. See Peter Burke, *Varieties of Cultural History* (Cambridge: Polity, 1997); Chris Humphrey, *The Politics of Carnival: Festive Misrule in Medieval England* (Manchester: Manchester University Press, 2001).

8. See John C. Chasteen, *National Rhythms, African Roots* (Albuquerque: University of New Mexico Press, 2004); Reid Mitchell, *All on a Mardi Gras Day* (Cambridge, Mass.: Harvard University Press, 1995).

9. See Philippa Jackson and Fabrizio Nevola, *Beyond the Palio: Urbanism and Ritual in Renaissance Siena* (Hoboken, N.J.: Wiley, 2006). Compare Brian W. Pugh, *Bonfire Night in Lewes* (London: MX Publishing, 2011).

10. See, for example, Jean-Marie Chauvet, *Dawn of Art: The Chauvet Cave Paintings* (New York: Harry N. Abrams, 1996); Chantal Conneller, "Becoming Deer: Corporeal Transformations at Starr Carr," *Archaeological Dialogue* 11, no. 1 (2004): 37–56. For medieval animal disguising, see the mummers pictured in Bodl.264. fo.21v., . . . image available at http://www.pinterest.com/pin/30962316159707971/, accessed September 10, 2016.

11. See Ronald Hutton, *The Stations of the Sun: A History of the Ritual Year in Britain* (Oxford: Oxford University Press, 1996), esp. 81–94. See also E. C. Cawte, *Ritual Animal Disguise: A Historical and Geographical Study of Animal Disguise in the British Isles* (Cambridge: D. S. Brewer, 1978); compare Ljubika Janković and Danika S. Janković, "Masked Dancers in Serbia," *Folk Music Journal* 1, no. 4 (1968): 227–35.

12. Millie Taylor, *British Pantomime Performance* (Bristol: Intellect, 2007). See also R. J. Broadbent, *A History of Pantomime* (London: Benjamin Blom, 1901).

13. See "horse-play" in *The Oxford English Dictionary Online*, http://www.oed.com/view/Entry/88658?, accessed August 13, 2014.

14. Johan Huizinga, *Homo Ludens*, trans. R. Hull (London: Temple Smith, 1971), 188–89.

15. Barbara Ehrenreich, *Dancing in the Streets: A History of Collective Joy* (London: Granta, 2007), 24.

16. Steven Mithen, *The Singing Neanderthals: The Origins of Music, Language, Mind and Body* (Cambridge, Mass.: Harvard University Press, 2006), esp. chap. 10.

17. Michael Heaney, "The Earliest Reference to the Morris Dance?," *Folk Music Journal* 8, no. 4 (2004): 513–15.

18. Michael Heaney, "Observations on Early Images of Morris Dancers," *Musical Traditions*, article 138 (13–03–2004/March 13, 2004); http://www.mustrad.org.uk/articles/e_morris.htm, accessed April 8, 2014. A picture of the Betley window is available on the Victoria and Albert Museum web site: http://collections.vam.ac.uk/search/?limit=15&q=Betley+Window&commit=Search&after-adbc=AD&before-adbc=AD&subject%5B%5D=24117&narrow=1&offset=0&slug=0, accessed September12, 2016.

19. See Forrest, *Morris and Matachin*, chap. 1; compare Hutton, The Stations of the Sun, chap. 25.

20. See Linda Colley, *Captives: Britain, Empire and the World 1600–1850* (London: Jonathan Cape, 2002); Nabil Matar, *Islam in Britain, 1558–1685* (Cambridge: Cambridge University Press, 2008).

21. Ben Jonson, *The Masque of Blackness* (1608), in Stephen Orgel, ed., *Ben Jonson: Complete Masques* (New Haven, Conn.: Yale University Press, 1969), 61–74. See also Elliot H. Tokson, *The Popular Image of the Black Man in English Drama, 1550–1688* (Boston: G. K. Hall, 1982).

22. On pagan origin theory, see Cecil J. Sharp and Herbert C. MacIlwain, *The Morris Book*, 2nd ed. (London: Novello, 1912), 11–14. For a critique, see Ronald Hutton, *The Triumph of the Moon: A History of Modern Pagan Witchcraft* (Oxford: Oxford University Press, 1999), 126–31. For comparison, see http://paganwiccan.about.com/od/beltanemayday/p/MorrisMummers.htm, accessed January 28, 2014.

23. See John Forrest, *The History of Morris Dancing 1458–1750* (Toronto: University of Toronto Press, 1999). See also Hutton, *The Stations of the Sun,* chap. 25.

24. See, for example, John Fletcher and William Shakespeare, *The Two Noble Kinsmen,* Arden ed., ed. Lois Potter (London: Bloomsbury, 1996), act 3, scene 5. See also Barbara Lowe, "Early Records of the Morris in England," *Journal of the English Folk Dance and Song Society,* 8, no. 2 (1957): 61–82.

25. On misrule, see Hutton, *The Stations of the Sun,* chap. 9; John Forrest and Michael Heaney, "Charting Early Morris," *Folk Music Journal* 6, no. 2 (1991): 178. On fools, see John Southworth, *Fools and Jesters at the English Court* (Stroud: Sutton, 1998). On animal disguise, see Cawte, *Ritual Animal Disguise.* On cross-dressing, see Hutton, *The Stations of the Sun,* 21, 96.

26. Philip Stubbes, *The Anatomie of Abuses,* London (1583), repr. London, New Shakespere [*sic*] Society (1879), part 1 (of 2), chap. 12. For an overview, see Ronald Hutton, *The Rise and Fall of Merry England* (Oxford: Oxford University Press, 1994), chap. 5.

27. David Underdown, *Revel, Riot and Rebellion: Popular Politics and Culture in England 1603–1660* (Oxford: Oxford University Press, 1987), 175.

28. Hugh Ripon, *Discovering English Folk Dance* (Princes Risborough: Shire, 1993), provides a brief guide. For further information, see Hutton, *The Stations of the Sun,* chap. 25.

29. For a fuller discussion, see Keith Chandler, *"Ribbons, Bells and Squeaking Fiddles": The Social History of Morris Dancing in the English South Midlands 1660–1900* (London: Folklore Society, 1993). For one individual's career, see Keith Chandler, "The Life and Musical Activity of Thomas Boswell, aka Thomas 'Gypsy' Lewis (1838–1910)," *Folk Music Journal* 10, no. 1 (2011): 102–22.

30. See Derek Schofield, "'Revival of the Folk Dance: An Artistic Movement': The Background to the Founding of the English folk Dance Society in 1911," *Folk Music Journal* 5, no. 2 (1986): 215. See also Michael Heaney, "Sharp, Cecil James (1859–1924)," *Oxford Dictionary of National Biography* (Oxford: Oxford University Press, 2004), online ed. (2008), http://www.oxforddnb.com/view/article/36040, accessed September 1, 2014.

31. See "Coronation of King George V and Queen Mary: Rejoicings in Kingston and the Surrounding Districts," *Surrey Comet,* June 24, 1911, http://www.springgrove morris.org/history/kingston-pageant-1911/1911-pageant-report, accessed April 30, 2014. On Stratford, see Roy Judge, "Cecil Sharp and Morris 1906–1909," *Folk Music Journal* 8, no. 2 (2002): 223. See also Keith Chandler, "Musicians in 19th Century Southern England No. 11: The Sturch Family of Shipston-on-Stour, Warwickshire," *Musical Traditions,* article 187 (2006), http://www.mustrad.org.uk/articles/sturch.htm, accessed April 14, 2014.

32. Maya Jasanoff, *Liberty's Exiles: The Loss of America and the Remaking of the British Empire* (London: Harper, 2011); Simon Schama, *Rough Crossings: Britain, the Slaves and the American Revolution* (London: BBC Books, 2005).

33. See, for example, Peter R. Vronsky, *Ridgeway: The American Fenian Invasion and the 1866 Battle That Made Canada* (Toronto: Penguin Canada–Allen Lane, 2011).

34. See, for example, John E. Moser, *Twisting the Lion's Tail: Anglophobia in the United States, 1921–1948* (New York: New York University Press, Macmillan, 1998).

35. For U.S. Austen mania, see "The Republic of Pemberly," http://www.pember ley.com/, accessed August 11, 2014. For American Pythonism, see Marcia Landy, *Monty Python's Flying Circus* (Detroit: Wayne State University Press, 2005), 24–30. For Gilbert and Sullivan, see Ray B. Browne and Pat Browne, eds., *The Guide to United States Popular Culture* (Madison: University of Wisconsin Press, 2001), 321; and the Massachusetts Institute of Technology Gilbert and Sullivan Players Web page, http://gsp.mit.edu/, accessed September 1, 2014. For the Beatles in America, see Jonathan Gould, *Can't Buy Me Love: The Beatles, England and America* (New York: Crown, 2007).

36. For the Baker Street Irregulars' New York Weekend, see http://www.bsiweek end.com/#sthash.He5iyQHO.dpbs, accessed April 10, 2014. For the Los Angeles Doctor Who Convention, see http://www.gallifreyone.com/, accessed April 10, 2014.

37. Eric Hobsbawm and Terence Ranger, eds., *The Invention of Tradition* (Cambridge: Cambridge University Press, 1983); Benedict Anderson, *Imagined Communities: Reflections on the Origins and Spread of Nationalism* (London: Verso, 2006).

38. Ronald Hutton, *Witches, Druids and King Arthur* (London: Hambledon & London, 2003), 1–37; Roy Judge, *The Jack-in-the-Green: A May Day Custom* (London: Folklore Society, 2000); Dave Harker, *Fakesong: The Manufacture of British "Folksong," 1700 to the Present Day* (Milton Keynes: Open University Press, 1985); Georgina Boyes, *The Imagined Village: Culture, Ideology and the English Folk Revival* (Manchester: Manchester University Press, 1993).

39. Michael Ignatieff, *Blood and Belonging: Journeys into the New Nationalism* (New York: Farrar, Straus and Giroux, 1994), 27.

40. See Gary W. Gallagher and Alan T. Nolan, eds., *The Myth of the Lost Cause and Civil War History* (Bloomington: Indiana University Press, 2000). See also United Daughters of the Confederacy, http://www.hqudc.org/, accessed April 17, 2014. On the heritage industry, see Dona Brown, *Inventing New England: Regional Tourism in the Nineteenth Century* (Washington, D.C.: Smithsonian Institution Press, 1995). For comparison, see Bill Bryson, *The Lost Continent: Travels in Small-Town America* (London: Secker & Warburg, 1989), 270–71.

41. See the Revels page, http://www.revels.org/about-revels/mission-values/, accessed April 15, 2014.

42. Thomas Morton, *The New English Canaan* (Amsterdam: J. F. Stam, 1637; repr., Boston: Prince Society, 1883), 276–79.

43. Edith Murphy, "Morton, Thomas," *Oxford Dictionary of National Biography* (Oxford: Oxford University Press, 2004); online ed. (2008), http://www.oxforddnb.com/view/article/19372, accessed September 1, 2014.

44. Rachel Lee Rubin, *Well Met: Renaissance Faires and the American Counterculture* (New York: New York University Press, 2013). See also the website of the Jane Austen Society of North America, http://www.jasna.org/info/about.html, accessed September 12, 2016; for U.S. Dickensian events, see http://dickensfair.com/, and http://www.dickensfestival.com/, accessed September12, 2016.

45. See American Civil War Historical Re-enactment Society, http://www.acwhrs .com/, accessed April 8, 2014. Compare California's Legion VI Victrix, http://legionsix .org/, accessed April 8, 2014.

46. For details, see the SCA Web site, http://www.sca.org/, accessed April 5, 2014. See also Mike Sutton, "Looking Forward to the Past," http://digitalcommunity.english diaspora.co.uk/?p=671, accessed July 12, 2014.

47. The PEERS Web site mentions "a Canterbury Tales Feast & Ball, a recreation of Lord Capulet's Ball from Romeo and Juliet, an outdoor Restoration Fete and Ball, an 18th-Century Scarlet Pimpernel Ball, a Mostly Mozart Ball set in the Amadeus universe, a Jane Austen Tea, Fete and Assembly, a Phantom of the Opera Masquerade Ball, a Sherlock Holmes Mystery Party and Ball, an Edwardian Music Hall, a 1941 Evening in Casablanca, a bi-lingual Moulin Rouge Ball, a Tango Tea, a 1920's Speakeasy, a 1930's Mystery Party, a Film Noir Black & White Ball, a variety of Victorian Balls and our famous annual Le Bal des Vampires"; see http://www.peersdance.org/, accessed April 13, 2014.

48. Cyndi Moncreiff, Greenwood Morris (Florida): survey response, 2012.

49. See Hutton, *The Stations of the Sun*, 126–28.

50. On collecting, see Russell Wortley and Michael Dawney, eds., "George Butterworth's Diary of Morris Dance Hunting," *Folk Music Journal* 3, no. 3 (1977): 193–207. Also informative is a fictional account based on firsthand observation in Edward V. Lucas, *London Lavender* (London: Methuen, 1912), 220–29.

51. Cecil J. Sharp, 1909 handbill, quoted in Judge, "Cecil Sharp," 223.

52. In the 1950s the "Lichfield tradition" entered the canon by this means; see Roy Judge, "The Morris in Lichfield," *Folklore* 103, no. 2 (1992): 131–59.

53. Roy Judge, "Mary Neal and the Espérance Morris," *Folk Music Journal* 5, no. 5 (1989): 545–91.

54. Mary Neale, interview in *New York Times*, January 22, 1911, quoted in Rhett Krause, "Morris Dancing and America prior to 1913," *American Morris Newsletter* 25 (July 2005), http://www.americanmorrisnews.org/pastissues/dec2005v25n4/current_issue/ rhettkrausev25n4morrisdancingandamerica.html, accessed August 28, 2014.

55. The "hoydenish gambols" remark occurred in a 1912 letter from Sharp to Harley Granville-Barker, quoted in Judge, "Mary Neal," 571.

56. On Florrie Warren in the United States, see Krause, "Morris Dancing". On Neal's later career, see Judge, "Mary Neal."

57. John Dexter, quoted in Rich Holmes, "Pre-1980s Morris Dancing in North America" (2005), http://morrisdancing.wikia.com/wiki/Pre-1980s_morris_in_North _America, accessed April 22, 2014.

58. See Daniel J. Walkowitz, *City Folk: English Country Dance and the Politics of the Folk in Modern America* (New York: New York University Press, 2010).

59. Martin Graetz, "Pinewoods Morris Men . . . the History" (25th Anniversary Programme, 1989), http://www.pinewoodsmorris.org/history.html, accessed April 11, 2014.

60. Personal communication between the author and Mitch Diamond, 2012.

61. Holmes, "Pre-1980s Morris Dancing." See also Graetz, "Pinewoods Morris Men."

62. Key recordings include Ashley Hutchings and Friends, *Morris On!* (Island Records, 1972), and Albion Country Band, *The Battle of the Field* (Island Records, recorded in 1973, released in 1976).

63. E. C. Cawte, "The Morris Dance in Herefordshire, Shropshire and Worcestershire," *Journal of the EFDSS* 9, no. 4 (1963): 197–232; D. Jones, "Morris Dances of the Welsh Border," *English Dance and Song* 48, no. 2 (1986): 14–15; Russell Wortley, "A Penny for the Plough Boys," *English Dance and Song* 36, no. 1 (1974): 23.

64. See Roy Dommet, "The Collected Border Morris," http://www.opread.force9 .co.uk/RoyDommet/BorderNotes/collectedmorris.htm, accessed April 1, 2014.

65. On creating new dances, see John Kirkpatrick, "The Shropshire Bedlams," http:// www.johnkirkpatrick.co.uk/mo_ShropshireBedlams.asp, accessed March 29, 2014. For critiques of inept performers, see Gordon Ashman, "Border Morris: Roots and Revival," *American Morris Newsletter* 25 (April 2005), http://www.americanmorrisnews .org/pastissues/april2005v25n1/current_issue/gordonashmanv25n1bordermorrisroot sandrevival.html, accessed September 9, 2016.

66. On female Morris dancers, see Chandler, *"Ribbons, Bells and Squeaking Fiddles,"* 26–27, 123.

67. Derek Schofield, booklet accompanying audio CD *Absolutely Classic: The Music of William Kimber,* EFDSS CD03 (1999), 6–7. CD track 24 contains the quoted Kimber interview (recorded by Peter Kennedy, December 4, 1951).

68. See http://morrisfed.org.uk/about/about-the-federation/, accessed August 20, 2014.

69. See http://morrisdancing.wikia.com/wiki/Morris_teams_in_United_States; and http://morrisdancing.wikia.com/wiki/Morris_teams_in_Canada, both accessed April 13, 2014.

70. For more on the English diaspora project, see www.englishdiaspora.co.uk, accessed October 22, 2014.

71. Steven Levene, Ramsay's Braggarts (Minnesota): survey response, 2012.

72. Jim Brickwedde, Ramsay's Braggarts (Minnesota): survey response, 2012.

73. Andrea Tarr, Wake Robin Morris (Massachusetts): survey response, 2012.

74. Rich Holmes, "Salt Springs Morris History," http://saltsprings.wordpress.com/ history/, accessed April 25, 2014.

75. Sarah Strong, Hart's Brook Garland Women (Massachusetts): survey response, 2012.

76. Peter Hoover, Heartwood Morris (New York): survey response, 2012.

77. Paul Handford, "A History of Thames Valley Morris," http://publish.uwo.ca/ ~handford/tvhist.html, accessed April 2, 2014.

78. Ibid.

79. Forest City Morris and Sword Dancers, http://www.freewebs.com/forestcity morris/aboutus.htm, accessed April 24, 2014.

80. See "Kirtlington" in Lionel Bacon, *A Handbook of Morris Dances* (Leicester: Morris Ring, 1974), 225–26. See also Kirtlington Morris Web page, http://kirtlington -morris.org.uk/, accessed April 27, 2014.

81. Tim Radford, "Duns Tew Chapter One: The Beginnings," *American Morris Newsletter* 25 (June 2005), http://www.americanmorrisnews.org/pastissues/july2005v25n2/current_issue/timradfordv25n2dunstew.html, accessed April 28, 2014.

82. Jocelyn Reynolds, Goat Hill Morris (California): survey response, 2012.

83. The Bessels Leigh tradition is analyzed in Barrand, *Six Fools*, 207–14.

84. Bob Oser, Berkeley Morris (California): survey response, 2012.

85. Roger Avery, Berkeley Morris (California): survey response, 2012.

86. Participant observation with Berkeley Morris (April–May 2012). For more information, see Mike Sutton, "Dancing up the Sun," http://digitalcommunity.english diaspora.co.uk/?p=585, accessed August 21, 2014.

87. Marjory Stevenson, Ladies of the Rolling Pin (Rhode Island): survey response, 2012.

88. Lara Friedman-Shedlov, Duck or Grouse Rapper Sword (Minnesota): survey response, 2012.

89. Steven Levene, Ramsay's Braggarts (Minnesota): survey response, 2012.

90. Steve Howe, Marlboro Morris and Sword (Vermont): survey response, 2012.

91. Cyndi Moncreiff, Greenwood Morris (Florida): survey response, 2012.

92. Lawrence Szydek and Ruth Olmstead, Pokingbrook Morris (New York): survey response, 2012.

93. Deirdre Bialo-Padin, Half Moon Sword (New York): survey response, 2012.

94. Sarah Strong, Harts Brook Garland Women (Massachusetts): survey response, 2012.

95. See Marlene LeGates, *In Their Time: A History of Feminism in Western Society* (London: Routledge, 2012); Rosemary Tong, *Feminist Thought: A More Comprehensive Introduction* (New York: Westview, 2009); Estelle Freedman, ed., *The Essential Feminist Reader* (New York: Modern Library, 2007).

96. Cynthia Whear, "The Way We Were: One True History of the Original Muddy River Morris," *American Morris Newsletter* 25 (December 2005), http://www.american morrisnews.org/pastissues/dec2005v25n4/current_issue/cynthiawhearv25n4muddy rivermorris.html, accessed April 2, 2014.

97. Jim Voorhees, "The Not-So-Long but Glorious History of Foggy Bottom Morris: The Beginning," *American Morris Newsletter* 25 (December 2005), http://www .americanmorrisnews.org/pastissues/dec2005v25n4/current_issue/jimvoorheesv25n4 foggybottom.html, accessed September 12, 2016.

98. Paul Handford, Thames Valley International (Ontario): survey response, 2012.

99. Pauline Greenhill, *Ethnicity in the Mainstream: Three Studies of English Canadian Culture in Ontario* (Montreal: McGill-Queen's University Press, 1994), 103.

100. Barrand, *Six Fools*, 74.

101. Greenhill, *Ethnicity in the Mainstream*, 95.

102. White Rats Morris (California) "saw ourselves as a sort of sexual pervert/street dyke/mildly neopagan/motorcycle gang/morris team"; see http://www.whiteratsmorris .org/history.html, accessed August 24, 2014.

103. Personal communication between the author and Steve Howe, Marlboro Morris Men (2014).

104. Bob Oser, Berkeley Morris (California): survey response, 2012.

105. See Geoffrey Blainey, *The Tyranny of Distance: How Distance Shaped Australia's History* (Sydney: Macmillan, 2001).

106. On politics and the revival, see Dick Weissman, *Which Side Are You On? An Inside History of the Folk Music Revival in America* (London: A & C Black, 2006); Gillian Mitchell, *The North American Folk Music Revival: Nation and Identity in the United States and Canada* (Farnham: Ashgate, 2013).

107. See Michael Heaney, "Tiddy, Reginald John Elliott (1880–1916)," *Oxford Dictionary of National Biography* (Oxford: Oxford University Press, 2004), http://www.oxforddnb.com/view/article/57228, accessed September 1, 2014.

108. Personal communication between the author and Michael Collins, Berkeley Morris (2013).

109. Cyndi Moncreiff, Greenwood Morris (Florida): survey response, 2012.

110. Patricia Montoya Donohue, Two Rivers Morris (Oregon): survey response, 2012.

111. Jim Brickwedde, Ramsay's Braggarts (Minnesota): survey response, 2012.

112. See Hutton, *The Stations of the Sun,* chap. 24. Compare Bob Bushaway, *By Rite: Custom, Ceremony and Community in England 1700–1880* (London: Junction Books, 1982).

113. Anthony G. Barrand, "The Marlboro Morris Ale at 30: Part I," *American Morris Newsletter* 25 (June 2005), http://www.americanmorrisnews.org/pastissues/april2005v25n1/current_issue/tonybarrandv25n1marlboroaleat30part1.html, accessed May 1, 2014.

114. Barrand, "Marlboro Morris Ale."

115. Mary Chor, Rock Creek Morris Women (DC): survey response, 2012.

116. Dick Bagwell, Deer Creek Morris (California): survey response, 2012.

117. Kalia Kliban, Apple Tree Morris (California): survey response, 2012.

118. Personal communication between the author and Jerry Callen, Pinewoods Morris Men (2012).

119. Lara Friedman-Shedlov, Duck or Grouse Rapper Sword (Minnesota): survey response, 2012.

120. Casey Garhardt, Oak Apple Morris (Wisconsin): survey response, 2014.

121. Jim Brickwedde, "Reflections of an Ex-Editor," *American Morris Newsletter* 25 (December 2005), http://www.americanmorrisnews.org/pastissues/dec2005v25n4/current_issue/jimbrickweddev25n4reflections.html, accessed April 2, 2014.

122. Personal communication between the author and Jerry Callen, Pinewoods Morris Men (2014).

123. Survey response: Deirdre Bialo-Padin, Half Moon Sword, New York, 2012.

124. Scott Higgs, Renegade Morris (Pennsylvania): survey response, 2012.

125. Sally Sprague, Maroon Bells Morris (Colorado): survey response, 2012.

126. Personal communication between the author and Bob Orser, Berkeley Morris (2013).

127. Personal communication between the author and Mitch Diamond (2012).

128. Barrand, *Six Fools,* 131.

129. Casey Garhardt, Oak Apple Morris (Wisconsin): survey response, 2014.

130. Steven Levene and Jim Brickwedde, Ramsay's Braggarts (Minnesota): survey response, 2012.

131. Bob Oser, Berkeley Morris (California): survey response, 2012.

132. Participant observation by the author, April/May 2013. For further details on Berkeley, see http://berkeley-morris.org/history.html. Accessed September 13, 2016. See also Lucy's Facebook page, https://www.facebook.com/lucy.bear.18, accessed August 29, 2014.

133. Personal communication between the author and John Shewmaker, Capering Roisterers (2012).

134. Steve Howe, Marlboro Morris Men (Vermont): survey response (2013).

135. Personal communication between the author and Jerry Callan, Pinewoods Morris Men (2012).

136. Barrand, "Marlboro Morris Ale."

137. See Maple Morris Web site, http://maplemorris.com/, accessed August 29, 2014.

138. For details, see http://www.morrisoffspring.org.uk/shows.htm, accessed August 29, 2014. For video, see https://www.youtube.com/watch?v=JaPdqWMueOk, accessed August 29, 2014.

139. Participant observation by the author, Sidmouth Folk Week, August 2011. Maple Morris members are shown dancing at Sidmouth at https://www.youtube.com/watch?v=PTCS-InUjDk, accessed August 28, 2014.

140. Participant observation by the author, California Ale, April 2013.

141. Tom Redman of Hexham Morrismen and Newcastle Kingsmen led dance workshops at Pinewoods Summer Camp, July–August 2014 (personal communication between the author and Tom Redman, 2014).

CONTRIBUTORS

DEAN ALLEN is a senior lecturer at Bournemouth University in the United Kingdom. Having lectured at universities in South Africa, Ireland, and Australia, he has published widely on the history and politics of sport and society throughout the British Empire, most notably in South Africa. His particular interests are colonialism, imperialism, and the identity of sporting groups and nations. His research for his essay here was in part funded by the Arts and Humanities Research Council (AHRC) of the United Kingdom research grant project "Locating the Hidden Diaspora: The English in North America in Transatlantic Perspective, 1760–1950."

TANJA BUELTMANN is associate professor of history at Northumbria University and the author of *Clubbing Together: Ethnicity, Civility and Formal Sociability in the Scottish Diaspora to 1930; Scottish Ethnicity and the Making of New Zealand Society, 1850 to 1930* (2014); and, with Andrew Hinson and Graeme Morton, *The Scottish Diaspora* (2013). Tanja's current research focuses on her Economic and Social Research Council (U.K.) Future Research Leaders project titled "European, Ethnic and Expatriate: A Longitudinal Comparison of German and British Social Networking and Associational Formations in Modern-Day Asia," for which she is the principal investigator. She was a coinvestigator on the AHRC (U.K.) funded research grant project "Locating the Hidden Diaspora: The English in North America in Transatlantic Perspective, 1760–1950."

DAVID T. GLEESON is professor of American history at Northumbria University. His most recent book, *The Green and the Gray: The Irish in the Confederate States of America*, was published as part of the University of North Carolina Press's Civil War America Series in 2013. He was a coinvestigator on the AHRC (U.K.) funded research grant project "Locating the Hidden Diaspora: The English in North America in Transatlantic Perspective, 1760–1950."

JOSEPH HARDWICK is a senior lecturer in history at Northumbria University and is a specialist in the history of the British Empire in North America and Asia. He is particularly interested in the religious aspects of British imperialism, especially the role of the Anglican Church. His first book, *An Anglican British World: The Church of England and the Expansion of the Settler Empire, c. 1790–1860*, was published in 2014. His research for this essay was in part funded by the AHRC (U.K.) research grant project "Locating the Hidden Diaspora: The English in North America in Transatlantic Perspective, 1760–1950."

KATHRYN G. LAMONTAGNE has an M.A. from the University of London, School of Advanced Study, and an M.A. and a B.A. from Providence College. She was a teaching fellow at Boston University–London, where she taught British history and popular culture. A native of Fall River, Massachusetts, Kathryn is a Ph.D. candidate at Boston University. Her research interests include English Catholic women's history.

DONALD M. MACRAILD is professor of British and Irish history at Ulster University. His most recent books are (with Kyle Hughes) *Ribbonism in Nineteenth-Century Ireland and Britain* and (with Tanja Bueltmann) *The English Diaspora in North America: Migration, Ethnicity and Association, 1730s–1950s.* He is the author or editor of numerous other books and articles, including *The Irish Diaspora in Britain, 1750–1939.* Donald edits the journal *Immigrants and Minorities,* which is published three times a year by Routledge. He was also principal investigator of the AHRC (U.K.) funded research grant project "Locating the Hidden Diaspora: The English in North America in Transatlantic Perspective, 1760–1950."

JAMES MCCONNEL is associate professor of history at Northumbria University. Since 2002 he has published a number of scholarly articles in journals such as *Historical Journal, Irish Historical Studies, War in History, Past and Present,* and *English Historical Review,* which look at various aspects of Edwardian Irish political history. In 2013 he published his monograph *The Irish Parliamentary Party and the Third Home Rule Crisis.* He is currently researching Ireland and World War I. His research for this essay was in part funded by the AHRC (U.K.) research grant project "Locating the Hidden Diaspora: The English in North America in Transatlantic Perspective, 1760–1950."

MONIKA SMIALKOWSKA is a senior lecturer in English literature at Northumbria University. Her current research explores the ways in which the three-hundredth anniversary of Shakespeare's death in 1916 was celebrated across the world. As part of this project, she was awarded a short-term Folger Shakespeare Library fellowship in 2014. She has published a number of book chapters and articles in journals such as *Critical Survey* and *Shakespeare,* and she is working toward a monograph on this topic.

MIKE SUTTON has a bachelor's degree in chemistry and a doctorate in the history of science from Oxford University. He taught history of science and history of ideas at Northumbria University (formerly Newcastle upon Tyne Polytechnic) for thirty-seven years. He is currently a visiting fellow in history at Northumbria. A former president of Oxford University's folk-song society, he has danced with the Hexham Morris Men since 1976. His publications include many articles on the history of science and several on folklore studies. His research for this essay was in part funded by the AHRC (U.K.) research grant project "Locating the Hidden Diaspora: The English in North America in Transatlantic Perspective, 1760–1950."

WILLIAM VAN VUGT is a professor of history at Calvin College, Grand Rapids, Michigan, where he teaches courses in English and American history. His books include *Britain to America: The Mid-Nineteenth Century Immigrants to the United States; Race and Reconciliation in South Africa: A Multicultural Dialogue in Comparative Perspective* (coauthor and editor); *British Buckeyes: The English, Scots, and Welsh in Ohio, 1700–1900;* and the four-volume *British Immigration to the United States, 1776–1914.* He has also written scholarly articles and chapters in books on migration and the economic history of the North Atlantic.

INDEX

CPSIA information can be obtained
at www.ICGtesting.com
Printed in the USA
BVOW08*0313310817
493200BV00002B/4/P